DWIGHT
MACDONALD

AND

the *politics* Circle

DWIGHT MACDONALD

AND

the *politics* Circle

———————

The Challenge of Cosmopolitan Democracy

———————

GREGORY D. SUMNER

Cornell University Press

ITHACA AND LONDON

First published 1996 by Cornell University Press.

Printed in the United States of America

Library of Congress Cataloging-in-Publication Data

Sumner, Gregory D.
    Dwight Macdonald and the *politics* circle / Gregory D. Sumner.
        p.   cm.
    Includes index.
    ISBN 0-8014-3020-8
    1. Macdonald, Dwight.   2. Politics.   3. United States—Politics and government—1945–1953.   I. Title.
E748.M147S86   1996
320.973—dc20   95-43999

To My Parents

Contents

Preface

My generation came to maturity after the 1960s, but I was nevertheless deeply moved by both the violent ruptures and the utopian yearnings of that decade. Despite the well-known excesses committed in the name of the latter, I remain convinced that the idealism and solidarity reflected in the best of that period hold something of enduring importance, and should at all costs be preserved, understood, and built upon. Even as it receded into mythology, I found myself drawn to the prehistory of "New Left" moralism, to artistic creations and critical works of the immediate post–World War II era united in expressing, with an urgent, stripped-down clarity, a protest against new dangers, new forms of dehumanization which in many respects have only worsened with the intervening passage of time.

The genesis of this book was my discovery that two of the writers I most admired—the New York Intellectual Dwight Macdonald and the French novelist Albert Camus—came to speak a remarkably similar language of dissent after the war, and even crossed paths briefly to act on their shared moral and political commitments. This intriguing, now-obscure collaboration proved, upon further investigation, to be only one facet of a much larger and richer transatlantic dialogue, centered around Macdonald's independent journal, *politics*. I have found the story of *politics'* brief rise and fall well worth the retelling, filled with interesting characters and dramatic moments, and highlighted by a creative debate about the road to peaceful, democratic reconstruction of a torn social order. My purpose is to obtain a fresh hearing for that debate, and I hope others will agree that it offers lessons for our own age of unparalleled crisis and opportunity.

I deeply appreciate the assistance and encouragement I received during this project. I am particularly grateful for the financial support of Indiana University, the John D. and Catherine T. MacArthur Foundation, the Andrew W. Mellon Foundation, and the National Endowment for the Humanities. Thanks are due to the many helpful people I encountered at the libraries of Indiana University, the University of Michigan, and the University of California at Los Angeles; to Yale University for permission to examine and quote from the Dwight Macdonald Papers; and to Vassar College for permission to quote from the Mary McCarthy Papers.

I was fortunate to visit personally with several members of the *politics* inner circle. I gained immensely from the reflections and insights of Lewis Coser, Niccolo Tucci, Lionel Abel, and, above all, Nancy Macdonald and Miriam Chiaromonte. I also benefited from the criticisms and suggestions of scholars familiar with Dwight Macdonald's place in the intellectual history of the 1940s, especially Robert Cummings, Robert Westbrook, Terry Cooney, and Michael Wreszin. I give warm regards to Robert Wohl and my NEH seminar peers for their interest and ideas during the summer of 1994. And my thanks to Peter Agree, Carol Betsch, Andrew Lewis, and the staff at Cornell University Press for their efforts in bringing this work to completion.

My professors and colleagues at Indiana University provided a lively and nurturing environment during the formative stages of this project, and I give special thanks in this regard to Jim Madison, Leonard Lundin, Dave Thelen, and my associates at the *Journal of American History*. Jeffrey Isaac's enthusiasm and good counsel have been invaluable. And I will never be able to repay the debts I owe to my teacher and friend Casey Blake. His rigor, generosity and patience inspired me throughout, and if this book has any value, a large measure of the credit goes to Professor Blake.

Let me also recognize at least some of the many individuals whose warm "sociability" has sustained me over the years: Robert Bennington, James Bertch, Thomas Brown, Kathleen Bush, Kenneth Cotter, Edwin and Anne DeWindt, Gretchen Galbraith, Sarah Gravelle, Anders Greenspan, Merrill Hatlen, Arlene Hill, Jean Kane, Donald Kroger, Elizabeth Lehfeldt, Molly Lynde, Deborah Piston-Hatlen, Michael Recchia, Arlene Shaner, Walter Ranney, Stephen Smith, and Diane Wilkerson. Finally, I thank my family, especially Richard Sumner, Jacki, Russ, Matt, John Baxter, and my beautiful mother Barbara, for their love and understanding.

GREGORY D. SUMNER

Detroit, Michigan

DWIGHT MACDONALD

AND

the *politics* Circle

Introduction:
Dwight Macdonald
and the "First New Left"

Dwight Macdonald found his annual holiday at Cape Cod especially welcome in the late summer of 1945, a respite from both the heat of New York City and the rigors of editing *politics*, the monthly "little magazine" he had begun a year and a half earlier, in the midst of the Second World War. At the remote seaside village of Truro, Macdonald enjoyed the company of his wife Nancy, the novelist Mary McCarthy, Italian émigré Nicola Chiaromonte, and a small number of other European and American friends. He was able briefly to forget about concentration camps, saturation fire bombings, and the other novel horrors that had consumed his attention in recent months. McCarthy's biographer writes that during their beach sojourn the vacationers "read Shakespeare aloud in groups, feasted on picnics in the moonlight, had talks at night by the fire, and went swimming in the phosphorescent water."[1]

Meanwhile, the conflict on the other side of the globe moved toward its spectacular conclusion. At the end of the first week in August, news reports of the atomic bomb shattered the tranquility of the Truro retreat with numbing suddenness. Outraged by this latest innovation in the science of mass destruction, Macdonald interpreted Hiroshima as ultimate proof of a turning point in human history, as a symbol of a terrifying new age in which traditional assumptions and categories of thinking were woefully out-of-date. An event of this magnitude required immediate response, and Macdonald stopped the presses of *politics* at the last possible moment to insert an editorial on the August cover, declaring to his audience: "THE CONCEPTS 'WAR' AND 'PROGRESS'

ARE NOW OBSOLETE." In his eyes, the nuclear incineration of a city—like the Nazis' Final Solution—raised the most troubling questions about modern technology and organization, about "the desirability *in itself* of man's learning to control his environment," about the Enlightenment faith in Progress through reason and mastery. "The underlying population," Macdonald warned, "should regard this new source of energy with lively interest—the interest of victims." The imperative for human survival was now clear and direct: "WE MUST 'GET' THE MODERN NATIONAL STATE BEFORE IT 'GETS' US."[2]

Readers of *politics* also felt shock at the news of the atomic bomb, but they would not have been surprised by the editor's vigorous reaction. For the contemporary observer, Dwight Macdonald's personal qualities made him a particularly appealing guide through the "rough country" of the 1940s. A founding member of the "New York Intellectuals," who came together under the banners of Marxism and modernism in the depression decade, Macdonald was the inveterate dissenter, by his own account "ever hopeful, ever disillusioned." Throughout his career he defied party lines and the rules of propriety to follow the facts as he saw them, wherever they might lead. In a milieu of exaggerated egos, Macdonald was willing to take chances and admit mistakes; and as his post-Hiroshima editorial illustrates, he had a talent for getting to the heart of things. Daniel Bell has observed that in the face of World War II, which he opposed from the start, Macdonald was among the few able to confront "changes in moral temper, the depths of which we still incompletely realize."[3]

Bridging the crucial years between 1944 and 1949, Macdonald's *politics* occupies a special, almost legendary place in the history of American radicalism. Scholars sympathetic to the New Left and the antiwar movements of the 1960s have referred to its pioneering discussions of modern warfare and the bureaucratic state as an enduring legacy, and recent monographs and memoirs about the New York Intellectuals express admiration for the vitality *politics* exuded during a period otherwise not distinguished for the quality of its public discourse. The problem with these accounts is that they are often superficial and incomplete, portraying the magazine as a one-man vehicle and dismissing its efforts to formulate a post-Marxist radicalism, however well intentioned, as a quixotic retreat from political engagement revealing little more than the editor's eccentric moralism.[4]

It is my view that *politics* offered a communitarian alternative to both Marxian socialism and cold war liberalism that deserves much more careful consideration than it has received to date. To encourage a fresh look at the journal's insights, I have done two things in this book. First, I have situated Macdonald in a broader, international context, as one of a handful of independent intellectuals in Europe and the United States who asserted a similar critique of modernity based on their exposure to totalitarianism and war in the 1930s and 1940s. This group, which includes such influential figures as George Orwell, Hannah Arendt, Simone Weil, and Albert Camus, has been variously described. James D. Wilkinson calls it the "Resistance generation"; Staughton Lynd uses the term "First New Left"; Jeffrey Isaac considers Arendt, Camus, and their contemporaries the earliest postmoderns. For all their differences, these dissidents shared a commitment to rescuing the individual from the collective abstractions and messianic ideologies—of the Left as well as of the Right—by which the excesses of the age were justified. Because Macdonald dedicated his journal to serving as a forum for this scattered community, *politics* is best seen as a collaborative project, a transatlantic meeting place unique in the twentieth century. In the shadow of the war, the magazine fulfilled the traditional New World function of refuge: by its second year, Macdonald characterized *politics* as a "transplanted spore of European culture." Besides offering an exciting exchange of ideas, this overlooked chapter in the larger intellectual migration of the war years contains compelling human stories, testaments to the resilience and solidarity of men and women in crisis, which I hope to convey in some measure through a sampling of personal correspondence and other writings.[5]

I also attempt to recover the historical significance of *politics* by taking seriously its efforts to define new radical directions after 1945. Drawing on the legacy of classical humanism and the modern libertarian tradition, Macdonald and his colleagues came to see World War II, with its monstrous scale and ethos of victory at any price, as an abuse of force, a consequence of the modern faith in the metanarrative of Progress. Assured of their grasp of the workings of the historical process and confident that things would inevitably "come out all right" in some final accounting, people on all sides of the conflict abandoned any notion of restraint in pursuit of their ends, with murderous results. After the war the *politics* intellectuals called for a renewed appreciation of the limits of knowledge and the contingency of human existence as the first step away from a world of untrammeled power and total violence. This ethic demanded the creation of a society radically different from the statist regimes then solidifying their hegemony—a decentered, pluralistic order founded on the dignity and moral autonomy of individuals linked by personal, rather than abstract, relations.

The *politics* agenda for reconstruction was far from fully developed, and it was not without its contradictions. One theme of this study, for example, is Macdonald's dramatic oscillation between hope and despair, the latter promoting impulses toward categorical denunciation and, ultimately, withdrawal. Still, the ideas he and his friends advanced in the 1940s bear striking affinities to the experiments in "participatory democracy" associated with the New Left two decades later, and they also anticipate current debates about the need for an independent sphere of civil society initiated by dissidents from the former Soviet bloc. I believe that it is especially useful to revisit the pages of *politics* now, as the cold war recedes and the struggle is joined over the nature of the "New World Order" that we shall be living well into the next century.

I begin by introducing the members of Macdonald's transatlantic circle, an assortment of heretics centered around his partnership with Nicola Chiaromonte, the refugee antifascist writer he came to know well during the Cape Cod summers of the mid-1940s. In Chapter 2 I examine Macdonald's reading of World War II, which by its end had degenerated, he argued, into a contest between automatized machines wreaking "the maximum physical devastation accompanied by the minimum human meaning." With the death of Progress and the bankruptcy of Marxism, Macdonald began a search for a new ethic, which he found embodied in the writings of Simone Weil and in exemplary acts of individual moral resistance during the war. In Chapters 3 and 4 I carry this search further, detailing his engagement, in the pages of *politics,* with European Resistance movements and American pacifists, civil rights activists, and cultural radicals—all seen as models of a new kind of political praxis.

In Chapter 5 I shift the analysis to a more theoretical exploration of the journal's efforts to formulate a humanist radicalism, discussing its use of the insights of libertarian "ancestors" as a basis for reconstructing a democratic sphere of public life. In Chapter 6 I focus on the efforts of the magazine's core voices—Macdonald, Chiaromonte, and the latter's mentor, Andrea Caffi—to define what I call a postmodern politics of limits, an approach rejecting the Enlightenment impulse toward absolute mastery and final solutions in favor of a world of contingent truths and circumscribed ambitions, of human dialogue and sociability. Of particular interest is the way Caffi's idea of "thinking outside politics" prefigured the antipolitical strategies of contemporary East European writers like Václav Havel. In Chapter 7 I consider the Packages Abroad relief program and Europe-America Groups, two practical endeavors that the *politics* intellectuals, in cooperation with Camus and others across the Atlantic, hoped would foster a cosmopolitan subculture of "sociability" as an alternative to the cold war. In Chapter 8 I describe the eclipse of "third camp" possibilities—and the demise of *politics*—by the end of the decade and conclude by tracking the Macdonald-Chiaromonte friendship to the death of the latter in 1972.

Historians have become accustomed to viewing the middle and late 1940s as a period of retrenchment and defeat for the American Left, a time when "deradicalized" intellectuals, bereft of new ideas, moved quickly to embrace the liberal anticommunist consensus taking shape by the end of the decade. But although World War II did irreparable damage to Old Left dreams of proletarian revolution, this did not mean the end of all hope for fundamental challenges to the status quo. Mary McCarthy spoke for Macdonald and others in their circle when she noted that the upheavals of those years ironically fostered an unusual optimism about prospects for a fresh start. "After the war was the very best period, politically, that I've been through," she later recalled wistfully. "It seemed possible still, utopian but possible, to change the world on a small scale." This study explores how the *politics* group, standing amid the ruins of disaster, tried to lay foundations for a new and better kind of human society.[6]

ONE

Preface to *politics*

Macdonald has turned his back on every kind of doctrine that implicitly would treat man as an object, even from a benevolent point of view. What he is concerned with is to create a modern humanism that can hold its own in the face of enormous bureaucracies and the atomic bomb. In so doing he has had to renounce many things which he had heretofore energetically championed. This is further evidence of what a really serious person he is.

—HANNAH ARENDT, 1946

An American Iconoclast

By conventional reckoning, the winter of 1943–44 was not an auspicious time to launch an antiwar "little magazine" in the United States. But Dwight Macdonald was a man used to going "against the grain," an instinctive nonconformist. Czeslaw Milosz once described Macdonald as "a totally American phenomenon" in the tradition of Thoreau, Whitman, and Melville—"the completely free man, capable of making decisions at all times and about all things strictly on the basis of his personal moral judgment." And for Norman Mailer, another admirer, Macdonald possessed a "quintessentially dialectical spirit" unique among his generation of intellectuals. Never was this iconoclasm more visible—and valuable—than in the difficult 1940s. Through his journal *politics*, born during that crucial winter, Macdonald helped to keep radical discourse alive in this country even as the Marxist hopes of the previous decade lay in ashes, and with the end of World War II he saw creative possibilities that escaped most of his peers. Because *politics* was such a personal vehicle, directly reflecting its editor's strengths and weaknesses as a critic, it is important to begin with some understanding of his early development.[1]

Dwight Macdonald was born in New York City in March 1906. His early life differed in important respects from the background of others among the founding generation of New York Intellectuals with whom he eventually became identified. He grew up, not as an outsider in a working-class Jewish tenement in lower Manhattan, but instead as a child of privilege in comfortable WASP surroundings on the Upper West Side. The central motif of Macdonald's formative years, therefore, was the emergence of a radically critical consciousness, a rejection of the culture to which he was born in favor of experience on the margins.[2]

Macdonald's father Dwight was a struggling lawyer; his mother, the former Alice Hedges, was the daughter of a wealthy Brooklyn merchant. Robert Cummings tells us that young Dwight exhibited an early temperamental preference for his father, with whom he shared the most intense emotional bond of his life. Dwight Sr.'s humanity—his affable spontaneity, self-deprecating sense of humor, and intellectual curiosity—seemed a stark contrast to Alice's more genteel, reserved, and status-conscious personality. The elder Dwight's relative lack of success in financial matters and the shattering blow of his sudden, premature death by heart attack in 1926 help to explain his son's later repudiation of the empty and unjust business ethos he associated with his maternal relatives.[3]

Dwight Jr. was a bright, precocious child. Encouraged by his father, the boy displayed a natural interest in books and the life of the mind, and from kindergarten to the Ivy League he enjoyed the advantages of a first-class formal education. At Phillips Exeter Academy, Macdonald won literary prizes and became "class poet," but he also began to cultivate a public identity as a dissident troublemaker. During his years in prep school, and later at Yale, he took part in a number of small aesthetic rebellions (an overt political consciousness was still in the future), protesting the petty and confining codes of an anachronistic institutional universe. He also gravitated to small oppositional enclaves like the "Hedonists," defiant admirers of Wilde and Mencken. It was in such youthful coteries, according to Cummings, that Macdonald first developed the habit of seeing himself as part of a cultural elite, besieged by the philistine masses.[4]

Upon graduation from Yale in 1928, Macdonald lacked a clear sense of direction, and, in order to help his financially strapped family, he decided to try his hand in the world of commerce. His six months as a thirty-dollars-a-week "executive trainee" for Macy's department store, culminating in the offer of a position as a sales clerk behind the necktie counter, stands as one of the more unlikely moments in American intellectual history, especially given Macdonald's notorious lifelong disregard for sartorial niceties. Macdonald unhesitatingly declined the job, now further convinced of the corruption and absurdity of marketplace values. Three decades later he recalled the experience: "I was appalled by the ferocity of interexecutive competition, I disliked the few big-shots I met (and doubtless *vice versa*) and I soon realized not only that I was without business talent but also that even a modest degree of success was possible only if one took merchandising far more seriously than I was able to."[5]

Macdonald was to return to the business world only a few weeks later, but this time at a remove from its front lines. With the help of a Yale classmate he landed a position as a writer for *Fortune*, then just getting underway as the latest entry in Henry Luce's burgeoning publishing empire. For Macdonald, the years spent in the Luce stable were a kind of graduate school, an opportunity to hone his prose and to develop his considerable journalistic instincts. Macdonald's view from the belly of the capitalist beast during the depths of the economic crisis of the 1930s also destroyed any remaining illusions he might have had about the virtues of American free enterprise. At the time he still couched his critique in the language of the previous decade's revulsion against provincial Babbitry rather than in any coherent theoretical framework. He later explained: "My undergraduate suspicions were confirmed—the men running our capitalist system were narrow, uncultivated and commonplace; they had a knack for business as unrelated to other qualities as a talent for chess ... their social and economic theories, or rather prejudices, were childish; their Republican Party was as unable to cope with the depression as they were."[6]

Macdonald's views began to take on a more political cast in the mid-1930s. Two developments precipitated his decision to embark on a career as a radical journalist. The first was his marriage to Nancy Rodman, a woman from an elite background whose libertarian disposition and tireless devotion to social causes exerted a moral influence on those around her which, according to Dwight Macdonald's biographer, Michael Wreszin, is difficult to overstate. Italian émigré Niccolo Tucci, a friend of the Macdonalds in the 1940s, called Nancy "the soul of *politics*." Fellow Vassar graduate Mary McCarthy once described Nancy Macdonald's impulse to help the less fortunate as "a vocation—a calling, such as happened to figures in religious history." In her memoirs, Nancy explained the peculiarly American, social-gospel roots of her "calling": "Helping was a kind of family tradition," she wrote, and "it was also the kind of work expected of women." Her grandmother ran a settlement house in New York City, and Nancy's mother arranged for her children to "adopt" two French orphans after World War I. Nancy vividly recalled her initial forays into the larger world: "At Sunday school at the Madison Avenue Presbyterian Church, I was given the assignment of visiting poor parishioners on East 72d Street. It was the first time that I climbed tenement stairs, tapped on strange doors, and listened to people's problems."[7]

During the 1930s, Nancy's sympathies led to activism in radical political circles (originally inspired by her discovery of Trotsky's autobiography) and an abiding sense of connection to the struggle of the Spanish republicans. These interests naturally rubbed off on Dwight Macdonald after their marriage and a honeymoon trip to Mallorca. He began to accompany his wife to the meetings she regularly attended, gaining initiation into the hothouse Marxist subculture of depression-era New York. Soon Macdonald was himself immersed in Marx, Lenin, and Trotsky; with his wife he became a "mild fellow traveler," participating in events sponsored by the Communist Party to raise money for southern sharecroppers, for the defense of Tom Mooney, and a number of other Popular Front causes.[8]

Dwight Macdonald once commented on the relative lateness of his arrival to the revolutionary camp, a consequence, in part at least, of attending Yale rather than City College or a similar bastion of radical education. "Many of my Trotskyist comrades had begun handing out antiwar leaflets while they were in short pants," he noted. "At thirty, when I first read Marx, they were scarred veterans." He justified his new political direction on "pragmatic" grounds: "I leaned toward the Communists because they alone on the American Left seemed to be 'doing something.'" In contrast to the experience of the other New York Intellectuals, however, Macdonald's embrace of Marxist doctrine was equivocal from the start. "The critical side attracted me, and also the protest against capitalist injustice," he explained, "but the dogmatism and the insistence on explaining everything by one system of thought repelled me (as did a certain moral callousness)." Revelations about the Moscow Trials in 1936–37 prevented Macdonald from developing the illusions about the nature of Stalinism held by American radicals of longer standing. Diana Trilling made this point to him during an interview decades later. "As soon as you were really learning about the Soviet Union," she remarked, "you were learning it in the spirit of dissent from it." In the years following his "conversion," Macdonald would be a most heretical Marxist.[9]

Resignation from *Fortune* in the late spring of 1936 signaled the end of the first phase of Dwight Macdonald's political awakening. Luce's writers enjoyed an unusual degree of editorial freedom during the New Deal decade; and in keeping with the Rooseveltian zeitgeist, articles with a moderately liberal tone often managed to find their way into print. Macdonald was drifting to the left further and faster than most of his colleagues, however, and he characteristically pushed his license of expression too far, introducing the final installment of an exposé about U.S. Steel with a quote from Lenin about the "inevitability" of socialism. Michael Wreszin writes that the suffering Macdonald saw while doing field research in "squalid company towns" affected him deeply. When his superiors decided that the piece could appear only in a drastically watered-down form, Macdonald, who had been looking for an excuse to move on, walked out in protest. He and Nancy now began what would be a "thirteen-year sabbatical" in the world of radical journalism.[10]

At the end of the following year Dwight Macdonald and two Yale friends, F. W. Dupee and George L. K. Morris, joined with Philip Rahv and William Phillips to revive their "little magazine," *Partisan Review,* as a voice of independent radicalism. Rahv and Phillips originally founded *PR* in 1934 as a literary organ for the Communist Party's John Reed Club in New York, but they soon became disenchanted with the Stalinist approach to culture, represented first by the commitment to a formulaic "proletarian literature" and, after the mid-decade shift to a Popular Front strategy, by an uncritical celebration of American mythic traditions. In 1936 Rahv and Phillips finally severed their ties to the Party, and *PR* folded. In its later incarnation it would become the most influential literary-political journal of the prewar anti-Stalinist Left.[11]

A major reason for the success of the new *PR* was the unique chemistry that existed between its editors. In his recent study of the New York Intellectuals, Neil Jumonville describes Macdonald as an "emissary" from an older tradition of Puritan Yankee moral dissidence, transformed and revitalized by contact with "the wave of radicalism from Europe and the second-generation American Jews." Rahv and Phillips accepted a partnership with Macdonald on the basis of his gifts as a writer, and although they worried about his lack of political experience and propensity to take risks, they could not help but admire his energy and passionate love of argument. William Barrett captured the common sentiment when he later recalled that "Macdonald had some kind of galvanizing power, either generating arguments or attracting them down on his own head, so that when he was present disputes seemed to go off like small firecrackers all over the place."[12]

As a group, the *PR* intellectuals styled themselves descendants of the cultural rebels of the 1910s. Alfred Kazin has vividly evoked this sense of a shared tradition:

> When I read Randolph Bourne and the young Van Wyck Brooks of *America's Coming of Age,* I could not feel that 1938 was so far from 1912. . . . I thought I could see across the wasteland of the Twenties to our real literary brethren in the utopians and Socialist bohemians of 1912. . . . We were in revolution, prodigiously on the move again, as

in that glorious season before the First World War, whose greatest spirits everywhere had been *literary* radicals, the *avant-garde* in every department of life.

In the face of the apparently inexorable advance of totalitarianism in the late 1930s and early 1940s, the editors of *Partisan Review* defined their mission as the defense of the possibilities of a radical politics and an autonomous, experimental modernist art first identified by their forebears a generation earlier. Although Macdonald involved himself on both fronts, he is probably best remembered for his crusade against the cultural regimentation he saw proceeding in brutal fashion in the Soviet Union and in more subtle forms in the United States. Macdonald devoted special attention to exposing what he condemned as the vulgar literary nationalism practiced by writers like Van Wyck Brooks (a betrayal of his youthful ideals, and perhaps the harbinger of a new wave of World War I–style repression) and the imperialist incursions of commercial mass culture.[13]

Several commentators have noted inherent tensions between *PR*'s political and cultural agendas during its heroic period. In fact, when they came into conflict, the *democratic* aspirations of the former often gave way to the *elitist* imperatives of the latter. David Hollinger has identified the guiding ideal of the New York Intellectuals as "cosmopolitanism," a breadth and openness to diversity derived from the "transnational" alternative to the "melting pot" articulated by Randolph Bourne in 1916. Hollinger argues that the WASPS and Jews around *PR*, in flight from what they experienced as the parochial limitations of their respective backgrounds, joined forces in the 1930s and 1940s to try to forge a perspective incorporating the best of Western traditions. Literary modernism and, for a time at least, Marxian socialism seemed to offer such a transcendent synthesis.[14]

This reading explains *PR*'s aggressively international flavor and the efforts by members of its circle to "Europeanize" what they perceived to be a backward, provincial domestic culture. Terry Cooney has argued, however, that the brand of cosmopolitanism practiced by the New York Intellectuals fell short of the Bournian ideal of a true dialectical interchange between the universal and the particular. Cooney properly concludes that throughout their careers the writers at *PR*, including Macdonald, tended toward too reflexive a dismissal of beliefs "that struck them as religious, mythic, rural, narrowly national, popular, simplistic, or restrictive."[15]

Macdonald remained active in Trotskyist circles throughout his tenure at *PR*. He valued Leon Trotsky, above all, as a model of the cultured, cosmopolitan intellectual, a man who had achieved the rare combination of radical thinking and effective action. Macdonald supported American efforts to exonerate Trotsky (by now exiled in Mexico City) from Stalinist charges of treason, and he worked with his co-editors in an unsuccessful attempt to recruit the renowned dissident as a contributor to *PR*. During the early stages of the war in Europe, Macdonald formally joined the Trotsky-inspired Socialist Workers Party, but the marriage was predictably stormy and brief. Macdonald objected to the group's authoritarian procedures and absurd sectarianism, and an unrelenting heterodoxy in factional disputes won him a reputation for frivolous "irresponsibility"—an epithet he wore as a badge of honor. In his memoirs, Sidney Hook, a critical admirer, recalled the nature of the problem: "Macdonald never got along with the professional revolutionists of the [SWP], not because he lacked fervor but because he lacked discipline. He would blurt things out—out of season and to the wrong people." Eventually Macdonald even drew the ire of Trotsky himself. Stung by the American upstart's criticisms of his suppression of the Kronstadt mutiny during the early days of the Bolshevik Revolution, Trotsky ended the discussion with a brutal retort. "Everyone has the right to be stupid on occasion," he wrote, "but Comrade Macdonald abuses the privilege."[16]

Partisan Review's editorial alliance was one of the many casualties of the Second World War. Initially there was agreement on the need to withhold support from the conflict, interpreted as another in a long succession of contests between rival imperialisms. Macdonald, joining the Workers Party in a break with SWP, adopted its "third camp" argument that, under the circumstances, the only cause worth fighting for was an international proletarian revolution. Even before the outbreak of hostilities, Macdonald declared the struggle a replay of the previous world war, the second half of a "tragi-comedy" promising "an orgy of slaughter and destruction compared to which the last war will seem idyllic." In a spring 1939 *PR* editorial, "War and the Intellectuals, Act Two," Macdonald spoke for his colleagues by attacking those who accepted the "progressive" justifications for a new mobilization. Echoing Randolph Bourne, he reserved special censure for American liberals willing to be fooled again, eager to offer their services as advertising men for a process over which they would have no real influence. Macdonald wrote:

> As the savage hopefully calls the dreaded volcano "the blessed source of all good things," so the intellectual believes in the power of verbal formulae to sweeten the ghastliest realities. The last war would have been a dirty business were it not for those glowing phrases of Woodrow Wilson: "Self Determination of Nations . . . A People's War . . . Open Covenants Openly Arrived At . . . A World Safe For Democ-

racy." Now once more we have in the White House a statesman who also knows how to use that rhetoric of heart-warming abstractions and moral earnestness which attracts the intellectuals. The President speaks their language.[17]

As the war unfolded, however, and the possibility of a Nazi victory became a frighteningly real one, cracks in *PR*'s united front began to appear. Rahv and Phillips came to accept the necessity of American participation in the anti-Hitler coalition, and they became nervous about Macdonald's stridently antiwar position. The schism deepened with each passing month. In the summer of 1941, just after the German invasion of the Soviet Union, Macdonald and Clement Greenberg issued "10 Propositions on the War," a defiant reiteration of their commitment to "third campism." Rahv responded several months later by rejecting the "morally absolutist" Macdonald-Greenberg program of "revolutionary defeatism," presenting a critique that, in retrospect, reveals a surer grasp of the available alternatives (which, for the moment, did *not* include revolutionary socialism). The war, he argued, "will either be won by the combined might of the Anglo-American imperialism and Stalin's Red Army, or else it won't be won at all; and the military defeat of Germany remains the indispensable pre-condition of any progressive action in the future." Rahv concluded: "Oracular appeals to history and a mere show of will on the part of a few literary intransigents will avail us nothing."[18]

Macdonald disagreed with his colleagues' lesser-evil, "realist" assessment, but what he found particularly frustrating was their desire to quash further discussion of the war in the pages of *PR*. Rahv and Phillips had no real appetite to press a stance that put them in the company of patriotic nationalists—Macdonald later noted that they lacked "a vocabulary for a critical defense of the war." Moreover, there was genuine concern that full-scale polemical exchanges might invite the kind of government suppression common in the last war. The skirmishes continued until mid-1943, when Macdonald finally submitted his resignation from the editorial board. He had long considered either taking over *PR* or starting his own magazine, "a more informal, disrespectable, and chance-taking" vehicle in which cultural criticism would be subordinated to political analysis, and a change in financial backing arranged by Rahv and Phillips that year made the latter course the practical one. Nancy Macdonald, *PR*'s business manager for six years, left with her husband, having demonstrated, among other things, a genius for operating on a shoestring budget.[19]

Macdonald hoped that his proposed journal would foster a renewal of the radical dialogue largely suspended in the wartime atmosphere of "national unity." In an early prospectus he explained: "Because of the tendency toward institutionalization, conformity, total integration of all groups and opinion into the 'official' pattern, which exists today so strongly everywhere, there is a special value in the expression of independent, dissident, nonconformist criticism." In addition, Macdonald felt that this was the "ideal historical moment" for a forum whose "crystalizing theme" would be the shape of the postwar world: "We seem to be heading into a period of great political-social stress and strain —liberals rapidly losing illusions, ready to listen to reason—labor movement on move again, so is blackest reaction—FDR govt.'s internal and international policies drifting rightward—a completely new magazine, wholly devoted to politics, with a left line, should find a wide and receptive audience."[20]

In the last months of 1943 the project began to come together. Macdonald consulted with sympathetic younger intellectuals he knew from *PR* and Workers Party circles such as C. Wright Mills, Paul Goodman, and German émigré Lewis Coser about the magazine's format, contributors, and even its title. Mills, then a young academic at the University of Maryland, protested the first idea Macdonald suggested as needlessly provocative: "For gods sake dont call it 'the radical review.' get some more innocuous name. maybe you do not realize how many people you estrange by such publicity of names . . . radicalism comes out in detailed and compelling analysis not in names and slogans. It wd cost many men in many institutions their jobs if they were to write for a journal with such a name." Mills offered "Politics" as an "innocuous" alternative ("the magazines that last and grow in influence have plain titles," he observed). Macdonald accepted the suggestion, adding to it the democratic flourish of a small "p." The first issue appeared on newsstands in early 1944, boldly stating its founder's aim to "create a center of consciousness on the Left" where none currently existed.[21]

In that first issue Macdonald contrasted his brand of engagement to Arthur Koestler's much-discussed call in the *New York Times* for a "New Fraternity of Pessimists,"individuals who would "create oases in the interregnum desert" designed to preserve humane values for a more hospitable day. Macdonald blasted Koestler's strategy to "lie low and fatalistically wait until the time is ripe" as shortsighted and "self-liquidating." He wrote:

> The next few decades require not an "oasis psychology" among Left intellectuals, but rather a more conscious, active intervention in the historical process. It will be a period of tremendous suffering, tremendous revolutionary *possibilities*, in Europe and in the colonial countries. One's endeavor should be not to withdraw into illusory "oases" but rather to go into the desert, share the common experience, and try to find a road out of the wilderness.

The task of "active intervention into the historical process" was to prove more difficult than Macdonald imagined in early 1944, however, and the temptations of the "oasis psychology" would not always be so easy to dismiss.[22]

Creating a New Left "Center of Consciousness"

A Radical Bridge

In the late 1960s, amid the social upheavals associated with Vietnam and the rise of the worldwide student insurgency, Dwight Macdonald's close friend Hannah Arendt observed that rereading *politics* was much more than an exercise in nostalgia. On the contrary, she found the magazine still fresh and lively, many of its insights of "astounding" relevance to contemporary debates. Much of the credit for this vitality naturally went to Macdonald himself. The questions he was asking in the 1940s—about individual responsibility in a bureaucratic, warmaking society, for example—anticipated the preoccupations of the New Left two decades later. In this connection, Arendt called *politics* a "premature dress rehearsal" for what was to follow. Just as important as Macdonald's own ideas in the success of the enterprise, however, was his "flair in the choice of contributors." Citing the remarkable list of European and younger American writers *politics* helped introduce to American readers, Arendt concluded that "if this was a one-man magazine, it was never the magazine of one man's opinion." Instead, *politics* became a refuge for homeless radicals like Macdonald himself, "a focal point for many who would no longer fit into any party or group."[23]

In late 1943, as Macdonald focused on the precise shape his new project should take, the question of contributors became fundamental. Years later he recalled that the initial range of possibilities considered "was not an inspiring list." He explained: "Almost all the names I could think of . . . were the familiar ones of the Old Left, anti-Stalinist section, of which [I] had been a part for so long. All good men, honorable men, and sound politically. Maybe too sound—was it worth all that trouble to get out another edition of so well-established a text?" Isolated from most of the leading figures in New York literary circles because of his antiwar stance, and intent upon giving his magazine an original flavor, Macdonald decided to experiment, taking advantage of untapped resources he saw readily at hand. In its first issue he committed *politics* to providing a forum for two marginalized groups in particular: "younger, relatively unknown American intellectuals," presumably less wedded to Marxist verities and habits of thought than their elders; and "those many leftist refugees who can produce informed analysis of European events but at present have no satisfactory means of communication with advanced American opinion."[24]

As Terry Cooney noted in his study of *Partisan Review,* defining an intellectual circle is necessarily an imprecise business. The *politics* "circle" presents special problems, owing to its unusually diffuse character. Many of the European participants never set foot in New York. Victor Serge, for example, spent most of the war years in Mexico City, and Andrea Caffi conversed with Macdonald and company only through occasional letters from his exile in southwest France. Simone Weil, arguably the most compelling voice in the *politics* circle, died in England six months before the journal first appeared. In addition, some of Macdonald's most notable contacts during the period, among them Arendt and George Orwell, offered only occasional or indirect contributions, whereas others less well known, especially the Italians Chiaromonte and Caffi, would exert a more profound influence. It is nonetheless appropriate to speak of a distinctive *politics* community, one that evolved very much along the lines set forth in Macdonald's founding blueprint. The best metaphor for the role the magazine came to play in the 1940s is that of a *bridge:* a bridge between radical generations, between "Old" Left and "New," and between Europe and America.[25]

Training Ground for the Next Generation

Macdonald demonstrated amazing prescience in his choice of new American faces. A large number of the "younger, relatively unknown" intellectuals who cut their teeth in the pages of *politics* went on to great prominence in the postwar decades. Macdonald first encountered most of these writers during his days at *Partisan Review*—literary critic Lionel Abel, for example, and the young novelist Mary McCarthy. Although McCarthy, who had served as *PR*'s theater columnist, rarely wrote for *politics,* she sided with Macdonald on the war question and became a lifelong friend and confidant. Their affinity is not surprising. Beyond agreement on particular issues, McCarthy was, in many ways, cut from the same privileged cloth as Macdonald: she was another outsider thriving in the predominantly Jewish milieu of the New York Intellectuals. McCarthy was also a relative latecomer to radical politics and, like Macdonald, was first inspired to activism by the injustices surrounding the Moscow Trials. McCarthy's recollection of how she stumbled into the Trotskyist camp provides a revealing glimpse into both her moral outlook and the world of 1930s Marxist sectarianism. She told an interviewer about attending a party given by James T. Farrell's publisher:

> There were a lot of Communists [there and] Farrell went around asking people whether they thought Trotsky was entitled to a hearing

and to the right of asylum. I said yes, and that was all. The next thing I discovered I was on the letterhead of something calling itself the American Committee for the Defense of Leon Trotsky. I was furious, of course, at this use of my name. . . . Just as I was about to make some sort of protest, I began to get all sorts of calls from Stalinists, telling me to get off the committee. I began to see that other people were falling off . . . and this cowardice impressed me so unfavorably that naturally I didn't say anything about my name having got on there by accident. . . . So I stayed.[26]

Other "younger generation" contributors to *politics* held more conventional leftist pedigrees. Daniel Bell, then at the beginning of a distinguished career as an academic sociologist, took time from his editorship of the *New Leader* to analyze socialism's declining prospects for his friend's new journal. Bell's pessimism, based on his sense that the American labor movement had irrevocably sacrificed its independence in the state-controlled wartime economic order, played a key role in Macdonald's accelerating flight from Marxism by mid-decade.[27]

Macdonald got to know Irving Howe in Workers Party circles during the early 1940s. As a draftee, Howe spent the later years of the war far from the internecine political feuds of New York City, reading books in the splendid isolation of a remote army outpost in Alaska. He returned to find the Trotskyist Left in a shambles and proceeded "down the slopes of apostasy" as a fifteen-dollar-a-week assistant at *politics,* writing a "Magazine Chronicle" and performing other editorial chores. During this apprenticeship Macdonald gave Howe the pseudonym "Theodore Dryden," described to readers as a "ferret breeder in Staten Island." Although Howe later acknowledged *politics* as "the liveliest magazine the American Left had seen in decades," his association with this ideological den of iniquity was not well received by his WP comrades. He recalled in his memoirs:

In my political milieu, *politics* was read with a nervous fascination, for while we were troubled by its accumulating "deviations," it was still a magazine one could actually read, which was more than could usually be said for our *New International*. . . . That I was now working for *politics* made some friends in the movement uneasy, as hard-shell Baptists must feel when a congregant succumbs to soft-shells.

Howe was permitted to maintain his WP credentials only on condition that he serve as Macdonald's "technical aide" rather than "editorial collaborator"—a distinction typical of the sectarian mentality with which he was becoming increasingly disillusioned.[28]

The two most important young Americans in the *politics* orbit were Paul Goodman and C. Wright Mills, fellow "troublemakers" who laid much of the groundwork for the radicalism of the student New Left of the 1960s. Goodman, the abrasive bohemian exile from City College later famous as an icon of the counterculture, was never a popular figure in New York Intellectual circles, but from their earliest contacts Dwight Macdonald felt drawn to his uncompromising heterodoxy. In some respects, Goodman was an extreme version of Macdonald, his views a volatile mixture of moral utopianism and pragmatic common sense, expressed in a style that as Theodore Roszak has observed, "annoys its way into being taken seriously." Macdonald conceded the defects in Goodman's writing. "I, too, wish he would write less and better," Macdonald commented in 1946, "would put more flesh on the apodictic bones of his ideas, and would haul down the banner: *Pour epater les bourgeois.*" Still, the editor of *politics* found many of Goodman's ideas profound and concluded that the hostility they elicited was a reaction to the breadth and freedom of his intellect, the ability to "follow his ideas"—whether about sexuality or city planning—"to their rational conclusion, no matter how 'absurd' it may turn out to be."[29]

Goodman sparked controversy at *Partisan Review* in 1942 by submitting for publication an aggressive call to draft resistance and "sedition." He was already articulating the anarcho-pacifist position on the war that Macdonald would embrace three years later. Goodman argued that the current crisis was only an acute form of the violence endemic to modern centralized states. "By the war," he wrote, "I do not mean something subsequent to the attack on Pearl Harbor, but the activity of decades which has adapted itself with such astonishing smoothness to the present worldwide national unities." Goodman's declarations earned him a permanent place on Rahv and Phillips's unofficial blacklist at *Partisan Review,* seriously damaging his literary aspirations. Although too hot for *PR* to handle, Goodman was perfectly suited for Macdonald's new magazine venture, where he appeared frequently.[30]

The 1940s was a productive period for Paul Goodman. It was then that he first developed the critique of postwar America's technocratic civilization that would stir a wider audience after the publication of his landmark best-seller, *Growing Up Absurd* (1960). The social alternative Goodman envisioned was a decentralized world of small-scale communities, where meaningful work and fulfilling social relationships replaced the atomizing routines of industrial production. His 1947 study *Communitas,* written in partnership with his architect brother Percival, brimmed with practical suggestions for urban and environmental reform (banning cars from Manhattan, for example) that remain fresh even decades later. To the eclectic search for a post-Marxist radicalism conducted in the pages of *politics* Goodman contributed early readings of Freudian revisionist Wilhelm Reich, proponent of a "psychobiological" theory of revolution. According to Reich and Goodman, it was through the liberation of repressed libidinal drives, rather than institutional change, that a new, anti-authoritarian society would be born. Commentators in the 1940s considered these ideas wild speculation; twenty years later they were popular discourse.[31]

C. Wright Mills, the maverick academic who posthumously inspired Tom Hayden and the Students for a Democratic Society, was also, as we have seen, a Macdonald intimate during the *politics* years. Born and raised in Texas, Mills took a Ph.D. in sociology at the University of Wisconsin, long a heartland bastion of radical thought, where he studied the ideas of Veblen, Dewey, and Max Weber. Mills met Macdonald in the early 1940s, soon after arriving on the East Coast to assume a faculty position at the University of Maryland. Macdonald later explained their mutual attraction:

> We took to each other partly because we were isolated radicals in a wartime period and misery loves company but also because of a temperamental affinity: we were both congenital rebels, passionately contemptuous of every received idea and established institution and not at all inarticulate about it. . . . Also we had in common a peculiar (and incompatible really — but there it was) mixture of innocence and cynicism, optimism and skepticism. We were ever hopeful, ever disillusioned.[32]

Mills was eager to support the new antiwar journal whose title he had suggested, and in its initial year he made two important contributions. One was an excerpt of a translation of Weber, featured in the October 1944 issue. Part of a larger volume Mills prepared in collaboration with H. H. Gerth, his Wisconsin mentor, this was the first exposure to the pioneering German sociologist for most American readers. Weber's pessimistic account of the processes of bureaucratic rationalization, a radical departure from Marxist orthodoxy, seemed especially prophetic in a period defined by Hiroshima and the Holocaust.[33]

In addition, Mills's essay, "The Powerless People," appeared in the third issue of *politics* in April 1944. Addressed to a demoralized Left, this manifesto for intellectual engagement proved to be a formative moment for the twenty-eight-year-old writer, representing, as James Miller has observed, "nothing less than a preview of Mills's life project." It also helped to define the central concerns of the *politics* community. Building on Weber, the essay described a tragic world of "organized irresponsibility," where "the centers of political initiative (become) less and less accessible" and "men in high places must hide the facts of life in order to retain their power," safe from "the violent results of their own decisions." "On every hand," Mills concluded, "the individual is confronted with seemingly remote organizations and he feels dwarfed and helpless," reduced to the role of passive spectator. Intellectuals, in and out of the academy, were implicated in the general corruption, buttressing the status quo either by retreat into private worlds of alienation and "busy work" or by hiring themselves out as standardized "commodities" available to the highest bidder. In either case, they succumbed to subtle but pervasive pressures to refrain from expressing unpopular views.[34]

What could the "powerless" dissident, interested in restoring a "politics of truth" and democratic responsibility, do in such circumstances? The answer went beyond traditional Marxist formulas for class struggle. Instead, Mills argued for an aggressive reassertion of critical independence, a politics of individual moral "resistance" to the machinery of oppression that would become increasingly attractive to Dwight Macdonald as World War II entered its concluding months. Artists and intellectuals, who were "among the few remaining personalities equipped to resist and to fight the stereotyping and consequent death of genuinely lively things," bore a special duty to awaken their less favorably situated fellow citizens to the realities of the crisis. Mills urged his peers to channel their private frustrations outward, to search for a grassroots public among the other "powerless" elements of society, wherever they might be found. Although he offered few specifics on how this might be done, Mills identified the urgent immediate task as the formulation of challenges to the top-down postwar order already being prepared by Allied authorities. This was a role Macdonald and others in his circle would attempt to fulfill in the years to come.[35]

"A Transplanted Spore of European Culture"

If Dwight Macdonald achieved his goal of building a generational bridge in the 1940s, he was even more successful in establishing links across the Atlantic. The Euro-American character of *politics,* made possible by the exigencies of the war, is what truly sets it apart from other journals in the annals of the intellectual Left. By providing a forum of expression for physically and ideologically displaced voices, by giving them, as Andrea Caffi observed from France, a "lighted torch around which to rally," Macdonald carried *PR*'s efforts to "Europeanize" a provincial American culture to new levels. The *politics* community—contributors and readers, Europeans and Americans—was a living experiment in "cosmopolitanism," bringing a wide variety of experiences and traditions into fruitful conversation about how to rescue the best features of a shared Western culture.[36]

In September 1945, Macdonald reflected on the shape his journal had somewhat unexpectedly assumed during its first eighteen months of operation. Letters from Europe extolling the magazine's critical independence often drew larger conclusions about the atmosphere prevailing across the Atlantic. The words of a correspondent from Paris were typical: "I must confess that there were times when we had great doubts about America. Most of the American soldiers we have known talked only of 'football' and were bored by the problems that preoccupy us. But 'Politics' shows that there is, in America, an elite which discusses freely the burning problems of today, and that it still exists, that spirit of free criticism which we had thought dead."[37]

Macdonald felt compelled to correct the mistaken impression that *politics* spoke for a broad cross-section of American opinion. He described his project's function in more modest terms: "The most I would claim for American intellectuals is that some of them are still sceptics and rebels—and that they are willing to learn. Furthermore, many if not most of the contributors to 'Politics' are refugees, so that the magazine is a kind of transplanted spore of European culture growing in an environment that is physically and politically more favorable to free thought than that of modern Europe." By nurturing these "transplanted spores," Macdonald felt that *politics* could help to preserve cultural values threatened by the crises of totalitarianism and total war.[38]

Macdonald had come to admire George Orwell as a kindred spirit in the early 1940s, when Orwell's regular dispatches from overseas provided discussions of the war otherwise absent from the pages of a divided *Partisan Review*. In a 1943 draft prospectus for his new magazine, Macdonald expressed his intent to model its political journalism after that of his English counterpart ("to try to do for [the] USA scene what Orwell does for London"), and throughout the decade the two men maintained an intimate personal correspondence. Macdonald saw in Orwell a fellow exile from the cloister of class privilege and private schools, a writer whose work combined empathy for the sufferings of the dispossessed (which he witnessed at close range, on the streets of Paris and London and among the POUMist forces in Spain) with a plain writing style purged of ideological cant and hyperbole.[39]

Like Macdonald, Orwell identified himself as a proponent of libertarian socialism; and also like his American friend, he earned the enmity of many on the Left for exposing perspectives that fell short of that ideal. Both writers crusaded against the "Russomania" gripping liberal fellow travelers during the war period, a problem that was particularly acute in

England. Orwell complained to Macdonald of the censorship pressures he faced for voicing the slightest reservations about his country's temporary ally to the east. Both men had concluded by the 1940s that the crimes of the Stalinist regime had deep roots in Bolshevik authoritarianism. This, as Orwell explained in a 1946 letter to Macdonald, was the theme of his best-selling allegory, *Animal Farm:*

> Of course I intended it primarily as a satire on the Russian revolution. But I did mean it to have a wider application in so much that I meant that *that kind* of revolution (violent conspiratorial revolution, led by unconsciously power-hungry people) can only lead to a change of masters. I meant the moral to be that revolutions only effect a radical improvement when the masses are alert and know when to chuck out their leaders as soon as the latter have done their job. . . . What I was trying to say was, "You can't have a revolution unless you make it for yourself; there is no such thing as a benevolent dictatorship."

Referring to his leftist critics, Orwell concluded: "If people think I am defending the status quo, that is . . . because they have grown pessimistic and assume that there is no alternative except dictatorship or laissez-faire capitalism." Macdonald concurred with this assessment, and he directed his efforts after the war to the task of defining such an alternative.[40]

Although from the beginning he was sympathetic to Macdonald's new magazine, following it closely and helping to secure British subscribers, Orwell was not a frequent contributor to *politics,* owing to his continuing commitments to *PR* and, later, to his deteriorating health (he died of tuberculosis in 1950). The two pieces that did appear in *politics,* however, were very much in accord with ideas advanced by others in its inner circle. "The Ethics of the Detective Story: From Raffles to Miss Blandish" (November 1944) was a small example of the kind of popular cultural criticism at which Orwell, like Macdonald, excelled. Orwell interpreted rising sales of lurid, "American-style" crime stories in England as the reflection of a general decline in public morality in the West—one of the disastrous consequences of the erosion of nineteenth-century social norms, however "foolish," corrupt, and embedded in hierarchy those norms may have been. Protagonists of earlier popular literature, he noted, acted within the well-defined limits of a shared code of behavior, a consensus that certain things were simply "not done." Characters in the pulp fiction of the "totalitarian" 1930s and 1940s, in contrast, felt no such inhibitions, obeying only the laws of power and success. The result, in books as in real life, was an insidious brutalization of human relations, a normalization of gratuitous violence. In "Catastrophic Gradualism" (September 1946), Orwell sounded another seminal *politics* theme, condemning the "progressive" narrative of history that allowed British intellectuals to defend Stalinism in the name of social advances that never seemed to materialize.[41]

Although they shared a common sensibility, Macdonald and Orwell did not see eye-to-eye on all matters. In a letter to the anarchist journal *Retort* in the late 1940s, defending Orwell's anti-ideological integrity, Macdonald acknowledged fundamental differences in their perspectives: "He's a liblab (tho of the finest quality, in my opinion), I'm a radical; he supported the late war, I didn't; he has hopes [for] the Labor [*sic*] Party, I haven't." For his part, Orwell considered Macdonald's third camp abstention from World War II, like his later flirtation with pacifism, fatally abstract and naive (a view shared by other Europeans in the *politics* camp). In 1947 Orwell succinctly reminded his friend of what, in his view, had been at stake in the face of Hitler's aggression. "The issue," he wrote, "was between having a war and letting Germany dominate Europe up to the Urals."[42]

A writer closer to Macdonald's brand of radicalism, and the most prominent British voice in the pages of *politics,* was George Woodcock. A conscientious objector during World War II, Woodcock later sent a semiregular "London Letter" to Macdonald, advising American readers about such topics as the state of civil liberties in Britain and the failure of the Labour Party to enact dramatic political change. His first article for *politics,* "The Tyranny of the Clock" (October 1944), was an imaginative analysis of the regimentation of modern life (inspired by American critic Lewis Mumford), the kind of non-Marxist social criticism Macdonald was increasingly interested in publishing. Woodcock helped to school Macdonald in the tenets of the anarchist tradition, and his periodical *Now* was in some respects a sister magazine to *politics,* sharing in its efforts to articulate a libertarian socialist alternative in the late 1940s. Woodcock and Macdonald commiserated about the trials of keeping an independent journal afloat, and in 1949 Woodcock finally abandoned the struggle, moving (with financial help from the Macdonalds) to rural British Columbia to set up an experiment in communal living.[43]

Woodcock's most important *politics* essay was a critique of his friend George Orwell in the December 1946 issue. In Woodcock's eyes, Orwell was a dinosaur, a "19th century liberal" willing to fight specific injustices but unable to mount a consistent attack on the root causes of society's ills. Woodcock conceded the symbolic importance of this latter-day Dickens: Orwell was "a rare survivor in the atomic age," and his "old-fashioned pragmatism," his "radical honesty and frankness, his respect for such excellent bourgeois mottoes as 'Fair Play' and 'Don't kick a man when he's down,' " served as necessary correctives to "the sneers of

Marxist amoralism." By 1946, however, for Woodcock as for Macdonald, nothing less than a principled resistance to state power in all its forms would do.[44]

Perhaps in their search for an oppositional stance in the wake of a catastrophic war, Woodcock, Macdonald, and others sometimes underestimated the ordinary, "old-fashioned" values Orwell represented and defended. Note, for example, Woodcock's dismissal of Orwell's views on local loyalties: "In *The Lion and the Unicorn* [Orwell] point[ed] out the power of patriotism over the English mind, and . . . claim[ed] that socialists should use this element in popular mythology as a means of gaining popular support. He failed to understand the fundamentally evil nature of patriotism as a producer of war and a bulwark of authority." This hostility to the particularist sentiments embodied in the notion of "patriotism" is a recurring motif in the discourse of some *politics* writers, and it seems to reveal a blind spot in their "cosmopolitan" vision. As Michael Walzer has argued, Orwell stands as a model of intellectual engagement—what Walzer terms "connected criticism"—precisely because of his grasp of the "national-popular" idiom of his culture. Orwell avoided the temptation of blanket condemnations, and he always conveyed an understanding that attachment to native rituals and traditions is part of what makes human beings whole and need not lead to chauvinism and war.[45]

A number of the new faces Dwight Macdonald recruited for his journal were European refugees, and *politics* deserves to be remembered as a significant chapter in the intellectual migration of the war years. Through their lives and their ideas these individuals, resilient bits of the "raw material of history," in Albert Camus's apt phrase, conveyed something of the depth of the human crisis abroad to insulated American readers.[46]

The Macdonalds had been active in emergency relief efforts since the war began. After the fall of France in the spring of 1940, Nancy Macdonald responded to a flood of desperate appeals for help by setting up the *Partisan Review* "Fund for European Writers and Artists," a project that raised hundreds of dollars and made a life or death difference for dozens of dissident refugees. While serving on this and other committees, Nancy learned skills in overcoming bureaucratic obstacles that were to make her an invaluable link in the transatlantic relief network for the next decade. She labored to obtain the money and documents needed for safe passage to America, typing biographies ("sometimes fanciful") to assure reluctant immigration authorities that the people she sponsored would make good citizens.[47]

The Macdonalds took special interest in the plight of the writer Victor Serge, a frequent *PR* contributor whom Nancy later affectionately called her "first refugee." Born in Belgium in 1890, Serge was, by the outbreak of the Second World War, a rare surviving member of the revolutionary generation of 1917. In Dwight Macdonald's words, Serge, like Trotsky, possessed "a breadth of culture and a personal integrity not very common among political figures." He was active in pre–World War I anarchist circles in Europe and in 1919 joined the staff of the Soviet Communist International, where he witnessed up close the degeneration of the Bolshevik experiment. By the 1930s Serge faced persecution as a Trotskyist, and only a concerted publicity campaign by Western intellectuals saved him from a death sentence during the Moscow Trials. While exiled in France, Serge published a series of works exposing Stalinism, and in 1940, as a well-known opponent of both the communists and fascists, he faced danger from a number of quarters as he and his family headed south, just ahead of the Nazi advance. A letter to Nancy Macdonald vividly conveys the experience common to the refugees she and her husband helped during the war. Serge wrote:

> By some luck I managed to flee Paris at the very last minute. We have been traveling in freight trains, spending nights in the fields. In a little village in the Loire country we were so tired that we lay down behind some stones and slept through an entire bombardment. Nowhere, in this completely chaotic world, were we able to find any asylum.
>
> Of all I once owned—clothes, books, writings—I was able to save only what my friends and I could carry away on our backs in knapsacks. It is very little, but fortunately includes the manuscripts which I have already begun. This letter is a sort of S.O.S. which I also hope that you will communicate to my known and unknown friends in America. . . . I don't at all know how long we are going to hold out.[48]

The Macdonalds invested enormous energy during the following months trying to save Victor Serge. They marshaled support for his case from prominent figures like Max Eastman, John Dewey, and Sidney Hook, and even made a special trip to Washington, D.C., in an unsuccessful effort to persuade State Department officials to grant entry to a man deemed undesirable for his past connections to the Communist Party. Serge finally obtained a Mexican visa, and in 1941 he and his son made the arduous journey (largely financed by the Macdonalds) from Marseille to Mexico City, where he spent the remainder of his life. The four chapters of Serge's memoirs that appeared in *politics,* together with pieces by Czech dissident Josep Gutman (writing as "Peter Meyer") and an excerpt from Anton Ciliga's *The Russian Enigma,* provided readers a detailed and authoritative history of the early development of the Stalinist dictatorship. When Serge died in November 1947, Dwight Macdonald paid tribute to his example as "a human being who struggled all his life against monstrous social institutions without himself becoming a monster."[49]

Before arriving in the United States, many of the Central European refugees who joined the *politics* circle spent time in some type of concentration camp, that "monstrous social institution" so representative of the horrors of the 1940s. These former internees included socialists like Henry Jacoby (who wrote under the pseudonym "Sebastian Franck") and the Viennese psychologist Bruno Bettelheim. "Behavior in Extreme Situations," Bettelheim's account of his year in prewar Dachau and Buchenwald, sent shock waves through the American intellectual community when it appeared in the August 1944 issue of *politics*. Macdonald discovered the essay buried in the academic *Journal of Abnormal Psychology,* and Daniel Bell later recalled that, more than any other article, it helped to "put *politics* on the map" for its "stunning" revelations about the process of personality disintegration in the camps—a phenomenon presumed to have implications for modern society at large.[50]

Hannah Arendt's experiences as an exile from Hitler's Germany and her brief stay in a French internment camp in 1940 inspired those inquiries into the nature of totalitarianism for which she became famous. Alfred Kazin has observed that Arendt's quietly passionate quest for understanding gave Americans "intellectual courage before the moral terror the war had willed to us." Although she never wrote for *politics,* Arendt's ideas, especially on the question of "collective guilt," influenced Dwight Macdonald's thinking in the 1940s profoundly. Robert Westbrook has noted that Arendt and Macdonald "recognized a shared set of interests and insights" after the war and were the first members of the New York Intellectual community to try to confront the meaning of the Holocaust. The two became close friends from the moment they met. Arendt, the grave, rigorous continental philosopher steeped in the ideas of her teachers, Husserl, Jaspers, and Heidegger, admired Macdonald's generous spirit and "fearlessness"; he represented the most appealing virtues of an American civic tradition she was just then beginning to discover. In a 1946 fellowship recommendation she offered this synopsis of her friend's mission: "Macdonald has turned his back on every kind of doctrine that implicitly would treat man as an object, even from a benevolent point of view. What he is concerned with is to create a modern humanism that can hold its own in the face of enormous bureaucracies and the atomic bomb." For Arendt, the fact that Macdonald approached the task with an open mind, willing to jettison earlier political commitments as they proved inadequate, revealed a rare "seriousness" of purpose rather than the frivolous irresponsibility alleged by his Marxist critics.[51]

Lewis Coser, another German exile, also became part of the *politics* circle in the 1940s, and he warmly remembered Dwight Macdonald as his "first guide to the American intellectual scene." Born in 1913 to an upper-middle-class Jewish family in Berlin, by the late 1920s Coser had become active in Weimar socialist politics. With Hitler's rise to power in 1933, Coser left Germany to join the burgeoning refugee community in Paris, where, between odd jobs, he was able to study at the Sorbonne. An early-morning knock at the door soon after the outbreak of World War II ended any semblance of a normal existence, however. French *gendarmes* arrested Coser, now, like Arendt, classified as an "enemy alien," and he spent a disorienting week with hundreds of others in the open-air *Stade de Columbes*, awaiting a gas attack from the German air force. In the months that followed, the authorities shuffled Coser from camp to camp, until "through a variety of tricks and maneuvers" he was able amid the chaos of the French collapse to escape to the south. In Vichy he was impressed by the simple acts of heroism and solidarity he witnessed among his fellow refugees, recalling especially how the Spaniards were able to sustain a sense of community under the most adverse circumstances. In 1941 Coser was among the "lucky few" to obtain an American travel visa, and he boarded one of the last ships to leave before the Germans occupied the entire country.[52]

Once in New York, Coser began to build a new life, marrying Rose Laub, his International Rescue Committee caseworker, and joining the Workers Party milieu. Coser also took a post with the Office of War Information, working beside fellow refugees ("a motley array of lyrical poets, economists and pacifists") translating smuggled Nazi literature. Eventually Coser met Nancy and then Dwight Macdonald, whom he came to esteem as "the most gifted journalist of his generation." Coser was one of a number of Europeans who regularly dropped in at the Macdonalds' small apartment on East Tenth Street, and he credited Dwight Macdonald with teaching him how to write in a stripped-down "American" style. From the beginning, Coser, under the pseudonym "Louis Clair," was a familiar voice in *politics*. His "European Newsreel" column passed along the latest international developments, fresh from the O.W.I. office or the informal émigré grapevine.[53]

Two decades after its demise, Dwight Macdonald described *politics* (in characteristically cinematic language) as an "Italian-American co-production." He was referring to his remarkable partnership with the antifascist writer Nicola Chiaromonte, which formed the heart of the journal's transatlantic community. During his years in New York in the 1940s, Chiaromonte became Macdonald's closest friend and adviser, and, as Irving Howe has noted, his breadth of knowledge and moral example gave Macdonald's search for a post-Marxist radicalism "a certain philosophical dimension" otherwise lacking. Chiaromonte's guiding principles were justice and freedom, and these unwavering commitments made him wary of the ideologies that went in and out of fashion during his lifetime. "When a line of political action was proposed to Nicola," Lionel Abel recalled, "he would ask himself, 'Will I be carried away by the deeds it requires?' " Mary McCarthy once wrote that "his ideas did not fit into an established category: he was neither on the left nor on the right. Nor did it follow that he was in the middle; he was alone." Chiaromonte's imprint on the thinking of the Americans in the *politics* circle was distinctive and profound. In a 1984 interview McCarthy explained: "Talking with Nicola Chiaromonte was an absolute awakening, and I never got over it." In an April 1947 letter to Chiaromonte upon his return to Europe after the war, Dwight Macdonald summed up his influence this way: "I've learned a great deal from you, Nick, and you've changed my whole intellectual outlook (you and the atom bomb)."[54]

Chiaromonte had suffered the archetypal twentieth-century European experiences of totalitarianism, exile, and war. Born into a middle-class family in the southern Italian town of Rapolla in 1905, Chiaromonte never lost his admiration for the strength, dignity, and innate anarchism of the rural peasantry that surrounded him. Although he enjoyed the benefits of a rigorous Jesuit education growing up in Rome, Chiaromonte developed an early preference for Greek humanism over theological abstraction, Catholic or Marxist. He also participated in the modernist cultural revolution of the 1910s and 1920s; the theater absorbed his deepest passions, and he was an especially ardent devotee of Pirandello. Following law studies at the University of Rome, Chiaromonte worked as a journalist, a career frustrated by the censorship restrictions in place under Mussolini. Chiaromonte became active in the underground opposition to the regime, and by 1934 he was forced to leave Italy, beginning a long period of exile.[55]

In Paris—the same city sheltering Arendt, Coser, and countless other refugees from all points of Europe in the 1930s—Chiaromonte again immersed himself in dissident political circles. His life came to center around the antifascist group *Giustizia e Libertà,* and it was in this milieu that he first met his intellectual mentor, Andrea Caffi. A veteran of heretical social causes dating back to prerevolutionary Russia, Caffi encouraged Chiaromonte's libertarian instincts, and as a group *Giustizia* embodied the elder man's idea of a spontaneous "sociable" community, existing "outside" the world of mass politics and official institutions.[56]

Despite his abhorrence of violence, Chiaromonte, like many others of his generation, felt duty bound to go to Spain in 1936 to fight on the side of the Republic. During the early months of the civil war he served in André Malraux's air squadron, surviving hazardous missions in its notoriously antiquated "flying coffins." Chiaromonte was the inspiration for the character Scali in Malraux's novel *Man's Hope*, the conscience-ridden intellectual out of place in a world of ruthless action, always reading Plato and raising difficult ethical questions. The courage and idealism of the ordinary Spaniards who came together to defend their revolution moved Chiaromonte deeply. In an essay published in the *Atlantic Monthly* in 1939, he wrote of the atmosphere:

> One sometimes has the impression among these people of being in the midst of a crowd of Patrick Henrys. "Give me liberty or give me death" seems to be everybody's motto. They have the common urge to liberate the whole world from the Fascist menace. This is often expressed by boasting and posturing. But there is also faith—a fanatic faith based upon this perfectly simple concept: a nation living in freedom, a society of honorable men obliged neither to go hungry nor to be clothed in rags. Could anything be simpler?

Chiaromonte broke with Malraux over the issue of Stalinism, and he returned to Paris dispirited, having witnessed a struggle originally motivated by a desire for justice devolve into uncontrolled ideological violence. For him, the Spanish tragedy was a model for the much larger conflagration about to begin.[57]

As Paris fell to the Nazis that terrible spring of 1940, Chiaromonte and his ailing Austrian-Jewish wife Annie joined the flood of refugees fleeing to the unoccupied south. The journey took its toll: Annie died soon after their arrival in the provincial city of Toulouse. Despondent over the course of events, Chiaromonte found sustenance in the simple virtues and solidarity of his fellow émigrés. In an essay appearing in *Commonweal* in 1941, he captured the ambience of the Italian enclaves that took him in:

> In Toulouse there were comrades, there were *compaesani* who could speak one's dialect, there were friends of friends; a man would find a bed, something to eat. They came from everywhere: from their homes, from foreign regiments, from labor battalions, and from concentration camps; from Lorraine and from Alsace as well as from the neighborhood of Paris, from Belgium, and even from England—via Dunkirk.
>
> We all gathered around a table in a dilapidated basement, and there was never enough room at the table, or enough chairs. Yet out of the abyss of disaster spaghetti had been resurrected. A dining room had been organized. . . . On the most elementary basis possible—the necessity to eat—a little community had immediately grown into existence, or, rather, a family of sorts had grouped itself together.

For Chiaromonte, a Mediterranean genius for small-scale informality was the key to the success of the Italian "families." He explained:

> Of course, the Belgian refugees and the Poles had their group kitchens, too. But it was not at all the same thing; they had big refectories for a hundred people . . . , while with us—apart from the fact that we would not have had the means to set them up—we never even considered the possibility of letting it grow beyond the proportions of a large family. If occasionally we were thirty or so at the table, there was instant chaos, ill temper, complaints, and argument. About twenty was the ideal number—enough for company, enough to feel among friends, but not so many that one would feel, in spite of their numbers and in their midst, alone. There was, too, a tremendous difference in organization between us and the men of the northern countries. They had budgets and directors, and they ran things on a timetable. With us it was a question of being able to improvise, or, rather, to reimprovise everything as each day came.

Chiaromonte would carry these lessons about social organization with him when he attempted, as a member of the *politics* "family," to define a humanist radicalism after the war.[58]

From Toulouse, Chiaromonte made his way to Algeria, where he enjoyed the hospitality of another small group of friends, among them the young writer Albert Camus. He eventually reached New York, via Casablanca, where he would remain until 1947. Chiaromonte adjusted quickly to his new environment. He married Miriam Rosenthal, a school-teacher, and established a niche in intellectual affairs, publishing essays on literature and politics in such magazines as *Partisan Review* and the *New Republic*. Italian critic and friend Enzo Bettiza later described the "exceptional" personal qualities that allowed Chiaromonte to make an impact in both Paris and New York. "His European culture, his personal rigour, his intransigence in political commitment, his rejection of what he called 'modern Jesuitry' and 'useless lies,' his very ability to write easily in English and French, had all equipped him to participate in the life of ideas at a very sophisticated and hard-headed level." In short, Chiaromonte was the quintessential cosmopolitan; in Bettiza's words, he was "a citizen of the world, a polyglot of the spirit as well as of tongues."[59]

Dwight Macdonald met Chiaromonte soon after his arrival in America. The precise details of their early relationship are unclear, but Macdonald later recalled that it was Meyer Schapiro who first informed him of an iconoclastic Italian émigré "in sympathy with my attitude in the editorial wrangle" at *PR*. William Barrett characterizes Macdonald's "adoption" of Chiaromonte—"one of the more quiet and striking figures around at the time"—as part of the American's search for "another and purer political ideology" beyond Marxism. He recorded William Phillips's contemptuous remark, "Dwight is looking for a disciple who will tell him what to think." In the first year and a half of the existence of *politics,* Chiaromonte contributed articles and insights on the European scene, but it was the summer holidays at Cape Cod in 1944 and 1945 that finally cemented his friendships with Macdonald, Mary McCarthy, and other members of their intimate circle.[60]

In McCarthy's words, the retreat near the village of Truro during the "Hiroshima Summer" was "a watershed, a dividing line" for all the participants. On their idyll away from the bustle of New York and the relentless pace of world events, this diverse group formed what she later described as a "secular monastic community," enjoying moonlit beach picnics, reading Shakespeare, and discussing literature and philosophy. Chiaromonte was taken by the openness and cheerful enthusiasm of his American friends, and they, in turn, became enthralled with the quiet wisdom of this "dark, handsome man who looked like a monk." Chiaromonte found a receptive audience for his passions: the ethical vision of Tolstoy, the Greek conception of "limit" espoused by an obscure French writer named Simone Weil, and the ideals of communal "sociability" embodied in the life and thought of his Paris mentor, Caffi. McCarthy biographer Carol Gelderman has written that on many days her subject "could be spotted on the beach with her typewriter, pounding out a translation of Weil's 'The *Iliad,* or the Poem of Force,' " the touchstone essay Macdonald published in *politics* late in 1945. Gelderman concludes that during this time "the notion that some resistance might be offered to the general mechanization in modern society took hold of everyone. In a way, this little company discussing the possibility of changing the world on a small scale was just the sort of embryo community Caffi and Chiaromonte had in mind" in their discussions before the war.

Eileen Simpson gives us a vivid portrait of life at the Cape, with Macdonald making the rounds, "talking in a loud and penetrating voice" about issues great and small, "agreeing enthusiastically, disagreeing vehemently and . . . gesturing with his head, arms and shoulders like a great bird." Evening get-togethers, she recalls, were "so heated, the fight to have one's say so boisterous, that often Nicola, whose tonsured head made him look like a monk in a sixteenth-century painting, was appointed to the chair": "In an attempt to keep a semblance of order, he, the most urbane member of the group, often had to impose a time limit for those who asked for the floor. Politics, foreign and domestic, Marxism, psychoanalysis, the poetry of Louis Aragon—there was no lack of subjects, nor of fuel to heat the arguments."[61]

Years later, Mary McCarthy reflected upon what she and Dwight Macdonald found so compelling in Chiaromonte that summer long ago.

"It was a kind of seriousness, a kind of thoughtfulness," she remarked. "We talked about Tolstoy and about Dostoyevsky, and the *change* from someone like Edmund [her estranged husband, literary critic Edmund Wilson] was absolutely stunning."

> Nicola did not like Dostoyevski and he had an absolute passion for Tolstoy. Anyway we would talk and it had never occurred to me before to think of those two writers as anything but two writers—as *Edmund* would have looked at them. One might have said of course T. was a much better stylist and D. wrote bad Russian and so on. But that was a completely empty literary point of view by comparison. And in some way a self-satisfied point of view: it really didn't involve thinking about what these writers were saying!

For McCarthy, Chiaromonte's engagement was an attractive alternative to the abstraction and complacency she sensed among American intellectuals. In a revealing aside, she noted that this invigorating moral "seriousness" was a trait possessed by both of the émigrés she befriended in the 1940s:

> I think that getting to know Hannah Arendt and Nicola Chiaromonte, and becoming very close to them—probably that was Europe! You know, I've never thought of that until this minute. Hannah and Nicola had one striking thing in common: they were both Europeans. They were both Platonists too, incidentally, or Socratics, rather. And when I was talking before about the radical difference I felt with Nicola from what I used to with Edmund and his circle, what I was listening to on the beach was Europe.

The cultivation and transmission of this European sensibility to an American audience became fundamental to the "cosmopolitan" mission of *politics*.[62]

Chiaromonte's message about the need to create decentralized societies of human proportions, aloof from the bureaucratization and runaway technology condoned by conventional notions of "progress," received unexpected confirmation with the shock of the atomic bomb in August 1945. McCarthy's reaction was undoubtedly typical: "I remember reading the news of Hiroshima in a little general store on Cape Cod, and saying to myself as I moved up to the counter, 'What am I doing buying a loaf of bread?' The coexistence of the great world and us, when contemplated, appear[ed] impossible." By the time the group returned to New York, Macdonald had decisively broken with Marxism and Chiaromonte was a full partner in his efforts to define a new direction for radicals.[63]

Among Chiaromonte's functions as the "co-producer" of *politics*, Macdonald later recalled, was that of "talent scout." Two of his most important finds—the other pillars of the journal's "Italian connection"— were Caffi, who spent the war in hiding in southwest France, and fellow émigré Niccolo Tucci, another member of the Truro entourage. Like Chiaromonte, these men were cosmopolitan wanderers, congeni- tally distanced from any type of routinized existence or intellectual orthodoxy.

Tucci, whose playfully sardonic column "Commonnonsense" became a *politics* institution, emerged from a background unique within the magazine's circle. As a young man growing up in Italy, he was more interested in literature than politics, and, like many in his generation, he supported Mussolini as a shallow patriotic reflex. Several visits to the United States in the 1930s (as a "minor itinerant lecturer at large" for the Fascist Ministry of Propaganda) eroded his loyalty, however, and by the early 1940s he had taken up permanent residence in New York, espousing an idiosyncratic brand of anarcho-pacifism more suited to his disposition. During his early years as an expatriate, Tucci began a career as a writer, publishing essays in magazines like *Harpers* and the *New Yorker*. He also became a friend and disciple to Chiaromonte, who introduced him to the editor of *politics*. Dwight Macdonald immediately liked Tucci's biting, irreverent wit, and he saw the Italian as just the person to give his magazine an extra dimension of liveliness and unpre- dictability.[64]

Like Paul Goodman, Tucci appealed to that side of Macdonald rep- resented by his membership in the "Hedonists" as a student at Exeter, the guerilla rebel committed to exposing by the most direct means possible the wrong-headedness of the stuffed shirts in power. Tucci's frequent contributions to *politics*—pieces consisting of anecdotes, aph- orisms, and stream-of-consciousness parodies—had a surreal quality that delighted some readers while leaving the more literal-minded baffled and annoyed. Tucci was more than the resident clown, however. The cumu- lative effect of his writing was subversive, inspiring skepticism toward the kind of hypocritical authority he had witnessed as a youth. During the war he conveyed a special sense of outrage about the way ordinary Europeans suffered under the realpolitik of the victors. Typical of Tucci's approach was a continuing feature, "Notes for a Political Dictionary," which, in the spring of 1945, shed light upon the following items from the official Allied lexicon:

> *Deemed:* necessary. Especially when it isn't. Usually "for the further- ance" of something (see *Furtherance*).
>
> *Furtherance:* commemoration of something that has ceased to exist.

Justice: shall prevail. As: "that —— shall prevail." Phrase used after Pie à la Mode at official dinners.

Unknown: usually a soldier. Never a civilian. If a civilian were unknown, he would know better than to become an unknown soldier. The "U.S." on American uniforms does not stand for "Unknown Soldier" nor even for "Unknowing Soldier." It means "United States," that is, the uniting of millions of States (of submission, of bewilderment, of utter confusion, of irritation, etc.) into One Army. The Communists call this "National Unity."

Crime: small-scale war. (Doesn't pay.)

Yes: affirmative for "no."

In 1975 Macdonald, who always believed the aesthetics of writing carried moral and political implications, remembered Tucci's "Common-nonsense" column as "anarchism w. a stylistically dandified lemon twist, like Oscar Wilde—but Tucci's mockery came from deeper, and more agonized, sources: he's half Russian, half Italian, an uneasy cocktail."[65]

Andrea Caffi, the most important influence in Nicola Chiaromonte's political development, was another volatile Russian-Italian "cocktail." Because he chose, as a matter of principle, to lead a private, underground existence, Caffi is an extraordinarily difficult figure for the historian to capture with any depth. His life was "rich in adventures, encounters, associations, and friendships," according to Chiaromonte, but its details remain "singularly sparse and fragmentary." Caffi's written legacy is similarly elusive, consisting of letters, notebooks, and a few articles scattered over the years in Italian, Russian, and American periodicals. With his erudition, originality of mind, and genius for conversation, however, Caffi left an indelible impression on the people he encountered personally. Chiaromonte once described Caffi as "the best, as well as the wisest and most just man I have known in my lifetime," an example of "what it means to live as a free man in a world where success and power hold sway." In his memoirs Lionel Abel recalled Chiaromonte's assertion in 1942 that "Caffi is the only man in the world who might come up with a new political line, one for intellectuals, who, after the war, may still want to be radical."[66]

Like Victor Serge, Caffi was a voice from an earlier generation of the European intelligentsia, one whose perspectives grew out of the searing experiences of the First World War and the Bolshevik Revolution. Born in St. Petersburg in 1887 to émigré Italian parents, Caffi attended the local International Lycée, where he enjoyed exceptionally broad exposure to Western cultural traditions. As a young man Caffi embraced a libertarian socialist politics based on an amalgam of Hellenic philosophy, Enlightenment freemasonry, and nineteenth-century Russian anarchism.

The social injustices he saw horrified him, and by the age of sixteen he was already involved in anticzarist activities, helping to organize the first typographer's union in St. Petersburg. Later Caffi was jailed for his collaboration with the Mensheviks in the unsuccessful revolution of 1905. Following his release from prison two years later, Caffi went to Germany to complete his university education. Although impoverished, he managed to travel widely during this period and found an agreeable place to settle in cosmopolitan Paris. Together with a group of French, Russian, German, and English students calling themselves *La Jeune Europe,* Caffi planned to write an "encyclopedia" of contemporary Western culture, a project interrupted by the outbreak of war.[67]

Chiaromonte later confessed his surprise at learning that Caffi had enlisted in the French army during the First World War. Caffi's participation, however, reflected a fatalistic sense of solidarity rather than any martial passion. "Confronted by a war which he, like many others in Europe, had felt inevitably drawing closer since 1911," Chiaromonte explained, "it seemed to him impossible to raise questions of principle. The catastrophe had come; there was nothing to do but undergo it." Despite being wounded twice, Caffi emerged from the war physically intact; his revolutionary optimism, however, had vanished forever. Chiaromonte described Caffi's feelings of disillusionment:

> August 2, 1914 had marked for him not only the end of his youth but also the collapse of a whole world of ideas and hopes. After the war, . . . the conviction formed in him that the European nations were now launched on the road to ever more radical crises which rendered futile all idea of the "restoration" of democracy and socialism as he had conceived them before 1914.

From then on, Caffi remained convinced that no "political" solution, whether emanating from above with the state or from below through the actions of the "masses," could remedy problems that were fundamentally social and cultural in nature. In his view, "culture, understood as the intransigent assertion of the values of truth and justice, became a secret cult, practicable only in small heretical groups."[68]

Caffi returned to Russia as a journalist, where, from his vantage point with a Moscow information bureau, he watched the Bolsheviks destroy "all that had been most purely libertarian and socialist, and also most European" in the nation's century-old revolutionary tradition. He soon found himself again under arrest for subversive activities and spent several precarious weeks at the Lubianka prison, where every night, he recalled, the guards carried out random executions. With the help of Italian friends, Caffi was released unharmed, and he eventually made his way to Rome to take a post with Mussolini's Ministry of Foreign Affairs. His tenure as a Fascist bureaucrat was brief and mischief-ridden, and with his resignation Caffi dropped out of the "official" world once and for all. He became a denizen of clandestine oppositional enclaves, sleeping "on an improvised pallet somewhere in the rooms of the National Library" and attempting, as Chiaromonte noted, "to transplant in Rome the conspiratorial methods he had become familiar with in Russia." In time Caffi attracted the attention of the police, and facing imminent detention, he escaped to France, returning to Paris in 1929.[69]

Throughout the next decade Caffi adopted what Chiaromonte characterized as the life of a "sociable hermit," eking out a miserable existence on translations and menial labor while cultivating a "singularly broad and diversified" circle of friends from the various émigré communities of the city. Chiaromonte gives us the flavor of those prewar years:

> [Caffi] lived in furnished rooms, his door, following the Russian custom, was always open to anyone who might call and start a discussion, he welcomed visitors as if all his time was at their disposal. But he met with heavy silence, or worse, gave only embarrassed monosyllabic replies to a variety of "important persons" who . . . tried to "fish him out" and restore him to a more normal mode of existence. Caffi's lonely existence was the outcome of his decision to enjoy only such company as he chose: it was simply an expression of the free spirit of a man unable to adapt himself to the ways of the world. . . . [He] lived the life of a philosopher in the ancient sense of the word, of a man devoted exclusively to the pursuit of truth and justice and convinced that such a pursuit must inevitably become tainted once mixed with concern for worldly success or making a career.[70]

Although not interested in conventional politics, Caffi regularly met with socialists from a variety of countries and intellectual traditions. It was during his involvement with the libertarian Italian group *Giustizia e Libertà* that he first encountered the young Chiaromonte, who became his most devoted spiritual companion. Their "teacher-disciple" friendship developed within the context of a small heretical "cult" embodying values of community and "sociability" sharply contrasting with what they saw as the direction of the larger world. Writer Gino Bianco has described their approach as "thinking outside politics": "The aim, they declared, has always been a more human society, and it could be achieved only outside the existing institutions."[71]

The Paris milieu began to fragment by the late 1930s, first with the disruptions of the war in Spain and, later, with the French defeat of 1940. Caffi fled with Chiaromonte to Toulouse, where he remained until after the war, participating in the activities of Italian, Spanish, and

French Resistance groups. Chiaromonte's decision to continue alone to North Africa and then to the United States meant a long and mutually painful period of forced separation from Caffi. By the time they were able to resume contact, at first only by occasional letters, Chiaromonte had introduced his teacher's philosophy of "thinking outside politics" to an enthusiastic new audience. Dwight Macdonald would broaden that audience by publishing excerpts from Caffi's postwar correspondence in his journal, under the apt pseudonym "European."[72]

"A Responsive, Irritable Readership"

No discussion of the transatlantic community of *politics* is complete without a consideration of the magazine's uniquely intimate and diverse readership—a "responsive, irritable" lot, Dwight Macdonald once recalled affectionately. In her 1968 tribute to *politics*, Hannah Arendt remarked that "the feeling of companionship among its readers had something almost embarrassingly personal about it," in part because the editor "regarded his readers . . . as his intellectual equals." The journal evolved into a forum for dialogue (sometimes escalating into pitched battles) between those who remained more or less attached to the creed of Marxism and others who had become fatally disillusioned, ideologically "homeless"—fallen Trotskyists and dissatisfied liberals, conscientious objectors housed in government CPS camps, and a fair share of cranks and crackpots of various stripes. The sparks generated in the letters column (which bore the pseudomilitary title, "The Intelligence Office") accounted for much of the vitality of *politics*.[73]

Like many "little magazines," *politics* had a small but influential readership. Its first issue sold only 2,000 copies, and circulation never rose much above 5,000. Raw numbers drastically understate the journal's impact, however. As Macdonald later observed, a small-scale operation tends to attract a more devoted constituency than larger, more commercially successful vehicles, "being a more individual expression and so appealing with special force to other individuals of like minds." In addition, copies of *politics* usually passed through more than one set of hands. Lewis Coser estimated that, on the average, at least three people read each issue.[74]

According to a survey prepared by C. Wright Mills in 1947, the majority of the magazine's subscribers were young, male, college-educated New Yorkers of an independent socialist bent. A substantial number of readers did not fit this profile, however. Some were older: one correspondent enjoyed *politics* "with the same keen pleasure with which I used to read the old 'Freeman,' 'The Nation' and 'The Dial' back in the days immediately following the last world war." A fifth of the survey's respondents were female, seven percent described themselves as business-men, and four percent even admitted to being Republicans. *politics* also had an audience outside Manhattan and was available at selected news-stands in large and medium-sized cities throughout the United States.[75]

Voices from the hinterlands, pro and con, often made themselves heard amid the din of insular New York squabbles. Many wrote to express frustration with the magazine's relentlessly "negativist" or utopian tenor. A letter from Urbana, Illinois, for example, criticized Macdonald for his dismissal of available organizational alternatives: "Not many people can express their political opinions by starting a magazine. Especially is this true for those of us who live out in the center of the country. We could either sit at home and wait for the perfect party to emerge or we can engage in the activity of the Socialist Party and help to make it emerge. We have chosen the latter role." Macdonald delighted in publishing colorfully hostile letters, such as this one from a bookseller in San Diego:

> Please do not send me any more issues of your magazine. It arrived on April Fool's Day and it was one on me. I thought it would serve to help some people find their way through these trying times. However, out here on the West Coast we let W. R. Hearst . . . spread the confusion. We think there is enough here without importing any of the special brand you have developed in the East.[76]

Two groups of readers, in particular, stood out as elements of the far-flung *politics* community. Coser reported having met a number of devotees of the magazine over the years who had spent the war in uniform, stationed "out there somewhere in the Pacific" or in a similarly remote place. For members of the armed forces, a subscription to *politics* (available at specially discounted G.I. rates) was a defining badge of dissent. Macdonald took special pains to publish letters from these men and women, valuable as firsthand accounts of conditions abroad or the state of race relations in the Jim Crow military. During the last months of the war *politics* featured a regular department, "The Soldier Reports," designed to take advantage of this important information resource. Mac-donald noted that the "informal, human, bottom-dog" perspectives these letters provided often carried "a personal emotion which the newspaper correspondents can rarely afford," thus rendering "the reality of things all the more accurately."[77]

Some items amounted to fan mail. A soldier from Fort Knox, Ken-tucky, wrote: "Your magazine is swell. You can't realize what it means to receive it here." Others offered insights of stunning thoughtfulness and eloquence. Consider, for instance, the testimony of an anonymous army sergeant in a letter to Macdonald from devastated Germany in April 1945:

The guilty have, of course, fled. . . . But the problem of guilt is, as you very properly put it, complicated and as profound as any question the war has posed for us. The other day I helped the Inspector-General interview some witnesses in a war-crimes investigation. The correspondents had picked up a story of a "horror hospital," and the War and State Departments wanted some kind of dossier. Well, for hours and days we tried to piece together a story, asking questions, going through the documents. But it came to something which bewildered the poor old IG, and left me only with the small satisfaction of a lesson learned. In modern war there are crimes not criminals. In modern society there is evil but there is no devil. Murder has been mechanized and rendered impersonal. The foul deed of bloody hands belongs to a bygone era when man could commit his own sins. Now innocence or guilt is a problem beyond the scope of court and legal decision. Here, as in many other cases, the guilt belonged to the machine. Somewhere in the apparatus of bureaucracy, memoranda, and clean efficient directives, a crime had been committed. Men died in a hospital, of starvation, of medical neglect. But the witnesses were very "unsatisfactory"—*who* was responsible, the IG would never discover. *What* was responsible could, I think, be established, and convicted, but I am afraid the old man is searching for a "suspect" he can sit down in the witness chair and ply with the routine of cross-examination. The chair will remain empty, and the crimes will go on. . . .

Macdonald and his colleagues would devote much effort to elaborating the issues so simply and directly raised by this young soldier.[78]

The other group of readers that made *politics* unusual during the war consisted of scattered individuals in liberated Europe, mostly socialist intellectuals, who managed to obtain a copy of the magazine despite censorship restrictions and other daunting obstacles. For such people, *politics,* with its irreverent, critical tone, was a precious lifeline to another kind of existence, an inspiriting reminder, after years of violence and cultural isolation, that freedom of thought and expression still remained a live possibility in the world. A 1946 letter from "Ernst X," a refugee then living in Paris, vividly conveys these sentiments: "I am one of the privileged over here who receive *Politics,* and I judge it the best paper of its kind I ever read. . . . What I liked most is that you are never afraid to call everything by its right name and that you don't mind to step on somebody's feet if it's necessary. . . . I like *Politics* because it says what the others don't say."[79]

Thanks to the transatlantic community surrounding *politics,* Dwight Macdonald enjoyed a unique set of advantages—and, in turn, felt special responsibilities—as he interpreted the final stages of World War II. Influenced and inspired by the homeless dissidents he had attracted as collaborators, and more attuned to the human experience of the conflict than others of his background, Macdonald would undergo a sea change in political orientation as his bold experiment in radical journalism matured. Given the moral crisis the war represented, he soon realized the urgent need to reconsider his ideas from the ground up.

politics and the Moral Crisis of World War II

There must be some irreconcilables left who will not even accept the war with walrus tears . . . some intellectuals who are not willing to use the old discredited counters and to support a peace which will leave all the old inflammable materials of armament lying about the world. There must still be opposition to any contemplated "liberal" world-order founded on military coalitions. The "irreconcilable" need not be disloyal. He need not even be "impossibilist." His apathy toward war should take the form of a heightened energy and enthusiasm for the education, the art, the interpretation that make for life in the midst of a world of death. The intellectual who retains his animus against war will push out more boldly than ever to make his case solid against it. The old ideals crumble; new ideas must be forged.

—RANDOLPH BOURNE, 1917

It was . . . a time of troubles: the terrible last years of the war, with the Nazi death-camps and the atomic bombings and the gray dawn of "peace," when the reality behind the illusions of the antifascist crusade began to emerge, with Stalin's Russia smoothly taking over the role of Hitler's Germany. All of this demanded attention, exposure, analysis, satire, indignation, lamentation.

—DWIGHT MACDONALD, 1957

An "Irreconcilable" Voice, a "Time of Troubles"

politics was a product of World War II, and that conflict and its consequences remained the defining concern throughout the magazine's lifetime. Dwight Macdonald and his American and European colleagues kept their readers uniquely informed about the flow of events during the last furious months of total war and the early years of an uncertain, hungry "peace." Their analysis of the war's deeper implications—the "depersonalization" of the individual, the mindless automatism of modern industrial society, the death of the Enlightenment faith in "progress" through human mastery—frames the journal's subsequent efforts to articulate a new political direction in the 1940s.

As we have seen, Macdonald strenuously opposed the war from the start, at first interpreting it as another episodic conflict between "rival imperialisms," part of a cycle that could be broken only by the emergence of an international working-class "third camp." The shock of Hitler's sudden, decisive victories in 1940 demonstrated the novelty of the war and forced Macdonald to reassess the nature of the threat. He began to describe the Nazi regime as a "strange new monster," an advanced form of postcapitalist, totalitarian "bureaucratic collectivism" toward which industrial society as a whole was evolving. Given this situation, he continued to refuse to support the "lesser evil" of the Allies, maintaining that a socialist revolution was the necessary precondition to any meaningful victory. Years later he admitted that this position was naive and misguided. In retrospect it was easy to see that hopes for such a revolutionary scenario had been chimerical.[1]

Although he ultimately acknowledged his error, Macdonald insisted that his principled rejection of the war had been a "creative" mistake. This is an apt characterization. By remaining on the margins of American discourse, outside the complacency and triumphalism of the dominant prowar consensus, Macdonald enjoyed a critical detachment not widely shared among his peers. That distance permitted him to be the kind of "irreconcilable" presence Randolph Bourne represented a generation earlier, a voice skeptical of official slogans, sensitive to the human costs of the conflict, alert to shifts in "moral temper," and generally free to explore questions invisible to mainstream observers.[2]

In 1944–45, as the scale of violence escalated beyond all precedent, Macdonald's war critique evolved and deepened, finally breaking loose altogether from its tenuous Marxist moorings. The revelations of Auschwitz and the shock of Hiroshima emphatically signaled to him that something much more serious than traditional realpolitik was at work. These events exposed once and for all an endemic, long-term moral crisis that even a seizure of power by the workers would not remedy. For Macdonald, as for the critical theorists of the Frankfurt School (another "transplanted spore of European culture"), the Holocaust and the Bomb fatally discredited Enlightenment assumptions that instrumental reason and human freedom were inherently joined within a historical metanarrative of progress. On the contrary, World War II culminated in a triumph of "rationalized" barbarism, with the highest achievements of scientific organization and technique employed in the service of meaningless destruction and wholesale "killing by remote control." The results could hardly be termed "progressive." In Simone Weil's words, the war left "a picture of uniform horror, of which force is the only hero."[3]

Now Macdonald began to speak of a world in which massive centralized structures and advanced technologies crush the living individuals who create them. Industrial society appeared to him as a vast *mechanism*, "grinding on without human consciousness or control." "More and more," he concluded, "things happen TO people" as they find themselves reduced to faceless "cogs" and stripped of autonomy and personal responsibility. In such a setting, men and women lose their natural capacities for empathy and solidarity; abstract, collective stereotypes and brute assertions of power prevent the formation of genuine social relationships. Albert Camus, the French *résistant* whose ideas paralleled and influenced those of the *politics* inner circle, put the problem succinctly in 1946. "The years we have been through," he wrote, "have killed something in us. Mankind's long dialogue has just come to an end."[4]

What could one oppose to the regimentation and unrestrained violence pervasive in the modern world? How could people extricate themselves from a catastrophic history, how could they foster the sense of community essential to a meaningful postwar reconstruction? What did it mean to be "radical" in 1945, as crews picked through the smoldering wreckage of European and Japanese cities, and millions of refugees faced imminent death by starvation or disease? For Macdonald and his friends, answers to these questions had to start with a challenge to the ideological foundations of what Weil called our "bragging technological age." Her writings on war seemed to offer the rudiments of an alternative ethic to the contemporary worship of power and mastery, the messianic "pursuit of absolutes" linked to a faith that things will "come out all right in the end." Weil argued for recovering the notion of the tragic *contingency* of history, most profoundly expressed in the literature of classical Greek humanism. Recognition of *limits* in the effort to subordinate "force" to our will, and of the universal vulnerability to blind "fate," was, in her view, the first step to a society of human scale and proportion, where dignity and mutual respect replaced oppression and mass murder.[5]

Was the rebirth of such a humanism *possible* after the atomic bomb? Could the machine be overcome? Macdonald's response was equivocal: sometimes the "masses" appeared as passive victims, with an all-powerful "Apparatus" ready to eliminate and replace faulty "cogs" that might interrupt its smooth operation. At other times, however, Macdonald discovered new potential for dissent in a world of rigid integration.

politics would devote its energies to identifying and encouraging such opposition, which, in any case, might be the only hope left for a civilization on the brink of extinction.

"Maximum Devastation, Minimum Meaning"

In the August 1945 *politics* Dwight Macdonald mockingly described George Patton as his "favorite general," a "psychotic" personality who perfectly embodied the barbarous "virtues" of the current war. Macdonald was reacting to newsreel footage of Patton's latest speech to his charges, an "atrocity of the mind" filled with undisguised sadism, racism, vulgarity, and self-promotion. Macdonald found the performance illuminating: "[It] will be considered by later historians as typical of the style of this war as Caesar's and Washington's and Trotsky's set speeches to their troops were in *their* wars. At once flat and theatrical, brutal and hysterical, coarse and affected, violent and empty—in these fatal antinomies the nature of World War II reveals itself: the maximum of physical devastation accompanied by the minimum of human meaning." This absurd and tragic combination of wildly destructive means and empty ends came to dominate Macdonald's critique as the conflict reached its final stages. Paul Fussell has noted the irony that "every war is worse than expected, because its means are so melodramatically disproportionate to its presumed ends." For the *politics* intellectuals, the war that began in 1939 would carry that disproportion to new extremes.[6]

Macdonald's early analysis of World War II reflected the skepticism (shared by his Workers Party colleagues) that anything constructive or liberating could come out of an antifascist struggle that was not primarily directed by the workers. This attitude contrasted sharply with the views of the liberal intelligentsia, who seemed to accept at face value the progressive vision elaborated by Roosevelt and Churchill in the Atlantic Charter. The war against Hitler, argued spokesmen for the *Nation* and the *New Republic,* provided an opportunity to redeem at last the Wilsonian dream of a rationalized and peaceful world order. At *Partisan Review,* and later at *politics,* Macdonald maintained a steady barrage of invective against such "liblab" commentators for their enthusiastic endorsement of the war. Like Bourne more than two decades earlier, he ridiculed both their pretensions to political influence and their public relations campaigns portraying the conflict as a democratic crusade, as a chance to "globalize" the New Deal, or, in Henry Wallace's famous phrase, as a catalyst for the birth of a "People's Century."[7]

In Macdonald's eyes, the war began to show its true character—as an old-style power struggle—once it began to turn decisively in the Allies' favor in 1943. The treatment of newly liberated territories, first in

North Africa and later in Europe, was something less than the advertised model of democracy. High-level summitry rather than grassroots self-determination was the order of the day, and consistent Allied support for conservative and reactionary elements confirmed for Macdonald the unofficial new "line": "This is not a revolutionary war, and so the people must not get 'out of hand.'" Sensing betrayal of the ideal of "Four Freedoms," Niccolo Tucci spoke in 1944 of the disappointment emerging in his homeland:

> Many Italians who received copies of those speeches dropped from Allied warplanes, and kept them in their pockets at the risk of their lives, are now exhibiting them at Allied Headquarters and saying: "Here are your promises, why don't you keep them?" This is what happens when communications are slow and badly organized. Those poor devils have not yet been freed from the spell of the above speeches, which was not meant to last that long and to create such strong illusions of good faith.

"The problem is not how to get rid of the enemy," Tucci later concluded, "but how to get rid of the last victor."[8]

Always sensitive to the nuances of style, Macdonald noticed that the official rhetoric had shifted to serve new geopolitical realities. He was struck by how British and American leaders seemed to abandon efforts to endow the struggle with any sense of meaning beyond mere military victory as their troops moved forward. On the contrary, he argued, "everything is done to *de-politicize* this war." In a June 1944 article, Macdonald interpreted Churchill's public endorsement of the Spanish dictator Franco as a symbolic watershed. After three years of high-profile salesmanship, of "idealism and big promises" from FDR, the prime minister would now take the lead in bluntly reasserting imperial objectives. "It is a sensible division of labor," Macdonald bitterly concluded, "New Deal rhetoric to get us to accept the war and tough Tory talk to prepare us for the peace." The rightward turn accelerated as the months passed, manifest in the British suppression of Resistance forces in Greece and in Stalin's murderous betrayal of the Warsaw underground, developments *politics* followed with muckraking outrage. The inadequate response of liberals to these events only confirmed for Macdonald the depth of their naïveté and cynicism, a dreary reprise of their performance from a generation earlier.[9]

Accompanying Macdonald's criticisms of "imperialist" machinations and military maneuvers was another, darker level of argument: that the war was taking on a destructive, irrational inertia of its own, outside the control of even those at the top of the command structures. That such a dynamic might develop had been implicit in Macdonald's writings as early as 1939, when he warned that the outbreak of war, like the eruption of a volcano, unleashed forces whose direction could not be safely predicted. By 1943, while still writing for *PR*, Macdonald expressed despair over the disturbingly "unconscious" way in which the war was being conducted, by the "democratic" belligerents as surely as by the "totalitarians." "The best wisdom of our leaders," Macdonald wearily observed, "is that it will take x tons of bombs to reduce y acres of European cities to rubble." His indictment owed less to conventional Marxist categories than to a visceral sense of moral revulsion. "As it grinds automatically on, as it spreads and becomes more violent," he concluded, "the conflict becomes less and less meaningful, a vast nightmare in which we are all involved and from which whatever hopes and illusions we may have had have by now leaked out."[10]

Two years later the situation had worsened dramatically. In the spring of 1945, as Anglo-American and Russian forces made their final push across Germany, Macdonald saw little reason for celebration. Thinking especially of the civilians who had perished in Hitler's concentration camps and in cities leveled by Allied bombers, Macdonald described a war "which in destructiveness of lives, property, and civilized values has had no equal since the religious wars of the 17th century." "To say that civilization cannot survive another such war is a truism," he added. "The question is whether it can survive this one." Macdonald saw a moral symmetry between the "two horrors" confronting each other in central Europe, the dying Nazi "horror of conscious, rationalized destruction of the fabric of Western culture and ethics," and the Allied "horror of vast technological power exerted in warmaking by nations with no positive aims and little social consciousness."[11]

It would be a mistake to accept too literally Macdonald's equation between the singular evil of the Nazi apparatus of destruction and the allied war machines. Nevertheless, as Robert Jay Lifton has observed, certain parallels can be usefully drawn between the implementation of the Final Solution and the indiscriminate bombing of civilians that took place in World War II, culminating in the use of nuclear weapons on Hiroshima and Nagasaki. The similarities between the two enterprises in terms of organization and psychology, how both enabled ordinary people to accept and even participate in mass murder, to adopt what Lifton calls a "genocidal mentality," were the focus of Macdonald's concerns in *politics*.[12]

Nazi Horrors

Robert Westbrook has observed that for a variety of reasons—not least his extensive network of refugee contacts—Dwight Macdonald was alone among the New York Intellectuals in his public efforts to think through the implications of the Nazi program of genocide as it was revealed in the mid-1940s. Macdonald later recalled that, like most Americans, he had initially dismissed rumors about the existence of death camps, interpreting them as direct descendants of the "atrocity stories" circulated by Allied propagandists during the First World War. "Precisely because the whole thing *was* so sensational, so beyond all Western experience," he explained, "the reports for some time were simply not believed." Macdonald's criticism of the war had in some ways prepared him for the worst, however, and by 1944 he could no longer ignore the mounting evidence of mass murder in occupied Europe. He recognized early a moral imperative to "come to some kind of terms" with this terrifying phenomenon, and through his journal he pioneered the importation to America of what Orwell would call a "concentration camp literature."[13]

During the last year of the war *politics* offered its readers two memorable treatments of the Nazi horrors: "Behavior in Extreme Situations," Bruno Bettelheim's firsthand account of the psychological climate within the camps, and "The Responsibility of Peoples," Macdonald's meditation on the idea of collective guilt. These efforts were ultimately more valuable for the questions they raised than for the specific answers they provided. They serve to highlight the oscillation between despair and hope that characterized *politics* after the war, the persistent tension between what Westbrook describes as "Macdonald's normative vision of humane, responsible resistance to dehumanizing evil and his deeply pessimistic vision of a modern society that was obliterating the very conditions of such resistance."[14]

Macdonald discovered the original version of Bettelheim's essay in a 1943 issue of the academic *Journal of Abnormal Psychology*. In a letter to the author, a clinical psychologist from Freud's Viennese milieu, now ensconced at the University of Chicago, Macdonald described the piece as a "moving and illuminating . . . glimpse into a new world," and its subsequent appearance in the August 1944 *politics* helped to shape early discussions of the camp experience for a wide cross-section of the American intellectual community. Bettelheim recounted his observations of the behavior of fellow inmates during a year's internment at Dachau and Buchenwald in 1938–39. Soon after his arrival he detected signs of disturbing personality changes in many of his peers, a reaction to the physical and mental terror imposed by the Gestapo. He asked himself: "How can I protect myself from becoming as they are?" To safeguard his sense of self-identity, Bettelheim assumed the posture of a scientist doing field work and, by his own reckoning, emerged from the trauma "approximately" the same person he had been before his detention.[15]

Others were not so lucky. Bettelheim devoted most of the essay to outlining the process of "infantile regression" normal to life in the camps. The personality disintegrated in distinct, predictable stages. From the "initial shock" of wrongful arrest, through the daily pressures of constant surveillance and gratuitous brutality, those inmates who survived succumbed to a state of "final adjustment," characterized by a consuming selfishness and childlike dependency. According to Bettelheim, "new" prisoners—those held for less than one year—displayed the greatest resources for resistance, maintained strong emotional attachments to the outside world, and looked forward to a day when they could resume their former lives. Like him, they focused their energies on one overriding objective: to endure with their personalities and values intact. In contrast, "old" prisoners—those held for more than three years—manifested radical, often unconscious changes in outlook and lost contact with anything beyond the self-enclosed camp universe. "Old" prisoners seemed to have accepted and even *internalized* the values of their oppressors, performing meaningless tasks and enforcing petty rules with unnecessary enthusiasm. Some even aped the aggressive verbal and physical gestures of camp guards. The victimization of such men was complete, Bettelheim concluded, the Gestapo's objectives largely achieved: "*to break down the prisoners as individuals,* and to change them into docile masses from which no individual or group act of resistance could arise."[16]

Many took Bettelheim's account not only as an authoritative look at the attitudes and behavior prevailing in the camps, but also as a cautionary description of life in mass society at large—in Nazi Germany and throughout the industrialized West. Macdonald was not yet ready to pronounce the world "one big concentration camp," but Bettelheim's model of passivity and atomized "regression" seemed to point toward a more general "extreme situation" on the near horizon. It certainly fueled his pessimism about the erosion of social bonds and resources for individual autonomy in a bureaucratic environment. Because it exerted such wide influence, however, it is important to note that "Behavior in Extreme Situations" ignored, or at least minimized, the myriad forms of resistance that did exist, not only in the prewar concentration camps Bettelheim experienced but even in the death camps operating after 1941.[17]

Writers like Terrence des Pres have noted that much of the vast literature on the Holocaust appearing since 1945 gives a very different, and more balanced, picture of camp life than the one advanced by Bettelheim. Many studies portray a world where sophisticated networks of communication and mutual support operated to mitigate the worst excesses of the Gestapo reign of terror. Although the space for such activity was quite limited, it was nonetheless almost always present, even in the "extermination" camps. Des Pres concludes that in the latter environment, mere "existence *was* resistance, every day, all the time." Perhaps reflecting his own ambivalence on the question, Macdonald did publish samples of the new "concentration camp literature" that stressed resilience rather than victimization. The June 1945 *politics* featured another personal history of life at prewar Buchenwald, this one lauding the "unshakeable solidarity" of socialist and communist political prisoners. At great risk they protected Jews; distributed food, clothing, and medicine; challenged criminal inmates; and even gathered for a clandestine May Day celebration. The special "French Issue" of *politics* (July/ August 1947) included an excerpt from David Rousset's fictionalized camp memoir, "The Days of Our Death," which offered a similar alternative to the Bettelheim model. The defiance of Rousset's *concentrationnaires* is captured by an older prisoner's words of courage to a new internee. "By not shooting right away," he insisted, "by not hanging or poisoning all of us at once, the S.S. permits a society to live." Men resisted, even in a world where "a choice of evils always had to be made" and "the majority had to die."[18]

Macdonald's ambivalence was also evident in his consideration of the perpetrators of the Nazi crimes, "The Responsibility of Peoples." The title of this essay, published in March 1945, was his friend Nicola Chiaromonte's expression for the idea of "collective guilt" with which modern governments justified their wars of annihilation. The essay can be read in a number of ways. On the most immediate level, it was a defense of innocent German civilians against those who, in the winter of 1944–45, pressed for an escalation of bombing, followed by the imposition of a "hard," punitive peace in Central Europe. Macdonald never lost sight of the living human beings who found themselves on the receiving end of the technologies of destruction, and he argued that the vengeance randomly exacted by weapons like the "blockbuster" violated the most elementary principles of human rights for which the war was allegedly being fought. In retrospect it is clear that Macdonald went too far in his efforts to separate the innocent from the guilty. Westbrook correctly observes that his attempt to limit culpability for the Final Solution to a "sharply differentiated sub-group" of German society (the Nazi leadership and its S.S. "killing elite") was naive and facile, ignoring the widespread knowledge and "passive" complicity of "desk murderers" that had to exist for that grandiose enterprise to function with such deadly efficiency. Still, Macdonald's humanitarian instincts in that moment of urgency were appropriate, and his insistence on drawing lines, however flawed, stands as a corrective to the monolithic abstractions of anti-German demonology. It reveals a sense of empathy, restraint, and proportion rare on this side of the Atlantic in the final stages of the war.[19]

At another level, "The Responsibility of Peoples" opened out into a wider critique of modernity, a prophetic warning about the breakdown of human relationships and the eclipse of individual moral autonomy taking place in societies on all sides of the conflict. Macdonald grasped the fact that the Nazi Holocaust was "something new," a signal of nothing less than the bankruptcy of the Western faith in the inevitability of progress, the dead end of the Enlightenment project of freedom through mastery. Hitler's network of death factories was a stunning triumph of rationalized technique dedicated to irrational and barbarous ends. Macdonald grimly advised his readers that, in places like the Maidanek camp, "reality has now caught up with Kafka's imagination." "In all the reports, the atmosphere is the same: rationality and system gone mad; the discoveries of science, the refinements of modern mass organization applied to the murder of noncombatants on a scale unknown since Genghis Khan." Macdonald concluded: "It all reads like a sinister parody of Victorian illusions about scientific method and the desirability *in itself* of man's learning to control his environment. The environment was controlled at Maidanek. It was the human beings who ran amok."[20]

What had happened to the people who served this insane machinery? Macdonald drew upon the insights of a then-unknown émigré writer, Hannah Arendt, who asserted that in a bureaucratic culture like the one perfected by the Nazis, individuals lost a clear sense of responsibility for their actions. Simply by performing a job or "following orders," a person became implicated in a murderous system where "guilt" was at once "universal" and "meaningless." Macdonald came to the conclusion that, given these circumstances, "it is not the lawbreaker we must fear today so much as he who obeys the law." This erosion of conscience was a theme Arendt would develop in her most famous works, from *The Origins of Totalitarianism* (1951) to the controversial *Eichmann in Jerusalem* (1963). In 1945 she found it vividly demonstrated by the testimony of a death camp "paymaster" who protested his Russian captors' intent to hang him by exclaiming: "Why should they? What have I done?"[21]

For Macdonald, the dehumanizing pressures that reduced the concentration camp functionary to a mindless automaton existed on "our" side as well. They were built into the architecture of contemporary industrial society. The principles effective in the mass-production economy — "centralization of authority, division of labor (or specialization of function), rigid organization from the top down" — now dominated the political sphere as well, leaving people in a state of abject impotence and isolation. Macdonald returned to the metaphor of the unconscious *machine* to describe the evolving new order: "Modern society has become so tightly organized, so rationalized and routinized that it has the character of a mechanism which grinds on without human consciousness or control. The individual, be he 'leader' or mass-man, is reduced to powerlessness vis-à-vis the mechanism. More and more, things happen TO people." During wartime this process of "depersonalization" was most apparent in the context of the military, where, in Macdonald's words, the soldier "is fought" as an interchangeable part. He cited the reflections of an American bomber pilot. "I'm a cog in one hell of a big machine," the young man observed. "It looks as if I'd been a cog in one thing or another since the day I was born. Whenever I get set to do what I want to do, something a whole lot bigger than me comes along and shoves me back into place."[22]

Macdonald viewed "the responsibility of peoples" ideology as one of the fictions used to veil the gears of the totalitarian social "mechanism," part of a modern mythology designed to give meaning to meaningless events and to shield people from an awareness of their own subjugation. In their rhetoric of "national unity," political leaders like Roosevelt and Churchill imputed individual human qualities—"will, consciousness, thought, personality"—to abstract, collective entities, dividing the world into heroic and villainous "peoples" as expediency required. Thanks to such encouragement, Macdonald concluded, Hegel's idea of the omnipotent, "organic" state was fast eclipsing the fragile Enlightenment tradition of individualism.[23]

Our Horrors: Toward a "Götterdammerung without the Gods"

Macdonald's commentary on the Allied "horrors," especially the bombing campaigns against "enemy" civilians, waged with increasing intensity in the last months of the war, explored many of the same issues raised by the Nazi Holocaust. The air assaults, a product of the "responsibility of peoples" fallacy in action, appeared to be driven by an automatic logic beyond human agency. Once again "law-abiding" individuals became "cogs" in an elaborate machinery of destruction, insulated in their bureaucratic niches from accountability for their behavior, "calloused" to the sufferings of other people. The application of scientific organization and technology to the project of efficient mass murder presented, for "us" as well as for "them," a challenge to the faith in progress through instrumental reason.[24]

Macdonald examined the implications of new techniques of violence in a perceptive essay, "Notes on the Psychology of Killing," in the September 1944 *politics*. He began by reminding his readers that despite the pretensions of modern civilization, ancient methods were still in use, as evidenced by *Kill or Get Killed,* an official U.S. Army manual prescribing in gruesome detail how to destroy an adversary in hand-to-hand combat. As disturbing as this kind of mayhem was, however, at least it forced the participants to confront, in a direct and immediate way, the consequences of their actions.[25]

More ominous, in Macdonald's view, was the array of sophisticated new means of "depersonalized" warfare, the growing arsenal of tools to accomplish what he aptly termed "killing by remote control." Exemplified by the long-range bombing tactics employed by Allied air forces to "dehouse" enemy workers, in Churchill's famous euphemism, here the perpetrators remained *abstracted* from effects. The moral ramifications of this distance were profound, because most people lacked the imagination to feel empathy for victims they never saw. Thus emerged a tragic paradox: the fantastic increase in the modern soldier's capacity to commit violence corresponded to a diminished consciousness of the results. Now, Macdonald wrote, a small group of trained technicians, protected in the womb of a high-flying aircraft, could release a payload of incendiary bombs over the center of a city and return to their home base in time for the next meal, scarcely aware of or troubled by the horrors they had wrought. An urban "target" could be wiped out quickly, cleanly, routinely, the whole affair "as impersonal as a thunderstorm."[26]

Robert Jay Lifton has described a process of "silent technological brutalization" similar in effect to the phenomenon of "killing by remote control" Macdonald discussed in the 1940s. Lifton used a quotation from Charles Lindbergh that perfectly conveys the sense of disconnection Macdonald warned about. "You press a button and death flies down," Lindbergh observed. "How can there be writhing, mangled bodies? It is like listening to a radio account of a battle on the other side of the earth. It is too far away, too separated to hold reality."[27]

Macdonald attempted in *politics* to make the suffering real. Month after month he condemned the Anglo-American policy of indiscriminate, "saturation" bombing against Germany and Japan as a victory of mindless inertia over the ideal of a common humanity. It was, in his view, a program of genocidal destruction, an obscene abuse of power utterly negating Allied claims to moral superiority over their "totalitarian" foes. Macdonald was also sensitive to the fact that bombs consumed — literally — the most precious symbols of the Western cultural heritage. In March 1944 he registered his anguish:

> One of the many things I cannot get accustomed to in this war is the fact that the most ancient, beautiful buildings of Europe may be blasted to bits in a few hours. Rome, Paris, Assisi . . . who knows when they will join Warsaw, Bath, Coventry, Nuremburg, Frankfort, Kiev,

Cologne, Palermo, Naples, Rotterdam, Cracow, London, and Berlin? It is like living in a house with a maniac who may rip up the pictures, burn the books, slash up the rugs and furniture at any moment.

Every day the carnage escalated, but the cumulative effect was too numbing, the damage too abstract, the victims too "deserving" of their fate to arouse significant public protest. For Macdonald, the sense of apathy was especially pronounced in Americans, smug and sheltered in their provincial isolation. "We have grown calloused to massacre, and the concept of guilt has spread to include whole populations," he lamented. "Our hearts are hardened, our nerves steady, our imaginations under control as we read the morning newspaper."[28]

The climax of the Allied bombing policy, and the fitting last act of the "unconscious" war, was the atomic destruction of Hiroshima and Nagasaki in the late summer of 1945. Word of the attacks pierced the idyllic solitude Macdonald had been enjoying with Chiaromonte, Mary McCarthy, and other close friends on their retreat at Cape Cod, and it marked a decisive turning point in Macdonald's political orientation, the final blow to his wavering Marxist faith. Macdonald reacted immediately, inserting a dramatic last-minute editorial about the meaning of the event on the cover of the August 1945 *politics*. It was an angry manifesto, declaring the irony that the long-awaited conclusion to the greatest war in human history had been rendered an afterthought. The development and use of nuclear weapons confirmed once and for all the deadly symmetry existing between the two sides of the conflict. "This atrocious action," Macdonald wrote, "puts 'us,' the defenders of civilization, on a level with 'them,' the beasts of Maidanek."[29]

Macdonald then set forth what he saw to be the basic principles of survival in the post-Hiroshima age, sharpening ideas he had been moving toward for many months. "THE CONCEPTS 'WAR' AND 'PROGRESS' ARE NOW OBSOLETE," he asserted, explaining that the means of destruction had become so powerful, so beyond humankind's control, that they corrupted *any* cause, vitiated *any* ends. Nor could the atomic bomb be dismissed as an emergency expedient, a tragically necessary scientific aberration. Instead it was a representative product of industrial culture, "as easy, normal and unforced an expression of the American Way of Life as electric iceboxes, banana splits, and hydromatic-drive automobiles."[30]

For Macdonald, the Manhattan Project demonstrated in the boldest possible way the reality that large, centralized aggregations of power, in whatever form and however labeled, represented the true "enemy" to be confronted in the twentieth century. Above all, he declared, "WE MUST 'GET' THE MODERN NATIONAL STATE BEFORE IT 'GETS' US."

He urged his readers to adopt an attitude of militant, uncompromising moral resistance—"negativism"—as a first step in the struggle. "Every individual who wants to save his humanity—and indeed his skin," Macdonald warned, adopting the rhetoric of a Spanish POUMist or a French *résistant,* "had better begin thinking 'dangerous thoughts' about sabotage, rebellion, and the fraternity of all men everywhere."[31]

Macdonald expanded his analysis of the nuclear assaults on Japan the following month, as more information about the immediate and long-term consequences became available and as government officials offered their explanations and justifications. He was especially disturbed by the lingering, mysterious threat radiation posed to victims who had managed to survive the initial bomb blasts. It was significant, Macdonald observed, that American military authorities had taken extra precautions to protect the workers who assembled the bombs from this danger, but had failed to extend such consideration to the faceless inhabitants of the "target" cities. In the end, the planes over Hiroshima and Nagasaki simply "dropped [their] cargo[es] of half-understood poisons and sped away." Such "irresponsibility and moral callousness" could only be explained by the bureaucratic tunnel vision of the individuals involved.[32]

Macdonald rebuffed every effort to normalize or "domesticate" the bomb, every attempt to promote its "benign" possibilities or to reduce it to human proportions. Contrary to official reassurances, the mastery of nuclear energy was an unmitigated disaster for the world. "Like all the great advances in technology of the past century," he argued, "Atomic Fission is something in which Good and Evil are so closely intertwined that it is hard to see how the Good can be extracted and the Evil thrown away." President Truman's characterization of the Manhattan Project as an inspiring model of teamwork between ordinary people gave cold comfort. The participation of unionized labor and the academy, in particular, only highlighted for Macdonald how complicit those sectors had become in the "permanent war economy." And the sheer *remoteness* of the decision-making process seemed to him to have the most disquieting civic implications. "There is something askew in a society in which vast numbers of citizens can be organized to create a horror like The Bomb without even knowing they are doing it. What real content, in such a case, can be assigned to notions like 'democracy' and 'government of, by and for the people?' " The self-congratulatory celebrations of the moment amounted, in his eyes, to a shortsighted hubris, distracting attention from the urgent practical questions that now had to be faced if human society was to continue.[33]

Macdonald argued that the problem of Hiroshima transcended traditional categories of political thinking, leaving "progressives," conservative, liberal, and Marxist alike, ill-equipped to understand the nature of the crisis it symptomized. Pointing to the experience of two world wars, he ridiculed hopes that the frightening destructive capabilities of atomic energy would somehow lead to the "abolishment" of warfare. And instead of being entrusted to some kind of enlightened international control, as many liberals promised, he correctly predicted that nuclear weapons would simply be incorporated into the escalating military competition between the United States and the Soviet Union. Macdonald found Marxist speculations about the "liberating" potential of atomic power equally misguided:

> It blunts our reaction to the present horror by reducing it to an episode in an historical schema which will "come out all right" in the end, and thus makes us morally callous . . . and too optimistic about the problem of evil; and it ignores the fact that such atrocities as The Bomb and the Nazi death camps are *right now* brutalizing, warping, deadening the human beings who are expected to change the world for the better; that modern technology has its own anti-human dynamics which has proved so far much more powerful than the liberating effects the Marxist schema expects from it.[34]

Macdonald ended his analysis by returning to a by-now familiar theme—the "unconscious" nature of World War II. He found it appropriate that the final horrors had been unleashed, not by the formidable Churchill and Roosevelt, but by Atlee and Truman, "colorless mediocrities, Average Men elevated to their positions by the mechanics of the system." The machine "ground on," no matter who was at the controls:

> All this emphasizes that perfect automatism, that absolute lack of human consciousness or aims which our society is rapidly achieving. As a uranium "pile," once the elements have been brought together, inexorably runs through a series of "chain reactions" until the final explosion takes place, so the elements of our society act and react, regardless of ideologies or personalities, until The Bomb explodes over Hiroshima. The more commonplace the personalities and senseless the institutions, the more grandiose the destruction. It is *Götterdämmerung* without the gods.[35]

Simone Weil and the Lost Ethic of "Limit"

When Dwight Macdonald described the atomic bomb as an abuse of force and condemned celebrations of its development as a dangerous example of hubris, he was adopting the language of Simone Weil, the solitary French thinker Nicola Chiaromonte had championed so energetically during that memorable summer retreat in 1945. Staughton Lynd has described Weil as the "patron saint" of *politics,* and indeed her prophetic writings on the "oppressive" nature of technology, bureaucracy, and above all, warfare, set the tone for much of the journal's critique of modernity. In 1952, Macdonald expressed the hope that Simone Weil, the moralist and social critic *politics* had introduced to Americans the previous decade, would not be forgotten amid the "cult" revival of interest in her sometimes bewildering theological speculations. For him, Weil's importance lay in "the originality and profundity with which her writings deal with the tragic historical crisis we live in." Just as inspiring was "her bold, even reckless, attempt to unite theory and practice, to *live out* her ideas."[36]

Weil's brief career is justly legendary as a model of how to overcome what Macdonald called "the curse of the modern intellectual," the "division between thinking and living." Born in Paris in 1909 to an assimilated middle-class Jewish family, Weil demonstrated from an early age an obsession with the problem of human suffering and an instinctive solidarity with those at the bottom of the social order. As a philosophy student at the elite *École Normale Supérieure* in the 1920s, she became involved in a variety of working-class causes, moving from a flirtation with the French Communist Party to less orthodox anarcho-syndicalist circles. After graduating at the top of her class, Weil eschewed the privileges of her background to live and teach among the poor in a succession of remote provincial outposts, frequently attracting official discipline for her activism. In the 1930s the eccentric, frail young woman spent long periods immersed in arduous physical labor. Her journals on the experience of factory work, an excerpt of which eventually appeared in *politics,* convey, in intimate fashion, what Macdonald would later term the "anti-human dynamics" of large-scale industrial organization and technology.[37]

In the second half of the decade Weil became preoccupied with the issue of warfare, which she viewed up close during her ill-fated service for Republican Spain. As war clouds gathered over the rest of Europe, Weil's work began to assume a more detached, pessimistic tone, focusing on the deep cultural roots of messianic creeds like Hitlerism. This was also the period when she embraced the consuming, mystical brand of Catholicism for which she is often remembered. With the fall of Paris in 1940, Weil entered the last phase of her life, traveling with her family first to the unoccupied South, where she was active with the embryonic Resistance, and then to the safety of New York City. Weil was restless during her few months of exile in America, however, and at the end of 1942 she journeyed alone back across the Atlantic, hoping to rejoin the fight against the Nazis. Reluctant Resistance authorities in England commissioned the woman they considered a bothersome crank to prepare a blueprint for the postwar regeneration of France, but in August 1943 she died, the victim of years of overwork and ascetic self-denial.[38]

Simone Weil's written legacy consists of correspondence, notebooks, and a number of essays scattered in left-wing periodicals like *Révolution Prolétarienne* and the wartime *Cahiers du Sud*. In 1940 an essay from the latter journal, a meditation on Homer's epic poem of the Trojan War, the *Iliad*, appearing under the pseudonym "Emile Novis," captured the attention of Nicola Chiaromonte, then engaged in his own demoralizing flight from the Nazis. Chiaromonte recalled its bracing effect:

> I was a refugee in Marseilles, living under the oppression of Hitler's victory in France, that nauseating and terrible event which then looked as if it might be the final triumph of the "faceless man" over the last fragile hopes of the West. At the time I did not know who Emile Novis was. The author was certainly neither an academic nor a *littérateur,* but someone who had suffered in spirit and had purged through intellect the sense of defeat that had been hanging over Europe for at least four years. That this person would and could express himself through a new reading of the *Iliad* was a sign that "humane letters" could still yield vigorous thought.[39]

By the end of the war, Chiaromonte had converted his friend Dwight Macdonald to Weil's reading of the contemporary cultural crisis, and in 1945–46 *politics* published translations of several of her most important essays. Weil's crystalline pessimism took on a special moral resonance in the wake of the Holocaust and Hiroshima, an antidote to the triumphalism prevailing in mainstream American discourse. Her indictment of the Western commitment to mastery, power, and ideological absolutes formed a critique of the progressive zeitgeist that would become central to the postwar experiments conducted in the pages of *politics*.

The February 1945 issue featured "Reflections on War," an article Weil wrote in the early 1930s, as part of her pioneering analysis of the evils of Stalinism. In it she condemned the Marxian dogma of "class warfare," and indeed any strategy involving collective violence, as misguided and self-defeating, reducing human beings to the "condition of passive matter in the hands of a bureaucratic and military apparatus." Weil argued that orthodox socialists had yet to learn the lesson taught by the degeneration of the French and Russian revolutions: that "force" is an *inherently* reactionary phenomenon, especially in a world dominated by large-scale, centralized structures of authority. With one eye on the Nazis's recent seizure of power in Germany, Weil insisted that "in war as in fascism, the essential point is the obliteration of the individual by a State bureaucracy serving a rabid fanaticism." Like Macdonald's soldier, Weil's modern combatant "was fought" as an interchangeable part in some vast, mysterious mechanism. Thus it was no longer possible to define the enemies of social justice merely in terms of class or nation. Now the contest was between human freedom and an ever-tightening system of rationalized control. "Whether the mask is labelled Fascism, Democracy, or Dictatorship," Weil concluded, "our great adversary remains The Apparatus—the bureaucracy, the police, the military."[40]

In "Words and War," a 1937 essay published in the March 1946 *politics,* Weil continued her criticism of "The Apparatus." Again she rejected formulations like "class struggle" as narrow and outdated: "What is legitimate, vital, basic," she wrote, "is the eternal struggle between those who rule and those who obey." Oppression was a pervasive fact of social existence, and "wherever authority exerts itself, it cannot respect . . . the human qualities of its instruments. It takes the attitude that men are (malleable) things, quite incapable of resistance." For Weil, the process of dehumanization was most acute during the kind of war that now threatened to engulf Europe. Once such a conflict was unleashed, it would become total and self-perpetuating, the possibility of dialogue, negotiation, and compromise destroyed by the "lethal nonsense" of official propaganda. Undoubtedly thinking of her experiences in Spain, Weil predicted that "men will spill torrents of blood and pile ruin on ruin for meaningless, upper-case words." The debased language of modern warfare, she concluded, revealed the "decadence" of "our bragging technological age":

> We seem to have lost the very rudiments of intelligence, the notions of measure, standard, and degree; of proportion and relation, of affinity, of consequence. To get a firmer grasp on human events, we people our political world with monsters and myths; we recognize nothing but entities, absolutes, finalities. Look at any word in our political and social vocabulary: Nation, Security, Capitalism, Communism, Fascism, Order, Authority, Property, Democracy.

In such an environment it was clear that "success" could have only one meaning: "the annihilation of whoever supports the enemy words."[41]

Weil's haunting, lyrical 1940 essay, "The *Iliad,* or, The Poem of Force," which appeared in the November 1945 *politics,* best defined the journal's evolving critique of the moral crisis represented by the Second World War. In order to make sense of totalitarianism in that dark moment just after the fall of Paris, Weil characteristically turned to the wisdom of the ancient Greeks, whose values of "measure, standard, and degree" presented a stark contrast to the modern worship of power and "pursuit of absolutes." Weil began her reading of Homer's war tragedy by insisting on its timeless relevance:

> The true hero, the true subject, the center of the *Iliad* is force. Force employed by man, force that enslaves man, force before which man's flesh shrinks away. In this work, at all times, the human spirit is shown as modified by its relations with force, as swept away, blinded, by the very force it imagined it could handle, as deformed by the weight of the force it submits to. For those dreamers who considered that force, thanks to progress, would soon be a thing of the past, the *Iliad* could appear as an historical document; for others, whose powers of recognition are more acute and who perceive force, today as yesterday, at the very center of human history, the *Iliad* is the purest and loveliest of mirrors.[42]

· Weil elaborated on the deforming, "petrifactive" qualities of "force," defining it as "that x that turns anybody who is subjected to it into a *thing*. Exercised to the limit, it turns man into a thing in the most literal sense: it makes a corpse out of him." Murder represented force only in its "grossest and most summary form," however. More insidious was "the force that does *not* kill, i.e., that does not kill just yet." In one of her most subtle and poignant passages, Weil drew on a lifetime of identification with the oppressed to describe the latter kind of dehumanization:

> From its first property (the ability to turn a human being into a thing by the simple method of killing him) flows another, quite prodigious too in its own way, the ability to turn a human being into a thing while he is still alive. He is alive; he has a soul; and yet—he is a thing. An extraordinary thing this—a thing that has a soul. And as for the soul, what an extraordinary house it finds itself in! Who can say what it costs it, moment by moment, to accommodate itself to this residence, how much writhing and bending, folding and pleating are required of it? . . . [T]here is not a single element of its nature to which violence is not done.[43]

What Weil found so compelling in Homer's epic of the Trojan War was that every character eventually found himself face to face with the humiliation, suffering, and loss imposed by the reign of "force." "Violence obliterates anybody who feels its touch," she observed. No one, regardless of privileged rank or temporary advantage, was able to "master" it; no one was exempt from its unpredictable and inhuman logic. Life or death, victory or defeat, freedom or slavery—all these circumstances seemed in the *Iliad* accidental, contingent, "less a matter of valor than of blind destiny," which "by its very blindness establishes a kind of justice."[44]

Weil thus interpreted the poem as a passionate appeal for solidarity rooted in a universal vulnerability to the vagaries of fate. "The human race is not divided up," she wrote, "into conquered persons, slaves, suppliants, on the one hand, and conquerors and chiefs on the other." The Greeks accepted this leveling reality and taught that those who ignored it faced a "retribution" for the abuse of power "which has a geometrical rigor." This classical concept of "Nemesis" survived in the East, in the notion of karma, but "the Occident . . . has lost it, and no longer even has a word to express it in any of its languages: conceptions of limit, measure, equilibrium, which ought to determine the conduct of life are, in the West, restricted to a servile function in the vocabulary of technics. We are only geometricians of matter; the Greeks were, first of all, geometricians of virtue."[45]

Here was Weil's diagnosis of the sickness of modern European civilization. In their embrace of messianic ideologies, their pursuit of absolute mastery and "total" victory, their spiritual hubris, the inhabitants of our "bragging technological age" lost sight of the ethic of human *limit* essential to a society of equality, solidarity, and dialogue. To Nicola Chiaromonte and Dwight Macdonald, recovery of that ethic seemed the only way out of a world of dehumanizing abstractions and "unconscious" processes, of "extreme" situations and "maximum" devastation, of death factories and atomic bombs. About the people of her age, now consumed by another war of annihilation, Weil wistfully concluded: "Perhaps they will yet rediscover the epic genius, when they learn that there is no refuge from fate, learn not to admire force, not to hate the enemy, nor to scorn the unfortunate."[46]

Chiaromonte was gratified by the response to Weil's essay on the *Iliad*. He later noted surprise at "how profoundly it could affect a readership of New York radicals, people not especially concerned with ancient Greece and, to all appearances, interested exclusively in ideological controversy." Macdonald recalled a similar reaction: "Except for a few Marxists, who could not understand why a political magazine should feature a 'literary' article, every one who read [it] seemed to grasp the point at once: that by writing about a poem written three thousand years ago, Simone Weil had somehow been able to come closer to contemporary reality than the journalists who comment on current events."[47]

Hope amid Catastrophe

Were human beings doomed to the role of passive victims or faceless "cogs" in the new order signaled by World War II? Had they already become the debased internees of Bettelheim's concentration camp universe? Were they, as the managers of Weil's "Apparatus" believed, "malleable things, quite incapable of resistance?" Because he used a "rhetorical style" one historian has called "the politics of fearful anticipation," Macdonald sometimes seemed to be answering yes to such questions. The line in his war writings between cautionary "metaphor" and literal description was often fuzzy indeed. Even at Macdonald's bleakest, however, another, more hopeful motif ran through his journal, an embattled faith in human agency. Weil hinted at this possibility in her reading of the *Iliad,* noting that the "monotonous desolation" of Homer's "poem of force" was occasionally punctuated by "luminous moments" of transcendence, when men reclaimed their souls and expressed impulses for love and solidarity.[48]

For Macdonald, opposition to the machinery of oppression was no longer to be found in the "class struggle." Labor unions, mass parties, and the other traditional vehicles of that struggle merely reproduced the bureaucratic and "collective" practices of the ruling "Apparatus." Instead, genuine resistance had to begin at the level of the individual conscience. Macdonald concluded "The Responsibility of Peoples" with this credo: "We must look both more widely and more deeply for relief from the dilemma of increasing political impotence accompanied by increasing political responsibility . . . to a more sensitive and passionate respect for our own and other people's humanity."[49]

In the wake of Hiroshima, Macdonald pointed to the scientists who refused to participate in the Manhattan Project as exemplars of this kind of humanist ethic. They were individuals still able to see beyond the blinders of function, still capable of entertaining "negativist," "dangerous thoughts" about rebellion and "the fraternity of all men everywhere." In contrast to their peers, Macdonald argued, these recalcitrant few insisted on acting as "Whole Men," refusing to serve as "raw material" to be "exploited like uranium ore" in a program of mass destruction.[50]

As heartening as the courage of these faulty "cogs" may have been, however, their refusal to cooperate did not prevent the production of the atomic bomb. Was individual moral assertion therefore merely of symbolic importance? It depended on the situation. A year earlier Macdonald found cause for optimism in reports of increasing levels of psychological "maladjustment" within the ranks of the U.S. Army. He speculated that many of those discharged for "mental unfitness" were in fact merely expressing a healthy revulsion against their environment, being "too sane to fit within the lunatic pattern of total war." The special "headaches" these "troublemakers" and "draft-dodger types" created for the military hierarchy seemed especially significant. Army officials found it prudent to discharge these problem cases rather than to punish them, Macdonald noted, because they recognized that for a tightly integrated order "a single cog with an antagonistic will of its own" had the potential to cause "friction out of all proportion to its size." In a period full of tragic paradoxes, here was one that offered hope, a "last line of battle" for the resisting individual: the more rigid the degree of bureaucratic control, the *greater* the disruptive potential of small-scale dissent. Perhaps, Macdonald concluded, this fact provided "an important principle of action" for contemporary radicals.[51]

As the "unconscious" war came to its dispiriting finish, and as the dominant "progressive" ideologies, liberalism and Marxism, revealed, once and for all, their moral bankruptcy, the writers of *politics* initiated a search for alternative models of political action based on opposition to centralized authority. Macdonald and his friends detected exciting new departures in the Resistance forces of liberated Europe and in the nascent movements for peace, civil rights, and cultural radicalism in the United States. What these disparate, grassroots phenomena shared—and what the Old Left so clearly seemed to lack—was an unwavering commitment to the integrity of the individual. That ethic would be the essential ingredient in any meaningful reconstruction.

■■■■■■■■

THREE

The Appeal of the European Resistance

Two new terms have emerged in this concluding phase of the war which are not (as yet) devaluated, which retain all their sharpness and moral purity: "collaboration" and "resistance." I think it deeply significant that these are becoming the great political watchwords in Europe today, since they indicate no specific, positive ideology, no aspiring faith, but simply the fact that people either "go along" or that they "resist." . . . To resist, to *reject* simply—this is the first condition for the human spirit's survival in the face of the increasingly tighter organization of state power everywhere. That this is not a sufficient condition is true: only a general, positive faith and system of ideas can save us in the long run. Such a faith and system are no longer held by significant numbers of people. But they will develop, if they do, from the seeds of "resistance."

—DWIGHT MACDONALD, MARCH 1945

"From Resistance to Revolution"?

A "semantic note" Macdonald wrote during the last months of the Second World War illustrates the two ways he used the expression "resistance" in the 1940s. The dichotomy between "collaboration" and its opposite represented, first of all, the point of departure for a new moral language, one that replaced the shallow and confusing collective categories of "left" and "right" with a more revealing inquiry into the nature of individual responses to totalitarianism. In this sense, "resistance" was an exemplary model of thought and behavior, a posture of relentless "negativism" essential to preserving spaces of autonomy in a world dominated by dehumanizing bureaucratic logic, the world of Weil's "Apparatus." Hope for cultural renewal rested on the survival of the scattered "seeds" of such a heroic, oppositional mentality—wherever and whenever they might appear. The larger task of developing a "positive faith and system of ideas" would have to wait for a later, less catastrophic day.[1]

At another level, "resistance" was a historically specific reference to new political tendencies emerging in country after country in Europe upon deliverance from Nazi occupation. *politics* followed these incipient, potentially revolutionary movements with great interest as the war reached its final stages, effectively becoming, as Robert Westbrook has noted, "an American outpost of the Resistance." As elsewhere these forces succumbed to more or less brutal suppression at the hands of their "liberators," the journal's attention came to focus on the radical possibilities in France, motherland of the modern revolutionary tradition. Macdonald and his colleagues enthusiastically endorsed the promise of the French Resistance, suffered with its early defeat, and shared throughout what they believed to be its core values and assumptions—at least as expressed in the rhetoric of its most prominent spokesmen.[2]

Identification with the cause of the French *résistants*—Macdonald would call their endeavors "the one great positive movement toward humanly progressive ends" to come out of the war—is not difficult to understand. As historian Howard Brick has observed, writers associated with clandestine organizations like *Combat* had endured "a very concrete sense of being trapped by overweening power, which echoed the marginal sensibility of American left-wing intellectuals unable to share in the triumphalism of war." French activists had been forced by events—the shocking defeat of 1940 and its prolonged, agonizing aftermath—to reexamine their basic ideas, "cultivating a new style of radical humanism," according to Brick, "that seemed to surmount the deadlock of the old prewar left." Those who survived the rigors of intimate, daily contact with Nazi oppression evinced an intensity, moral purpose, and solidarity that Macdonald and his friends, observing from the comfortable security of New York, could only envy. Most important, substantial elements of the Resistance remained committed after the Liberation to working for a profound transformation of French—and ultimately European—society, a project succinctly expressed in the credo of *Combat*'s daily newspaper: "From Resistance to Revolution." For a few dramatic months in 1944 and early 1945, their heady ambitions appeared to be within reach.[3]

What was the content of this new "radical humanism" espoused by veterans of the French Resistance? The writers the *politics* circle most admired called for the creation of a society that subordinated material objectives like industrial production to the freedom and self-fulfillment of the individual. Drawing on anarchist, small-group models improvised during the occupation, their "socialist" vision linked grassroots localism and direct democracy to an international superstructure designed to maintain lasting peace. The Resistance "new order" was to end Europe's cycle of conflict by eliminating militarist nationalism and its chief instrument, the centralized state. Significantly, those who advocated this "new order" could provide only the barest outline of its architectural details.

Irving Howe concluded years later that "the Resistance movements in Europe, which we had hoped would 'deepen' into socialist politics, dissipated their energies in dispute and nostalgia." The inability of libertarian elements of the French Resistance to implement their postwar goals resulted from a number of factors, some beyond their control but others, as Howe implies, intrinsic to their approach to the world of politics. Those who saw themselves as a new moral elite, natural leaders of a unified, broad-based movement for radical reform, were bound to be disappointed by the behavior of an exhausted populace after the war. And although the *politics* intellectuals' reading of what the Resistance wanted provides valuable insights about the shape of their own emerging radicalism, their failure to grasp certain realities of the European situation reveals limitations in their perspective as well. In the end, for *résistants* on both sides of the Atlantic, a vision founded on simple dichotomies, however attractive for its "sharpness" and "moral purity," would prove inadequate to negotiating the difficult terrain of the late 1940s.[4]

"The France of Tomorrow"

Dwight Macdonald founded *politics* as a vehicle to publicize and encourage possibilities for radical change he saw developing, both at home and abroad, as the war moved to its climactic stages. In an editorial comment for the July 1944 issue, he reiterated the now-familiar "third camp" scenario. "Our best hope for a better, or even a humanly tolerable world after this war," he maintained, "is for the common people to take things in their own hands in a series of popular revolutions which will be socialist as to economics and democratic as to politics." By that point, however, he was already close to writing off the American working class as hopelessly conservative amid its prosperity, concluding that domestic revolutionary prospects were "as close to nil as at any time in our history."[5]

Given this bleak prognosis, Macdonald characteristically fixed his gaze outward, across the Atlantic. With the defeat of the Nazis only a matter of time in the wake of the D-Day invasion, he urged his readers to monitor closely events in the newly liberated quarters of the continent, presumably now ripe for revolution. "There," he argued, "four years of war and unbelievable suffering under German occupation have at least cleared away the institutions, ideologies and property rights which Marx called 'the muck of ages'; have at least forced the common people to think deeply—or 'radically,' i.e., in a going-to-the-root way—about how they can avoid these horrors in the future."[6]

As Allied armies rolled forward, however, Macdonald's hopes for a "series of popular revolutions" in Europe quickly evaporated. Soviet and Anglo-American efforts to contain "dangerous" radical energies generally succeeded, whether through the ruthless measures of Stalin in Poland and Churchill in Greece or through the more sophisticated political manipulations appropriate to Western Europe. The pattern of realpolitik was apparent everywhere. During the critical period of transition in each country, Allied authorities backed restoration of the most reactionary, pliant elements—native "Quislings," in Macdonald's view—while bypassing and isolating independent Resistance forces. These transparently antidemocratic policies met with little organized opposition; the "years of war and unbelievable suffering" had apparently not produced the revolutionary temper Macdonald had been anticipating. On the contrary, even after the fighting subsided, the exigencies of daily survival so preoccupied most of the exhausted European masses that engagement with larger political issues was out of the question. Amid the general deprivation and chaos, the showdown between grassroots Resistance and the representatives of the prewar order never really materialized.[7]

The situation in Italy offered, at first, the promise of a meaningful confrontation, especially as Anglo-American armies began to evict the Germans from the industrialized North, hotbed of militant working-class activity. But here, too, the Resistance "revolution" aborted almost before it began. British-inspired efforts to reinstall an unpopular monarchy and to disarm scattered partisan forces combined with conditions of desperate poverty to prevent a genuine contest over the country's postwar direction. In the December 1944 *politics,* Macdonald pronounced Italian prospects irretrievably lost, political life on the peninsula having been stripped of "both dignity and significance." In the face of reports of widespread "starvation, prostitution, and demoralization," he confessed to his readers that "the Italian tragedy has reached such a depth of squalor, shame and misery that it is painful to think about it."[8]

By late 1944, the only remaining chance for a popular left-wing revolution along the lines favored by Macdonald appeared to be in France. In the months following its liberation, during the late summer and fall of 1944, *politics* tracked the fortunes of sympathetic elements of the French Resistance as they attempted, against formidable odds, to seize the initiative of leadership. The journal's network of European contacts—individuals like Victor Serge, Andrea Caffi, and the Delecourts, two independent French socialists identified at the time only as "Gelo and Andrea"—proved to be an especially useful resource in interpreting shifts in the political climate. The most important correspondent in *politics*'s Resistance coverage was Lewis Coser, whose regular columns as "Louis Clair" presented information about transatlantic developments smuggled from his post with the Office of War Information.[9]

Hopes for political and social regeneration in France rose even before Hitler's armies had been driven out of the country. In a letter published in the August 1944 issue of *politics*, Serge, writing from Mexico City, reported: "All I hear from abroad indicates that in France, . . . where political energies were at a low ebb between 1937 and 1941, an extraordinary revival is now taking place." "This has not yet taken the form of any conscious political movements," he conceded, "but it seems impossible that consciousness will not develop later on."[10]

News that month of the liberation of Paris aroused euphoria among intellectuals throughout the West. An armed uprising by the city's residents against retreating German soldiers—although militarily insignificant —held great symbolic importance, redeeming a measure of French national honor and reassuring Resistance leaders that they would be influential as a new day dawned at last. Young Albert Camus's editorial for the first openly available issue of *Combat* captured the sense of righteous mission, the exhilarating feeling of possibility felt by many in that transcendent moment. "Paris is shooting all her bullets in the August night," Camus wrote. "No one can hope that men who have fought in silence for four years . . . will agree to the return of the forces of surrender and injustice under any circumstances. The Paris that is fighting tonight intends to command tomorrow. Not for power, but for justice; not for politics, but for ethics; not for the domination of France, but for her grandeur." Sincere, stirring rhetoric—but the precise meaning of these noble aspirations, and the strategies necessary to achieve them, remained, as yet, unclear.[11]

Macdonald shared in the initial wave of enthusiasm about the French rebirth. In the October 1944 *politics* he expressed his "surprise" at the strength and independence already demonstrated by the underground French Forces of the Interior (F.F.I.). Particularly heartening were reports of the Paris uprising, an unscheduled show of defiance that disrupted official blueprints for an "orderly" transition of power. "The Allied High Command," he wryly observed, "like the Red Army High Command, does not approve of cities spontaneously liberating themselves without waiting for the duly constituted military authorities. Most irregular, most irregular!" The atmosphere in Paris in the days following the Liberation remained fluid, even "revolutionary," Macdonald noted, with authority residing in the armed street patrols of the F.F.I. rather than the police forces of the provisional military government. General de Gaulle was alarmed enough by the situation to request assistance from Allied head-quarters, which promptly diverted two tank divisions through the capital for a conspicuous show of force.[12]

Macdonald was cautious in his estimate of the outcome of the initial jockeying for power. "All of this does not mean that a revolution has begun," he warned his readers. "The passion has so far been pretty negative, directed against the old collaborationists . . . and not in favor of any positive programs." Still, the events in France revived, at least for the moment, his wavering faith in human resilience. "It is enormously encouraging that the French people retain so much vitality after the 1940 debacle and the years of German occupation," he observed. "The re-serves of a people are inexhaustible, it would seem." Whether the proto-revolutionary energies loose in France would coalesce to produce genuine change or become mired in a "stagnant marsh," as in Italy, remained for Macdonald an open question, especially given the "deep divergences" that had already begun to manifest themselves between de Gaulle and the various underground factions. But perhaps certain natural advantages would permit the Resistance here to succeed where movements in other countries had failed. Of particular importance was the heightened po-litical consciousness of the French masses, a consequence, in Macdon-ald's view, of "the tradition of 1789, 1848, the Commune, [and] the 1936 general strike."[13]

Macdonald's concern about rifts within the Resistance coalition was based largely on Coser's survey for the September 1944 *politics*, "The France of Tomorrow: What the French Underground Wants." In exam-ining the nature and relative strength of the forces competing for control in the post-Liberation vacuum, Coser noted the feeling, almost univer-sally expressed in the organs of the Resistance press, that France must undergo a profound process of self-examination and renewal—political, economic, and spiritual—in order to root out the deeper causes of its wartime nightmare. A comment in the March 1943 journal *Libération* typified reactions against the malaise of the Third Republic that had made France such easy prey for Hitler's designs: "It would be really scandalous if the terrible years which have recently convulsed the world should result in there being some miserable restoration of pre-war insti-tutions and pre-war men."[14]

Perhaps most striking to Coser was the apparent consensus—across traditional class and party lines—behind an assault on liberal capitalism in the name of a broadly "socialist" economic agenda. Resistance pro-nouncements routinely called for the confiscation of key industries, con-demning "private interests" and concentrations of power as antithetical to the health of "the Nation." Coser remained suspicious about what lay "hiding behind this equivocal and magical word," however, and he wondered about the durability of this fragile, "classless" alliance for radical reform. "Most discussions have been very vague as to particular policies and means," he wrote. "The Underground knows what it opposes, [but] there is less clarity on what is to replace it."[15]

Coser concluded that the sweeping rhetoric of "national unity" masked explosive conflicts over France's future that threatened to resurface once the external enemy was gone. Battle lines were already forming. Most commentators agreed that an easy return to the *status quo ante bellum* was impossible, and that extraordinary emergency measures would be required to repair the country's devastated infrastructure. But what kind of measures, and, equally important, "Who is to control?" As to the latter question, Coser observed: "The underground provides two answers, sometimes simultaneously, sometimes separately: the workers on the one hand, and a new strongly centralized and authoritarian state on the other."[16]

The *politics* intellectuals naturally identified anarchist proponents of the first of these tendencies—what Coser called the "revolutionary socialist left wing"—as the rightful claimants to the Resistance mantle of leadership. Groups like *Libérer et Fédérer*, a loosely organized amalgam that included "revolutionary Marxists" and "syndicalists drawing their main inspiration from Proudhon," advocated principles "close to Guild Socialism," with political and economic power dispersed in networks of autonomous worker and peasant councils. These bodies resembled the clandestine Resistance committees that had proliferated during the occupation years, which many participants viewed as the basic cells of a new society rather than as a temporary wartime expedient. This brand of radicalism was far removed from the structured, large-scale class warfare of the 1930s, and prescriptions for specific institutional reforms took a back seat to celebrations of individual freedom and self-fulfillment. *Libérer et Fédérer*'s manifesto from the spring of 1944 urged "a popular movement for the liberation and rebirth of France—as a part of a unified Europe—rebuilt on the foundations of a socialism guaranteeing to the individual the full development of his personality within collectivities founded on a community of interests, and enjoying the largest possible autonomy within this framework."[17]

The new society these radical *résistants* envisioned would be a true participatory democracy, its overriding aim the elimination of the distance between rulers and the ruled. In May 1943, a journalist for *Libérer et Fédérer*'s underground newspaper expressed the common frustration: "For too long already," he wrote, "has the life of the nations been a comedy played by the governing few for a mass audience of citizens who, after having paid at the box office, have had no other rights than to applaud or to hiss, or to ask for a change of actors."[18]

From the *politics* perspective, one of the most attractive features of "advanced" elements of the "Left" Resistance was its cosmopolitanism. Hannah Arendt spoke of this in a letter to Karl Jaspers in 1946. "Now, all of a sudden," she wrote, pointing to individuals like Camus, "there is a new type of person cropping up in all the European countries, a type that is simply European without any 'European nationalism.' . . . They are at home everywhere." In France the repudiation of nationalism reflected itself in calls for a federated Europe and for reconciliation with Germany. Reviving a socialist dream that had been suspended for a generation, many Resistance spokesmen now seemed to understand that a council-based system of local self-government could survive only within an *international* framework—a "United States of Europe." Further, such a federation had to include central Europeans in order to be viable. In a clear reference to American liberals, Coser contrasted voices "far removed from the horrors of occupation," who sought the dismemberment or deindustrialization of Germany—thus "employing Hitler's logic about the racial bastardy of a whole people"—with the general absence of demands for a vengeful "hard peace" within the French underground press. A commentator in the December 1943 *La Revue Libre* took an admirably long view. "Hatred is healthy if it contributes to assure the defeat of the invader," he observed, "but we must lift ourselves above national hatreds if we want to avoid cycles of war and social convulsions." This poignant message of solidarity in the March 1944 *Combat* conveyed a similar immunity to the "responsibility of peoples" fallacy: "We have not forgotten that the German resistance movement was the first to rise against the Nazis and the first to be martyrized. We have not forgotten Dachau and the many militant Socialists, Catholics and Communists who 'disappeared without a trace.' We shall not forget you, our murdered friends. We shall try and help your children create a new fatherland."[19]

The calls for a council-based "United States of Europe" did not represent the view of all segments of the French Resistance coalition, however. Others favored—if initially in muted, qualified tones—the consolidation of a new centralized state and the reassertion of France's prewar status in international affairs as the solution to its national identity crisis. Whereas "rightist" elements traditionally dominant in French political life—industrialists, conservative Catholics, aristocrats of various stripes—had suffered severe blows to their legitimacy since 1940, Coser warned that they had by no means disappeared, and after a period of lying low were now preparing their own claims to leadership. The priorities for this faction included the early restoration of hierarchical "order" and a crash program of national rearmament. One group expressed the desire "to give to France an imperial consciousness and give her back her will to greatness and expansion."[20]

The "authoritarian" Resistance enjoyed a number of crucial advantages in its struggle against the "libertarians." First, the traditional Right already had experience in manipulating the levers of economic and political power. In addition, it could count on the backing of Allied authorities, who shared an overriding interest in quelling radical ferment and who would certainly have a large say in how "order" was ultimately to be reestablished. Finally, right-wing forces were better organized and, in General de Gaulle, had a compelling leader to rally behind. Although virtually all elements of the Resistance had recognized de Gaulle as the leader of "France at war," spokesmen for the libertarian Left were understandably skeptical of his rhetorical overtures to democracy and social reform. A traditional military background and intimate ties to conservative prewar elites made him an uncertain ally at best. Coser predicted that de Gaulle and his supporters would try to create a bonapartist dictatorship—a "sort of French national-socialism"—at the first opportunity. The popular appeal of the Gaullist "cult" probably presented the most serious obstacle to revolutionary possibilities in France.[21]

The wild card in the contest between authoritarian Right and libertarian Left was the French Communist Party. Although it had strong anti-Nazi credentials within the working class, the intellectuals at *politics* regarded the CP, in France as elsewhere, as an external threat to indigenous popular aspirations. In July 1944 Macdonald had warned: "These fifth columnists in the camp of revolution are much more dangerous than the open enemies." Coser explained the omission of the CP organ *L'Humanite* from his review of the Resistance press by the fact that it represented "policies not determined by the needs or tendencies within France, but dictated from the outside." In its slavish adherence to Stalinist realpolitik, the CP was a divisive and ultimately treacherous member of the Left coalition, muddying the distinction between "resistance" and "collaboration" Macdonald had originally found so appealing in European insurgency. Reflecting Moscow's hostility to the rise of a socialist rival in the West—especially one committed to building an international confederation—the French CP was willing to jettison commitments to a reform agenda in favor of cooperation with the forces of "order." It also worked to encourage what Coser interpreted as the most retrograde nationalist attitudes among its constituency, and he decried the continuing inability of French workers to grasp the CP's "counterrevolutionary" character.[22]

With the future direction of France in the balance, could the diverse "libertarian" elements of the Resistance join together to defeat their Gaullist opponents? Would they be able to capitalize on their post-Liberation momentum by articulating a coherent program for change, one capable of enlisting popular support? Would French workers wake up from their confusion in time to reject the false promises of the CP? Even with the hurdles to be overcome in the next critical months, and the fact that "many theoretical problems remain to be solved," Coser felt that important breakthroughs had already occurred. His analysis ended on a note of optimism:

> The socialist forces are extremely powerful in France, they have more vitality today than they have had in the last fifty years. Society in turmoil is receptive to revolutionary ideas, the stagnation of the interwar years has been definitely overcome. . . . Socialist thought has made a return to its humanist source; some of the best have come to reject the statist idea and to rediscover the essentially democratic conception of a federation grown from below, not imposed from above.[23]

The mood of hopeful anticipation continued in the November 1944 *politics*. In an article based on Coser's latest information, Macdonald argued that the classic prerevolutionary situation of "dual power" now existed in France. Although the Big Three allies had extended formal recognition to de Gaulle as head of a provisional government (seeking to use him as "a prop of conservatism"), the General's forces were experiencing enormous difficulties establishing authority, especially in the central and southern provinces. In these areas—isolated from the capital by the poor state of communications—local, independent Resistance committees created their own municipal and legal apparatus, with "no intention of abdicating peacefully in favor of the central government."[24]

According to the few on-the-scene reports that managed to evade a tight news blackout, street battles now raged in Marseille. In the southeastern part of the country, a group of Resistance committees went so far as to issue a resolution of mutual aid, invoking the model of the States General in 1789. This confirmed for Macdonald that "in no other nation today do revolutionary traditions seem so alive as in France: 1789, 1830, 1848, 1871—such dates are vibrant with political meaning to the man in the street." In response to government calls for order and "national unity," the Resistance paper *Combat* defiantly declared: "Disorder is preferable to injustice."[25]

Bowing to steady pressure from the Left, de Gaulle announced his support for a number of reform measures in the direction of democracy and "planned economy," but each contained a heavy dose of state control from Paris. Such concessions were not enough for the provincial "Liberation Committees," who insisted in their manifestos on a radically decentralized order, founded on a redistribution of wealth and workers' control of production. The national government was not yet strong enough to quash these challenges to its sovereignty; and with its efforts to disarm independent Resistance forces, the "see-saw struggle of Dual Power" seemed about to intensify.[26]

But even though local committees held fast to their revolutionary objectives and sought to give them concrete form, Macdonald was concerned about the lagging state of mind of the working classes. The CP, "by far the most powerful single group in the Resistance movement," continued to command widespread support, and thus remained a potential Achilles heel for the radical Resistance camp. One observer, noting the French Left's enduring admiration for Russia and the communists, remarked ominously: "They do not yet know who their enemies are."[27]

Macdonald also expressed misgivings about the apparently conservative instincts of the French populace as a whole. He correctly interpreted de Gaulle's push for early elections as an attempt to dilute the power of left-wing activists and worried that the strategy just might work. Macdonald took this opportunity to note the limitations of parliamentary forms:

> Elections are only one way by which the popular will expresses itself — and a method furthermore, which has the weakness that it may be more easily manipulated by conservative forces than such alternative methods as revolutionary committees. The trouble with elections is that they do not measure the intensity with which people hold views. Who is to say that ten men and women who will die for their beliefs are not as "deserving" of realizing those beliefs as a hundred who will do no more than mark a cross on a ballot?

Implicit in Macdonald's argument was a fear that the mood of the French "man in the street" might not be "revolutionary" after all.[28]

Interpreting the Post-Liberation Defeat

By the winter of 1944–45, radical Resistance hopes — on both sides of the Atlantic — began to fade precipitously. In an editorial comment for the December 1944 *politics*, Macdonald confessed frustration that a divided, impotent Left was squandering the "unparalleled objective *opportunity*" for revolution in Europe, created by the Nazis's systematic dismantling of the institutions of capitalism. The communists were, of course, beyond redemption, Stalinist puppets "prepared to sell out any popular movement for a little ready cash in the great game of imperialist power politics." Noncommunist forces, on the other hand, found themselves crippled both by their lack of experienced leadership and the absence of a "clear political consciousness" among the masses. Like the European "revolutions" of 1918–19, the Revolution of 1944 was in danger of aborting—with similarly tragic long-term consequences.[29]

In France, the window of opportunity was fast closing as proponents of centralization pressed with ruthless urgency to contain the scattered rebels. In his "European Newsreel" column for February 1945, Coser reported that "the atmosphere . . . has changed completely" in the brief period since the radicals announced their most ambitious aims. The Gaullists had already achieved important, if not yet decisive, victories in their crusade against the forces of anarchy and "disorder." A spokesman for the Liberation Committees expressed the mood of demoralization in a January 3 radio broadcast:

> We were going to increase the food supply—but people are hungry and cold while food and fuel go to waste nearby. We were going to purge the collaborationists—but the big ones escape and traitors are still at large, ready to do more harm. We were going to build a clean and unselfish community—but the same men still take advantage of positions to look after their own interests or to win votes just as before.[30]

The "miserable restoration of pre-war institutions and pre-war men" that many had sworn to oppose during the early days of Liberation now proceeded apace. Individuals with dubious wartime backgrounds resurfaced, after a decent interval, in the National Assembly, and through a variety of legal maneuvers the machinery of the central government began to supplant its provincial rivals. De Gaulle's Ministry of the Interior replaced local Resistance committees in municipal administration; an official labor bureaucracy effectively eliminated worker control of factory production; and independent "people's militia" cells dissolved, their members absorbed into a strengthened national police force.[31]

Coser pointed to "a lack of political insight and ideological homogeneity" as the primary reasons for the "temporary defeat" of the libertarian Resistance. Echoing Macdonald, he argued that French radicals continued to be naive about the nature of their enemies now that the Germans had been expelled. The CP's recent, sudden shift, at Moscow's behest, to a policy of "national unity" predictably fomented a sense of "disorientation and confusion" among its admirers. And the patriotic figure of de Gaulle still blinded many to the realities of his vision of national rebirth. Coser spoke of the plight of grassroots activists: "Never did they even dream of having to defend their local organs of power against the Central Government. Wasn't this government 'their' government?" Other factors in the Gaullist success included pressures to delay internal debate until the war's end and the desperate material scarcities, which, as elsewhere in Europe, "turn[ed] people's energies toward the immediate goals of finding enough to eat for the next day, diverting them from political activity."[32]

Coser was not yet prepared to give up all hopes for revolution, however. The de Gaulle regime still struggled against the same conditions that prevented local Resistance groups from achieving consensus and coordinating strategy, "communication difficulties ... so great that (as yet) there could be no country-wide exchange of ideas, no real crystallization of political thoughts." In some areas the F.F.I. retained its arms and continued to resist the directives of the government in Paris.[33]

Coser's reports over the next months recorded the final process of retreat for the radical Resistance. In a March 1945 *politics* article, "The Stalintern over Europe," he complained again of the pernicious communist influence over revolutionary movements throughout the continent, citing in particular French CP chief Thorez's January announcement—in the wake of de Gaulle's diplomatic pact with Stalin—of support for the provisional government, a dramatic turn to the right justified on the grounds of "public security." This sellout of the local Committees of Liberation reaffirmed for Coser that, like the Nazis ("the other great totalitarian party of our times"), official communist organizations had no goals beyond the advancement of their own political power. The French CP was a cynical "salesman of Russian wares" for whom, in pursuing its objectives, no means was too unethical, no ally too reactionary, and "nothing ... too stupid for the masses."[34]

Yet even in the face of such obvious duplicity, millions of Europeans continued to allow themselves to be swayed by Stalinist slogans, still looked to the CP as a vehicle of revolutionary socialism. Coser attributed this misplaced loyalty to a "cultural lag" fed by unconscious authoritarian impulses. In a footnote he explained how the demoralized masses, reduced by their hardships to a dangerous state of dependency, might be rendered susceptible to carefully crafted totalitarian appeals:

> Revolt against existing authorities is not necessarily revolt against all authorities. Craving for leadership is a deep-rooted tendency in modern man. To transfer one's craving for authority from one powerful source to another demands less psychological energy than to stand freely in rebellion against existing conditions. This is especially true of sections of the working class which have suffered through starvation and unemployment and who carry the burden of many previous defeats. Many of those, tired by scores of battles, now tend to await passively for liberation to be brought from the outside.[35]

In his June 1945 "European Newsreel," Coser described the steadily deteriorating situation in France, a nation of "fluttering banners and empty bellies" where the economic devastation of the war seemed finally to have destroyed the remnants of Liberation optimism and vitality. The Left was more paralyzed and divided than ever, permitting de Gaulle to position himself as the only alternative to chaos. The French revolution had entered the same "stagnant marsh" as the Italian, and the time for bold initiatives had all but run out.[36]

In the September 1945 *politics*, Coser warned that the reappearance of that fearsome bogey, nationalism, in France and every other corner of Europe, threatened to end for good the Resistance vision of a united continent. He condemned the outbreak of "fratricidal wars," manifest in petty border disputes and demands for the expulsion of ethnic minorities. These conflicts only advanced "Big Three" efforts to prevent the rise of another rival superpower. "The resurgence of nationalism on a mass scale . . . is a profoundly reactionary phenomenon," Coser concluded. "Every new exacerbation of national hatreds over the Aosta Valley, over Teschen or Silesia, over Saloniki or Klagenfurth, can but serve the interests of those who thrive on the Balkanization of Europe."[37]

Coser argued that for Europe to regain its independence, ancient particularisms, with their narrow horizons and "provincial quarrels," had to give way to the creation of a universal socialist order. Otherwise the continent was doomed to becoming "a new China," a feudal pawn "revert[ing] into a period without history." Although prospects for an international federation were receding, Coser offered the hope— ultimately a vain one—that the election of the Labour Party in Britain might revive "advanced" forces and provide a radical left alternative to Stalinist leadership.[38]

By late 1945 it was clear that the libertarian Resistance challenge to the old order in France was over. The central government had consolidated its authority, and the prewar parties were once again open for business, firmly in control of a political discourse that offered few choices outside the status quo. The sense of idealism and revolutionary possibility that marked the Liberation period was dead, at least for the moment. The *politics* commentators offered their postmortems on the defeat.

In his correspondence from Toulouse in southwest France, Andrea Caffi offered his diagnosis of the depressing climate he saw enveloping the country. Macdonald published translations of two of Caffi's letters in the November 1945 *politics* under the revealing title, "The Automatization of European People," introducing them as "the most profound analysis, in intellectual and moral terms, of the political psychology of postwar Europe" he had yet encountered.[39]

In July Caffi had written to Macdonald detailing the "wretched" physical conditions prevalent in France, hardships that reminded him of his experience in postrevolutionary Russia in the early 1920s. Widespread "filth" and hunger, made worse by skyrocketing inflation, were having a numbing, brutalizing effect on all spheres of daily existence. In such an environment, Caffi observed, people were able to "bring to their regular work and social life nothing more than a mechanical assent."[40]

Political conditions were similarly wretched. "Dissident minorities" found themselves excluded from the monopoly of "mass" parties, handicapped both by censorship restrictions and by such material factors as the shortage of paper and printing facilities. But scarcity of resources alone, Caffi emphasized, did not explain the utter lack of vitality in French civic culture, "the paralysis of spontaneous, daring, passionate initiatives, the absence of that swarming of 'clubs' and plans however naive, bizarre, messianic, which characterize a truly revolutionary ferment." In his view, the malaise was a symptom of a much deeper problem: the degeneration of the elite stratum known as "society" in Enlightenment France and nineteenth-century Russia. The contemporary crisis was the result of the abdication of responsibility within such "society,"

> the strange will to obey, to be subject to a hierarchy and *not have to reflect,* shown by those who would ordinarily be the active nuclei of the nation and form the cadres of the organized parties. What is clamored for is "unity" (of the Resistance, of "antifascists," of the Republic); the fusion at no matter what cost of the Socialist and communist parties . . . ; the maximum centralization of the State apparatus; and the maximum homogeneity in the nation.[41]

Caffi opposed his conception of "society" to that of the "masses," whom he dismissed as "by definition . . . sheeplike and simplistic," desiring "only peace and goods." Mass culture helped to create and sustain the general torpor. "There are," Caffi wrote, "the habits of automatism, of *zusammenmarschieren*, of responding to slogans that are as imperative as they are trivial, habits which the cinema, the radio, the newspaper headlines, the rationalization of work and pleasure, the tyranny of schedules, have spread and developed to a maximum point."[42]

Caffi found an "almost complete dislocation" of independent standards of judgment in modern industrial society, a divorce between behavior and morality, between "immediate, intimate experience and the formulas or schemes (more or less abstract) which purport to express the reality of the world in which we live." People turned to ritualized "slogans" and "formulas" in a desperate attempt to supply meaning to a meaningless existence. Caffi concluded:

Compounds like "Nation-country-State," or "technological progress-civilization-humanism," all such "realities" are today a kind of indigestible and qualityless broth, made of *ersatz* and false syntheses, but which must be gulped down and then praised to the skies, if one is to avoid an agonizing and unsustainable hunger, the frightful condition of having to live, spiritually, on nothing, and being, so to speak, left naked in an empty space.[43]

In a letter to Chiaromonte in early September, Caffi painted a similarly bleak picture of European politics and culture, observing that by now "the chances of a Resistance still embodying something of the true spirit of the French people to Hitlerism and Pétainism are very slim indeed." Cooperation with communists, Gaullists, and Anglo-American capitalists was necessary to defeat the Nazi war machine, but the postwar fruit of such compromises appeared to be the victory of some other variant of fascism. Thus the martyrs of the recent struggle died for something less than a new era of social justice and were now being exploited for political advantage in a desultory competition for power. To Caffi, the betrayal of their legacy was complete:

Resistance to totalitarianism will remain as an imperishable honor to mankind. It was to individuals and groups of very dissimilar origin and nature, and it was carried out with makeshift means, under circumstances which were mostly atrocious. The final result can even be considered providential, but in itself it is certainly not a conquest: men have remained men (or nearly so), they have not become robots, they have not all perished in the crematoriums of Hitlerland. The resistance—with a capital R, and an accompaniment of trumpets, drums, manifestos, bids for profitable jobs, and plans for new totalitarian arrangements—is a very elastic compound of sincere messianic hopes, demagogical totems and taboos, very noble and very abject ambitions, dreams of liberty, and will-to-power. It is an artificial mythology choking and perverting authentic "epos," which is born in the depths of consciousness and in the real communion of a people.[44]

Once again Caffi expressed a mixture of contempt and fear toward the popular desire to end the political turmoil. He interpreted indifference to libertarian radicals in the darkest possible way:

The people cannot understand an indefinitely prolonged resistance, in the same way that they cannot understand a "permanent revolution." After all the struggle and the suffering, the people do not ask either for honors or (much less) for the continuation of an exceptional strain. They want a rest, enough to eat, to get married, and to be able to dance and go to the movies. Of course, if they do not get these things, there will be trouble again. But the exhaustion is such that one can legitimately wonder if, given a moderate amount of normalcy, an authoritarian regime would not be able to organize a triumphant plebiscite in its favor.[45]

In the April 1946 *politics*, Coser offered his own account of the reasons for the "Left-Socialist" Resistance defeat. While reasserting sympathies for a movement he considered "in many respects the most hopeful we have witnessed in recent years," Coser concluded that fatal weaknesses undermined its prospects from the beginning. Like Caffi, he pointed to Resistance dependence upon Allied material and military aid as a basic, if unavoidable, flaw, corrupting and deforming its autonomous development. "It is difficult to write consistently on the need for a social revolution with printers' ink furnished by the [British] intelligence service," he noted. Many came to see the Resistance as "primarily an auxiliary force of an army attacking from the outside" rather than as an indigenous social movement. "Blowing up trains (became) more important than the slow building of conscious political forces."[46]

Intrinsic deficiencies also contributed to the postwar failure of the radical Resistance. Its spokesmen, while perhaps heroic figures during the period of clandestine opposition, were also, in one observer's phrase, "political babies," naively presuming consensus and popular support behind a set of goals that they themselves only dimly understood. "Their many wonderful ideals were floating in mid-air," Coser declared, "and they were completely unprepared for the harsh political and social realities which they had to face after the liberation." "Until then," he explained, "everything had been very uncomplicated. One knew who the enemy was and who was one's friend." But as the extraordinary moment of occupation began to fade, the lines between "collaboration" and "resistance" became hopelessly blurred. In the ensuing confusion, rival factions, more experienced in the demands of realpolitik, easily outmaneuvered the forces of the libertarian Left.[47]

Coser argued that the class diversity of the Resistance—perceived by Hannah Arendt and other observers as a unique advantage—in fact helped to sabotage any hopes for revolutionary change after the war. Although a broad coalition would be necessary for its ultimate success, Coser contended that "a movement that [was] not primarily rooted in the self-activity of the workers" was bound to lose its radical soul. Although representing only one of many strains of thought, "the left-wing intellectual leaders of the Resistance tricked themselves into the belief that their newspaper articles and programs represented the movement; and thus they thought that since they, in their great majority, expressed some sort of vaguely socialistic ideology, the movement as a whole was not only a military organization to drive out the foreign invaders but also a socialist movement." In the end, Coser concluded, "it was not enough to proclaim on paper the solidarity of all Resistance men." Once the common enemy was gone, it was inevitable that conflicts along class lines—between the "forces of order" and the "forces of anarchy"—would reappear. Coser added that this lack of consensus also prevented the radicals from articulating a consistent "theoretical" direction to guide them through the "mixed up" postwar political landscape.[48]

At bottom, then—in spite of the "socialist phraseology" of its public declarations—the glue that held the Resistance together, in France and elsewhere, was *nationalism*. Coser admitted that he himself had initially been fooled into believing "that a new . . . European spirit had been animating the Underground in the various countries." In fact, it was now clear that "only a very thin if articulate layer of Resistance leaders really believed in the internationalist slogans." The masses, he asserted, had been motivated by national loyalties which were "easy for the DeGaulles . . . to direct . . . again into safe channels," and which often reverted into ugly chauvinisms.[49]

Coser ended his discussion by returning to the theme—"important above all"—of the passivity and "totalitarian" longings of the population at large. Here he borrowed fellow émigré Erich Fromm's recently coined phrase, "escape from freedom," to describe the prevailing state of mind, a product of the exhaustion and insecurity wrought by years of extreme situations. Widespread feelings of "impotence and powerlessness" explained for Coser why only a few engaged in Resistance activities in the first place, and the "desire to be protected by powerful organizations" was crucial to understanding the appeal of the Communist Party. Coser speculated: "It may very well be that the Fuehrer cult, which was supposedly smashed when Hitler killed himself in the Reich's Chancellery, is as strong as ever today among the frustrated, deceived, powerless and embittered masses of Europe." The continued hardships—perhaps, in Coser's view, consciously fostered by the Allies, given the small amount of emergency relief forthcoming—only deepened the sense of despair and the accompanying will to submission.[50]

Coser concluded that given its internal flaws, its rivals for power, and the political inertness of the masses, the libertarian "revolution" in Europe was never more than a mirage. The interwar crises of the Left had not really been surmounted, and the latest defeat simply represented "the culmination of a [long-term] process of deterioration of both spontaneous mass activity and independent socialist ideology." Although the

Resistance may have "marked something of a spring-tide of human emotions," it did not provide the foundations for a genuine socialist movement—at least in the immediate future.[51]

Coser's critique coincides in many respects with the interpretation later offered by historian James D. Wilkinson in his study, *The Intellectual Resistance in Europe*. Wilkinson's analysis of the postwar failure of Resistance movements in France, Italy, and Germany offers insights that apply with equal force to their American "outpost" in New York. "Its greatest contribution," Wilkinson concludes of the Resistance, "remained a moral one: the defeat of nihilism and the creation of an ethical consensus based on the principle of human dignity. Its most serious failure was the inability to implement its values in the political or social sphere." In short, this transatlantic community of dissidents was never able to move "from resistance to revolution," from "negativism" to positive program.[52]

The Resistance perspective Macdonald, Coser, and their colleagues found so exciting certainly had something important to offer to reconstruction efforts after World War II. As Wilkinson observes, spokesmen for the Resistance, in their articles and manifestos, restored a moral dimension to politics too often missing from the sectarian quarrels of the 1930s. Their rhetoric shifted the focus from historical abstractions such as nation, class, and party to a concern for the experience of the individual, for his or her capacities for growth and spontaneous action. Such programs as the Resistance offered possessed many attractive features, above all a commitment to participatory democracy and an attempt to marry anarchist decentralization with an overarching international framework. These goals were a promising start, deserving exploration and serious debate. They offered answers to many of the problems that had helped produce the cataclysms of 1914–45.[53]

Unfortunately, such a debate never really took place in the 1940s. Part of the reason was, of course, the configuration of power in postwar Europe. Getting a full hearing for radical alternatives would have been difficult, perhaps impossible, under the best circumstances, given the constraints of Allied hegemony and the developing cold war. Still, flaws in the Resistance vision helped to cripple any attempt to advance its agenda, leaving its leaders cut off from a constituency, their ideas, in Coser's apt phrase, "floating in mid-air." As Wilkinson has written, "there were many rivals for power in 1945, of whom the Resistance intellectuals, as it proved, were least able to make good their claims."[54]

Because of their activities in defiance of the Nazis, Resistance spokesmen came to see themselves as a new ethical "aristocracy." Wilkinson compares the experience of the *résistant* to a "religious conversion," both for "the depths of the transformation it induced and the feelings of personal election that resulted." Wilkinson also describes the Manichaean universe many came to inhabit, in which values had been reduced to elemental "pairs of opposites: positive and negative, evil and good." Dwight Macdonald expressed this binary vision in his contrast, majestic in its "sharpness and moral purity," between "collaboration" and "resistance." Although this kind of thinking undoubtedly had its advantages during the exigencies of the war, it fundamentally deformed reality and rendered Resistance intellectuals peculiarly ill-prepared to handle the complexities and compromises of the post-Liberation European environment.[55]

The Resistance movements in France and elsewhere were never able to define a program or goals beyond vague exhortations for "workers' control" and "economic justice." As "Gelo and Andrea" demonstrated, the one item they discussed with any depth — the "nationalization" of key industries, also known under the rubric "planned economy" — ironically worked, in practice, to enhance the consolidation of state power. H. Stuart Hughes has described the undeveloped nature of their ideas: "For all the heroism and sacrifice that went into it, the social thought of the Resistance lacked specific content. Most of the time, it did not go beyond a reiteration of the principles of fraternity, moral regeneration, and the transcending of factional quarrels. . . . [T]he social doctrine of the Resistance was more a state of mind — a mystique — than a tangible program." Macdonald, in flight from what he saw as stifling Marxist orthodoxy, found the fact that the Resistance represented "no specific, positive ideology" a virtue, at least in the short run. But as the false consensus of the occupation disintegrated, this lack of ideological focus proved to be a severe handicap against rivals from both the right and left.[56]

Although the aversion of Resistance intellectuals to conventional political means — as Wilkinson notes, a reflection of their "anarchist belief that all government is bad" — had its healthy aspects, it left them perhaps too isolated from the political process. "Time and again," he observes, "it prevented them from identifying within the government potential allies with whom to join in the pursuit of concrete goals. Their distrust of the state and of corporate interests within the state — parties, the bureaucracy, pressure groups — robbed them of the opportunity to seek organized political expression of their ideals after 1945." Their brief for an anarchist localism within an international federation ignored, at great cost, intermediate levels of power. "They failed to supply a link connecting present and future," Wilkinson concludes. "They elected to look below, or above, but not *at* the social institutions with which any attempt to change society (even by abolishing those same institutions) would eventually have to deal."[57]

Finally, Resistance leaders sometimes displayed a self-righteous contempt for the recalcitrant "masses" they sought to persuade, dismissing their countrymen as hopelessly "totalitarian" when they failed to respond to calls for radical social change. Members of the *politics* circle also indulged in this practice as Resistance fortunes declined. At one moment the people were valorized for their "inexhaustible reserves"; at another, they stood condemned as atomized, pathological reactionaries, prone to "automatization," "Fuehrer cults," and "escape from freedom." This analysis reached a level of absurdity with Caffi and his portrait of "simplistic," "sheeplike" hordes.[58]

Even granting the widespread sympathies for fascism that may have survived into post-Hitler Europe, it does not follow that the failure of radical Resistance forces to attract popular support was entirely the public's fault. Certainly a desire for "peace and goods," as Caffi derisively characterized it, was understandable and legitimate in the devastated landscape of the mid-1940s. A focus on private concerns in such circumstances, an attempt to achieve, for perhaps the first time in one's life, a modicum of "normalcy," can be seen as heroic in its modest way, an expression of human resilience rather than a retreat to totalitarianism. And, for all their obvious flaws, at least the mainstream political parties —including the communists—had concrete programs and a record of experience that might help to fulfill those aspirations. What did the radical Resistance really have to offer, other than calls (often in pious tones, and always short on details) for a sweeping social and "spiritual" revolution promising further hardship and "disorder"? To expect people battered by years of war to sign on to such a cause seems unrealistic.

Instead of dismissing the "masses" and withdrawing from political debate—a strong temptation for disillusioned Resistance radicals— perhaps the obligation was to continue trying to connect with the public, to create an agenda and a "national-popular" idiom that spoke in a more positive, specific way to its needs and desires—in short, to build a viable alternative to the mainstream choices. Perhaps that would have been the best way for the members of Caffi's demoralized "society" to rescue the people's martyred "epos." Such engagement, however, would have required a strategy of patient, grassroots movement-building for which the romantic Resistance sensibility was less than ideally suited.

To the observer half a century later, at the far end of the cold war, the rise and decline of the Resistance moment of the 1940s—from liberation euphoria to compromise, dissension, and a kind of gray paralysis—bears striking similarities to the story that has unfolded in postcommunist

Central and Eastern Europe after 1989. But this more recent experience also reminds us that social change is an elusive, mysterious affair, and that "antipolitical" activities of the kind Resistance intellectuals favored, "outside" the boundaries of corrupt parties and government institutions, can set in motion forces that are not immediately apparent. In pursuit of signs of life amid the Caffian "society" that was the remnant of the radical Resistance, *politics* continued to monitor events in Europe even after the victory of the forces of authority was assured. As a whole, the stream of letters and articles from France, Italy, Germany, and other places in its burgeoning transatlantic network made for depressing reading. In addition to an overwhelming food crisis, the postwar atmosphere throughout the continent seemed fatally poisoned: black market economies flourished, politicians jockeyed for petty advantage, and the superpower stalemate cast an ever-deepening shadow over every aspect of daily life.[59]

The picture was not uniformly bleak, however. Some correspondents saw a reappearance of radical possibilities as popular discontent with the new order mounted. For instance, in a December 1945 article describing the recent erosion in working-class support for the French CP, "Gelo and Andrea" asked whether this unexpected volatility might offer the chance for "a new beginning" for independent European socialists. The problem was that despite "a certain revival of apolitical syndicalist tendencies and small Trotskyist groups," disaffected leftists as yet had no clear alternative to rally around. In their "French Letter" for the April 1946 *politics,* "Gelo and Andrea" reported further signs of a "growing critical spirit" among workers and other sectors of the populace. In the wake of de Gaulle's resignation early in the year, the dominant political institutions —parties and unions as well as the central government—again faced a legitimacy crisis amid the general restlessness and frustration. By now, in addition to the enclaves of "Trotskyists" and "syndicalists," "Gelo and Andrea" observed that "new little groups of a political or of a more intellectual character, less ossified in their thinking, have sprung up here and there. These groups most of the time have as yet no connection with each other and are still groping toward new ideas, new ways."[60]

Could these scattered groups coalesce into something more substantial? Were they the harbingers of a wave of "spontaneous, daring, passionate initiatives," which, in Caffi's view, signaled genuine "revolutionary ferment?" Was a "third camp" socialist alternative to the cold war still possible? Macdonald and his colleagues embraced encouraging bits of evidence like the ones "Gelo and Andrea" provided as a sign that the European "Resistance spirit" was not completely dead after all. The *politics* intellectuals would devote much of their energy after 1945 searching for ways to nurture these fragile new growths.

FOUR

Domestic Alternatives: New Directions in American Radicalism

Radicals must be more concerned about individual morality
than they have been in the past.

—DWIGHT MACDONALD, 1944

Looking to the Margins

In a July 1944 "Comment" to his readers, Dwight Macdonald justified
an increasing focus on developments abroad as a response to the dearth
of encouraging prospects at home. In contrast to the situation in Europe,
where, for a time, the Resistance seemed to promise immediate opportunities for radical change, Macdonald found the domestic political
climate static and reactionary. As the war entered its final year, he
considered the chances of a socialist revolution in the United States
anytime soon "close to nil."[1]

One reason for Macdonald's gloom, and a primary factor in his
disenchantment with Marxian ideology, was what he and others in the
politics circle interpreted as the demise of the proletariat as an agent of
social transformation. When he launched his journal earlier in 1944,
Macdonald still hoped that American workers would take advantage of
the war crisis to create, at the very least, an independent third party as
a challenge to the capitalist status quo. Within a few months, however,
it was clear that such a challenge was not forthcoming, and explanations
for labor's failed promise soon became a *politics* staple.

Daniel Bell and economist Walter Oakes argued that the American
trade union movement had come to accept its place as a junior partner
in the state-directed "Permanent War Economy," its institutions now
functioning as organs of control rather than opposition. Macdonald
agreed, decrying the fact that the CIO had already repeated the "devo-
lution" from "youthful rebellion to bureaucratic conservatism" that had

characterized its older European counterparts. He concluded that the unionized rank-and-file, blinded by appeals to patriotism and distracted by the benefits of war production, was content to follow the directives of its leadership, enthusiastically building atomic bombs and other weapons of destruction in the interest of "more work, better pay." Even the occasions when workers acted on their own initiative provided little cause for hope. The wildcat walkouts of the late war period seemed to be about narrow wage and hour issues, and a strike staged by Philadelphia transit employees in August 1944 was motivated by the most disgusting kind of racial antagonisms, dashing any romantic visions of worker solidarity. In short, by war's end Macdonald and his colleagues believed that the labor insurgency of the previous decade was spent. The class struggle central to Marxist prophecy had turned out to be a "mirage."[2]

A second, related reason for Macdonald's pessimism was his view of the influence of a debased and manipulative mass culture in American life. In the first issue of *politics* he carried forward the pioneering critique he had begun earlier at *Partisan Review,* describing the incursions of a market-driven, standardized "popular" culture against older "high" and "folk" traditions founded on individual freedom and spontaneity. Although not yet as resigned as Frankfurt School émigrés Horkheimer and Adorno (he still held out for the possibility that a "*human* culture" might emerge sometime in the classless future), Macdonald saw popular culture as a frighteningly effective "instrument of social domination" whose political implications could be seen in the successes of Nazism and Stalinism. In the United States, Macdonald warned, "the deadening and warping effect of long exposure to movies, pulp magazines and radio can hardly be overestimated," and a descent into some native variant of totalitarianism was therefore not out of the question. In any case, prospects for a radical left agenda under current circumstances appeared to be severely limited.[3]

The portrait in *politics* of a barren domestic landscape was too one-dimensional, its arguments about coopted workers and mesmerized masses based more on caricature than reality. Although Americans were certainly not in a revolutionary temper during this period, their acceptance of the evolving new order was far from complete. Historians like Staughton Lynd and Nelson Lichtenstein remind us that although labor organizations did indeed become more bureaucratic and conservative during World War II, class conflict persisted and rank-and-file militancy continued to bubble beneath the surface. The wave of wildcat actions interrupting the industrial harmony of the mid-1940s represented real struggles over power that deserved more systematic and sympathetic scrutiny than they received from *politics* magazine. In addition, the interpretation of "popular" culture as a one-way "instrument of social domination," forged by Macdonald and others in the shadow of mid-century totalitarianism, ignored the complex ways in which people interact with and reshape their environment. As a wealth of recent scholarship demonstrates, cultural meanings are always contested.[4]

Like his opposition to the war, however, Macdonald's premature dismissal of workers and the mainstream "masses" can be seen in retrospect as a "creative" mistake. It prompted him to move beyond conventional boundaries in his search for the seeds of a new radicalism, to fix his attention on movements and ideas on the margins that might eventually attract a wider constituency. Again, one is struck by the prescience of Macdonald's explorations. Already in the 1940s he understood that debates about militarism and the bureaucratic state, race and gender relations, and the moral autonomy of the individual were eclipsing the class issues that had preoccupied the Old Left. His engagement with the nascent pacifist and civil rights movements, and with new currents in "cultural" radicalism, make *politics* a uniquely interesting window on the post-Marxist New Left that would come to maturity by the 1960s.[5]

Conscientious Objectors and
Revolutionary Pacifism

In a May 1946 report to his readers, Macdonald reflected on the unexpected directions his journal had taken during its first two years of existence. He noted that as the question of warfare became central, *politics* found itself "in the absurd position, from a Marxist point of view, of devoting more space to the ideas and acts of the Conscientious Objectors than to those of the whole U.S. labor movement." Indeed, after some initial hesitation, Macdonald became an enthusiastic publicist for the small subculture of "revolutionary pacifists" emerging from World War II, and his magazine served as an important forum of discussion and debate among C.O.'s. Besides being outraged by the injustices war resisters suffered, Macdonald found inspiration in their example of individual and small-group resistance to the state and was intrigued by the tactical potential of their brand of direct action. Attempts to build on this model after 1945, however, forced him to confront difficult questions about the relationship between morality and politics that pacifism—at least in its more absolute forms—could not fully answer.[6]

Following a period of mainstream acceptance in the isolationist 1930s, the American peace movement dwindled after Pearl Harbor to a hard core of committed dissidents. Of this group, the young men who refused to submit to military conscription paid a special price for sticking to their principles. Under the Selective Service Act of 1940, the government consigned those individuals classified as Conscientious Objectors (about 12,000 in all) to "alternative" duty in Civilian Public Service (CPS) work camps, scattered in remote locations throughout the country and administered by officials of the "Historic Peace Churches"—the Christian Brethren, the Mennonites, and the Society of Friends. Those who declined or were denied C.O. status (about 6,000) faced criminal prosecution as draft resisters and usually served time in the federal prison system.[7]

Ironically, these artificially enclosed environments served as breeding grounds for further dissent and civil disobedience. A communal ethos quickly developed among the inmates of the various camps and prisons, and intimate contact with arbitrary bureaucratic authority radicalized their pacifism. Maurice Isserman describes C.O. internment during World War II as "a formative experience for a new generation of pacifist leaders, providing them with the equivalent of a post-graduate education in applied Gandhianism." Through organized walkouts, slowdowns, work or hunger strikes, and other means of noncooperation, modeled on the factory sit-down strikes of the 1930s and consistent with Gandhi's ethic of *satyagraha,* C.O.'s won a series of small but dramatic victories over their beleaguered caretakers. In the process, they developed networks of communication and mutual support that many believed would serve as the basis for a more ambitious movement after the war.[8]

Dwight Macdonald was a late convert to the strategy of conscientious objection. He admired the courage such a choice required, but he was initially troubled by the disengagement it seemed to imply. In the second issue of *politics* in March 1944, Macdonald rejected University of Chicago official Milton Mayer's pacifist response to the war as self-defeating. Mayer's ideas were "sensible and sensitive," his willingness to risk jail for his convictions "refreshing and inspiring." Still, Macdonald could not agree "that the best way to act if one has profound political objections to this war is to become a C.O. or to go to jail." "One can more effectively fight for one's ideas," he maintained, "if one does not isolate one's self from one's fellow-men, and the army is a better place to learn, and to teach, than either a C.O. camp or a jail. Only for a few symbolic leaders, like Debs, does going to jail seem to me the wisest course."[9]

Four months later, *politics* published a reply to Macdonald submitted by Don Calhoun, another University of Chicago pacifist. In "The Political Relevance of Conscientious Objection," Calhoun disagreed that C.O.'s necessarily isolated themselves, an assumption based on an outdated stereotype of the pacifist as an otherworldly religious ascetic, "a somewhat unreal or asocial or apolitical character." On the contrary, Calhoun insisted that many C.O.'s were political radicals, interpreting their experience as part of a broader struggle to overturn an oppressive social system. The new pacifism of the 1940s was not merely an excuse for withdrawal or inaction. It was "a positive technique practiced and trained for," involving "drama and danger, self-discipline and self-sacrifice." It was the foundation for a vigorous and tough-minded campaign of *resistance* to coercive institutions that might ultimately have widespread popular impact.[10]

Calhoun admitted that inmates at CPS camps spent their days performing useless make-work, but added that the evening "bull sessions" crackled with argument and debate, often resulting in coordinated, well-publicized—and therefore politically "relevant"—campaigns of nonviolent protest. He cited a recent work action against racial discrimination in the Danbury, Connecticut, federal prison and a hunger strike directed at censorship of the mails in a Lewisburg, Pennsylvania, jail as examples of C.O. militancy with ramifications for American society at large. Calhoun praised the harmony between values and action achieved by C.O. activists, and he emphasized, in language Macdonald himself would later adopt, "the utterly disproportionate nuisance value" a handful of individuals employing the tactics of "moral jiu-jitsu" could have in a rigidly structured system of authority. By demonstrating that its "supply of cannon fodder" was not unlimited, Calhoun concluded, these resisters posed a direct challenge to the legitimacy of the ruling order. "Today the conscientious objector, and the conscientious objector alone, stands out as the nucleus for the only movement which can shatter the confidence of the state in its ability to effectively make war *if and when it chooses*."[11]

Macdonald responded skeptically to the idea that the C.O. community could be the germ of a wider insurgency, given both the limited scope of its successes and the peculiar character of its membership. Betraying his own urban-secular biases, he worried about the fact that many of those involved were religiously motivated farmers—"not a normal cross-section of American society, nor . . . a particularly promising group to try to influence in a radical direction." Still, Macdonald confessed that Calhoun had presented "a much stronger case for Conscientious Objection as a political anti-war tactic than I should have imagined possible." Macdonald was impressed above all by the "moral advantage" such resistance offered:

In a period like the present in this country, when there is no immediate prospect of effective political action to realize ultimate principles, there is something very attractive about the C.O.'s kind of individual moral stand. His day-to-day life and his long-range convictions, if they do not wholly coincide, are at least on speaking terms with each other.[12]

Referring to his own sense of impasse and frustration, Macdonald contrasted the C.O.'s posture of defiance to the "psychologically dessi-cating" outward conformity of the Trotskyist during a conservative period. The latter's cautious behavior might, he acknowledged, be a defensible strategy for survival; but as time passed it fostered a cynical resignation to and even acceptance of the values of the status quo. The C.O., on the other hand, "like the European anarchist or our own old-time Wobblies, at least reacts spontaneously, immediately against the evils he fights, and shapes his everyday behavior to fit his principles. This is a great thing."[13]

Macdonald began to follow journals like *Fellowship* and *Pacifica Views* with intense interest, urging his audience to take note of "how much serious and original thinking" was occurring within pacifist circles. In turn, *politics* developed a loyal readership among C.O.'s, and it regularly featured their letters describing conditions in CPS facilities and criticizing religious officials for their cooperation with the government. One correspondent condemned the work camps as "laboratories in forced labor," not far removed in principle from those operating under Hitler's regime. The June 1945 issue reprinted excerpts from a news-letter circulated at Germfask, a government-run camp in Michigan's northern peninsula that Macdonald termed the "Siberia" of the CPS system, the last destination for disciplinary "problem cases." At Germ-fask, one inmate observed, the lines were clearly drawn. "The labor conscripts face their overseers directly; there is no church opiate to hide the fundamental nature of the program." Work stoppages were a chronic problem at the camp, and the newsletter encouraged rebellious inmates to see themselves as front-line defenders of individual freedom against the advances of totalitarian regimentation:

> Slowly, but almost inevitably, the people of this country and the world are being cast into a mold: authority from the top, unquestioning obedience to that authority. . . . CPS men are in a position to strike a very effective blow at areas of uncontrolled authority—and the grow-ing public complacency and acceptance of such authority—if they are willing to consider themselves as expendable for their principles as is the soldier expendable (less voluntarily) for the purposes of the State.

Echoing Macdonald, the paper observed that "a majority of human beings are rapidly falling into two categories: those who resist and those who collaborate." For all their hardships, it concluded, C.O.'s who decided to join the fight against "uncontrolled authority" enjoyed an exhilarating sense of freedom and solidarity unknown to "collaborators."[14]

The task facing the pacifist community after the war was to translate its moral opposition to militarism and the centralized state into a positive political program with a coherent organizational structure. This would not be easy in the chill of increasing tensions between the superpowers, however. In the April 1946 *politics,* Don Calhoun reported the results of a meeting of pacifists, many of them veterans of CPS or prison internment, earlier that year in Chicago. After four days of discussion the ninety-five participants from around the country launched the "Committee for Non-Violent Revolution" (CNVR), a loosely knit coordinating body to be headquartered in New York. Its manifesto condemned efforts "to create a world government from the top down, either through military alliance of capitalist states or through the creation of a monster world state." It also declared members' intentions to work *outside* the traditional institutions of power, to create grassroots alternatives to the "deals or reformist proposals directed to the present political and labor leadership." To achieve their goals the signers of the charter dedicated themselves to using the direct action techniques practiced and refined during the war, including "demonstrations, strikes . . . and underground organization where necessary." Like the pronouncements of radicals in the European Resistance, however, the CNVR's founding statement was sketchy about the nature of those goals. It called for a "decentralized, democratic socialism" with "worker-consumer control" of the economy as part of a peaceful international order, and it encouraged small-scale experiments in cooperative or communal living, so long as they avoided "the tendency of many such groups to isolate themselves" from larger struggles. The CNVR's guiding principle was a commitment to human rights against the intrusions of government authority. "We deny the right of the state to dictate the conditions of labor, to conscript, to spy on individuals, or to interfere with basic civil liberties."[15]

Calhoun regarded the CNVR conference as "one of the more significant political developments to come out of the war," confirmation that pacifists could transcend their traditional quietism in favor of militant social engagement. Although he agreed with the group's rejection of conventional politics, he expressed reservations about the vagueness of its direction. In words that might be applied to the *politics* project in general in the 1940s, Calhoun wrote that CNVR's anarchist "picture of the post-revolutionary society seemed more a miscellaneous collection of objectives than an analytical attempt to present a plausible sketch of a working economic system." Many practical questions remained unanswered, and "the gap between the existing highly interdependent world economy, and the desired society based on locally autonomous economic and political groups, was hardly bridged on more than a purely verbal level." Despite such shortcomings, Calhoun gave the Chicago meeting a favorable review:

> It was the first effort at a systematic synthesis of elements which have hitherto been generally considered incompatible—rejection of statism (either capitalist or collectivist), rejection of reformism, and rejection of violence. . . . Until those many orphaned leftists who are tired of old approaches can produce something better, the Committee for Non-Violent Revolution may well serve as a rallying point from which to work out a new revolutionary program and technique.[16]

At least one "orphaned leftist" was less impressed with CNVR's potential, however. In a letter to Calhoun, Macdonald expressed disappointment with the "pious and familiar generalities" emanating from Chicago, dismissing the founding declaration as "the dullest collection of political platitudes since the last Trotskyist convention I attended." "All through," he continued, "one is struck by the discrepancy between the handful of people making Big Statements and the hugeness of the issues they toss around."[17]

Macdonald's skepticism would prove justified. Isserman has observed that CNVR "led a short and unspectacular life" in the hostile atmosphere of the 1940s, sponsoring a few small public demonstrations (supporting imprisoned C.O.'s, protesting the "neo-imperialism" of the United Nations) but never expanding its base or working out a sharper sense of purpose. In the July 1946 *politics*, Macdonald vividly illustrated the air of futility surrounding the typical CNVR meeting by quoting from this account by a *Pacifica Views* correspondent in Philadelphia:

> We proceeded to get down to the business at hand, the first item of which was an evaluation of . . . two recent CO demonstrations. . . . All agreed they were damn good demonstrations. . . . The group displayed the greatest interest in a discussion of Dwight Macdonald's recent article, "The Root Is Man." Every one agreed it is a damn good article and that the world is in a helluva shape. At 9:45 some intemperate person slipped in a question about "what can we DO?" There was a momentary silence, someone mentioned cooperatives and there was a general agreement that cooperatives were very valuable. Then it was 9:50 and time for the meeting to break up. A half hour later, as I leaned against the bar and fondled my glass of beer, the thought occurred to me that the evening's discussion had ended at the same place all the articles I could recall having read in *Pacifica Views* or *politics* had ended.

The problem of "what to DO," of how to connect talk to some type of effective action, would continue to bedevil Macdonald and his friends throughout the postwar years.[18]

Pacifist cooperative experiments—one solution to the problem of action—did develop in the 1940s, but they had a hard time avoiding the temptations of isolation cautioned against in the CNVR manifesto. The August 1946 *politics* featured a firsthand account by George Woodcock of the "community movement" then proliferating in England, a phenomenon he interpreted as the latest incarnation of a "perennially" recurring impulse in socialist thought. Earlier in *politics* he had noted the emergence of a "revolutionary consciousness" among C.O.'s in Great Britain, a group paralleling (and actually exceeding in numbers) its counterpart in the United States. Although not segregated in camps like their American peers, British resisters nonetheless constituted a distinctive oppositional subculture united by "common problems and a common enemy, the state." Woodcock believed that the process of radicalization he had undergone reflected the experience of many other C.O.'s:

> During this period of . . . contact with the state machinery . . . my whole attitude had crystallized from a vague humanitarianism into a clearly-understood revolutionary anarchism. From a somewhat airy feeling that war was due to "something wrong in society," I had come to realize that it could only be ended by a really radical change in the whole social structure, both economic and political.[19]

According to Woodcock, some British resisters went "on the run" for the duration of the war, evading the police thanks to the help of a C.O. underground "closely linked . . . with the fringe of the criminal underworld." Others gathered in small, largely self-sustaining agricultural communities. Because these latter individuals saw their activities, at least initially, as "a solution to an urgent personal problem rather than the fulfillment of a political ideal," Woodcock observed that "theories tended to be developed after rather than before the formation of communities," leaving their ideological dimensions "nebulous." Still, participants began to feel a shared "missionary purpose" about their settlements, rooted in a desire to avoid contact with the state and to create "an alternative pattern of social organization" built on cooperation rather than "acquisitive values."[20]

By 1946, more than a hundred of these rural enclaves remained viable. Many more, however, had collapsed in the face of economic and organizational problems. Chief among the handicaps undermining the experiments in their early stages was a general ignorance about farming methods and other mundane details of subsistence—a difficulty compounded, in Woodcock's eyes, by a lack of experience in the interpersonal dynamics of small-group living. The failure of many English communities to establish organic contacts with their neighbors heightened the problem, often with fatal consequences. "The feeling of isolation caused the life of the group to turn inward," Woodcock wrote, "creating a hothouse emotional atmosphere where personal differences assumed monstrous proportions, and the most bitter feuds were started over trivialities." Although he admired the communities that had managed to overcome these obstacles, Woodcock concluded that they were not likely to mature into a broader movement for radical social change because of their insularity and "almost deliberate neglect of wider issues."[21]

Similar difficulties plagued communal experiments in the United States. The winter 1948 issue of *politics* contained David Newton's profile of the hardiest of these groups, the farm cooperative in Macedonia, Georgia. Originally founded in 1937, Macedonia attracted C.O.'s like Newton who wanted to continue the "comfort [of the] enforced solidarity against a hostile society" they had experienced in CPS camps and prisons during the war. Newton described the crises, large and small, the eighteen participants encountered as they eked out a spartan existence by dairying, farming, and woodworking. Their mutual commitment to the Quaker model of consensus democracy meant long hours of intense debate about the most basic budgeting and administrative matters, and, as with Woodcock's British communities, minor frictions sometimes threatened to explode into divisive confrontation. "When a number of individualistic pacifists are gathered together," Newton explained, "what you get may be something other than sweetness and light."[22]

In spite of its growing pains, Newton pronounced Macedonia a kind of "good life." The cooperative's financial situation was finally beginning to stabilize, and internal cohesion, as well as relations with suspicious neighbors, seemed to be improving by the month. Newton concluded with a rebuttal to the charges of escapism lodged against the group by its urban, "lib-lab" critics. "For the life of us," he wrote, "we can't feel that we've escaped from anything except the insuperable handicaps to decent living imposed by the megalopolis. We walk to work through evergreen woods; we work with friends whom we know and trust; we work at jobs the immediate value of which we can see and feel."[23]

Although it is difficult to imagine that the city-dwelling cosmopolitans around *politics* could be long content taking to the woods in this manner, small-scale communitarian experiments like those described by Woodcock and Newton appealed to a utopian strain prominent in their thinking. Macdonald idealized these enclaves as spaces of *personal* human interaction, sharply different from the abstract relations prevailing in "mass" society. But he and his colleagues were never able to resolve the tendency to claustrophobia, withdrawal, and disintegration these communities faced in practice—problems Mary McCarthy would examine at the end of the decade in her satirical novel, *The Oasis*.

American C.O.'s continued to face persecution even after the war, and *politics* followed their cause closely. A July 1946 cover story, focusing on the plight of dissidents at the Glendora, California, CPS camp, publicized the fact that a year after the end of hostilities, 6,500 resisters remained in federal custody. Macdonald reviewed in detail the grievances prompting current outbreaks of C.O. militancy—organized actions that, according to James Peck, took on deeper political significance in the wake of Truman's interventions against striking railway workers and coal miners. Macdonald declared that the objectors' courageous show of defiance against the state "must enlist the sympathy and active support of every radical," and he issued an amnesty petition and appeal for legal defense funds as a way to demonstrate that support. C.O.'s around the country showed their appreciation by preparing *politics* relief packages to Europe.[24]

Soon the wartime energies of the radical C.O. community began to flag, however. In the September 1946 *politics*, Albert Votaw reflected on why local rebellions like the one at Glendora failed to produce a wider campaign of resistance. One answer lay in the confusion sown by the Peace Churches, who ran and legitimized the CPS system. Votaw observed that many C.O.'s—especially the "religious" ones—felt inhibited from joining protests against abuses like unpaid labor by a misguided sense of obligation to "serve" their country. In an explicit analogy to Bettelheim's model of behavior in the Nazi concentration camps, Votaw noted that many CPS inmates came to "identify themselves with the administration":

> This usually took the form of pride in doing the work well, in meeting high work quotas, and in a—to me—excessive concern with the elimination of administrative problems. During the hey-day of C.P.S. assignees spent an incredible amount of time attempting to implement Selective Service objectives, even when it meant taking action against fellow assignees. . . . A few . . . wore Army uniform or Forest Service green, called their fellow assignees "the boys," and in general finked for the administration.[25]

Another factor limiting the impact of the insurgency, in Votaw's view, was the deep-seated hostility to organization prevalent among CPS activists. As with the European *résistants,* commitments to personal spontaneity and radical democracy (which Votaw termed "organization without official leadership") stymied the planning necessary to mount a more ambitious challenge to government authority. The individual, ad hoc nature of most protests frustrated efforts at intercamp cooperation. "This anti-organizational attitude made it impossible for national coordination on any issue," Votaw concluded. "Any successful action took place locally, over a short period of time, and on specific, local grievances."[26]

The Truman administration's push for a permanent conscription bill briefly injected new life into radical pacifist ranks. Macdonald jumped at the chance to do something concrete to advance his principles, joining such figures as A. J. Muste, David Dellinger, and Bayard Rustin to protest this latest step in cold war mobilization. Their joint appeal, published in the January 1947 *politics,* condemned the peacetime draft as "an integral part of a consistent pattern of competitive power developing throughout the world, including the maintenance of huge military machines, the development of atomic and biological weapons, the scramble for colonies and raw materials." "It will lead by its own logic," the statement warned, "to the final world war and the extinction of the human race." Signatories pledged to defy the state's power to conscript its citizens by returning or publicly destroying their draft cards, an act of civil disobedience they encouraged others around the country to emulate.[27]

The following month, *politics* reprinted the text of a speech Macdonald made to an anti-conscription rally in New York City titled "Why Destroy Draft Cards?" Macdonald characterized draft resistance as an important symbolic assertion of individual morality in an age of bureaucratic irresponsibility. "I am willing to compromise with the State on all sorts of issues which don't conflict too oppressively with my own values and interests," he told the crowd.

> But when the State—or rather, the individuals who speak in its name, for there is no such thing as the State—tells me that I must "defend" it against foreign enemies—that I must be prepared to kill people who have done me no injury in defense of a social system that has done me considerable injury—then I say I cannot go along. I deny altogether the competence—let alone the right—of anyone else . . . to decide for me a question as important as this.

Macdonald took this occasion to voice some pragmatic qualifications to his pacifist creed, admitting that force might be a necessary last resort in "concrete limited situation[s]" where the perpetrator "know[s] to some extent what will be the results." This was a far cry, however, from the machinery of mass "murder by remote control" some now wanted to expand on the old pretext of "the responsibility of peoples." Macdonald referred to the lessons of the recent war: "How does it punish the Nazis for massacring helpless Jews and Poles to massacre ourselves helpless Germans in saturation bombings? But if we use the instrumentality of the State and organized warfare, the only way we can prevent massacre and atrocities is to commit them ourselves—first. This is a kind of book-keeping which I don't accept."[28]

The anti-conscription movement failed to generate much popular support over the next months, amid growing, genuine fears about the Soviet threat. In April 1948, in a last-gasp attempt to articulate a peaceful alternative to the cold war, three hundred activists met in Chicago to form a new nationwide organization they called "Peacemakers." Its founding charter, reprinted in *politics*, invited the public to join in a concerted campaign of militant, nonviolent resistance to the state military apparatus, suggesting the use of disruptive tactics like strikes, draft evasion, and refusal to pay taxes in order to slow the momentum toward armed conflict. Executive committee member Dwight Macdonald admitted to his readers that "the whole thing is still pretty vague," however; and indeed the Peacemakers' broader program, consisting of a brief reference to "political and economic democracy," must have seemed a rehash of the CNVR "platitudes" he had criticized only two years earlier.[29]

By this point Macdonald entertained larger doubts about the "political relevance" of pacifist moralism—and, indeed, of radical thinking in any form—in a world of totalitarian dictatorships and irrational violence. News of Gandhi's assassination in January 1948 only fueled those doubts. The winter 1948 issue of *politics* featured reflections on the meaning of Gandhi's life and martyrdom by members of the journal's inner circle, along with representative excerpts from the Indian leader's own publication, *Harijan*. Mary McCarthy described her feelings of "perfect impotence" and "futility" upon learning of the murder, a reminder of humanity's boundless capacity for evil. Nicola Chiaromonte argued that the directness and simplicity of Gandhi's ethics, the harmony between his ideals and his actions, made him "profoundly unintelligible to us in the West." Niccolo Tucci satirized the empty and hypocritical expressions of tribute flooding the mass media now that the revolutionist was safely dead.[30]

Macdonald's thoughts on the killing revealed an overwhelming personal sense of loss. The reign of "maximum violence with minimum meaning" seemed to continue without a pause. "Three historical events have moved me deeply of recent years," he wrote, "the murder of Trotsky, the atomic bombing of Hiroshima, the murder of Gandhi. That all three should be simply catastrophes—hopeless, destructive, painful—is the style of our period." Macdonald compared the careers of Trotsky and Gandhi, noting the irony that each man was killed gratuitously, after his moment of world-historical influence had passed and "after his ideas—or at least [his] tactics—had been shown by the brutal logic of events to be inadequate." Even in decline, however, "both men were still giving, by their personal example and still more by their unwearied experimenting with general principles, some kind of meaning, of *consciousness*, to modern political life. Their assassins killed not only two men, but also two cultures."[31]

Macdonald found human virtues in Gandhi that were rapidly disappearing in an era of massification and totalitarian manipulation. He wrote:

> Gandhi was the last political leader in the world who was a person, not a mask or a radio voice or an institution. The last on a human scale. The last for whom I felt neither fear nor contempt nor indifference but interest and affection. . . . He was dear to me because he had no respect for railroads, assembly-belt production, and other knick-knacks of liberalistic Progress, and insisted on examining their human (as against their metaphysical) value. Also because he was clever, humorous, lively, hardheaded, and never made speeches about Fascism, Democracy, the Common Man, or World Government. And because he had a keen nose for the concrete, homely "details" of living which make the real difference to people but which are usually ignored by everybody but poets.

Of particular note here is the way Macdonald contrasted Gandhi's "concreteness" and sense of complexity (characteristics obscured by "Sunday Supplement" hagiography) to the "boring" and "dull" attitudes of many of his followers. Macdonald's increasing disaffection from the latter was palpable: "Intellectually, their ideas lack subtlety and logical structure. Ethically they are *too* consistent; they don't sense the tragedy of life, the incredible difficulty of putting into practice an ethical concept. They have not succumbed to temptation because they have never been tempted; they are good simply because it has never occurred to them to be bad. They are, in a word, unworldly."[32]

For Macdonald, the pacifist faithful appeared especially ill-equipped to respond to the realities of the cold war as it entered its acute phase in 1948. His commitment to revolutionary nonviolence ended with the Soviet blockade of Berlin in the summer of that year, an event that prompted him to renounce the political relevance of any kind of "utopian" or "ultimatist" morality. Pacifism, in Macdonald's view, was utterly inadequate to meet the threat posed by an adversary like Stalin, who would interpret any gesture of "brotherly love" as a sign of weakness inviting further aggression. Macdonald now spoke of a tragic impasse: failure by the United States to take a stand meant appeasement, but the alternative risked a war of mutual annihilation. Radicals faced a historical "dilemma" with no satisfactory answers.[33]

Macdonald complained that many of the pacifists he knew, clinging to their "ultimatist" principles and secure in their "unworldliness," seemed blind to the difficulties presented by the Berlin crisis. The withdrawal of American troops they called for would only deliver the city's residents to the bloodbath of Soviet reprisals. "When I made [this] point at a pacifist meeting," he later recalled, "several speakers from the floor expressed amazement that I, as a pacifist, should consider the consequences of an action. If the act is good in itself, they argued, then it should be done, regardless of consequences." In the end, Macdonald was too much of a Deweyan pragmatist to accept this kind of thinking. He replied to his challengers: "It seems to me that it is almost entirely by its consequences, whether immediate or long-range, that we evaluate an action."[34]

What are we finally to make of the movement for "revolutionary non-violence" that Macdonald and *politics* found so attractive in the mid-1940s? Certainly the amalgam of ideas emerging from CPS camps, communal experiments, and organizations like CNVR and Peacemakers had flaws as a successor to Marxism, especially in its programmatic vagueness and tendencies toward moral absolutism and disengagement. Radical pacifism served better as a basis for criticism and "resistance" than as a fully developed political doctrine. These deficiencies help to explain why its adherents aroused so little public response in their doomed efforts to counter the forces of the cold war.

Even with its failures, however, the pacifist subculture *politics* admired pioneered tactics and advanced arguments about the relationship of the individual to the state that would take on increasing importance in the postwar years. Perhaps Macdonald himself offered the best defense of this fledgling peace movement, in his February 1947 speech condemning official plans for a new military buildup. When he confessed to his listeners that burning a draft card was an imperfect and probably ineffectual means of political protest, he added that "it is the only action I can think of which directly expresses my opposition to conscription. A beginning must be made somewhere." Two decades later Macdonald would draw on the lessons of this "beginning" as he participated in much larger rallies protesting the war in Vietnam.[35]

The Struggle for Racial Democracy

The Second World War was the catalyst for profound social changes in the United States, and among those at the forefront of reform were African-Americans. The manpower shortage caused by the emergency mobilization drastically increased the black community's political and economic leverage, and the egalitarian rhetoric of the crusade against fascism presented it with new opportunities to push the problem of racial injustice toward the center of the national agenda. The dramatic victory won by A. Philip Randolph's March on Washington Movement (MOWM) in 1941 encouraged the new spirit of militancy, signaling that, their patience during World War I notwithstanding, blacks would not be content to defer discussion of their long-festering grievances for the duration of World War II.[36]

The gains achieved by the new assertiveness were at first more symbolic than substantive, however. Although the Roosevelt administration made landmark concessions in response to the MOWM's threat of large-scale direct action, its overall approach to the "Negro problem" remained conspicuously timid, captive to the need to appease the Southern "white supremacist" wing of the fragile Democratic Party coalition. The Fair Employment Practices Committee, created by executive order to eliminate discrimination in war industries, never received the funding or enforcement powers to do its job effectively, and token administrative appointments had little real impact. Most telling with respect to the weight of Southern political influence was the War Department's decision to continue traditional practices of segregation in raising and deploying an army.[37]

This latter policy inflamed Dwight Macdonald's sense of outrage, and it was the racial issue to which he devoted most of his muckraking energies in the 1940s. In a February 1943 *Nation* article, later appearing as a pamphlet for MOWM, Macdonald condemned the Jim Crow armed forces as "the war's greatest scandal." He detailed reports of the unequal conditions and harassment (often violent) endured by the half-million black Americans then in uniform, especially those stationed at bases in the South. Macdonald described the massive logistical effort required to implement the government's policy:

> Every regiment, every ship, every battery, every flying squadron and medical staff and jeep company is either all white or all colored. The most ingenious planning, the most complicated and voluminous quantities of paper-work, the tireless efforts of thousands of officers are devoted to the great task of keeping apart the two races. The instant he puts on the uniform of his country, the Negro becomes a deadly plague-carrier, to be quarantined, isolated at all costs from his white comrades in arms.

Under the regime of segregation, blacks invariably found themselves relegated to positions as "servants and laborers" and subject to a variety of humiliating restrictions. The policy of "quarantine" reached absurd extremes: Macdonald noted that the American Red Cross processed and stored blood plasma separately based upon the race of the donor, and Arlington National Cemetery interred black soldiers in a specially designated area for "colored graves."[38]

Macdonald found this state of affairs supremely ironic, "a fantastic situation in an Army supposedly dedicated to wiping out Nazi racialism." The doctrine of white supremacy on which this systematic discrimination rested was, in his view, "simply Hitler's 'Nordic Supremacy' in cracker lingo," senseless on both pragmatic and moral grounds. "If you are interested in winning the war," he concluded, "this is a criminal waste of human resources. If you are interested in democracy, it means spreading the poison of legalized, official jimcrow from the deep South throughout our entire national life and even overseas."[39]

Macdonald argued that military segregation was not only "shameful" and impractical but also illegal—a clear violation of the antidiscrimination section of the 1940 Selective Service Act. That provision had been ignored, however, because of the black community's "mistaken" reliance on liberal white politicians to protect its interests. For Macdonald, the MOWM success demonstrated that "the Negro gets something from the Roosevelt Administration only when he kicks up a fuss." Wartime exigencies provided no excuse for inaction or delay. "The colored people of America, and their white friends," Macdonald insisted, "must begin *right now* to make a real fight on this issue."[40]

One individual willing to risk that fight was Winfred Lynn, a young black landscape gardener from Long Island who had recently refused induction into a segregated army, choosing instead to press a legal challenge to the government's policies with the help of his brother Conrad, an attorney. Macdonald admired the Lynns' actions as an example of heroic resistance to the state, and he followed their case as it worked its way through the courts, hoping that it might eventually become a watershed challenge to *Plessy*'s "separate but equal" doctrine. He joined civil rights activists like Randolph, Roger Baldwin, and Alain Locke in cosponsoring a fund-raising body called the "Lynn Committee to Abolish Segregation in the Armed Forces." In addition, "Free and Equal"—a regular *politics* column devoted to race relations, described by Macdonald as "the most dynamic social issue of today"—reproduced the text of Conrad Lynn's brief to the New York Court of Appeals on behalf of his brother. The document asserted the stigmatizing and inherently discriminatory effects of racial segregation, an anachronistic "regional habit" that military authorities had now raised to the level of national policy. It concluded: "How shabby is the conduct of an agency of the government which bends all efforts to aid in establishing the 'Four

Freedoms' abroad while maintaining a rigid barrier to achieving them at home!" Despite Macdonald's initial hopes, however, the Lynn challenge ultimately died a quiet death, victimized, in his view, by a liberal failure of nerve in the face of potentially divisive racial issues. In *politics* he scored Arthur Hays, the intervening ACLU attorney, for redirecting the suit to narrow questions of procedure, effectively gutting it of social relevance and "educational" value. The Supreme Court's refusal to overturn the dismissal of the case only confirmed Macdonald's sense of betrayal.[41]

During the final months of the war Macdonald continued to use his magazine to expose, through journalistic accounts and firsthand testimony, the "scandal" of Jim Crow in uniform. Besides bringing home the nature of the hardships and indignities endured by black soldiers, and confirming the effectiveness of direct action tactics, these materials gave witness to the power of face-to-face human contacts to overcome bureaucratically encouraged barriers of race, nationality, and other characteristics of difference—a key *politics* insight in the 1940s.

The June 1944 issue featured a profile of Isaac McNatt, one of nineteen black Seabees summarily and dishonorably dismissed for speaking out against the unfair treatment they received in every aspect of their lives in the Navy. "We are casualties of war," McNatt concluded.

> When we volunteered ... we had in mind a number of bad things which could happen to us, but not this. We knew we faced death, maiming, or other serious injury by gunfire, bombardment or torpedoing. But we never considered ... discharge without cause. We didn't expect to come back to civilian life as heroes, but at least we wanted to be proud of the fact that we had offered to do our bit to help win the war, and have those we love proud of us. ... The country which we worked and fought to save has stigmatized us.

The following April, thanks in part to the publicity generated by the Lynn Committee, a Navy Board of Review decided to remove this "stigma," upgrading to "honorable" the discharges of most of the Seabees, including McNatt.[42]

The June 1944 *politics* also contained an article (borrowed from the *Pittsburgh Courier*, a prominent African-American journal) written by an anonymous member of the 477th Bombardment Group, an all-Negro unit of the prestigious Army Air Corps assembled, with much fanfare, to satisfy mounting public pressures for reform. Macdonald noted the great symbolic value the 477th had for the black community, and he saw the absence of segregation in its initial training phase as an important step in the right direction, adding that the arrangement had produced "no racial friction, as has generally been the case when the military authorities permit the men to get to know each other as human beings." Unfortunately, the innovations of this "outpost of democracy" would be short-lived. "Bombardier" recounted how a visiting general overruled local officials by ordering segregation in the mess hall. Embittered black pilots responded by boycotting the facility, taking meals at their own expense at the base PX.[43]

The trials of the men of the 477th continued after they were transferred to a post in Michigan. There the commander publicly condemned blacks who applied for membership in an all-white officers' club as "agitators." Before a promised recreational facility for Negroes could be constructed, the unit was once again suddenly relocated, this time to an antiquated air base in Kentucky. "Bombardier" argued that, beneath the official pretext of training requirements, "the real reason for the move was to shift the 477th to a Southern field where the local jimcrow laws and sentiment would be used to back up the Army's jimcrow policies." Despite deteriorating conditions and low morale, however, the black pilots, conscious of their visibility, remained dedicated to their work and maintained a model performance record.[44]

In the next issue, Macdonald again drew upon the experiences of soldier-correspondents like "Bombardier" to question the "practical" justifications usually advanced for a segregated armed forces. He rejected the assumption that a racially mixed army would inevitably produce violent internal conflicts. On the contrary, cooperation and harmony seemed to be the rule in those places where blacks and whites lived and worked together under the same conditions. In such an environment, Macdonald argued, even people from white supremacist backgrounds came to "discover . . . that Negroes are human beings also, who may be liked or disliked as individuals and not as embodiments of an abstract racial quality." The troops seemed to be ahead of their commanders on the race question. A soldier stationed at a desegregated post in Fort Lee, Virginia, wrote: "Even between Southerners and Negroes the most amazing friendships spring up. . . . It is a great pity that this doesn't prevail throughout the Army. It would end race prejudice in America. The fact is that if you put two human beings in fatigues in the same kitchen, they will fraternize."[45]

Macdonald was impressed by more general evidence of a natural human impulse to solidarity in adverse circumstances. Soldiers' shared sense of fear, hardship, and a common enemy ("their officers in the training period, the opposing armies in the combat period") often evoked "feeling[s] of cooperation and group loyalty" capable of effacing the petty prejudices of civilian life. As Simone Weil had understood in her reading of the *Iliad,* the kingdom of "Force" imposed a tragic equality on all its subjects. A story by the *Pittsburgh Courier*'s war correspondent vividly illustrated how race consciousness tended to evaporate under fire. It described how, during an intense period of fighting in Italy, blood plasma carefully separated by the Red Cross began to run out, forcing medics overwhelmed with wounded to use donations taken indiscriminately from troops in the field. When the reporter asked some G.I.'s at hand how they felt about this irregular practice, he was "startled by the ferocity with which they answered." A "big rawboned Texan," rolling up his sleeves to reveal skin grafts he had received from a black coworker after being burned in an oil field accident before the war, spoke for the majority: "Now about that there blood. Them slobs back home had better forgit that stuff in a hurry. We're fighting a war over here, and if it takes a black man's blood to save a white man's life, he's gonna git that blood, and we don't care what they say back there."[46]

As the war approached its conclusion, Jim Crow's days in uniform appeared to be numbered. An increasing number of successful direct action protests, paralleling the disruptions taking place in CPS camps, hastened the demise of segregation in the military. "Free and Equal" chronicled many of these actions, examples of moral resistance to which the authorities responded with an uncertain mixture of heavy-handedness and conciliation: a sit-down strike protesting unfair treatment at an airfield near Tucson, Arizona; a similar work stoppage by a group of sixty black WACS stationed at a Massachusetts hospital; a walkout at a base in Hawaii; the "invasion" of an exclusive officers' club by the men of the 477th Bombardier Group "exiled" in Kentucky. Political pressures fueled by these activities gradually forced the military leadership to back away from its antiquated race policies. A skeptical Macdonald interpreted the assignment of 2,500 Negro troops to "mixed" combat units in Europe in early 1945 as "a last-hour token gesture," but it was in fact a sign of things to come. Three years later, in the context of a new "emergency" mobilization, the Truman White House found it prudent to abolish the practice of segregation in the armed forces once and for all.[47]

The intensity of the engagement in *politics* with the problem of discrimination in the military did not, on the whole, carry over to the home front. The space devoted to coverage of African-Americans' newly revitalized struggle for civil rights perceptibly declined after the war, owing largely to the magazine's preoccupation with the European food situation and the cold war crisis.

"Free and Equal" did preview some of the class and ideological debates within activist circles that would become so explosive in the 1960s. One theme was a sharp rejection of impulses toward black nationalism. George Schuyler set the tone with his approving review of

Gunnar Myrdal's landmark study, *An American Dilemma,* in July 1944. Schuyler concurred with its reading of the black insurgency as an effort simply to redeem "the democratic and equalitarian values of the American culture," adding:

> The so-called Negro is sick and tired of being booted about by those he does not regard as his betters. . . . Today he wants all the rights and privileges any other American enjoys, and he means to have them. . . . All along the Negroes have been much clearer-visioned than the whites; and in the larger sense they have even been more patriotic because they have persistently fought for the American Creed—the principles which white America has loudly pronounced but grudgingly practiced, if at all.

While congenial to the universal standards of *politics,* Myrdal's conception of African-Americans as shock troops for a transcendent "American Creed" had its limitations, attracting critics from a variety of quarters. Among the most persuasive was novelist Ralph Ellison, who pointed out that *American Dilemma*'s assimilationist premises ignored and denigrated the distinctive virtues of the subculture it purported to understand.[48]

In May 1944, Wilfred Kerr, chairman of the Lynn Committee, scored moderates like the NAACP's Roy Wilkins for their reflexive condemnation of disturbances in Harlem the previous summer as rank "hoodlumism," devoid of context or provocation. Three months later, however, Kerr was himself adopting the role of a "moderate," assailing as chauvinist demagoguery the separatist rhetoric of a new generation of black leaders, most notably Harlem's Adam Clayton Powell Jr. Kerr interpreted actions like the MOWM's 1943 exclusion of whites from membership as dead-end "Negroism," "a doctrine so wrong and so full of dangers that it must be hunted down to the earth, killed and buried. The Negro Problem is not just the Negro's problem. . . . [It is] the problem of the American people. Unless the Negro is aroused, encouraged and aided by the progressive whites and the labor movement of this country, his efforts are doomed to failure." Kerr worried that nationalist posturing only fueled the embers of a "holy race war" in the United States, perhaps linked to the incipient anticolonial rebellions of the Third World.[49]

While hostile to black separatism, the commentary in *politics* on domestic civil rights issues usually projected a healthy populist militancy. The best example in this regard was the July 1945 installment of "Free and Equal" by William Worthy, a unionist and organizer for the interracial CORE. Worthy began by questioning the commitment to reform among liberal politicians, who had failed to speak out during the war when Japanese-Americans and Conscientious Objectors were being interned. He also wondered about the reliability of elite black lobbyists, beholden for their prerogatives to their white "patrons" and hopelessly aloof from the experience of the masses they claimed to represent. Such individuals, he cautioned, could not be counted on to press for radical changes in the status quo. For Worthy, the only strategy promising genuine black empowerment was grassroots self-help. He reminded his readers:

> Once away from the efficient National Headquarters and Washington Bureaus of various Negro organizations, we discover a segment of secondary leaders steering clear of kings and remaining in daily touch with the Abraham Lincoln Johnsons and the Matilda Goulds: the Negro manager of a co-op whose enthusiastic members murder the King's English but put an A & P across the street out of business; a Negro CIO organizer who leads a wartime strike against Joe Pew's Jim Crow shipyard; a Baptist minister who walked dangerous picket lines way back when Negro leaders were water boys for the Republican party.

Worthy concluded by insisting, as Martin Luther King Jr. would a few years later, that "as with Silone's peasants, the last and the final hope for racial emancipation lies in the unscheming good works—the *bona fide* mutual aid—of poor and humble blacks." Indeed it was just this kind of ferment that would become a revolutionary force in postwar American society.[50]

politics and "Cultural" Radicalism

According to Richard King, one strategy available to radicals who saw their hopes frustrated in the political and economic sphere in the 1940s was to shift their focus to questions of values and attitudes, to the task of "transforming consciousness." The engagement in *politics* with "cultural" radicalism, although a relatively minor motif, nevertheless further establishes the journal as a crucible for the post-Marxist "New Left" of the 1950s and 1960s. Especially in their attention to changing perspectives on human sexuality (fostered, in part, by the dislocations of the war), Macdonald and his colleagues demonstrated a grasp of the political "relevance" of personal mores that directly anticipated the insights of a wide array of "counterculturalists" who would gain prominence in the years to come.[51]

A bold example of Macdonald's efforts on this front was his publication of poet Robert Duncan's confessional essay, "The Homosexual in

Society," in the August 1944 *politics*. Although Duncan strongly condemned the dominant culture's persecution of those with "deviant"
sexual preferences, most of the article was a polemic against an exclusive
and insular "cult of homosexuality" that fit perfectly within the journal's
overall "cosmopolitan" agenda. Duncan criticized the retreat into a
ghetto mentality indulged in by many of the artists and writers he had
encountered in the gay underworld of New York, marked by "the
cultivation of a secret language, the *camp*, a tone and a vocabulary that
is loaded with contempt for the human." He saw this retreat as a betrayal
of broader moral responsibilities. "Sensing the fear in society that is
generated in ignorance of their nature," Duncan argued, "they have
sought not to bring about an understanding, to assert their equality and
their common aims with mankind, but they have sought to profit by that
fear and ignorance, to become witchdoctors in the modern chaos." In
words that could have been written by Macdonald himself, Duncan
urged homosexuals to transcend their parochial walls, to join with
blacks, Jews, and other pariah groups in a shared struggle for universal
emancipation. "Only one devotion can be held by a human being a
creative life and expression," Duncan wrote, "and that is a devotion to
human freedom, toward the liberation of human love, human conflicts,
human aspirations. To do this one must disown *all* the special groups
(nations, religions, sexes, races) that would claim allegiance."[52]

politics rarely took up questions of gender, but Dwight Macdonald's
acceptance of women like Simone Weil, Hannah Arendt, and Mary
McCarthy as intellectual equals is evidence of an inchoative feminist
consciousness—a sensibility undoubtedly encouraged by his wife and
collaborator, Nancy Macdonald. Even so, the single article explicitly
broaching those questions evinced the same universalist hostility to difference articulated by Robert Duncan. In "The Independent Woman: A
New Course," published in the May 1946 *politics,* Ethel Goldwater
renewed the call to end the Victorian ideology of "separate spheres,"
arguing that advances in domestic technology had rendered obsolete the
"Career vs. Babies" dichotomy still subscribed to by conservatives and
feminists alike. She dismissed most gender-specific characteristics as cultural constructs and asserted that men and women should enjoy the same
choices and bear the same responsibilities, in and out of the home.
Goldwater's approach rejected identity politics or any other form of
"special allegiances." The problems facing her "independent woman,"
like those of Myrdal's Negro and Duncan's homosexual, were "human"
ones. Perhaps the most interesting feature of Goldwater's essay was her
insistence that "reactionary" and "bourgeois" sexual attitudes persisted
"even in left-wing intellectual circles"—an observation that struck a
chord with at least some of the female readers of *politics*.[53]

The most sustained attempt to examine the political dimensions of sexuality, and the one with the clearest connections to the 1960s counterculture, was Paul Goodman's effort to articulate a "psychobiological" basis for revolutionary action. In "The Political Meaning of Some Recent Revisions of Freud," published in the July 1945 *politics*, Goodman criticized Karen Horney and Erich Fromm for minimizing the role of instinctual drives in the development of the human personality. To Goodman, their notion that "character *directly* reflects the social pattern" appeared as a prescription for what Comte had earlier termed "sociolatry," the complete "adjustment" and integration of the individual into the status quo. Goodman argued that such ideas reduced people to cogs, molded by advanced social "engineering" techniques to act exclusively in the service of "the smooth functioning of the industrial machine." In the context of the 1940s, Horney and Fromm were ideologists for accommodation to bureaucratic statism in its various forms, from Stalinism to the New Deal.[54]

Like Macdonald, Goodman was in search of an alternative to this totalitarian model of human behavior, and he found it in the writings of a third Freudian revisionist, Wilhelm Reich. Unlike Horney and Fromm, Reich held to Freud's original views on the centrality of instincts in the human psyche, especially those related to sexual gratification, and he argued that those instincts provided resources for individual transcendence and self-assertion. People exposed to systematic sexual repression, Goodman wrote, exhibited attitudes of passive submission to authority in every aspect of their lives. Those encouraged to satisfy their biological drives, on the other hand, tended to adopt a posture of creative rebellion against their surroundings. Goodman saw evidence to support this claim in clinical studies demonstrating that men and women "restored to sexual health and animal spirits simply will not tolerate the mechanical and routine jobs they have been working at, but turn (at whatever general inconvenience) to work that is spontaneous and directly meaningful." Thus, as Richard King observes, libidinal instincts served for Goodman as "both a powerfully conservative force in providing a bulwark against social and cultural pressures and a revolutionary force insofar as they are the source of free action by the individual." Goodman incorporated Reichian precepts into his blueprint for a decentralized, "natural" social order, calling, in the December 1945 *politics*, for an enlightened commitment to "the sexual satisfaction of the young." In his eyes, without the fundamental change in attitudes such a commitment promoted, the superficial institutional reforms traditionally advocated by radicals remained forever doomed to failure.[55]

Goodman's attempt, through Reich, to locate some residue of human existence safe from a catastrophic history and exempt from determination by totalitarian "social and cultural pressures" bears striking affinities both to Lionel Trilling's use of Freud in the 1950s and 1960s to define a part of man "beyond culture" and to Macdonald's efforts, in his 1946 essay, "The Root Is Man," to describe a "vital core" of personal moral autonomy. For each of these writers it was essential to show, in the shadow of Hitler and Stalin, that the human consciousness was not, as King put it, "a tabula rasa and hence infinitely malleable." Although Goodman's defense of the complexity of individual psychology offered a valuable corrective to conventional notions of determinism, it also carried with it the dangers of withdrawal into the self to which many of his followers would eventually succumb. The details of how to translate individual rebellion into coherent public struggle still remained to be worked out.[56]

In the 1940s Dwight Macdonald and his colleagues looked to the margins of American life for a new kind of politics, one far removed from the bankrupt collectivism and realpolitik of Marxian class warfare. From their perspective, the most exciting thing about the fledgling pacifist and civil rights movements, and the latest manifestations of "cultural" radicalism, was a shared faith in the power of individual moral assertion to make a difference—to oppose and undermine an increasingly oppressive social order. Striking CPS inmates, soldiers standing up to Jim Crow in Uniform, and sexual libertarians each in their own ways exposed spaces of freedom in an apparently closed system, testifying that men and women did not have to become faceless cells in an "organic" state or interchangeable parts of some massive, inhuman "Apparatus." They embodied the ethic of "resistance" essential to any meaningful reconstruction after 1945.

FIVE

"Ancestors": Reconstructing the Radical Canon

I have long thought ... that our over-specialized culture
would profit if amateurs were more daring in rushing in where
experts fear to tread. In any case, the course which our society
is taking is so catastrophic that one is forced to rethink for
himself all sorts of basic theoretical questions which in a
happier age could have been taken more or less for granted.
                                                —DWIGHT MACDONALD, 1946

"Last Epigones of the Nineteenth Century"

After the war *politics* shifted its focus from event-oriented reportage to
an effort to "rethink basic theoretical questions" relevant to the mid-
century crisis of radicalism. From the outset, Macdonald cautioned his
readers not to expect full-blown blueprints anytime soon. "We can hope
for the present," he wrote in 1946, "only to clear the ground, to criticize
the old methods that have landed us in a blind alley, and to grope in a
new direction." In this chapter and the next I chronicle the shift in focus,
a project whose point of departure was the bankruptcy of the Enlightenment faith in progress so powerfully demonstrated by Auschwitz and
Hiroshima. The goal of its ground-clearing, criticism, and "groping" was
to define a political vision respectful of the diversity and contingency of
human existence, rescuing the individual from the messianic ideologies
and collective abstractions of a catastrophic history. Such a vision called
for the development of an independent, pluralistic public sphere outside
the world of rigid hierarchies and the rule of force, an environment
where the spontaneity, free expression, and dialogue essential to the
survival of Western civilization could establish new roots and flourish.[1]

The first task the *politics* intellectuals set for themselves was excavat-
ing the libertarian, humanist dimensions of the modern radical tradition.
It was time to reclaim impulses for a better world from the grip of

authoritarian, allegedly "scientific" doctrines dominant since the nine-teenth century; time to recall, in Nicola Chiaromonte's words, that "socialism . . . did not spring fully-armed from the head of Karl Marx." The alternative canon Macdonald and his colleagues identified in the 1940s, the assortment of "ancestors" they found helpful to the aim of a fresh start, reveals the promise as well as the blind spots and fault lines of their emerging vision.[2]

In the late 1960s, Dwight Macdonald chastised leaders of the student insurgency (for whom he also had a measure of paternal admiration) for their willful ignorance of the insights and lessons of the past. Macdonald contrasted the attitudes of earlier radicals with the militant antihistori-cism then apparently in vogue:

> I assumed the next generation would have the same respect we had for the positive achievements of the bourgeoisie, following the lead of our 19th-century ancestors—Marxist, Anarchist or Utopian-Socialist. For we were the last epigones of the 19th century, the last who were able to believe in a universal, general solution. . . . Also, like our ancestors, we considered ourselves the legitimate heirs of bourgeois culture, and an heir may detest his parents, even murder them, but he is not in-different to his heritage, nor does he smash it up.

Although New Leftists had perhaps understandably abandoned faith in "universal" solutions, Macdonald felt no sympathy for their lack of historical consciousness. "I can't understand the apathy at best—and the destructive rage at worst—that makes many of them reject their cultural inheritance *en bloc*," he lamented. "Even if they believe it's been thrown out on what we used to call 'the scrap heap of history,' couldn't they pick over the ruins a little? There are some useful things there for the dis-criminating scavenger."[3]

Here Macdonald offered a characteristically "conservative" defense of eroding cultural standards, holding out for the possibilities of a unifying cosmopolitan dialogue against the centrifugal forces of particularism and an increasingly apocalyptic rhetoric. His own reevaluation of the bat-tered socialist tradition two decades earlier had been no simple demoli-tion job, but rather an effort to salvage what was still useful even while discarding outmoded dogmas. In the January 1945 *politics*, Macdonald rejected a reader's suggestion that radicals look to religion to find moral values by commenting: "We have a secular—and indeed rather sharply anti-religious—libertarian tradition which can be traced from the 18th century French Enlightenment through the Utopian socialists to impor-tant elements of Marxian and anarchist thought; and . . . we should turn not to God but to this tradition to find again the link between the individual and society."[4]

Eight months later "Ancestors" appeared, a short course designed to "supplement and reshape the Marxist heritage" by exploring the work of writers whose ideas had been overlooked since the triumph of "scientific" socialism. The first installment examined the life and thought of Proudhon and promised future profiles on an assortment of thinkers also loosely associated with the "libertarian" tradition, including Diderot, Condorcet, Tom Paine, Saint-Simon, Fourier, Herzen, Kropotkin, Tolstoy, Daniel De Leon, and Rosa Luxemburg. Although most on this ambitious original list never received formal "Ancestors" treatment, the series as it henceforth (irregularly) appeared nonetheless became an important *politics* institution.[5]

The writers ultimately chosen as "Ancestors" were by no means all socialists, or even "radicals" in the conventional sense of the term. Proudhon, Herzen, Tolstoy, Godwin, and even Kurt Tucholsky were each in their own way "anarchists," men of the Left, but Max Weber was a nationalist liberal and Alexis de Tocqueville an avowed conservative. In addition, efforts to isolate or explain away the "unattractive" features of its subjects—Tolstoy's religiosity, for example, and Proudhon's "peasant" prejudices—were not always wholly successful. Still, the diversity of the series underscored Macdonald's belief that traditional political categories were now obsolete. Perhaps what united these individuals was their resolute, prophetic "negativism," their misgivings about proto-"totalitarian" changes they saw developing around them.

The construction and interpretation of the past is anything but an objective procedure. Alasdair MacIntyre has observed that "[a] living tradition is an historically extended, socially embodied argument, and an argument precisely in part about the goods which constitute that tradition." The radical canon as redefined in *politics* is therefore less important for the biographical details it provides than for what it tells us about the values of those who assembled it in the 1940s. The "Ancestors" series presented an "argument" with two primary features. First, there was the by-now familiar indictment of the modern fetish for mastery, a critique of the scientific rationality and bureaucratic centralization that mainstream "progressives," Marxist and liberal, still reflexively equated with social advance. Second, the argument called for the rebuilding of a vital, diverse, and democratic associational life, independent of and opposed to those dehumanizing processes.[6]

In one sense, the "Ancestors" project, as a forum for an international array of voices, represents the cosmopolitan mission of Macdonald and his *politics* collaborators at its eclectic best. But, as we shall see, it also serves to highlight persistent flaws in their efforts to articulate a post-Marxist political alternative. The positive prescriptions offered by the "Ancestors" were vague and general, far short of a comprehensive program for action. The series gave short shrift to the rich traditions of American radical thought. And, finally, by the end its "negativist" tone had degenerated into bleak despair, reflecting a strain of elitist alienation that sometimes threatened to overwhelm the search for new directions.

Critics of Modernity: Tolstoy and Weber

Two "Ancestors" influenced *politics* largely because of their critical insights. Both Leo Tolstoy and Max Weber dissented from the progressive zeitgeists of their times, convinced that the scientific and technological accomplishments heralded by their contemporaries invited not millennial paradise but disaster. Their opposition came from different sources: Tolstoy represented a romantic, idiosyncratic blend of Christian anarcho-pacifism, whereas Weber was a pioneer in the rigorous methods of European social science. At bottom, however, each man was a moralist, a modern Jeremiah concerned about the fate of the free individual in a world of oppressive, large-scale social structures. Each foresaw with uncanny accuracy the "abyss" toward which Western civilization, intoxicated with its powers, was rapidly heading.

The May 1946 "Ancestors" featured an introduction to the thought of Tolstoy (1828–1910), an intellectual of world-historical stature from prerevolutionary Russia. Tolstoy had been a hero to generations of reformers, including figures as diverse as Gandhi and Jane Addams. Macdonald's career as a latter-day "Tolstoyan" in the 1940s came as a result of the encouragement of his friend, Nicola Chiaromonte. Macdonald offered Tolstoy to his readers as both a "great moral teacher," able to convey profound messages with amazing simplicity, and as an extraordinary "journalist of ideas" whose writings on such subjects as anarchism and "passive resistance" remained "wonderfully to the point . . . in the age of atomic fission and bureaucratic collectivism."[7]

It is noteworthy that Macdonald took care to qualify his endorsement of the sage of Yassnaya Polyana, labeling as "absurd" Tolstoy's ascetic "obsession with the evils of drink," for example. "Nor," Macdonald confessed, "can I go along with the religious sentiment that [he] considered the heart of his values." This caveat was consistent with Macdonald's defiant secularism, but it reflects an unfortunate insensitivity to the critical insights and social experimentation of the religious left. Despite his disclaimers, Macdonald found himself on the defensive against charges of spiritual "escapism" for his growing interest in thinkers like Tolstoy, Gandhi, Simone Weil, and Dorothy Day. He usually interpreted this response as evidence of the modern aversion to moral questions. In a 1957 memoir he recalled that *Time* magazine clumsily profiled the discovery of Weil by *politics* in its "Religion" department, "simply because the 20th-century mind seems unable to conceive of any other pigeon-hole for ethics." Macdonald took the opportunity to reaffirm his secular credentials: "In actual fact, *politics* showed slight interest in religion. My own record is impeccable: I am not now and have never been a member of any church. Nor have I ever, not even in this late adolescence, believed in God or an afterlife or a power or consciousness beyond this world that is interested in this world. . . . Religion, in short, bores me even more than Marxism."[8]

The "Ancestors" feature on Tolstoy resurrected essays from the 1890s in which he had condemned two of the prevailing "superstitions" of the late-nineteenth century: scientific instrumentalism and the Western cult of activity. In "Modern Science," Tolstoy challenged the belief that advances in "experimental science" were always liberating, somehow inherently connected to humankind's spiritual progress. Instead he charged that scientists too often blinded themselves to their wider responsibilities, ignoring urgent first questions like "how should a man live?" in favor of mercenary service to the ruling classes or the investigation of irrelevant "trifles." Thus, despite its aura of triumph, Tolstoy argued that "no science in any age . . . has stood on so low a plane as the present one. One part of it, that which should study the means of making human life good and happy, is occupied in justifying the existing bad order of life, and the other is absorbed with the solution of questions of idle curiosity." Where a privileged minority dominated the masses, he concluded, "every victory over nature will inevitably only serve to increase this power and oppression." Less than a year after the success of the Manhattan Project, Tolstoy's concerns about scientific irresponsibility seemed more relevant than ever.[9]

In a second essay, Tolstoy admonished his readers—who perhaps included a few scientists—to awaken themselves from mental inertia, to look up from the deadening routines of their working lives to "Stop and Think!" about the need for radical change in a society hurtling toward catastrophe. His pessimism was unambiguous. "No one doubts but that if the present order of things be prolonged for some dozens of years the result will be ruin, imminent and general," he wrote. "We have only to open our eyes to see the abyss toward which we are advancing." Like Simone Weil, Tolstoy invoked Eastern values of balance and moderation (for him embodied in the teachings of Lao-Tze) to discredit the Occidental mania for mastery, the cult of "work for its own sake." Once again he urged his contemporaries to inquire into the ends of their endeavors, warning that in an irrational and immoral "bad order," mindless industry would not necessarily translate into social improvement: "Work, yes; but at what are we to work? Manufacturers and sellers of opium, tobacco, and brandy, every gambler on the Stock Exchange, all inventors and manufacturers of engines of destruction, all the military, all jailers and executioners—all work, but it is evident that humanity would be the gainer if all these workers ceased their work." By the 1940s, the same could be said of bomber pilots and concentration camp functionaries. In Tolstoy's view, work in the modern world had become a narcotic, a "means of moral anesthesia" used for "drowning thought and hiding from ourselves the disorder and emptiness of our lives." If people would only pause and reflect, they would realize the folly of the "egoistic conception of life" and embrace instead Christ's ideals of mutual love. Although he eschewed any religious foundation, Macdonald's call to individual moral assertion, "resistance," and solidarity after World War II closely paralleled the position Tolstoy advanced half a century earlier.[10]

Although not included in the series, German intellectual Max Weber (1864–1920) was a central influence on the *politics* circle and merits consideration as a full-fledged "ancestor." Even as late as the 1940s American audiences were just beginning to encounter Weber's ideas, and Macdonald's journal played a role in that discovery. The October 1944 issue presented a fragment of Weber's sociological writings, "Class, Status, Party," excerpted from a forthcoming volume of his works translated and edited by C. Wright Mills and his Wisconsin associate, H. H. Gerth.[11]

Like Frankfurt School émigrés Horkheimer and Adorno, Macdonald and his circle found Weber's dark evaluation of modernity compelling in the context of death camps and atomic warfare. In the concluding paragraph of his pivotal 1946 essay "The Root Is Man," Macdonald identified Weber's concept of "rationalization"—"the organization from the top of human life"—as the fundamental problem of the twentieth century. By this time Weber appeared to be a much better prophet than Karl Marx, having concluded that the processes of bureaucratization and centralization—not "class struggle"—were the driving dynamic of contemporary history.[12]

Unlike Marx—or American "progressives" like John Dewey—Weber saw the pervasive "rationalization" of maturing industrial societies as anything but liberating. In his later works, he evinced a Nietzschean fear that human spontaneity might soon disappear altogether within an "iron cage" of ossified bureaucratic structures. For his tragic sensibility Wolfgang Mommsen has characterized Weber as a "liberal in despair"; more recently, James T. Kloppenberg called him "the most desperate of progressives." In *politics*, Gerth and Mills introduced Weber as the "Jeremiah" of Wilhelmine Germany, a man who felt as though he was "seated in an express train and in doubt as to whether the next switch will be set right." "Disillusioned in a disenchanted world," they continued, "he was ready to face the 'icy darkness' that he saw settling over Europe after the first world war." By the end of his life Weber was asking the question now posed by the *politics* writers, occupants of the same misguided "express train": "What do we have to oppose to this machinery, so as to keep a residue of humanity free from this parcelling out of the soul?"[13]

Weber's diagnosis of the problem of bureaucratic rationalization may have been correct, but his solution—a slender hope in the revitalizing power of "charismatic leadership"—troubled many *politics* readers, given the course of German history after his premature death in 1920. The magazine's advocacy was therefore a matter of some controversy. In the February 1945 issue, Meyer Schapiro portrayed Weber as a proto-Nazi whose sympathies for authoritarian nationalism fatally tainted his political ideas. For Schapiro, Weber was an antidemocratic figure whose pessimism was more the result of mandarin nostalgia for an eroding bourgeois social hierarchy than a genuine concern for human freedom. But although Weber certainly had an "aristocratic," even authoritarian side, Gerth effectively dismissed as superficial any affinities between his ideas and Hitler's program for German "rebirth." Despite Weber's "Machiavellian" impulses, Gerth and Mills argued that "his humanism, his love for the underdog, his hatred of sham and lies, and his unceasing campaign against racism and anti-semitic demagoguery" would have made him an unlikely Nazi.[14]

Revitalizing the Public Sphere: Godwin, Tocqueville, and Proudhon

Was there an alternative to the dehumanizing, "totalitarian" world foreseen by Tolstoy and Weber? Other "Ancestors" sketched the outlines of a social order outside the machinery of hierarchy and "rationalization," a reconstructed public sphere where "a residue of humanity" might remain free. William Godwin (1756–1836), English *philosophe* and founder of the modern school of "libertarian" socialism, had spoken of such a sphere in his 1793 treatise *Enquiry Concerning Political Justice*, a work George Woodcock pronounced a timeless "masterpiece of social criticism" in the September 1946 *politics*. Written as a defense of the French Revolution (in its pre-Jacobin phase) against Edmund Burke's conservative attacks, *Political Justice* was a critique of all the "authoritarian" institutions of society—government, the legal and educational systems, and anticipating Proudhon, the apparatus safeguarding accumulated private property—institutions Godwin felt perpetuated unnatural inequality and conflict. He opposed any kind of coercion, any doctrine that reduced the individual to a means rather than an end. Of particular concern to Godwin was how nation-states manipulated sentiments of patriotism: "Society was instituted, not for the sake of glory, not to furnish splendid materials for the page of history, but for the benefit of its members. The love of our country, if we could speak accurately, is another of those specious illusions which have been invented by impostors in order to render the multitude the blind instruments of their crooked designs."[15]

For Godwin, government was a dangerous usurpation of individual rights. To the extent that some kind of formal organization was necessary, he insisted that its power be dispersed and restricted to the smallest possible scope in order to contain its mischief. "Popular commotion is like the waves of the sea," he observed, "capable where the surface is large of producing the most tragical effects, but mild and innocuous when confined within the circuit of an humble lake. Sobriety and equity are the obvious characteristics of a limited circle." Godwin provided little guidance on the nature of his small-scaled social order, however, beyond vague references to a decentralized federation of autonomous units he called "parishes."[16]

Godwin's communal vision presents other immediate problems. It seems that he considered the abolition of government and private property as sufficient by itself to inaugurate the good society. "It is property that forms men into one common mass and makes them fit to be played upon like a brute machine," he wrote. "Were this stumbling block removed, each man would be united to his neighbour in love and mutual kindness a thousand times more than now." But such a romantic, utopian opposition between innocent men and evil institutions, based on faith in human perfectibility, was too simple for an age in which, as Dwight Macdonald would himself assert, the tragic complexity of social existence lay newly exposed.[17]

In addition, Godwin assumed that his enclaves would practice a cosmopolitan "enlightened localism," ultimately turning the world "into a single great republic in which men could move and discuss freely without the impediment of national barriers." Throughout his career Macdonald also retained this eighteenth-century belief that localism and universalism could somehow be reconciled. In a 1959 letter to Woodcock he commented that "as an anarchist, I favor breaking up large political units, but as a literary man I deplore provincialism. Political units can hardly be too small, while cultural units can hardly be too large." Yet one of the recurring frustrations for the *politics* group was the discovery that commitments to a decentered localism sometimes went hand-in-hand with less "desirable" particularist sentiments. As we have seen, for example, the rank-and-file of the libertarian Resistance in France seemed, in retrospect, less motivated by visions of an integrated European culture than by the "provincial" imperatives of nationalism. Neither Godwin nor Macdonald ever fully resolved the tensions between their ideals of localism and universalism.[18]

In the April 1946 *politics*, German émigré Henry Jacoby ("Sebastian Franck") presented Alexis de Tocqueville (1805–59) as the "prophet of the total state," and in Tocqueville's discussions of the dangers of "mass" society one can discern some of the features of the renewed public sphere Macdonald and his friends had in mind in the 1940s. Focusing on the then-overlooked second volume of *Democracy in America*, Jacoby asserted that "perhaps only today, when so much of what Tocqueville dared to predict . . . is becoming a hideous reality, can its full import be understood."[19]

For Tocqueville, a vibrant, pluralistic "associational" life was the essence of healthy democratic culture. A variety of mediating associations provided the only effective bulwark against the expansive tendencies of the modern nation-state. Tocqueville modeled his ideal of small, self-constituted enclaves on the medieval world, with its complex networks of clubs, guilds, communal organizations, and other *pouvoirs secondaires*. But in Jacksonian America, crucible of liberal, capitalist democracy, Tocqueville witnessed how competitive pressures worked to destroy such ferment, "dissolving all community spirit" and encouraging people to turn inward, to adopt what Veblen would later call "the private and acquisitive point of view."[20]

A century before Stalin and Hitler, Tocqueville worried that the erosion of this middle stratum would permit the rise of new despotisms, leaving atomized and politically "apathetic" subjects naked and helpless before the "rational domination" of a new Leviathan. Undoubtedly thinking of his own experiences in Germany, Jacoby concluded that "its power would be unlimited, since millions of individuals who stand apart in solitary weakness are nothing but human dust." Tocqueville understood that the decline of public life ultimately undermined the possibility of an autonomous private life as well. In Jacoby's words, "the more . . . everybody sticks to his own business, the more the general interest becomes the business of a class of experts on whom the mass of the people have to rely." Tocqueville's dystopia anticipated Orwell's, featuring a paternal, technocratic ruling apparatus that "would provide for security, facilitate our pleasure, direct our industry and spare us all the care of thinking." The survival of minimal forms of "democratic" participation, such as the ballot box, would do little to impede the slide down this "road to servitude."[21]

Had we reached the Tocquevillian nightmare of total administration by the middle of the twentieth century? The examples of the Soviet Union and Nazi Germany demonstrated that we were perilously close, but Jacoby was heartened by recent evidence of a grassroots "counter-movement" embodied in the workers' councils, committees of national liberation, and other organs of local self-government associated with the European Resistance. Although these forces had suffered temporary defeat, Jacoby reminded his readers that "a new trend in history does not assert itself successfully in a few years." The democratic reconstruction of Western culture, if it occurred at all, would be a gradual, long-term affair.[22]

What were the characteristics of the intermediate layer of *pouvoirs secondaires* Tocqueville championed? *politics* never defined this sphere precisely, but in its engagement with Chiaromonte's hero Pierre-Joseph Proudhon (1809–65), some features become apparent. Proudhon shared with Godwin and Tocqueville an abiding hostility to the encroachments of *étatism* or *le principe gouvernemental* on the liberty of the individual, and he argued throughout his lifetime for a decentralized, international confederation of small-scale "natural associations" committed to justice and equality rather than the aggrandizement of power. Although proponents of this "anarcho-syndicalist" program lost the struggle over the direction of mainstream socialism to the Marxists in the First International, eighty years later J. Hampden Jackson observed, in the October 1945 *politics,* that Proudhon's influence remained alive, inspiring Paris Communards, anti-Bolshevik Russian revolutionaries, and in the 1930s, Catalonian rebels in the Spanish civil war. In addition, as Lewis Coser pointed out in his surveys of the post-Liberation European scene, radical *résistants* often styled themselves disciples of Proudhon. Jackson called for a wider revival of Proudhon's ideas as an antidote to the depressing "fatalism" afflicting all sectors of the political spectrum in the face of "the prospect of a bureaucracy which must be entailed by bigger units, political, economic and social."[23]

The "Ancestors" showcase presented excerpts from Proudhon's masterwork, *The General Idea of Revolution in the Nineteenth Century.* Writing from prison in the wake of the failed uprisings of 1848, Proudhon condemned acceptance of the centralized state as "the natural organ of justice, the protector of the weak, the preserver of the peace" as a "superstitious" faith reproducing the patriarchal oppression of the family. He observed: "The prejudice in favor of government having sunk into our deepest consciousness, stamping even reason in its mold, every other conception has been for a long time rendered impossible, and the boldest thinkers could but say that Government was no doubt a scourge, a chastisement for humanity, but that it was a necessary evil!" For Proudhon, this statist "prejudice" explained why modern revolutions betrayed the goals of human emancipation, finally spawning novel forms of tyranny that served only the interests of privileged minorities. He insisted that a genuine working-class revolution could never be achieved by authoritarian methods. "The history of governments," he wrote, "is the martyrology of the proletariat." Proudhon's indictment was total: "No authority, no government, not even popular, that is the Revolution."[24]

In place of the inherently hierarchical relationship between governors and the governed, Proudhon envisioned a society founded on horizontal, "contractual" exchanges between individuals and groups enjoying equal status. In the January 1945 *politics*, Chiaromonte explained that the rules for such an order would be *immanent*, emerging naturally from consensual human interactions rather than external coercion. He highlighted Proudhon's insight that "human society allows for no privileged point of view from which a law can be promulgated except the point of view of the mutual relationships of which society consists." From this it followed that "all organized superstructures are to be judged by the degree to which they are open to the living experience of justice, to the Social Law of the groups on which the existence of the superstructures themselves is based."[25]

Proudhon also recognized, according to Chiaromonte, that for the free individual "there exist . . . as many particular societies as there are particular interests," and that a "just" society is therefore "a plurality of groups and interests or it is nothing at all." Chiaromonte suggested that radicals promote diversity as a way to contest the prerogatives of centralized state and corporate authority and to reverse "the progressive disarticulation of society into masses of individuals." "If the eternal principle of power politics is 'Divide and Conquer,' " he argued, "the principle of pluralism could be expressed by saying: 'Multiply your associations and be free.' "[26]

It was common in the 1940s to interpret historical figures with illiberal attitudes as predecessors to Hitler and Stalin, and this was the case for Proudhon as it was for Weber. In the January 1946 *politics* Chiaromonte defended Proudhon against charges that he was, on closer inspection, a "harbinger of fascism" rather than a defender of human rights. Chiaromonte conceded that Proudhon's denunciation of Jewish "financiers," like his thoroughgoing "antifeminism," represented "the worst side of his peasant nature." Still, Proudhon's misgivings about the uprisings of 1848–49 (watching the workers rush to the barricades, he protested that "they have made a revolution without ideas" and are doomed to failure) hardly made him a supporter of authoritarian alternatives. Although it was a mistake to situate Proudhon on the wrong side of history in 1848, as later critics did, Chiaromonte readily accepted the charge that he was

an "enemy of the Common Man." In an age of dehumanizing abstractions and reductive platitudes, this seemed a refreshing virtue rather than
a sin. "Proudhon hated the 'common' man," Chiaromonte observed, "he
hated the 'average' man, he hated the 'class' man, he hated profoundly
and mercilessly any kind of fiction by which straight, unalloyed, naked
human reality could be hidden, distorted, warped—hence oppressed and
repressed." Chiaromonte concluded with a tribute to Proudhon's mili-
tantly *provisional* approach to social questions, his understanding that
concrete reality could never be encompassed within *a priori,* totalizing
systems like orthodox Marxism. "What one finds at the root of Proudhon's thought is the unshakable conviction that human society consti-
tutes an ever present and ever resurgent problem, which might or might
not have a final solution, but in any case requires above everything else
that it be kept open throughout the vicissitudes of history."[27]

Although the "libertarian" tradition the "Ancestors" series sought to
identify is distinguished more for its criticism than for the clarity or
consistency of its positive suggestions, some of the characteristics of the
revitalized public sphere *politics* came to advocate can be gleaned from
its treatment of Godwin, Tocqueville, and Proudhon. In opposition to
the trend toward centralization of power within gigantic bureaucratic
structures, and to the corresponding "disarticulation" of society into
anonymous "masses," this new order would consist of "federations" of
small-scale "natural associations," linked across geographic and other
boundaries with a minimum of administrative machinery. Membership
within these groups would be open and voluntary, and they would be
numerous and diverse enough to reflect the multitude of interests held by
whole, autonomous human beings. Recognizing that individual rights
can be guaranteed only within an egalitarian and mutualistic social
context, these clubs, guilds and other *pouvoirs secondaires* would be
committed to fostering personal, face-to-face relationships based on
genuine friendship and solidarity. They would encourage democratic
participation and dialogue and operate according to fluid, provisional,
"immanent" principles derived from concrete experience rather than
rigid coordination from above ("Whatever name," Chiaromonte added,
"the 'above' might have—God, State coercion or Class Dictatorship").
Finally, it was clear that this new order must evolve organically from
below, "outside" the existing apparatus of authority. Efforts aimed at a
violent seizure of power, like the strategies of conventional electoral
politics, only reproduced the evils of a corrupt status quo. While these
disparate ingredients hardly made for a mature social philosophy, they at
least provided a starting point for discussions of how to extricate Western culture from the "blind alley" apparently reached by the 1940s.[28]

Into "The Darkness": Herzen and Tucholsky

In 1946 Dwight Macdonald observed that the progressive optimism shared by Left intellectuals of all stripes in the nineteenth century—even "negativist" radicals like Proudhon—limited the value of their ideas in an age of death factories and nuclear weaponry. A faith that oppressive conditions would only hasten the inevitable triumph of a better world rendered them unequipped to deal with a society like the present one, which, in Macdonald's view, had become perhaps "*too* irrational and humanly destructive" to be redeemed. Where earlier generations thought they saw clarity and light, Macdonald saw enveloping darkness. "The process of history," he wrote, "appears now to be a more complex and tragic matter than it appeared to be to the socialist and anarchist thinkers, who were, after all, children of *their* age, not of ours. The area of the unpredictable, perhaps even the unknowable, appears far greater now than it did then."[29]

This tragic sensibility infused *politics* for most of its lifetime, but by the late 1940s it had become the dominant note. The trajectory of "Ancestors" reflected a deepening mood of alienation and impasse. Following a period of semiregularity in 1945–46, during which the rudiments of a "libertarian" social renaissance began to emerge, no new installments of the series appeared until 1948, the year the cold war seemed to foreclose hopes for a grassroots "third camp" irrevocably. The last two "Ancestors" featured, Russian anarchist Alexander Herzen and German social critic Kurt Tucholsky, stand out more for their bleak pessimism than for any kind of systematic analysis. Richard King has interpreted the series's descent from Proudhon's revolutionary vigor to Tucholsky's despair and suicide as symbolic of the *politics* group's larger "failure" to define a fresh start in the face of world events.[30]

Macdonald came to see Herzen (1812–70) as his nineteenth-century alter ego, owing both to stylistic affinities and to a shared disillusionment amid the collapse of revolutionary prospects. Macdonald had already for some time been drawing explicit parallels between the drift and sterility prevailing during World War II and the paralysis men like Herzen experienced in the years after 1848. "It is remarkable," Macdonald wrote in 1943, "how many of the issues of this period (and the ... reactions to them) anticipate those of our own time."

"There are no more general ideas"—what better describes the intellectual atmosphere today? Most political thinking has abandoned not only the old optimism of progress, but also the very notion of any consistent attempt to direct the evolution of society in a desirable direction. Submission to the brute force of events, choice between evils rather than between positive programs, a skepticism about basic values and ultimate ends, a refusal to look too far ahead—this is the mood.

In Macdonald's view, radicals in the 1940s, like their counterparts a century earlier, had to come to terms with the end of "progress" and the decline of Enlightenment aspirations for universal human emancipation. Perhaps this time the diagnosis was not premature.[31]

In the winter 1948 issue of *politics*, Macdonald introduced excerpts of Herzen's multivolume memoir, *My Past and My Thoughts*, noting his surprise that American intellectuals—"who have long paid more attention to Russian politics than to their own"—had almost entirely overlooked the legacy of "the first great Russian revolutionary." This neglect, he concluded, was a product of the radical optimism of the 1930s:

> Then the outrages of rationality and human feeling which we read about every day in the newspapers . . . were stimulating more than they were depressing, since they showed how absurd and hateful (therefore intolerable, therefore soon to be overthrown) the status quo was, and since we knew very well both the kind of social system that should replace it and how to go about the replacing. Marx was our man then—the systematic genius who had with Titanic labor worked out History's "law of motion," the great Believer in the workingclass proletariat as our savior and redeemer.

Since then, however, chastened radicals had shed their millennial hopes. "We are a world war and a few aborted revolutions the wiser," Macdonald grimly observed. "Now we don't much believe in Titans and even suspect Historical Laws." Because of his grasp of the irrationality of history and an "unsystematic, sceptical, free-thinking" approach to social issues that made him the antithesis of Marx, Herzen might be, Macdonald argued, "our man in the forties."[32]

Early sections of the memoirs present Herzen as an aristocrat with instinctive sympathies for the poor and victimized, deeply outraged at the bureaucratic corruption and brutality that permeated all aspects of life in czarist Russia. It is easy to see why Macdonald would identify with such a figure. Here is a typical example of Herzen's style: "What monstrous crimes are buried in the archives of the infamous reign of Nicholas! We are used to them, they are committed every day, committed as though nothing were wrong, unnoticed, lost in the terrible distance, noiselessly sunk in the silent bogs of officialdom or shrouded by the censorship of the police."[33]

Exiled in the 1840s for his subversive activities, Herzen roamed throughout Europe, absorbing Western ideals of individual freedom that he hoped one day to meld with the communal traditions native to his homeland. The decisive reversal of those ideals in the false dawn of 1848 came as a shattering blow, signaling to Herzen an indefinitely prolonged era of despotism. Although he remained politically active in the following decades, collaborating with Proudhon, Bakunin, and other anarchist revolutionaries, the defeat plunged Herzen into a despair from which he never recovered. He became, in his own words, a "man of negation," distanced from friends who could not understand "what it is to tear out by the roots the cherished convictions of a lifetime."[34]

The concluding excerpts from *My Past* display Herzen at his bleakest. His explanation for the decline of the West revealed sentiments hard to reconcile with his earlier faith in democracy. There are echoes here of Andrea Caffi's categorical disdain for the "masses," an attitude Macdonald himself sometimes adopted during moments of crisis and doubt. Herzen decried the unbridgeable gulf between the European intelligentsia (a cultured "secular clergy") and the larger public (denizens of a little-understood "heavy substratum of popular life formed by the ages") whom they sought to lead by force of persuasion and example. Whereas intellectuals "represented the *highest* thought of their time," Herzen wrote, they did not represent its "*common* consciousness." When, with the French Revolution, they led a successful assault on the "oppressive edifice" of monarchy,

> the gates [were] flung open and the crowd rush[ed] in. But it was not the crowd they expected. Who are these men? To what age do they belong? . . . An overwhelming wave of filth flooded everything. The inner horror of the Jacobins before this flood was expressed in the Terror of 1793 and 1794. They saw their mistake and tried to correct it with the guillotine; but however many heads they cut off, they still had to bow their own before the might of society that was rising to the top. Everything gave way before it.

Macdonald shared Herzen's ambivalence about the accession of the masses to the stage of history. Compare, for example, his account, a century later, of the disappointing results achieved by the victory of liberal values:

> Everyone can read and write, popular education is a reality—and so the American masses read pulp fiction and listen to soap operas on that triumph of technology, the radio, and the German and Russian masses are the more easily indoctrinated with a lying and debased official culture. The freeing of man to develop himself has had the effects which Erich Fromm described in *Escape From Freedom:* craving to be

rid of this empty "freedom," the masses turn neurotically to totalitarian leaders. The struggle for universal suffrage is won, and the result is
the rise of plebiscitary dictatorships, in which the State authority
becomes sacred precisely because it claims to represent "the People"
against the individual.[35]

For Herzen, as for Macdonald, the betrayal of Enlightenment dreams
for a better world called for a sober stock-taking by the dreamers. "It is
time to perceive," Herzen confessed, "that in nature as in history there
is a great deal that is fortuitous, stupid, unsuccessful, and confused. . . .
We are only now beginning to feel that all the cards are not so well
shuffled as we thought, because we ourselves are a losing card, a failure."
Herzen found the reality that there was "no escape" from "discordance"
and "disharmony" in human affairs admirably expressed in Byron's
prophetic early nineteenth-century work, *The Darkness*. He concluded
with a statement of the obligation to bear witness that could easily have
been written by Macdonald after World War II: "Our historical vocation," Herzen asserted, "our work lies in the fact that by our disillusionment, by our sufferings, we reach resignation and humility in the
face of truth, and spare following generations from these troubles. With
us, humanity is regaining sobriety, with us recovering from its drunken
orgy."[36]

The final "Ancestor," satirist Kurt Tucholsky (1890–1935), represents
an extreme of the intellectual posture of alienation that attracted Macdonald and his *politics* colleagues in the late 1940s. Tucholsky is remembered as a critic of German bourgeois society during the troubled
years of the Weimar Republic. He maintained an unrelenting, often
vicious attack on what he saw as the selfishness, venality, and cowardice
of middle-class Berliners—especially the assimilated Jews he grew up
with—in a political atmosphere poisoned by violence and racist nationalism. Tucholsky's caricature of "Herr Wendriner" described a "Jewish
Babbit," who, like Bettelheim's concentration camp inmate, comes to
accept the values of his oppressors, reassuring friends that "things aren't
so bad after all" even while Nazis march in the streets and the authorities
stamp his "yellow ticket." With the artist George Grosz, Tucholsky was
one of the few to foresee, in his own phrase, "the tribal fires of immo-
lation" soon to engulf his country.[37]

German émigré Hans Sahl, whose biographical sketch introduced the
profile of Tucholsky in the summer 1948 issue of *politics*, called his
subject "the pessimist par excellence," the "eternal fault finder, the man
in the fourth row of the political theatre who interrupted the proceedings
on the parliamentary stage with his ironic interpellations, the lone wolf
who was always 'against.' " Exiled, despairing, and in poor health,

Tucholsky took his own life three years after Hitler seized power. Although uncompromisingly critical voices like Tucholsky's can be valuable, his status as *politics*'s final "Ancestor" indicates the paralysis that had overtaken Macdonald and his circle by the end of the decade. The depth of their gloom, however, like that of Herzen and Tucholsky, was based on an unnecessarily dismissive view of the "masses." They indulged in a sense of absolute alienation that can easily result in the death of hope and the abandonment of the search for alternatives. Even the "negativist" intellectual has a responsibility to avoid this kind of dead-end posture.[38]

An Incomplete Dialogue

One of the immediately striking characteristics of the revised radical canon we have been examining is its Eurocentrism. In his study *The Party of Eros,* Richard King offered this observation: "Most surprising in retrospect was the failure of the *politics* intellectuals to make use of American thinkers and an American intellectual tradition of anarchism and communitarianism. . . . Of the 'Ancestors' series, not one profile dealt with an American thinker: no Emerson, Thoreau, or Wendell Phillips, no William James, Dewey or Veblen, and only passing reference to Randolph Bourne." Other names could be added to this list of omissions, but the point is that by ignoring indigenous resources in their "scavenging" efforts, Macdonald and his colleagues engaged in just the sort of antihistorical thinking that he would rightly condemn in the New Left twenty years later. Especially grievous was their disregard for the rich vein of American pragmatism, a tradition that, as Cornel West has recently argued, contains many of the elements necessary to a radically reconstructed, democratic public sphere. In their calls for an order small and flexible enough to protect individual freedom and spontaneity, writers like Emerson and Dewey articulated a social vision very close to the one Macdonald and company tried to find in Tocqueville, Proudhon, and other continental writers, an egalitarian world rich in mediating *pouvoirs secondaires,* governed by "immanent" standards of justice, suspicious of absolutes, and "open to the living experience" of its inhabitants. The failure of *politics* to explore this body of materials rendered its "cosmopolitan" dialogue incomplete.[39]

Macdonald expressed admiration for native rebels like the Wobblies, and he once speculated that anarchism ought to have a special appeal for Americans, given their "lawless and individualistic" temperament. But he never pursued these stray thoughts, even in a vehicle as conducive to that purpose as the "Ancestors" series. Perhaps Macdonald's flight from the cultural nationalism of Van Wyck Brooks and his supporters in the 1940s explains this oversight. At another level, one can detect a feeling within the *politics* circle that American intellectual life, sheltered and immature, was not up to coming to grips with the radical evil then at large in Europe. Macdonald's apprentice Irving Howe recalled the prevailing attitude: "If you felt that you were living in a moment of historical apocalypse—say, in 1939 or 1946—and were trying desperately to define ... what new kind of society had emerged that had traduced your socialist hopes, then Emerson's Concord could seem extremely thin, even genteel."[40]

Macdonald did respect the vitality of Emersonian America, but he also felt that its promise had been in eclipse for many decades. In the June 1944 *politics,* he intimated that reviewing a new study of America's early nineteenth-century "golden age" aroused feelings of wistful nostalgia. At a time "when all moral energy has gone out of our public life and America has become the most timidly conservative force in world politics," reading the book was "both depressing and exhilarating—the former because we have lost so much, the latter because we were once a people with a heart and a will, and may become so again." Macdonald waxed lyrical with his portrait of a young nation that "seethed and bubbled with a champagne effervescence of reform (both religious and secular), social experimentation, humanitarianism, democratic optimism and just plain crackpottery." America in its infancy was, in his view, a culture striving to embody Enlightenment aspirations for a society built on reason and human equality. The Civil War, and the ensuing triumph of industrial capitalism, effectively destroyed this Arcadia.[41]

Macdonald's tragic narrative of decline does an injustice to the diverse, contested history of politics and culture in this country and seems to reflect a pattern of disconnection that has plagued our intellectual life throughout the twentieth century. Christopher Lasch spoke to this problem when he observed that American radicals, frustrated by the absence of a constituency, have too often turned abroad for sustenance. A true cosmopolitan dialogue would engage indigenous traditions more fully in it efforts at creative synthesis.[42]

Photos

The editors of *Partisan Review*, circa 1940. *Standing, left to right:* George Morris, Philip Rahv, Dwight Macdonald. *Seated:* F. W. Dupee, William Phillips.

Dwight Macdonald at his *politics* desk. (Courtesy Macdonald Papers, Yale University Library.)

Nancy Macdonald, the humanitarian "soul of *politics.*" (Courtesy Nancy Macdonald.)

politics

25¢ a copy   May, 1945

Contents

Cover Design: "Totenkranz", from "Der Weltchronik von Doktor Schedel" (Nuremberg, 1493)

VICTORY ! ! !

VICTORY. Comes, lights up the horizon and the hearts, and before you know it, it's gone; you have just the ashes and the dead, and instead of ambush, hostage-killing, fight and vengeance, a good chance to grieve, to starve, to see your children die in peace. Makes me sad for those soldiers who are there, in the line, with ideals all theirs, reserved to the military, "requisitioned for the exclusive use of our boys", and forbidden to everybody else at home or abroad. Their job is that of transforming a torture-chamber into a cemetery; a place of terror and of hope into a place without terror and without hope. VICTORY.

(Niccolo Tucci in "Politics", November, 1944.)

The cover of the May 1945 *politics*, expressing dissent from celebrations of the costly Allied triumph in Europe.

Nicola Chiaromonte and Dwight Macdonald on holiday at Cape Cod during the "Hiroshima Summer" of 1945. (Courtesy Nancy Macdonald.)

Chiaromonte relaxing at the Cape. (Courtesy Miriam Chiaromonte.)

Andrea Caffi, Chiaromonte's mentor and proponent of "thinking outside politics." (Courtesy Miriam Chiaromonte.)

Caffi and Chiaromonte, together again in Toulouse, 1947. (Courtesy Miriam Chiaromonte.)

Simone Weil, *politics*'s "patron saint," in Marseilles in 1942, the year before her death. Weil's meditations on the lost ethic of "limit" inspired much of the journal's critique of modernity.

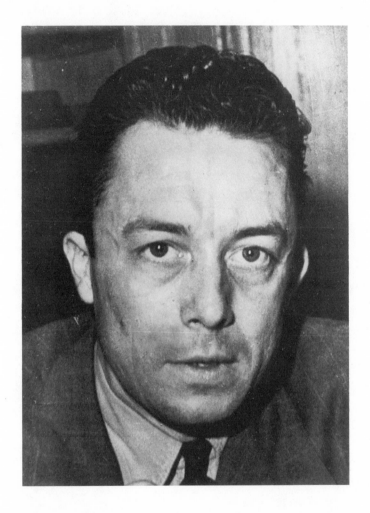

Albert Camus. His spring 1946 discussions with Macdonald and Chiaromonte about the need for a transnational "new left" served as the basis for the "Europe-America Groups" initiative. (Courtesy Bettmann Archive.)

Mary McCarthy and Bowden Broadwater with friends at their East 57th Street apartment, late 1940s. *Rear, from left:* Broadwater, Lionel Abel *(standing)*, Elizabeth Hardwick, Miriam Chiaromonte, Nicola Chiaromonte, McCarthy, and John Berryman. *Front:* Dwight Macdonald and Kevin McCarthy. (Courtesy Vassar College Libraries.)

EAG's "utopian" faction. (Courtesy Miriam Chiaromonte.)

Mary McCarthy and Nicola Chiaromonte at a Madrid literary conference sponsored by the Congress for Cultural Freedom, 1963. (Courtesy
Vassar College Libraries.)

A 1966 reunion. *Standing, from left:* Heinrich Blucher, Hannah Arendt,
Dwight Macdonald, and his second wife, Gloria. *Seated:* Nicola Chiaro-
monte, Mary McCarthy, and Robert Lowell. (Courtesy Vassar College
Libraries.)

"New Roads":
Toward a Postmodern
Politics of Limits

I think it is time for socialists to face the situation that actually
exists instead of continuing to fix our ideas on a distant future
in which History will bring us at last what we want.

—DWIGHT MACDONALD, 1946

I remember (in 1940) being totally obsessed with a single
thought: we had arrived at humanity's zero hour, and history
was senseless; the only thing that made sense was that part of
man which remained outside history, alien and impervious to
the whirlwind of events. If, indeed, such a part existed.

—NICOLA CHIAROMONTE, 1960

What is left? A few scattered individuals, and groups, that
might find in a resolute pessimism about the immediate future
the courage not to despair of the "eternal good cause" of man.

—ANDREA CAFFI, 1947

A Part of Man "Outside History"?

Our examination of the efforts at *politics* to define a fresh approach to
radical activism now turns to sustained consideration of the ideas of its
three most important voices—Dwight Macdonald, Nicola Chiaromonte,
and Andrea Caffi. The first two contributed installments to the year-long
"New Roads in Politics" series, introduced by Macdonald in December
1945 as a forum to "criticize the dominant ideology on the left today—
which is roughly Marxian—in the light of recent experience" and to
explore other means to achieving the "humanly satisfying" society Marxism promised but failed to deliver. Although he did not formally participate in that series, Caffi's letters from Europe appeared in the journal

with frequency after the war, and his proposals for reconstruction occupied a central place in its debates about how to build a postwar "new left."[1]

Macdonald, Chiaromonte, and Caffi agreed that the overriding challenge in the "zero hour" signaled by the Second World War was the rescue of "that part of man which remained outside history." But what was this "history" to which they so often referred? Macdonald offered this definition in 1949: "The process of hauling the individual about like a bale, or a corpse, and cramming him into some badly fitting context of ideology or action—this is what is euphemistically called 'history.' " History in this sense was an artificial and disastrously flawed way of looking at the world. It was the faith in historical *rationality* prevalent in the West since the Enlightenment, the optimistic confidence that attempts to "master" the environment contributed to inexorable social "progress" and human emancipation. This faith infused both of the "dominant ideologies of the left," Marxism and liberalism (at least in the reductive, instrumental forms in which *politics* tended to interpret them), and it explained their accommodation to ever larger aggregations of power, ever more refined techniques of regimentation and destruction. According to Macdonald this idea—that advances in science and organization would one day produce an earthly millennium, that events like Auschwitz and Hiroshima were only temporary aberrations in that forward march, that everything will "come out all right in the end"—fostered a callousness to the more troubling consequences of "rationalization" that he dedicated his journal to exposing.[2]

In *The Paradox of History,* a collection of essays published two decades after the end of World War II, Chiaromonte likewise criticized the modern fixation with what he called "History with a capital 'H,' " the grandiose metanarrative of rationality and inevitable progress that spawned messianic ideologies, "total" wars, and the cult of revolutionary violence. Time and again since the French Revolution, Chiaromonte observed, the inhabitants of the world of "real life" found themselves submerged into the vast "technicolor 'spectacular' " of such History, overwhelmed by processes operating outside anyone's control, crushed by a machinery that had jettisoned the constraints of "ordinary morality" in favor of the narrow logic of power and success. People in the twentieth century lived in "bad faith," he concluded, because they continued to cling to the superstition of "progress through mastery" that events had so clearly debunked.[3]

According to both Macdonald and Chiaromonte, to move beyond a catastrophic "History" one had to first recognize the *contingency* of that "History"; to renew modern society one had to embrace the lost ethic of limit identified by Simone Weil and acknowledge that there were no immutable "laws" of history to be discovered, no guarantees that things would somehow ultimately "come out all right." Furthermore, in the wake of the rationalized mass murders of recent decades, one had to recognize that it was time to reconsider the possibility and even desirability of controlling our environment. Although these innate "limits" had an undeniably tragic dimension, Chiaromonte noted the "paradox" that historical contingency was also *the necessary precondition to human freedom*—perhaps the most important insight offered by the *politics* intellectuals in their postwar speculations. "We are free," Chiaromonte wrote, "and this means literally that we do not know what we are doing."[4]

Acceptance of human limits—and freedom—implied a profound shift in moral bearings with a number of immediate corollaries and consequences. First, and most significant, it mandated rejection of absolutism in any form, whether asserted by church, nation, state, or political party. Human beings invited disaster when they presumed to play God, and they had to end at last their blind worship of power and the pursuit of ends that justified any means. In his seminal "New Roads" essay, "The Root Is Man," Macdonald captured this imperative in the simplest of terms: "We should not *push things too far*." In addition, the ethic of limit called for a healthy skepticism toward science and technology, a renewed vigilance to ensure that these "means" remained subordinated to human ends. Finally, it encouraged empathy and solidarity among men and women based on realization of a common vulnerability to the vagaries of fate. Social relations under such conditions would begin to reflect a fundamental equality rather than the calculations of advantage and force; individuals would view each other on their own terms rather than as impersonal objects to be manipulated or feared. This reorientation, in short, provided a radically different set of principles by which to judge actions and institutions and on which to base criticism and "resistance."[5]

Macdonald and Chiaromonte agreed that human values existed at a level "outside" (and beneath) the overarching logic of historical rationality, but they differed on the precise nature of their origins. Macdonald looked to a "transcendent" dimension in the heroic individual conscience —an ill-defined synthesis of the universal and the subjective that some read as an escape to quasi-religious mysticism. Chiaromonte was more successful in locating an alternative "locus" of values. Following Proudhon, he argued for "immanent" standards of justice, arising from the concrete experiences of associational life. But, he admitted, a pluralistic and autonomous stratum of "civil society" had been in eclipse in the West for many decades. By the late 1940s, it seemed that Tocqueville's premonition of an unfettered Leviathan ruling over atomized masses was close to reality. How, then, could radicals challenge the power of tightly integrated, "totalitarian" structures of authority? In the absence of a revolutionary "class" or a "mass" constituency, who would be the agents of change for a humanist alternative?

The *politics* program for the rebirth of an independent public sphere found its most complete expression in the ideas of Chiaromonte's mentor, Andrea Caffi. Caffi argued for the long-term subversive potential of a grassroots, "underground" counterculture, consisting of networks of small groups of individuals ("popular communities") practicing and preaching the threatened Enlightenment virtues of cosmopolitan "sociability"—friendship, equality, mutuality, tolerance, and open dialogue. It was hoped that this saving remnant, this ferment of a "few scattered individuals," would act, as Macdonald put it, as a "leavening in the dough of mass society," and that its values would spread organically as these communities matured and multiplied across national boundaries. Although Caffi's vision of revolutionary "sociability" carried overtones of insular elitism, it also offered exciting creative possibilities in a moment of demoralization and defeat.[6]

Macdonald, Chiaromonte, and Caffi were not rigorous social philosophers; and being a product of the turbulent emergency atmosphere of the 1940s, *politics* was not a place to find definitive solutions or detailed programs. Its effort to salvage a future from the deadly automatism of progressive "History" was self-consciously preliminary and "amateur," and its key insights amounted to moral intuitions rather than elaborate theoretical constructions. The credo of its search for "New Roads," for a human-scaled, postmodern politics of limits, was perhaps best articulated by Macdonald in October 1946: "All I can suggest," he explained, "is that we get down to something small enough to handle, real enough in terms of what we ourselves as individuals think and feel in order for us to be able to know whether it is serving our purposes or not."[7]

Creating a New Political Vocabulary

In his critical assessment of *politics,* Richard King observed that "Marxism hung over the journal like the ghost of a deceased and distant relative whose effect lingered on after death." Indeed, during its lifetime Macdonald and his colleagues expended much ink attacking the remnants of the Marxist ideology of the 1930s, still a powerful force in American radical circles and among the grassroots left in Europe. Macdonald was never doctrinaire, of course, but when *politics* made its debut in February 1944 he still retained commitments to a heretical brand of Trotskyism, declaring the magazine's orientation to be Marxist "in the sense of a method of analysis, not of a body of dogma." Its values, he asserted, would be "scientific, materialistic, this-worldly, democratic, humanist—in the tradition of Rousseau, Jefferson, Darwin, Marx, Freud and Dewey." Marxist verbiage about "class struggle" and "revolutionary defeatism" permeated articles appearing during its first year.[8]

As we have seen, the cumulative shocks of the Holocaust and Hiroshima prompted Macdonald to scrap Marxism altogether. After August 1945, he later recalled, only Freud and Jefferson remained of his original cultural heroes—"like two ill-assorted creatures cast up as sole survivors in a flood." He now intensified the search for models of action, for a line of "ancestors" and for theoretical "new roads" more relevant to an age of state-engineered, "rationalized" oppression and violence. "The Root Is Man," Macdonald's keystone essay of the postwar period (published in installments in April and July 1946), represented his attempt to confront the implications of the "death" of the faith in Progress undergirding both Marxism and liberalism. It was his effort to apply the Tolstoyan injunction "Stop and Think!" to a social order racing headlong toward final destruction.[9]

The critique of technology, bureaucracy, and Old Left collectivism offered in "The Root Is Man," along with its emphasis on the moral responsibilities of the individual, anticipated in many ways the humanist radicalism of the student New Left of the early 1960s, embodied in another, more widely remembered manifesto, the "Port Huron Statement." Although flawed and tentative, especially in its programmatic sections, Macdonald's essay is still interesting as an unblinking evaluation of unpleasant realities, a "conscientious attempt," as Macdonald himself later said, "to reshape theory to fit the concrete facts instead of doing the opposite in this over-ideological age." It was a microcosm of Macdonald's strengths and weaknesses as a social critic.[10]

Macdonald shrewdly began his case against Marxism by invoking standards set forth by one of its own high priests, Leon Trotsky. Trotsky maintained to the end of his life that the Soviet Union under Stalin remained a salvageable, if "degenerate," workers' state, and he interpreted the war that erupted in 1939 as an opportunity for the proletariat to regain lost momentum and to seize power throughout the industrialized West. Should this redemptive scenario not materialize,, however, Trotsky—the intransigent ideologue—acknowledged for the first time the possibility of the *failure* of the Marxian-socialist project. The ensuing "regime of decline," he conceded, would herald "the eclipse of civilization," leaving isolated radicals no choice but to try to forge a "new minimum program" for "the defense of the slaves of the totalitarian bureaucratic society."[11]

Writing in 1946, Macdonald bluntly concluded: "Trotsky's deadline is here and is revolution is not." The late war had, as expected, shattered the old class order of Europe and disrupted its imperial structures around the world. Yet nowhere did a revolution from below emerge triumphant. The laboring masses somehow failed again to achieve their "historical mission." In light of what amounted, in Trotsky's own terms, to a "decisive" defeat, Macdonald urged his fellow socialists to join him in abandoning optimistic illusions about the future of class struggle and to "face the situation that actually exists." Although Marxism was a "magnificent system," its predictions had gone unfulfilled once too often for it to remain a viable guide to action.[12]

Why the disjuncture between Marxist prophecy and the recent course of events? Macdonald argued that as a result of their Victorian faith in historical progress, Marxists had assumed that social crises and the dislocations they produced only hastened the day when workers would be able to direct the power of large-scale political and economic structures to beneficent ends. They focused their energies on strategic questions and "external" changes, ignoring the lesson taught by Max Weber and confirmed by the degeneration of the Bolshevik Revolution: that the centralized state was itself inherently oppressive and dehumanizing, regardless of who claimed to be in charge of its operation.[13]

Industrial capitalism had indeed suffered the succession of breakdowns anticipated by Marx, but its "death throes" turned out to be the birth pangs of an even more onerous and efficient system of authority, a top-down administrative order that writers like Anton Ciliga dubbed "bureaucratic collectivism." This "third alternative," Macdonald observed, existed in mild forms in Labourite Britain and New Deal America, and in more nearly "total" incarnations in Hitler's Germany and the Soviet Union under Stalin. Of the latter, site of Marxian socialism's most spectacular failure, Macdonald noted that in a matter of a few years it had molded a culture where "science is worshipped and production is God," a dystopia in which the omnipotent state reduced its citizens to the status of "docile instruments."[14]

Another, related reason Marxism lay exposed as bankrupt by midcentury was its inadequacies on the question of violence. As Trotsky demonstrated in 1939, "scientific" socialists, still thinking in terms of abstract, "world-historical" calculations, continued to view warfare, whether between classes or nations, as a legitimate and ultimately "progressive" phenomenon—an attitude Macdonald found indefensible in the age of death camps and nuclear weapons. The last years had ended for him any illusions that mass violence could be a blessing in disguise, a means to advance "class interests," or a source of "revolutionary opportunities." Instead, as Simone Weil had written, it was an irrational, self-perpetuating process that ultimately consumed victor and vanquished alike. Macdonald pointed to the failure of the European Resistance movements as evidence that "modern warfare is so insanely destructive that the seeds of a new order are wiped out along with the old order." "Nerves twisted by saturation bombing raids," he wrote, "feelings numbed by massacre and suffering, vigor sapped by too little food for too many years—out of these thistles we must not expect figs."[15]

Macdonald concluded that because of its tolerance of immoral means to achieve dubious ends, Marxism was flawed to the core. The smug confidence displayed by its initiates that they apprehended with "scientific" certainty the "laws" of a Progressive history was now untenable, and it was time for radicals to reorder their priorities accordingly. Macdonald argued that the starting point for a revitalized, "libertarian" alternative was recognition, belated and born of painful experience, that "ends . . . cannot safely be treated only as functions of materialistic factors," but must be engaged directly, rooted in a separate sphere, and "defined and communicated in their own terms." The "touchstone" of a fresh start would be an imperative to approach questions from the viewpoint of "the individual to society rather than the other way around," an attitude of enlightened "self-ishness" respecting the unique "talents and personality" of every member of the political community. "Why not begin with what we living human beings *want*," Macdonald asked, "what we think and feel is *good*? And then we can see how we can come closest to it—instead of looking to historical process for a justification for our socialism?" In short, "we must emphasize the emotions, the imagination, the moral feelings, the primacy of the individual human being once more, must restore the balance that has been broken by the hypertrophy of science in the last two centuries."[16]

The next step in this radical reorientation involved clarifying the language. Macdonald explained that since "the first great victory of Bureaucratic Collectivism," manifest in Stalin's consolidation of power in the late 1920s, old distinctions between "Left" and "Right" had lost their meaning, becoming a source of confusion rather than insight. Stalinism and National Socialism developed as novel, hybrid organisms, combining a "revolutionary" assault on the institutions of private capitalism with an unprecedented apparatus for state oppression. Traditional political vocabulary was simply incapable of describing these regimes.[17]

Macdonald's updated typology divided the "Left" into two opposing camps, "Progressives" and "Radicals," reflecting their different conceptions of the role of the state, the relation between science and ethics, and the nature of history. The majority, encompassing a spectrum from hard-core Stalinists to moderate New Dealers, unreconstructed "scientific" socialists to Deweyan liberals, were "Progressives," looking to the centralized state as the primary agent of positive change. They viewed events in collective rather than individual terms and focused attention on the "objective" flow of "historical process" rather than "subjective" questions of morality. For all their differences, "Progressives" were united in holding as an article of faith the inexorable improvement of modern society under the aegis of scientific advance. In Macdonald's words, they regarded "the increase of man's mastery over nature as good in itself," dismissing "its use for bad ends, as atomic bombs, as a perversion," a temporary deviation.[18]

The "Radical" camp, on the other hand, occupied the margins of political discourse. At present it consisted only of those "few individuals —mostly anarchists, conscientious objectors, and renegade Marxists" like Macdonald himself—who opposed both the incursions of bureaucratic statism and the routinization of mass violence. These stubborn malcontents worked to accomplish immediate rather than metaphysical ends, and they directed their concern to individual realities rather than collective abstractions, eschewing what Macdonald derided as the Marxian "fetishism of the masses."[19]

"Radicals" condemned the comfortable fiction of historical progress as morally corrupting, and they considered it "an open question whether the increase of man's mastery over nature is good or bad in its actual effects on human life." They favored equilibrium over endless growth and viewed science with the utmost caution, as a tool whose uses must be carefully circumscribed, "even if it means—as may be the case—a technological regression." Macdonald described his antiprogressive dissidents as a new generation of "human materialists" whose influence might expand in the wake of recent man-made disasters. Perhaps, he argued, they could educate their fellow citizens about the symbiotic connections between the Western cult of consumption and an oppressive social order:

> Is it fantastic to imagine that large numbers of people may, as life grows increasingly unbearable in our scientifically-planned jungle . . . conclude that they don't want electric ice-boxes if the industrial system required to produce them also produces world war III, or that they would prefer fewer and worse or even no automobiles if the price of more and better is the regimentation of people on a scale which precludes their behaving humanly toward each other?

Later Macdonald reiterated the advantages of the more intimate, decentralized order he championed:

> If effective wars cannot be fought by groups the size of New England town meetings, and I take it they cannot, this is one more reason for giving up war (rather than the town meeting). If automobiles cannot be made efficiently by small factories, then let us make them inefficiently. If scientific research would be hampered in a small-unit society, then let us by all means hamper it.[20]

In sum, Macdonald's chastened "Radicals" shared an ethic of limit, based on their renewed awareness of the imperfection and contingency built into human existence. People had proven themselves capable of evil as well as good, "not only today but in any conceivable kind of society." The pursuit of absolutes, however packaged, therefore amounted to dangerous overreaching, a manifestation of hubris that always risked terrible retribution. In a world infused with various messianic ideologies, Macdonald concluded that the first principle of the true "Radical" was that "we should *not push things too far.*" He joined Weil in urging rediscovery of the virtues of "moderation," touchstone of the "flair for the *human* scale" characteristic of the ancient Greeks, and he offered some ideas about how to adjust to the surrender of metaphysical guarantees:

> The trick in living seems to me precisely to reject all complete and wellrounded solutions and to live in a continual state of tension and contradiction, which reflects the real nature of man's existence. Not the object at rest but the gyroscope, which harmonizes without destroying the contradictory forces of motion and inertia, should be our model. Perhaps the most serious objection to Marxism is that, in this sense, it is not dialectical *enough.*

In Macdonald's view, this sense of limit and provisionality was the only appropriate response to the death of old idols, whether in the form of "Marx's History," "Dewey's Science," or "Tolstoy's God."[21]

Macdonald performed a valuable service for his readers by outlining, step-by-step, the bankruptcy and moral vacuity of progressive historicism, and his call for smallness, "self-ishness," and an ethic of limit was certainly a useful correction to Old Left habits of thought. His arguments in "The Root Is Man" were not without defects, however. One was his superficial reading—and conflation—of the ideas of Marx and Dewey. Macdonald should have made clear that his critique of "scientific" socialism applied less to the founder than to his literal-minded, deterministic progeny. He acknowledged that Marx understood the need for normative values in any system, and had in fact demonstrated admirable instincts in that regard. The socialist future he contemplated was a world of peaceful cooperation and individual fulfillment consistent with the best in the humanist tradition. The problem, Macdonald pointed out, was Marx's ambiguity on ends: preoccupied with materialism and "science," he "smuggled" them into his framework without proper definition. As a result, his ideas lay vulnerable to wildly varying interpretations, permitting regimes like the Stalinist dictatorship to appropriate the mantle of his authority. Macdonald's position on this point is well taken, as evidenced by a wealth of recent scholarship. Steven Lukes, for example, has spoken of Marxism's "historic unreflectiveness about moral matters," concluding: "Despite its rich view of freedom and compelling vision of human liberation, it has been unable to offer an adequate account of justice, rights, and the means-end problem, and thus an adequate response to injustice, violations of rights, and the resort to impermissible means, in the world we must live in."[22]

The dismissal of Dewey as an avatar of a bloodless, scientific-instrumental logic was a more grievous error. Macdonald's characterization here echoes Randolph Bourne's critique during World War I, but it ignores the complexity and subsequent evolution of this seminal philosopher of radical democracy. In fact, many of the ideas Macdonald presents in "The Root Is Man" can be found in Dewey's ethical pragmatism: the rejection of the pursuit of metaphysical absolutes (what Dewey called the "Quest for Certainty"); the call to embrace contradiction and contingency, expressed by the metaphor of the "gyroscope"; the insistence on the interdependence of means and ends; and the concern for the relationship between scale and a participatory public sphere (Macdonald even invokes the "New England Town Meeting"—Dewey's own point of reference—as an ideal political model). Finally, Macdonald's indictment of Marxist determinism and expediency mirrors almost exactly the objections Dewey himself advanced in a famous polemical exchange with Trotsky in 1938. Macdonald's caricature should be seen as part of a more general decline of Dewey's reputation by midcentury —an injustice that is only now beginning to be rectified.[23]

Macdonald also foundered when he attempted to define more specifically the nature of the values he claimed existed "outside History." He began on solid enough ground, arguing that even in a world approaching total integration there persisted in human beings a "vital core" of moral autonomy, a well-demarcated sphere of "free choice intrinsically impervious to scientific examination" and beyond the determination of large-scale social forces. In this sphere, according to Macdonald, reside the resources necessary "to stand up against overwhelming odds for one's idea of what is right." In the unprecedented conditions of the twentieth century, however, even this resilient core has been compromised. Macdonald warned that, as a result of neglect, individual ethics have degenerated into abstract and empty platitudes, "no longer *experienced*, but ... simply assumed." In his eyes, postwar hand-wringing about death camps and atomic bombs appeared in many cases to be a hollow reflex, operative "only on a superficial, conventional, public-oration and copy-book-maxim plane" even while such evils were "accepted or at least temporized with on more fundamental, private levels." In the wake of years of uncontrolled violence, Macdonald decried the readiness of millions of ordinary citizens to " 'go along' with their government in World War III and kill as many helpless enemy people as possible." This was all the more reason to make explicit—as "progressives" would not—the inner dynamics of this embattled sphere of moral freedom.[24]

Macdonald proposed that the heroic ethics necessary to "resistance" had its roots both in the inner recesses of the individual conscience (the realm of the "subjective, personal, even arbitrary") and in an external, *absolute* dimension. "Each man's values," he wrote, "come from intuitions which are peculiar to himself and yet—if he is talented as a moralist —also strike common chords in other people's consciences." To be sure, these timeless, archetypal values found full expression "only in a few individuals and cultures throughout mankind's long history." They appeared most prominently in the teachings of Tolstoyan "prophets" such as Lao-tzu, Socrates, Christ, and Thoreau, men who, each in his own way, articulated a shared humanist vision that countered and transcended the debased mores of their societies and appealed to "something in common" to persecuted and persecutor alike. "In this sense," Macdonald concluded, "we may say that Truth, Love, Justice, and other values are absolute: that, in addition to the variations in these conceptions which appear under different historical circumstances, there is also an unchanging residue which is *not* historically relative."[25]

In addition to being vague and inconsistent, Macdonald's account of the realm of moral autonomy has two characteristic flaws. First, it casually depicts ordinary people as passive, transparent victims, easily conditioned by exploitative institutions "to want such things as to be fed in return for submission to authority, or to play God in their own family circle, or to despise the weak and honor the strong." Although recent events had certainly shown that people could be so "conditioned," the observation was overdrawn, reflecting one pole of Macdonald's tendency to either romanticize the "masses" or to write them off as hopeless. Second, it reflects Macdonald's vulnerability to the temptations of disengagement. Searching for values "outside" the historical process, and wary of coercion in any form, he found what he was looking for in a conception of personal "intuitions" almost entirely divorced from the interdependent, *social* dimensions of human existence. Absolutes such as "Truth," "Love," and "Justice," without more of a context, seemed just the kind of platitudes Macdonald was hoping to replace.[26]

"The Root Is Man" attracted many critics after its publication, among them Macdonald's collaborator, Nicola Chiaromonte. By training and temperament more comfortable than his American friend in the arena of dense philosophical speculation, Chiaromonte found the essay, for all its good intentions, naive, confused, and fatally imprecise. He was especially unconvinced by Macdonald's loose rejection of "ideologies which require the sacrifice of the present in favor of the future," admonishing Macdonald in a letter that "morality is nothing at all if it is not giving up something in the present in favor of not only the future, but even of the purely ideal." Moreover, Macdonald's case for a suprahistorical ethics was specious and circular. "No fresh argument is offered," Chiaromonte wrote, "no attention paid to the difficulties involved. Your argument runs somewhat like this: Science and Marxism do not provide us with Values; we are up against such 'overwhelming odds' that we need Absolute Values; hence Absolute Values must exist." "In what way," he dryly concluded, "to *assume* the existence of Absolute Values would distinguish us from the demoralized multitudes is not discernable to me."[27]

Chiaromonte, *The Paradox of History*, and "The Idea of Justice"

Chiaromonte offered his own analysis of Marxism in a February 1946 "New Roads" essay, "On the Kind of Socialism called 'Scientific.' " He decried the evils of Marx's economic and historical determinism, and like Macdonald, he urged a renewed commitment to the dignity of the individual and the classical ethic of limit. In contrast to Macdonald's notion of a "vital core" of human nature, however, Chiaromonte firmly rooted his "locus of value-choice" in the concreteness and plurality of a reconstructed "civil society."[28]

Chiaromonte began by condemning Marx's continued influence as an obstacle to checking "the present rush of mankind toward disintegration." In spite of the reversals of the twentieth century, socialists still accepted Marxism's basic conceptual framework, explaining away developments like Stalinism as the product of strategic miscalculation or "inadequate" historical conditions. "It is always possible," Chiaromonte wrote, "to show that, far from being general and essential, the failure is on the contrary local and temporary." He called for an end to this tradition of mental gymnastics, pronouncing Marxism inherently flawed, its claims to privileged, "scientific" status utterly fraudulent.[29]

Chiaromonte argued at length that Marx's "dialectical materialism" was an arbitrary and narrow account of human existence, founded on a "breathless sequence" of unverifiable assertions that collapsed when subjected to critical scrutiny. Following Hegelian metaphysics, Marx placed his hopes for a better world in "laws" of "historical process," subordinating individual consciousness, morality, and the myriad phenomena of social life to the so-called essential realities of economic structure and "class struggle." This "materialistic conception of history" relied on collective categories in a way that obliterated the individual subject. "With remarkable brusqueness," Chiaromonte wrote, "men are deprived of the right to be heard." In his view, Marxism's theoretical flattening of experience directly fostered the current crisis of totalitarianism, "reduc[ing] to pure illusion and empty make-believe all the relations which constitute what is usually called 'human society.' In fact, there is no reality left, but the dialectical mechanism of the productive forces. A mechanism that is, to say the least, impersonal."[30]

For Marxists, the exclusive goal was the collective ownership of the means of production, initially administered by a "dictatorship of the proletariat." But exactly how such a regime would prove "liberating" remained curiously unexplained. Chiaromonte had trouble distinguishing the Marxian dictatorship—a temporary, "emergency" compromise with coercive, centralized power—from other varieties of despotism. Beneath semantic adjustments, it seemed to him merely an exchange of masters, leaving an oppressive bureaucratic apparatus in place: "What is the use of changing the label of power . . . if, under the yearned-for dictatorship of the proletariat, and after, men shall continue to be the slaves both of the inscrutable and unmeasurable needs of economic reorganization (determined by technicians whose exclusive concern will be with a transcendental 'whole') and of the ruthless political power required to enforce and safeguard the new economic structure?" The belief that authoritarian means would produce a free and "classless" society required a decidedly unscientific leap of faith, Chiaromonte argued, and was therefore "Utopia(n) . . . in the most disparaging and most Marxist sense of the word."[31]

To Chiaromonte, the basic problem with the Marxist scheme was its reduction of "socialism"—for him an essentially *moral* concept—to cold *economic* terms. With Macdonald, he saw Marx's ambiguity and even hostility to ethical principles as a fatal flaw, an omission that allowed the worst crimes to be excused in the name of human liberation. Marxism, by Chiaromonte's reading, denigrated moral concerns as somehow less than "real," "a kind of unsubstantial and sentimental echo of historical facts."[32]

At a deeper level, Chiaromonte agreed with Macdonald that Marxism was the offspring of the pernicious Western confidence in linear human progress. His most complete discussion of this problem appears in a volume of essays appropriately titled *The Paradox of History*. Drawn from his 1966 Christian Gauss lectures at Princeton University, the themes Chiaromonte outlined in *Paradox* had been gestating in his mind for many years, and they reflect a lifetime of meditation about ordinary people and the man-made catastrophes that periodically engulf them. As an original and profound illumination of the crisis of modernity, and as the consummate expression of its author's moral outlook, *Paradox* is essential to understanding the postwar search for "New Roads" that was conducted in *politics*.[33]

"The individual who has lived through a great historical upheaval," Chiaromonte wrote, referring to his own memories of exile and war, "has sensed the reality of a Power which nobody can control." Critic Joseph Frank has commented that *Paradox* reveals the "peasant" side of Chiaromonte's sensibility (which he shared with his friend Ignazio Silone), a stubborn "unwillingness to lose sight of, and betray, the simple, humble, pathetic bedrock realities of human experience" in the name of ideological abstractions. Chiaromonte's purpose, as always, was to defend the concreteness and "inexhaustible multiplicity" of that experience against the ruthlessly reductive logic of historical rationality.[34]

The "paradox" to which Chiaromonte referred was the fact, self-evident by the middle of the twentieth century, that despite all our attempts to master historical forces, "things never turn out as they should." In the aftermath of the French Revolution, a consciousness of "History with a capital 'H' " was born in the West, a belief that men rather than God controlled the (forward) movement of events, epitomized in Hegel's famous description of Napoleon as "the *Weltgeist* on horseback." Chiaromonte was able to identify a line of writers who rejected this belief as an arrogant delusion, a countertradition whose most important spokesman was Tolstoy.[35]

Chiaromonte's reconstruction of this countertradition begins with Stendhal's portrait, in *La Chartreuse de Parme,* of Fabrizio's tragicomic attempts to become "an actor in the Napoleonic pageant" at Waterloo. Searching for grandeur, the luckless protagonist instead found only chaos and absurdity. After his horse was commandeered, Fabrizio slept through most of the battle, awakening, disillusioned, to discover that "the . . . drama had ended before he [had] even understood what it was all about." Fabrizio's war was not the stuff of heroic narratives; despite expectations, his experience was instead a "swarming mass" of random facts and occurrences that no description seeking to impose a "final unity" could begin to capture.[36]

According to Chiaromonte, Stendhal meant to explode the idea that human affairs were held together by coherent, discernible laws of causality—a notion that underlay the "optimistic faith in history," in "the preordained harmony between man's aspirations and the tide of events," dominant throughout the nineteenth century. Such rationality could be achieved, Chiaromonte warned, "only when events are reduced to a web of concepts in an abstract construction designed to give them a single meaning. But to do this, one must completely disregard the specificity of the event whose 'true' meaning one claims to be seeking." This approach also ignored the "specificity" of living individuals—with murderous results. "The catastrophes suffered by myriads of human beings," Chiaromonte wrote (using the cinematic language dear to his friend, Macdonald), "become episodes in a kind of technicolor historical 'spectacular,' whose meaning is expressed not in any single scene but in the unwinding of the whole film."[37]

Tolstoy also understood the dangers of the modern faith in "History with a capital 'H.' " Referring to Simone Weil's *Iliad* essay of 1940, Chiaromonte called *War and Peace* "the second great 'poem of force' in Western literature." For Chiaromonte, this epic masterpiece depicted, above all, the consequences that invariably follow when individuals attempt to ride the tiger of History, confident of their grasp of its workings and of their ability to direct it to their own narrow purposes. In contrast to the humility characteristic of the ancient Greeks, who acknowledged a limit beyond which lay a realm subject only to "Fate," Chiaromonte charged that post-Enlightenment Europeans suffered from a condition Bertrand Russell called "cosmic impiety." They saw power in strictly materialistic, utilitarian terms, as a means to be employed like any other rather than as a phenomenon to be feared and treated with caution. Chiaromonte wrote: "Not only does modern man admire force, but thinks he is by definition capable of turning it to good use. In other words, force, for us moderns, is essentially a physical, quantitative affair, a certain amount of power, the more of which one has at his disposal, the more good one is in a position to do to oneself and to society as well."[38]

Tolstoy challenged this hubris, presenting the characters in *War and Peace* as frequent victims, like Homer's warriors and Stendhal's Fabrizio, of irresistible and seemingly random forces, often triggered by the "utterly ironic detail." Throughout its pages we see "the image of the crushing might of historical events; of the fluctuation of chance and circumstance in them; of the irrevocable that takes place without anybody having anticipated it; . . . of the individual (bewildered and) lost in the turmoil." The novel is, in short, an elaborate demonstration that "laws" of history, if any exist, are inaccessible to humankind, and that attempts to seize or wield power based on presumed knowledge of those laws are doomed to failure. Tolstoy maintained that certainty and predictability were not features of human society, which consists of autonomous yet interdependent beings who can never be finally or completely understood. This limitation explains why, time after time, "history seems to escape entirely from the control of those who are supposed to be its makers. The force released by human actions is stronger than any idea we might form of it, upsets any previous calculation or design and finally reveals the ultimate obscurity of things rather than their rationality."[39]

Chiaromonte noted that events were especially likely to defy expectations during revolution and war, each an ultimate "release of force" signifying, as Macdonald would put it, that men had "pushed things too far." For Chiaromonte, "History with a capital 'H' " was synonymous with such violent "enterprises," unleashing "the dark element in life," sooner or later sweeping away "everything and everybody, from Napoleon to the merest soldier."[40]

Chiaromonte's endorsement of Tolstoy's dichotomy of "war" and "peace" was perhaps his clearest statement of the nature of the "part of man outside history" he sought to locate and defend in the 1940s:

> There is on one side "peace," the real life of individuals, made up of a succession of feelings, impulses, and everyday occurrences. On this level of "real life," historical events—wars, battles, the decisions of rulers—appear as a series of happenings that have neither meaning nor rationality, insofar as they do not spring directly from the "normal" existence of individuals, and have no clear connection with their ordinary motives. On the other side, above and beyond all this, there is history, the great movement that carries individuals and peoples away as if they were completely necessitated by it.

Chiaromonte's social ideals emerged from the layers of spontaneous "real life" that existed, in Tolstoyan terms, *beneath* "History" (or, as Randolph Bourne expressed it during World War I, "below the battle"). This was a world far removed from the logic of the state, the requirements of "class struggle," and other abstractions that inevitably involved the use of "naked force" on a massive scale.[41]

In the end, the limitations of historical knowledge, the inability of ideological constructions to predict human behavior and to account for the mysteries of "fate" was, for Chiaromonte, a source of *relief* rather than despair. In fact, his entire moral and political orientation flowed from the insight that *contingency and autonomy are interrelated*. He explained:

> If we could get to know all the consequences of our actions, history would be nothing but an idyllic and constant harmony of free wills, or the infallible unfolding of a rational design. We would then always act rationally, that is, we would not act at all, since we would simply follow a preestablished and sterile pattern. But then we would not be free. We are free, however, and this means literally that we do not know what we are doing.

Free men, in Chiaromonte's view, have to learn to live without the security of "progressive" fictions, whether inspired by religion or science. They have to pull back from their attempts to control opaque and dangerous historical forces operating above the terrain of "real life."[42]

Although belief in the rationality of the historical "process" became untenable after 1914, Chiaromonte argues in *Paradox* that people in the contemporary "age of bad faith" have sought, through various strategies, to avoid facing the difficult new responsibilities—and freedoms—such a state of affairs imposes on them. Some, like Chiaromonte's comrade-in-arms in Spain, André Malraux, have immersed themselves in a cult of action, becoming "nihilists with a cause," who embrace "the great heresy of our time: the attempt to control force by becoming its servant."[43]

More commonly, the hollow shell of progressive faith survived in industrial societies as a desperate material consumerism, a "cult of the automobile, television, and machine-made prosperity in general" founded on the impoverished notion of man as nothing more than "an animal . . . completely absorbed in the satisfaction of his appetites and in unlimited self-aggrandizement." In such a world, culture becomes "part of a deadly, automatic search for novelty," individuals move thoughtlessly "from one vainglory to another, from satiety to satiety, from tedium to tedium." The inadequacy of such pursuits lead to complaints of spiritual emptiness and "alienation."[44]

The deeper "sickness" of modernity, in Chiaromonte's view, was the individual's persistent "egomania," his or her desire to remain at "the center of the universe," denying bonds to community and to "all that is ineffable, secret and arcane in the world."

> The most striking image of this egomaniacal inflation of the individual produced by modern society's indiscriminate extension of his physical power is the face of a man behind a steering wheel. Tensed in his effort to sustain the weight and prestige of the power at his command and arrogantly shooting ahead at full speed, overbearing and scornful of anything slow or stationary, he has all the appearance of a supernormal . . . being.[45]

Chiaromonte concluded *The Paradox of History* with a plea for restoration of the sense of limit lost on such "supernormal beings," a return to a "cosmic piety" respecting the irreducible plurality and mystery of the universe that make freedom possible. Human beings must outgrow their preoccupation with "more-than-human aims," with abstractions and absolutes—above all, the absolute of "History with a capital 'H.' " They must confront again "the immediacy of nature and experience," engaging in direct "contact with things, one by one, in their primal disorder." They must abandon for good the effort to impose a false rationality on that disorder, the misguided Enlightenment project of mastery. Chiaromonte challenged his contemporaries to step outside the murderous "technicolor 'spectacular' " they had created, and to look instead to the communal world of "real life" and "ordinary morality" for guidance and spiritual sustenance.[46]

What principles govern this subterranean world of "real life"? Chiaromonte provides some preliminary clues toward the end of his "New Roads" essay, reasserting the vitality of Proudhon's "idea of Justice." He offers few specifics on the meaning of this concept except to propose that it always contained both an absolute, ideal dimension and an immanent, "experienced" dimension, embedded in the concrete. "An experience of Justice," he declares, "is real only insofar as it is the experience of a definite social fact, in a definite social situation." Although Chiaromonte's ethics exist "outside history," this explicit grounding in social life avoids the resort to humanist essentialism taken by Macdonald in "The Root Is Man." Macdonald responded to his Italian friend's arguments with skepticism, however. He naturally concurred with the polemic against "scientific" socialism, but complained privately about the essay's normative vagueness. "You criticize Marx for refusing to examine what kind of a world he wanted and the moral bases of his choice," Macdonald observed, "but here you have written [many] pages without giving even a hint of the kind of Justice, or the kind of 'better society' you favor. Not even by implication, as Marx did."[47]

Chiaromonte attempted to address this problem on two occasions in *politics*. In a note in the July 1946 issue, he intimated that a "just" future hinged on the rebirth of the eighteenth-century notion (later employed by Hegel) of *civil society*, defined as "the multiplicity of human relationships, norms, customs, ideas, culture, as opposed to and independent from any machinery of coercion, *raison d'État*, military ferocity, ecclesiastical dogmatism, material brutishness and such." Again, in Chiaromonte's reading, Marx had betrayed the thickness and diversity of social experience by reducing it to *one* of its aspects—"political economy." Acceptance of this narrow vision of society was "the source of actual injustice," marking the first step down a road to totalitarian regimentation.[48]

Chiaromonte's "Remarks on Justice" in the May/June 1947 issue of *politics* was a further elaboration of his pluralistic ideal. He began with the caveat that "justice" resisted general definition and could be described only indirectly and by negation. Justice was a standard that offered the possibility of restoring human community in a world of extreme ideological violence, of vengeful victims and tyrannical executioners who, as in a Homeric or Tolstoyan epic tragedy, suddenly and unpredictably exchanged places. The excesses of the age could be diminished, he argued, by measuring each action, on its own terms and within its particular context, by the simple query, "Is it just?"[49]

Injustice was, for Chiaromonte, another word for *dehumanization*, a consequence of the "petrifactive" qualities Simone Weil had identified in the abuse of "force." With injustice, empathy and solidarity ended and the individual lost his or her human qualities, "becom[ing] for another ... something like a stone, a volcano, or a plague, ... a subject for wonder and horror." Injustice was the common, humiliating fate where people repudiated reason and dialogue in favor of random, unrestrained assertions of power. Chiaromonte vividly captured its essence: "From the child that is forbidden a pleasure without being given a reason for the prohibition, to a man who is barred from a course which he deems reasonable by a power that is merely strong, and does not care to persuade, the unjust ultimately appears as ... the act of a power whose ways are beyond comprehension: a stark *blow*." Injustice, endemic to the modern age, arose with the atrophy of those things essential to civil society: safety, stability, proportion, and communication based on tolerance and mutual respect. Their disappearance left people atomized and alone, exiles at the mercy of large, mysterious forces. "At practically every step," Chiaromonte wrote, "we, as individuals, become foreigners in society, being told that we are nothing but numerical units in a transcendental calculation."[50]

"Justice," on the other hand, possesses three related qualities distinguishing it from the conceptions of Marxists and other "progressives." They also contrast sharply with Dwight Macdonald's formulations in "The Root Is Man." First, and most fundamental, justice is *immanent* in individual experience and interpersonal relationships. It is "not at all an intellectual scheme to be imposed on society with more or less violence, on the pretext that it is required by reason or history." Like Proudhon, Chiaromonte condemned standards enacted from above—by church, state, party, or ideology—as inherently artificial and coercive. "Justice ... cannot be regarded as the projection of something entirely new, something whose shape lies entirely in the future: an 'historical task'; but rather, to begin with, as the recollection and clarification of an experience which, however dimly, already contains the norm of what is to be done." The guidelines of justice, according to Chiaromonte, are not connected to grand millennial schemes, nor are they conceived and handed down on stone tablets by prophetic "teachers." Instead they emerge from the intimate experience, "which no man is so wretched as not to have had at some moment of life, of love, of friendliness, of the *right* behavior on the part of other men." Justice does not require, as Macdonald seemed to imply, "so drastic a break with past traditions" that only the initiated few could grasp its dictates. Instead it involves the cultivation of values already universally practiced and understood.[51]

Second, the requirements of justice reveal themselves in particular situations rather than in a priori abstractions. Chiaromonte asserted: "Doing justice is, first and foremost, the defense of a specific right (that of the Egyptian serf, of Alfred Dreyfus, or of the modern proletarian) which defines and limits any action on our part. Outside of this, the realization of justice becomes a confused and questionable business, and finally loses meaning." For Chiaromonte, the ethic of "limit" always depended on close contact with the concrete world of "real life."[52]

Finally, a genuine commitment to justice requires vigilant understanding of the *immediate,* human consequences of any action. Rejecting the assurances of the progressive teleology, Chiaromonte refused to condone present wrongs committed in the name of future goals. Individual injuries were irremediable, and corrupt means, however justified, always vitiated noble ends. Again it was a question of respecting the moral imperative of moderation, of recognizing the unavoidable constraints of the human condition. "If we give up the notion of what we want," he queried, "and of the limits within which we want it; if, when confronting the risks of the real world, we make of what is ruthless in action, and unpredictable in events, a stern rule, what will remain?"[53]

Chiaromonte recognized that complete justice was impossible to achieve, especially in the realm of political action. At times values collided, and the risk of committing unjust acts was unavoidable. Marxists and other "progressives," however, imbued with certainty about the ultimate success of their cause, seemed unaware of this tragic complexity. Recent history, Chiaromonte noted, was soaked with the bloody results of this hubris. The Bolsheviks, for example, defended the brutal suppression of the Kronstadt insurgents in 1921 as necessary to preserve their revolution, exalting the act as "just." A terrible violation thus became "normal," opening the way for the Stalinist crimes to follow.[54]

Chiaromonte's arguments for the revitalization of "civil society," based on Proudhonian commitments to "immanent" justice and pluralism ("Multiply your associations and be free"), anticipated in important ways the widespread interest in forms of associational life outside the reach of centralized state power—a preoccupation intensified by the disintegration of communism in the last decade. But although his socially grounded ethics offered clear advantages over Macdonald's approach, it was not without its own deficiencies. Most obvious, again, was the problem of vagueness. As a matter of principle, Chiaromonte left the substantive content of his notion of "justice" largely undefined.[55]

More fundamental, it would be a mistake to characterize Chiaromonte, on the basis of his "peasant" instincts and the democratic implications of his theoretical commitments, as the resident radical populist at *politics.* In fact, he shared Macdonald's vision of heroic transcendence, along with an accompanying pessimism about modern "mass" culture and its ability to stifle human potential. A good example of the elitist, even aristocratic strain in Chiaromonte's thought is his description in *The Paradox of History* of how the denizens of the world of "real life" reacted to the outbreak of World War I. In that "extreme situation," he saw few resources for resistance to the pressures of conformity, of what his friend Caffi might call "automatization." "Except for a few dissenters," Chiaromonte wrote, "the majority of people, deprived as they are of ordinary cares, act as if they were under hypnosis." Passages like this one raise doubts about the extent of Chiaromonte's faith in "ordinary morality" and "immanent" justice.[56]

"Join the Church"

The assault on the progressive-Marxist edifice and the forays into the realm of ethics that appeared in the "New Roads" feature of *politics* aroused intense feelings among the magazine's readership. Many supported its efforts to redirect socialism, but others felt uncomfortable with what they saw as an exercise in abstract moralizing, divorced from engagement with real political struggles. Critics directed their most heated fire at Macdonald's subjective-absolutist ethics, an amalgam they interpreted—not without reason—as an escape hatch rather than a "new road." A few readers even sensed a religious impulse in this formulation. One correspondent offered Macdonald the blunt suggestion, "Join the Church; it has the answers tailor-made—for YOU."[57]

An insightful commentator on these matters was pacifist and fellow "New Roader" Don Calhoun, who, while sympathetic to the idea of an ethically informed "libertarian" socialism, balked at the blanket indictment of "Deweyan" science advanced in "The Root Is Man." Calhoun also rejected Macdonald's arguments in favor of a separate, "transcendental" moral sphere.

> Values are not . . . "non-historical" in the sense that they come to us through divine revelation or some other source outside human experience. The goals of truth, love, justice, toward which Macdonald and the rest of us choose to work, are, as Dewey says, *projections* of the love, truth, and justice that we and other men have experienced. . . . Thus, when he comes to solve a moral problem, to make a choice, such as whether to refuse the draft, or whether to "throw his vote away" on Norman Thomas, or whether to choose the lesser of two evils or choose the Good regardless, he comes equipped with a system of values which reflects and projects his social experience and that of his group.

Here Calhoun echoed Chiaromonte in describing values as socially constructed and "immanent." Moreover, Calhoun demonstrated an understanding of affinities between this approach and the ethical pragmatism of John Dewey—connections largely ignored by others in the *politics* inner circle.[58]

The strongest criticisms of the "New Roads" feature came, predictably, from Marxists. Reflecting on a series of public "Friday Evening Discussions" he helped to sponsor, Macdonald discerned a deep schism between Trotskyists and "anarchists" in the audience and expressed surprise at the virulence of the attacks by those in the former camp against the journal's allegedly "utopian" tendencies. "One impression I formed from the meetings," he wrote in early 1946, "is that the intellectual influence of Marxism, qua scientific socialism, is greater than one expected, especially among the readers of a magazine like *politics*, which has been nibbling away at some of the taproots of Marxism, and is taking bigger bites all the time."[59]

In his memoirs, Lionel Abel recalled the night in 1946 when Chiaromonte presented his case against "scientific" socialism in a Greenwich Village basement crowded with "the leftist intellectual elite of New York City," a group that included James T. Farrell, Mary McCarthy, Meyer Schapiro, William Phillips and Philip Rahv, Hannah Arendt, Niccolo Tucci, and, of course, Dwight and Nancy Macdonald. "The response that night to [Chiaromonte's] views, which were by no means dogmatically offered," Abel wrote.

> Nicola's views were rejected by almost everyone in the audience . . .
> Farrell declared, with the brutality of one who thinks he cannot
> possibly be wrong, "At least Marxism isn't boring and you are." . . .
> and then . . . Schapiro, a very particular friend of Nicola's, intimidated
> almost everyone who might have wavered, or gone over to his side,
> with his ominous prediction: "If you follow Chiaromonte tonight you
> won't know what to do in a week, month or year; you won't even
> know what to do tomorrow morning." It was then that Mary McCar-
> thy intervened dramatically, beseeching the audience thus: "In the
> name of humanity, stop attacking Chiaromonte."

According to his account, Abel later took the floor himself to argue, "if one is going to reconsider his whole political outlook, why should it matter if he didn't know what to do on the very next morning?" Indeed, he added, "I did not realize then that few who heard Chiaromonte that night knew what to do politically the next morning, or on mornings after that."[60]

In *politics*, Marxists charged that Macdonald and his circle abdicated their responsibilities by writing off the working class as a revolutionary force. Henry Jacoby ("Sebastian Franck") grasped a subtle point when he blamed the journal's retreat on American conditions. "The hunt for a magic formula," Jacoby observed, "is understandable in a country where, because radical thought is not connected with a radical movement, the problems posed for the intelligentsia lack definition and a distinct content."[61]

Detroit labor activist Frank Marquart excoriated Macdonald for the "cynical" aloofness of *politics* from workers—in his eyes, precisely the kind of vanguardist attitude "by which fascist and bolshevik-elites try to justify their dictatorships." Instead of working to build a mass movement, he argued, the journal occupied itself with fabricating "bohemian incantation[s]" of interest to "only a handful of intellectuals."[62]

Macdonald dismissed these criticisms as the ravings of "Marxist sectarians and trade-union fetishists" who refused to acknowledge new realities. Although Marquart's activism was admirable, his continued belief that the revolutionary consciousness of the workers would eventually "mature" seemed to defy the lessons of recent history. To his argument that people would not go on starving forever in a world of potential plenty, Macdonald darkly responded: "Marquart lacks faith in human capacities. . . . How does he know they won't? If a single generation can absorb two World Wars plus Hitler and Stalin plus saturation bombing and atomic warfare without being goaded toward a better society—quite the reverse, indeed—how does Marquart know that people cannot adapt themselves indefinitely to starvation?" To the charge of elitism, Macdonald replied that it was a "Fact of Life that, in the USA at least, 'only a handful of intellectuals' ever get excited about any idea or ideal at all." Wedded to outmoded thinking, organized labor seemed uninterested in addressing questions of fundamental interest to the *politics* readers—issues like war, for example, on which its record was "utterly 'respectable' and hence alien." Noting the lack of response from the labor movement to his calls for discussion, Macdonald concluded that, in reality, "the class struggle is aloof from me."[63]

The harshest exchange over "New Roads" apostasy involved James T. Farrell. Still a Trotskyist after the war, Farrell unleashed a torrent of personal invective against Macdonald and his group in a letter published in the March 1946 issue of *politics*. He charged that the magazine had become a vehicle for Macdonald's "egomania," its political shifts mirroring the shallow, "flighty" character of the editor's thinking. Farrell found its recent debates to be "a joke if not a disgrace," an unmethodical pastiche reflecting "the moral priggishness of a little clique." In his view, *politics* had all but given up on the public sphere, claiming now that "the social problem is reducible to a series of personal problems" solved by resort to an arbitrary "Moral Absolutism" and "frivolous psychiatry."

"The only practical proposals you have," he added, "are those of self-betterment. One can try to better oneself without having to dredge the writings of Dwight Macdonald and Nicola Chiaromonte in order to try and make a little sense out of them." Farrell pronounced the New Roads critique of Marxism a waste of time in the absence of "alternative explanations which are empirically verifiable." In a final, contemptuous thrust he demanded: "Where, precisely, is *politics* going?"[64]

Macdonald responded with sarcasm to the attack, contrasting his willingness to explore new directions with the rigid certitude of "those lucky people like Farrell who are in possession of a foolproof, money-back-guarantee system." Although Marxism still contained valuable critical insights—and the task of articulating a "precise" alternative remained to be accomplished—Macdonald defended his journal's "irreverent and even hostile" attitude toward its dogmas. "We are groping around, changing our minds, doubtless often making fools of ourselves," he admitted, "but until a drastic break is made with the old tradition—which involves the risk and discomfort of being so to speak ideologically homeless—a new approach will not be found."[65]

Macdonald protégés Lewis Coser and Irving Howe also combined to criticize, if in tones somewhat less purple than Farrell's, *politics*'s flight from Marxism, which they interpreted as a retreat from political engagement altogether. Coser ("Louis Clair") assailed the New Roads pioneers as a "league of frightened moralists" (a play on the title of Farrell's book, *The League of Frightened Philistines*), dilettantes who chose to "shut off the radio" in order to "escape from the ugly noise of a world in agony . . . into a world of purity and cleanliness."[66]

For Coser, the New Roaders' preoccupation with personal ethics at the expense of mass political action only helped to bolster the status quo. He was especially unimpressed with the communitarian aspirations Macdonald described in "The Root Is Man." "Concern for morality and justice," he observed, "so long as it remains a private concern, may be considered an inoffensive hobby. There may well exist exemplary model colonies cultivating simple living right next to the Bomb Laboratories." Like fellow émigré Jacoby, Coser saw the weaknesses in Macdonald's ideas as a product of the traditional isolation of intellectuals in the United States, "the paradise of the patent solutions and crackpot schemes, the paradise of the 'model community.' " Commitments to the working class in such an environment, he correctly observed, were prone to be highly abstract and romanticized. "For most American radical intellectuals," Coser wrote, " 'Class Struggle' was not the uninspiring routine of organizing, the painful and tedious process of education, the slow building up of a circle, of a group, of an organization; it was barricades and red flags, bloody battles and resounding proclamations."[67]

Howe—shedding his "Theodore Dryden" pseudonym—called Macdonald "the 13th disciple" in light of the quasi-religious tone he detected in "The Root Is Man." He found the essay "a grab-bag of modern confusionism," its discovery of Absolute Values "a mere platonic utopian assertion." Howe criticized Macdonald's abandonment of the working class as premature and "snobbish," given the unrest and ferment still in evidence, especially in Europe.[68]

Although many of these broadsides found their targets, Macdonald expressed disappointment that his young adversaries directed their attacks not at his critique of Marxism but instead at the easy prey of his admittedly inadequate alternatives. In the absence of a mass constituency, he asked, was a renewed focus on individual moral assertion and small-scale activism any less "realistic" than the course still being pursued by Marxists? Here Macdonald scored points of his own:

> Both my critics write as though they were engaged in mass activity, were really "doing something," while I perversely refuse to act. . . . But, so far as I can see, they are both doing just what I am doing: namely, writing about politics for small predominantly intellectual audiences. They aren't making revolutions, or influencing the masses through propaganda, or building socialist societies, or storming barricades, or even capturing trade unions.

Macdonald protested once again that his retreat was not a permanent one. His statement of the postwar dilemma was frank and poignant:

> When large numbers of people begin to move toward some basic social change which seems to me at all desirable, then naturally I'll go along and take part as far as I honestly can. But this is not the case today, and so we must find some way to continue to exist as people with unpopular political ideas. All I can suggest, and God knows it's not as exciting as the grandiose perspectives of Marxism, is that we get down to something small enough to handle, real enough in terms of what we ourselves as individuals think and feel in order for us to be able to know whether it is serving our purposes or not.[69]

What was Macdonald's strategy for keeping alive radical hopes in an arid climate? Was it possible for a small group of "ideologically homeless" dissidents—"people with unpopular political ideas"—to foment real change in a world of unparalleled state power and mass apathy?

The unconventional "program" advanced in *politics* for a revival of democracy owed much of its inspiration to the ideas of Chiaromonte's enigmatic mentor, Andrea Caffi—the third member of the journal's "vital core."

Caffi and the Ideal of "Sociability"

Caffi's correspondence from Europe, fragmentary, pessimistic, but full of wisdom and defiance, captured Dwight Macdonald's imagination as he struggled to define ways for radicals to move against the grain of a murderous "History." For the *politics* circle, Caffi was a voice from an earlier generation, a living "ancestor" whose life and ideas embodied the best of a damaged cultural tradition. They listened carefully as he spoke about how to preserve its remnants.[70]

Caffi agreed with the deconstruction of modern metaphysics set forth by Macdonald and Chiaromonte. He shared their "anarchist" abhorrence for the products of Western "rationalization"—centralized nation-states, massive bureaucracies, out-of-control scientific technique—and, as a resolute pacifist, he condemned anything remotely connected to the prosecution of organized warfare. Caffi was particularly critical of Marxian authoritarianism and visions of collective "class struggle," as well as the Left's romantic glorification of violence. Revolutionary realpolitik was antithetical to the humanist goals of true socialism, in Caffi's view, and represented, rather, the misplaced priorities of a narrow, profoundly "*antisocial* mentality." "The French Jacobins and the Russian communists saw society exclusively in terms of certain power relationships," he explained, "aiming at governmental organization or controlled economy in the name of the people or the proletariat, while considering as mere by-products the manners, sociability, justice, happiness which constitute the immediate content of real existence and real freedom."[71]

Caffi maintained that the radical changes necessary for a just society could not be brought about in a single apocalyptic stroke, nor would they occur as the result of structural reforms initiated from above. The problems of modernity reflected a deep-seated social crisis, and any real solution required long-term organic shifts in the "moral" and "psychological" climate. Toward that end, Caffi advocated a strategy Italian critic Gino Bianco later termed "thinking outside politics." Here the task was not to try to challenge the state on its own terms, but rather to begin rebuilding, from below, an independent, democratic public sphere.[72]

Caffi's guiding principle in that project was the Enlightenment ideal of cosmopolitan "sociability." Following Georg Simmel, his teacher from pre–World War I Berlin, Caffi defined sociability as the quintessential form of voluntary, spontaneous association, the ethos of an intimate realm of human relations independent from the power of the state, the pressures of the market and other manifestations of coercive, instrumental logic. This recalled the ambience of the bourgeois public sphere of the eighteenth century, which has recently attracted the attention of scholars like Richard Sennett and Jürgen Habermas, a world of critical reflection, open discourse, and democratic participation that ultimately helped to undermine the foundations of monarchical absolutism in Europe. Within the small, informal institutions of that sphere, the clubs, cafés, literary salons, masonic lodges (Caffi himself was a devoted Freemason), and other *sociétés de pensées* of prerevolutionary France, men cultivated the "sociable" virtues of convivial friendship, politeness, and free expression that were threatened not only from above, by the monarchy, but also from below, by the "masses." These spaces of "free sociability" fostered a living alternative, across national boundaries, to large-scale, hierarchical organization, to relations based on manipulation and "will to power."[73]

For Caffi, these values survived within the clandestine circles of the nineteenth-century Russian intelligentsia, the oppositional milieu he experienced directly as a youth. In fact, Caffi spent most of his life in such marginalized, "underground" enclaves—as a Menshevik; as a member of *La Jeune Europe* before 1914; as an antifascist agitator in Mussolini's Italy; as a guiding voice of Chiaromonte's group, *Giustizia e Libertà*, in 1930s Paris; and, during the Second World War, as a *résistant* in southern France. It will be recalled that Caffi identified the post-Liberation "automatization" of the elite, activist substratum to which he belonged —the absence of "spontaneous, daring, passionate initiatives," of a "swarming of 'clubs' and plans however naive, bizarre, messianic"—as evidence that a Resistance-led "revolution" had aborted. Caffi remained committed to the underground, "sociable" mode of living, however, inhabiting the cafés of Paris and remaining aloof from the ambition and vulgarity he saw around him as the war faded into memory. Lionel Abel, who encountered Caffi in the late 1940s and early 1950s, later observed: "To me, Caffi represented, and tried in his own way to reestablish, the kind of atmosphere that may have prevailed in the circles of atheists and libertines in the seventeenth century, and the salons of the *philosophes* in the eighteenth. He stood for all those places . . . where men came together and enjoyed themselves, hiding their 'hateful' egos behind the mask of good manners and of 'pure' ideas."[74]

"After the ravages of the [war] . . . the city was visibly going to pieces: social customs, political institutions, and spiritual life were disintegrating; private interests were irreconcilable with public welfare; philosophical speculation was losing contact with popular beliefs." Caffi's portrait of cultural decay, presented in a letter Macdonald published in the January 1947 *politics* under the title, "Violence and Sociability," referred to Athens at the time of the *Republic* rather than postwar Rome or Berlin, but the parallels to the current situation were clear. For Caffi, "civilization" in any meaningful sense of the word faced extinction by the middle of the twentieth century, and the diagnosis Plato offered more than two thousand years earlier had the greatest contemporary relevance: "For the time being, there is no solution; one can only wait for some unpredictable turn of the historical tide." The late 1940s, in short, seemed to Caffi one of those "moments in history when it is reasonable and farsighted to give up hope in any kind of immediate, large-scale results."[75]

Caffi posed the natural question for such a moment: "What is left?" What can a small number of heretics do to nurture humanist values in such a forbidding climate? The answer lay "outside" conventional politics, in the patient efforts to rebuild an autonomous public life by a "few scattered individuals, and groups, who might find in a resolute pessimism about the immediate future the courage not to despair of the eternal 'good cause' of man." Caffi proposed the formation of small groups of friends ("popular communities"), committed to practicing and proselytizing the besieged virtues of "free sociability." They would act in the spirit of a long line of subterranean enclaves struggling to maintain the spark of civilization, "*outside of* the network of existing institutions" and regardless of historical circumstances. Caffi traced this tradition back to Plato's notion of "model cities" and through a wide variety of thinkers, beliefs, and arrangements: the monasteries and sects of early Christianity; the "Utopia" of Thomas More; the peasant "free cities" and "cantons" of the Middle Ages; the communal experiments of the Quakers and Anabaptists; the writings of early socialists like Saint-Simon, Owen, and Proudhon. Again, the closest prototype to the kind of "new International" Caffi advocated was the elite milieu of the eighteenth-century *philosophes*, "the cenacles of *libertines* and 'encyclopaedists'; the small 'societies of atheists'; the masonic lodges and the *salons* where 'people conversed,' developed an irresistible propaganda, and established contacts between men from one end of Europe to the other."[76]

The common element in each of these examples was the attempt to create spaces where cosmopolitan "free sociability" could survive, flourish, and—when a more auspicious "moment" developed—help to inspire peaceful and genuinely liberating change. They achieved lasting impact because they had their priorities in proper order, working first to alter "attitudes rather than things, society rather than institutions." Following their inspiration, Caffi's "New Road" to revolution was a long and arduous one, beginning at the level of grassroots *personal* relations. He concluded: "Today, the multiplication of groups of friends, sharing the same anxieties and united by respect for the same values, would have much more importance than a huge propaganda machine. Such groups would not need any compulsory rule. They would not rely on collective action, but rather on personal initiative and effective solidarity, such as can be developed only by friends who know each other well."[77]

These "popular communities" would remain as visible as possible, reaching out to try to activate the capacity for "sociable" living latent even among members of the inert "masses." Here was Caffi's lyrical version of Chiaromonte's "immanent justice":

Each one of them has been a child. Each one has made, *by* himself and *for* himself, the discovery of the world and of his own consciousness. Each one, as an adolescent, has experienced "unique" moments of love, friendship, admiration, joy of living or unmotivated sadness. Even in the greyest existences, there are traces of aspiration to a life less debased, to a real communion with one's neighbors. One can hardly imagine a human life without some moments of carefree enjoyment and enthusiasm, or without dreams.

The challenge for radicals was to provide outlets for these utopian impulses denied by the present system of bureaucratic organization.[78]

How should we evaluate Caffi's notion of "free sociability" as a model of a politics of human limits, a basis for a revived "civil society," a vehicle for the expression of "that part of man outside history"? In some respects it was not a promising direction, bearing the usual flaws of postwar "Resistance" initiatives. As a blueprint for action the idea lacked substantive content, and it may well have amounted to a prescription for coterie elitism, especially given the aristocratic prejudices shared by Caffi, Chiaromonte, and other members of the *politics* inner circle.

Perhaps a more generous reading of the ideal of "sociability" is possible, however. The most exciting aspect of Caffi's ideas, preliminary as they may have been in the 1940s, is that although they jettisoned the Enlightenment project of mastery and its supporting metanarrative of historical rationality, they kept alive its vision of a universally shared culture. Unlike other "postmodern" formulations that celebrate essentialist differences, identity politics, or the recovery of various populist traditions, "free sociability" — potentially, at least — implies a decentered but *inclusive* sphere of intimate and voluntary association, *transcending* (though not effacing) the boundaries of class, race, ethnicity, gender, and geography. It may therefore retain relevance as part of a strategy for reconstructing common ground where people with diverse characteristics and orientations might meet and engage in fruitful dialogue, fulfilling the best aspirations of the cosmopolitan ideal.

What of Caffi's insistence that his "popular communities" operate at a remove from existing governmental structures and "mass" organizations? Once again, the idea of "thinking outside politics" could easily be dismissed as a cover for withdrawal and monastic isolation, the very "oasis" mentality Macdonald condemned in the first issue of *politics*. This criticism is strengthened by the fact that Macdonald and his colleagues, including those associated with the European Resistance, ultimately did succumb to the temptations of disengagement as the cold war tightened its grip by the end of the decade. But was such a retreat inevitable? Does the idea of "a few scattered individuals and groups" cultivating alternative values outside the realm of "politics" as traditionally understood always lead to the dead end of the "oasis"?

Decades after the demise of *politics,* we have historical examples of how grassroots activism "outside politics" can have profound political consequences in a repressive social environment. The American civil rights and peace movements of the 1950s and 1960s teach this lesson, as do dissident groups active in the former Soviet bloc. Just before his death, Dr. Martin Luther King Jr. looked to "that international coalition of socially aware forces, operating outside governmental frameworks" as the key to his efforts to "planetize" the movement for racial and economic justice.[79] And, like Macdonald in the 1940s, Czech writer Václav Havel has devoted much of his attention in recent years to the dehumanizing "self-momentum" of modern systems of power, "blind, unconscious, irresponsible." Like Chiaromonte, he found the problem tied to a faith in historical metaphysics, "as though, from age to age, history were drifting somewhere high above us in a kind of fatal superworld, . . . taking its own course, which had nothing to do with us and was utterly impenetrable." And, like Caffi, Havel decided to turn his focus to activities on a small scale. In his 1978 essay, "The Power of the Powerless," a classic of *samizdat* literature written and circulated during the grayest days of neo-Stalinist repression in Eastern Europe, Havel offered some prophetic observations about the subversive potential of "prepolitical" behavior in a tightly integrated ("post-totalitarian") system of authority.[80]

Havel argued that real changes under such conditions emerge from the continuous ferment of "the hidden sphere" of everyday social interaction rather than from dramatic frontal challenges to the apparatus of power. A small underground of individuals asserting, in myriad ways, a measure of personal independence—a self-constituted moral elite "living in truth" —had the capacity, in Havel's view, to shake to its roots a social order founded on lies and ritual conformity. The confrontation this kind of dissent precipitates, he wrote, "does not take place on the level of real, institutionalized, quantifiable power which relies on the various instruments of power, but on a different level altogether: the level of human consciousness and conscience, the existential level." Havel added that "the effective range of this special power cannot be measured in terms of disciples, voters, or soldiers," and that "it is utterly unimportant how large a space this alternative occupies." Its transformative possibilities consist not in "physical attributes but in the light it casts on [the] pillars of the system and on its unstable foundations."[81]

Building on these insights, Havel called for the formation of a rich "parallel *polis*" strikingly similar to the Caffian vision of underground enclaves of "free sociability," a world of intimate circles of friends devoted to fostering an atmosphere of "trust, openness, responsibility, solidarity, love"—values that would slowly erode the hegemony of impersonal "official" mores. These circles would demonstrate, in concrete and immediate ways, that "a different life can be lived," and, far from being "a retreat into a ghetto," Havel insisted that they would remain open and "potentially accessible to everyone." Hungarian writer György Konrád carried the notion of a "parallel" dissident subculture a step further in his 1982 book *Antipolitics,* applauding the rise of dense communication networks within a transnational "intellectual aristocracy" opposed to the machinery of the cold war. "We speak of circles of friends," Konrád explained, "in which the free and equal relations of autonomous individuals are more valuable than the alleged effectiveness of the organs of power." It was from this "uncontrollable sea of private conversations," he correctly predicted, that real alternatives to the status quo would ultimately take shape.[82]

Caffi's proposal for immanent, natural, small-scale "revolutionary action" was a recurrent motif in *politics* magazine in the 1940s. A good statement of how such a "*pre*political" (as distinguished from *anti*political) strategy works, anticipating figures like Havel and Konrád, is the following declaration by Paul Goodman, cited with approval by Macdonald in November 1946:

> A free society cannot be the substitution of a "new order" for the old order; it is the extension of spheres of free action until they make up most of social life. . . . The libertarian . . . does not look forward to a future state of things which he tries to bring about by suspect means; but he draws now, as far as he can, on the natural force in him that is no different in kind from what it will be in a free society, except that there it will have more scope and will be immeasurably reinforced by mutual aid and fraternal cooperation.

For "revolutionaries" like Goodman, Macdonald, and others in the *politics* community, "success" was to be measured by standards other than the numbers of "disciples, voters or soldiers" their ideas might attract. Goodman concluded:

> Merely by continuing to exist and act in nature and freedom, the libertarian wins the victory, establishes the society; it is not necessary for him to be the victor *over* any one. When he creates, he wins; when he corrects his prejudices and habits, he wins; when he resists and suffers, he wins. . . . Consider if several million persons, quite apart from any "political" intention, did only natural work that gave them full joy! The system of exploitation would disperse like a fog in a hot wind.[83]

In May 1946 Dwight Macdonald admitted his growing "fatigue" with the "rarefied atmosphere" overtaking the pages of *politics* during its debates about post-Marxist "New Roads." By this point he and his collaborators were becoming preoccupied with the task of converting words into action. The following chapter considers how they attempted to meet that challenge.[84]

SEVEN

The Search for a Vehicle

After the war was the very best period, politically, that I've
been through. . . . The war was over! Certain . . . mistakes had
been realized. The political scene looked free. It seemed possible still, utopian but possible, to change the world on a small
scale.

—MARY McCARTHY, 1962

"What Is to Be Done?"

In the months and years following the war, Dwight Macdonald and his
colleagues hungered for concrete means of action, some way to implement the vision of a cosmopolitan "personal" politics emerging from
their theoretical explorations in "Ancestors" and "New Roads." A sense
of urgency haunted this search. The moment of opportunity between
World Wars II and III—the possibilities for "changing the world" to
which Macdonald's friend Mary McCarthy later referred—would not
last forever. Foundations for an international, grassroots "new left"
would develop soon or not at all.[1]

The *politics* intellectuals came up with two answers to the postwar
query, "What Is to Be Done?" Each solution exploited the transatlantic
networks already in place by 1945, especially with scattered remnants
of the defeated Resistance movements, and each embodied the kind of
small-scale (as against "mass") activity Macdonald advocated in the
concluding sections of "The Root Is Man." Each, in its own way, was an
effort to create Caffian spaces of "free sociability," linked by dialogue
and fraternity *across* national boundaries and *beneath* the dehumanizing
bureaucratic structures of governments and parties. Each offered a way
for people of diverse backgrounds to interact on the basis of equality
and mutual respect, outside the reach of violence and power politics.
If, as hoped, significant numbers of Americans and Europeans could get
to know each other directly, as living, variegated human beings rather
than faceless abstractions of nationalist propaganda, perhaps a new and

lasting spirit of community would develop from below to challenge the automatism dragging the world toward a final conflict.

The first answer, the "Packages Abroad" relief initiative, was an improvised response to the continuing suffering in Europe. Beyond saving lives, its purpose was to break down the provincial isolation that prevented Americans from seeing the shared concerns and humanity of their brethren across the Atlantic. Packages Abroad blossomed into a notable success: at one point in 1946, Macdonald told his readers that "the chance to carry out this project alone has made it worth all the effort of putting out *politics*." The second, more ambitious project, "Europe-America Groups," sought to promote an international confederation of intellectuals opposed to the polarizing forces of the cold war. The project as originally conceived was to be guided through a partnership between Macdonald's circle and French writer Albert Camus, whose ideas about the need to restore human dialogue closely paralleled those of Caffi. EAG was a distinct expression of the "third camp" impulse widespread after World War II and represented the most fully developed blueprint for a post-Marxist "new left" to appear in *politics*.[2]

Both Packages Abroad and EAG ran their course by the end of 1948, the watershed year when the creative possibilities sustaining the entire *politics* enterprise seemed to recede rapidly. Packages had already fulfilled its immediate function, and in any case was being supplanted by the vast machinery of the Marshall Plan. EAG collapsed almost before it began, a victim of both the pressure of world events and a lack of internal consensus about its direction and goals. These experiments nonetheless stand as examples of cosmopolitan ideals in action, and they retain interest for the lessons they teach about building a vital "sociable culture" in the contemporary world.

The "Packages Abroad" Relief Effort

"Starvation! America's Gift to the European Peoples"

For Dwight and Nancy Macdonald, the tragedy across the Atlantic did not end with the formal cessation of hostilities in the spring of 1945. In their view, the crisis merely entered a new phase, and callous Allied treatment of native populations throughout the continent, especially in Germany, merely continued the brutal logic that had characterized the war in its acute stages. Thanks to reports from their European contacts—and from American soldiers on the scene—the Macdonalds were uniquely situated to communicate, in intimate and vivid terms, the grim aftermath of the greatest display of organized violence in history. By criticizing occupation policies and giving voice to those who still suffered, the *politics* community demonstrated a sense of moral outrage, of sympathetic identification with the vanquished, not widely shared in the victors' camp.

Typical of this coverage was the installment of "European Newsreel" for the May 1945 *politics*, in which Lewis Coser contemplated the bleak future facing his homeland as the Allies mounted their final offensives. Coser mocked the air of triumphalism coloring most American accounts. "Rejoice!" he declared, "We have created a vast no-man's land in the center of Europe." Months of relentless pounding from the air had reduced Germany to a smoldering "wasteland," every city and town of any size rendered a "rubble heap" unfit for human habitation. Coser warned that the long-term cultural consequences of this indiscriminate devastation were profound and ominous. "Not a conquering army in search of living space, but famine and disease will spread from there," he wrote. "Just as war could not be localized, so this disease cannot be localized. It will . . . eat away at the body of Europe. It will attack the very lifestreams of European civilization."[3]

The immediate political consequences were also disastrous. Coser noted that this time, in contrast to 1918–19, there was no indigenous opposition picking up the pieces in Germany, no "threat" (from the Allied perspective) of revolutionary alternatives issuing from workers' councils or other grassroots organizations. The desperate, daily scramble for survival precluded such possibilities. Ironically, with the "bewildered youngsters" of the occupying armies incapable of governing, local Nazi functionaries were already resurfacing to fill the power vacuum. Coser concluded that conditions were ripe, not for the democratic rebirth portrayed in liberal rhetoric, but for the emergence of new forms of authoritarianism—perhaps even another Hitler. "What the Nazis began has been completed," he observed, and, in language once again reminiscent of Erich Fromm, he added: "The population is now an atomized mass of docile, isolated individuals, helplessly craving for protection, tired and benumbed, mere puppets waiting for anybody to pick up the broken wires."[4]

Dwight Macdonald shared Coser's pessimism about the European situation. The Allies' costly military triumph offered, for him, little reason for celebration. The cover of the same May 1945 *politics* graphically conveyed his disgust, its announcement of "VICTORY!!!" undermined by a medieval German depiction of disemboweled, skeletal corpses dancing over a landscape of death and destruction. For millions of people on the shattered continent, the day of victory was indeed the beginning of "another Dark Ages."[5]

Almost every issue of *politics* in the year following the war contained eyewitness accounts of the European catastrophe. They spoke of charred corpses filling the streets of Dresden and other unlucky places targeted, by some mysterious logic, for incendiary raids; of elderly women pushing their few pathetic belongings across roads choked with refugees; of U.S. troops in Cologne firing on a crowd of 5,000 civilians who had gathered to welcome political prisoners returning home from Buchenwald; of rape and pillage—the exception in the American sector, the norm in areas held by the Red Army.[6]

The scale of the crisis in Central Europe was, in Macdonald's view, a natural result of the ideology of "collective" responsibility. This was the abstraction used to justify the tactic of terror bombing, the policy of "unconditional surrender," and the Morgenthau and Baruch plans for the dismemberment and deindustrialization of Germany. Macdonald castigated liberals like *PM*'s Max Lerner for their willingness, through such means, to punish *all* German citizens—including children, veterans of concentration camps, and other innocents—for the crimes of the Nazis.[7]

To combat this kind of thinking, Macdonald had for some time been publicizing whatever evidence he could find of native resistance to Hitler: reports of the youth movement "Edelweiss," for example, and Coser's essay, in the July 1944 *politics*, describing indirect expressions of opposition in contemporary German literature. Although these did not amount to the wider dissent he had expected, still Macdonald was making an important case in the defense of the individuality and human rights of a people with very few friends abroad, especially in the United States.[8]

Belief in collective responsibility lived on during the early occupation period, taking the form of prohibitions on organized political activity and on correspondence with the outside world—clumsy, ill-considered policies that in Macdonald's eyes only prevented democratic forces from developing alternatives to the Nazi leadership. Macdonald was particularly angered by the "No Fraternization" rule issued by Allied authorities, a directive that encouraged occupation soldiers to look on their charges with blanket contempt and hostility. He was cheered by reports that G.I.s routinely ignored the regulation.[9]

An American sergeant wrote from Germany praising Macdonald's "Responsibility of Peoples" essay and describing the discomfort he experienced trying to follow orders not to show empathy, "staring past passers-by on an avenue, coldly ignoring occasional smiles of old folk and the playful greetings of children waving at the columns going by." Like many of his friends, he soon decided to disobey rules against fraternization, in his estimation "politically futile and wrong-headed, and morally part of the deep and terrible emptiness of the whole war." He was moved by the encounters that followed:

> There was a doctor in Frankfurt who helped me find the old museum at Goethe's birthplace (which was shattered bricks and stone, with not even a fragment of a wall standing). For an hour on the rubble we talked, and his earnestness and passion (and broken heart) touched me more than perhaps anything I have ever known. (But then he was something of a political or developed person.) There were two simple fellows in Darmstadt who understood little beyond the outline and substance of the events which had rained in on them; but the events themselves had been destructive and tragic enough. Even they, non-Nazi and petty-bourgeois, left me full of hope—not perhaps for a new Germany or a healthier European order, but for something much more practical and even immediate: a returning sense of the dignity of people, of the independence and honesty and character of a human being.

Humbly eloquent letters like these seemed to Macdonald to offer an antidote to the prevailing atmosphere, a way of restoring the sense of connection and meaning that had been so badly damaged by the machinery of total war. "A returning sense of the dignity of a human being"—these simple words beautifully captured the essence of the *politics* group's postwar aspirations.[10]

As the months passed, and summer turned to fall, the *politics* group focused on the desperate shortages of food, clothing, and medicine, which, barring a massive Allied relief effort, promised, in Macdonald's words, to make for "the hardest winter in centuries," especially in central Europe. The Truman administration's abrupt cancellation of Lend-Lease aid in August, together with the meager funding provided for the United Nations Relief and Rehabilitation Commission (UNRAA), was a disquieting indication that once again the actions of the officials in charge would not measure up to their humanitarian rhetoric.[11]

By December 1945, Macdonald was sounding the tocsin even more emphatically. In "Starvation! America's Christmas Gift to the European Peoples," he warned that the continent was on the brink of "a catastrophe which has no precedent since the Black Death of 1348," citing evidence of epidemics, famine, and skyrocketing infant mortality— problems the coming cold weather would only make worse. Yet despite the emergency, and even as warehouses at home bulged with the rotting produce of a record agricultural surplus, American relief efforts continued to lag.[12]

Why the inadequate response? There were a number of factors at work, among them the distractions of the unfinished Pacific war and popular pressures for rapid demobilization and a return to normalcy. After the German surrender, the situation in Europe was no longer a priority for American policymakers. It is also clear that from the start, occupation officials simply miscalculated the dimensions of the coming shortages, which would be magnified by the first of a series of unusually harsh winters in 1945–46.

Macdonald detected more sinister, deliberate reasons for the neglect, however. Geopolitical considerations, for example, almost certainly intruded into the management of postwar relief. As with Herbert Hoover's programs after World War I, it seemed likely that government officials saw food as a "weapon," a commodity to be distributed selectively—in order to buttress the forces of "stability" rather than on the basis of need. This time, however, not even Hoover-type initiatives were in the works. "We're just pulling out," Macdonald wrote, "turning our back on the whole business."[13]

Greed was also part of the equation. Macdonald argued that consumer industries, concerned only about their economic self-interests, had successfully lobbied Congress for a premature easing of wartime rationing restrictions. Maximum profits came from the sale of luxury goods like perfumed toilet soaps—not from ambitious overseas relief programs. Macdonald bitterly observed: "That the people of Europe have skin diseases because they have no soap at all, that their most serious diet deficiency now is fats and oils—these facts do not enter into the businessman's calculations."[14]

But for Macdonald there was a still deeper explanation for the American abdication of responsibility. The lack of concern over the postwar European crisis was, in his view, simply the latest manifestation of a congenital defect in the national character: a parochial narrowness of vision, an inability, laced with know-nothing bigotry, to see the outside world on its own terms. This blindness afflicted political leaders from Harry Truman (whom Macdonald dubbed the "Happy Hypocrite") to the isolationist Republican conservatives in Congress, who reflexively opposed all foreign aid—"the reactionaries who don't want Uncle Sam 'to play Santa Claus to a lot of wops and reds.'"[15]

Such a failure of imagination also explained the apathetic response of the American public at large, for whom the problems in Europe were simply too distant and abstract to inspire the urgent concern warranted. There was no American equivalent to the British "Save Europe Now" campaign, for example, and although an April 1945 Gallup Poll reported 65 percent of those surveyed willing to continue wartime rationing to alleviate suffering overseas, Macdonald complained that good instincts somehow did not translate into action. "The people as a whole," he observed, "while their hearts seem to be 'in the right place,' have not themselves known severe privation during the war . . . and thus seem to have little sense of what things are like abroad this winter." Although the recent conflict provided a convincing demonstration of the unprecedented and irreversible interdependence of nations, Macdonald bemoaned the fact that the lesson appeared lost on most of his countrymen. Here was a powerful restatement of his ongoing "cosmopolitan" critique of the native sensibility:

> Our armies think the rest of the world is just funny, and want nothing out of the war except to get back home as fast as possible. Our businessmen still think in terms of a self-sufficient domestic economy. . . . It would seem that the rest of the world is simply not real to us Americans, that we are neither imperialists nor internationalists but just—provincials. It is not the least grim aspect of Europe's tragedy that the one nation able to give her economic help should not even know that she exists.[16]

Even as Americans prepared to celebrate their first postwar holiday season, preoccupied with spending binges and assured of a "rich, fat and prosperous" future, Macdonald reminded his readers that millions of Europeans faced imminent death through disease, starvation, and exposure to the elements. He highlighted this obscene disparity by juxtaposing advertisements for mink coats and other frivolous items from the *Lord and Taylor* Christmas catalog with anecdotal portraits of the hardships facing hungry Berliners that cruel winter.[17]

The situation continued to deteriorate over the next year, and Macdonald devoted a section of the January 1947 *politics* to "The German Catastrophe," supplementing new first-person accounts with a "Hunger Map of Europe." Again Macdonald emphasized American culpability, declaring "we are responsible," and he was not shy about comparing the debacle, at least in its potential effects, to the Nazi program of genocide. As with the bombing raids of the war, the resulting human misery was universal. "This 'cold' pogrom," Macdonald charged, "is applied by the Allies to *all* Germans, indiscriminately: Brown Shirt veterans and five-year-old kids, ex-Nazis and lifelong Socialists, former guards in concentration camps and the political prisoners they tortured there."[18]

Macdonald reiterated the bureaucratic obstacles, the desires for vengeance or profit, and the general apathy and narrowness of vision that conspired to prevent Germans from receiving even minimally healthful rations. He argued that ordinary Americans, immersed in private concerns and feeling no immediate sense of connection to the vast, faceless crisis in Europe, had little reason to question the malfeasance of their government or to think critically about their own behavior. Macdonald condemned maritime workers and coal miners (oddly enough, members of the same working class he routinely wrote off as hopelessly passive) for walking off their jobs without consciousness of the deadly impact their actions might have overseas.[19]

In addition to presenting various moral arguments for aid, Macdonald pointed out that the demands of international realpolitik required a more forceful commitment to European relief and reconstruction. He was a step ahead of Washington in recognizing practical reasons for helping Germans back to their feet quickly, noting the anti-American hostility, the potential for extremism, and the drain on the U.S. Treasury promoted by the current policy of neglect.[20]

Macdonald was sensitive to the cultural as well as physical deprivation prevailing in central Europe, the result of a quarantine still imposed on the inhabitants by occupation authorities. "There are TWO hungers in Europe today," he told his readers, "a hunger for food and a hunger for information," and the letters he received—mostly from socialist intellectuals—"emphasize[d] the second almost as much as the first." One correspondent described the sense of isolation this way: "Of course we are hungry. But believe me, our intellectual hunger is even greater. For a decade we have been mentally cut off from the world. Books from the outside are absolutely unattainable. It makes one desperate. Will you help us to throw a bridge across this intellectual chasm? Will you help get books through to us?" With the Packages Abroad project, Macdonald and his *politics* colleagues had already embarked upon their own efforts to "throw a bridge across the chasm" and respond to Europe's misery.[21]

"Here's ONE Thing We Can Do!"

politics went beyond merely reporting the postwar European crisis. Dwight and Nancy Macdonald reacted creatively to the problem, mobilizing members of the journal's far-flung community to take matters into their own hands, to fill the breach left open by official mismanagement and inaction. From the beginning, they conceived of the Packages Abroad relief program as much more than a conventional "charity" drive. By giving the crisis a human face, by encouraging participants to form reciprocal, lasting relationships, the effort would serve to restore genuine "fraternity and solidarity" across geographic and other barriers. It would remedy the cultural isolation plaguing individuals on both sides of the Atlantic, providing, at last, opportunities for spontaneous, constructive action, for "building order out of chaos."[22]

Packages Abroad started informally, a natural outgrowth of the Macdonalds' earlier work to aid European refugees. With the war's end and the reopening of transatlantic lines of communication, *politics* received a flood of new appeals for help. As the first postwar winter approached, and its potential for disaster became apparent, the Macdonalds decided to invite their readers to join in an emergency relief effort. Dwight Macdonald introduced the Packages scheme in the October 1945 issue, telling his audience, "Here's ONE Thing We Can Do!" The inadequacy of the American government's response to the situation in Europe was a scandal, he reaffirmed, "but—for once—it is a disgrace that each of us can do something about personally. What 'our' Government will not do, the individual can do. What will not be done on a big, organized scale, can be done on a small, personal scale. Not so effectively, more wastefully—but still, to some extent, done."[23]

politics supplied the names of needy individuals and families to readers willing to make a commitment to send packages of food, clothing, and other necessities on a regular basis, either directly or through the magazine. The enterprise would have minimal overhead, operating exclusively through volunteer efforts coordinated by Nancy Macdonald. It would target independent, radical intellectuals and activists for aid— "fighters for the ideals the readers of *politics* believe in," Dwight Macdonald asserted. "Some of them have returned from years in German concentration or even death camps, all of them have suffered and struggled for OUR cause. They are Socialists, Trotskyists, Anarchists, leftists of every shade. They are French, Italian, Dutch, German, etc."[24]

The Macdonalds sought to prevent bureaucratic imperatives or condescension from infecting the project. They designed Packages, in part, as a political experiment, to be founded on the friendship and mutuality that could only exist within an atmosphere of intimacy. The initial appeal encouraged Americans to "adopt" Europeans—"a particularly human way" to demonstrate solidarity, Nancy Macdonald later recalled. Dwight Macdonald wrote:

> It is hoped that, in addition to mailing packages to "your" family, you will also be able to correspond with them. Letters from people over here, we know from experience, are eagerly welcomed by Europeans, who have for years been cut off from contact with the rest of the world. By your packages, by your letters, you can show them that they are not forgotten, that they have friends over here, and that international fraternity is not *completely* destroyed.[25]

Individual attention was the keystone of the program, and the Macdonalds took pains to match donors with recipients sharing common interests. Under this approach, each party had something to gain: Europeans would receive desperately needed material and moral support, and Americans would be able to learn something about the world beyond their borders, in the process reclaiming a sense of empowerment in an age when "gigantic impersonal institutions . . . grind on to impersonal and uncontrollable ends."

The Packages Abroad appeal struck a chord with the *politics* readership. The response was immediate and enthusiastic, far exceeding the Macdonalds' modest expectations. The accumulating frustration of years of bad news had apparently taken a toll, and many people jumped at this concrete outlet for "personal" moral assertion. Nancy Macdonald kept meticulous financial records for the project, and during three years of peak activity it raised over $23,000 and distributed over 20,000 parcels overseas. Although aid reached individuals and families in a number of countries, two groups whose problems were particularly acute — antifascist Germans and Spanish republican exiles living in southwest France — received special treatment over the life of the program.[26]

The December 1945 *politics* published a sampling of first reactions. A subscriber from New York exclaimed: "This IS a project! Everyone ought to be glad of an opportunity to make up, however feebly, for the sins of our government." A reader from Berkeley expressed similar sentiments: "It is a personal relief to be able to do something about one of the endless tragedies of this war era. Thank you for giving your readers this opportunity." A Washington, D.C., correspondent appreciated the fact that Packages was a grassroots initiative, untainted by official sanction: "We have long hoped for a way to help our European friends without, at the same time, implementing U.S. foreign policy." A disillusioned soldier based in Minnesota offered to do his part: "I am going to leave the army after more than six years of service," he wrote, "during which I have learned a few of the political facts of life the hard way. To me your appeal seems like a real opportunity. I expect to have plenty of trouble with money when I get out . . . but I know I can manage at least one package a month."[27]

Dwight Macdonald could already predict that Packages would fulfill its larger aims. Although given the scale of the crisis, the food, clothing, medicine, and other items sent amounted to little more than an emergency stopgap, the effort was at least "a token of fraternal feeling across national boundaries." Perhaps this would be its most profound legacy. "The idea of corresponding with individuals abroad," Macdonald concluded, "seems to appeal strongly to people. The human ties whose formation the arrangement makes possible may turn out to be at least as important as the material help provided."[28]

Subsequent regular reports, prepared by Dwight and later by Nancy Macdonald, kept readers advised of the project's evolution. In addition to financial information, shipping instructions, and other practical details, they featured generous excerpts of letters from both sides of the exchange, giving a feel for the intensely personal, transformative experience participation became for many people. Decades later this correspondence, filled with autobiographical data, family photographs, and other artifacts, still gives voice to the extremity of the European situation, still resonates with the dignity and resilience of the human spirit, and still testifies to the restorative capacities of small acts of friendship.

Donors came from diverse quarters, a sign of the reach of *politics* magazine. East Coast college students, Conscientious Objectors, and church groups were well represented, but the May 1946 issue published excited testimonials from Indiana, Michigan, Ohio, Colorado, and California. One group of reader-participants lived in Johannesburg, South Africa. European members of the *politics* inner circle like Chiaromonte, Tucci, Coser, and Woodcock facilitated contacts between donors and worthy recipients.[29]

As the months passed the Packages project rapidly expanded, occupying Nancy Macdonald full-time and threatening to overwhelm the limited resources of the magazine. In the May 1946 report, Dwight Macdonald observed that "New York City readers have been bringing in their old shoes and clothes to the office at such a rate that the place looks more like a haberdashery than an editorial office." He joked, "Sometimes it seems that *politics* is a house organ for the Package project rather than a magazine on its own. Some people will say that this is just as well." Mary McCarthy later captured the informal ambience of these years:

> The *politics* clothes barrel . . . was famous in our circles of the 1940s and early 1950s: old clothes were collected from sympathizers by Nancy and her helpers for mailing (after due cleaning) to needy European intellectuals. Anyone who wanted a suit of clothes or a jacket could buy one from the barrel and the money—more efficiently—sent in its place to Europe. The barrel could be examined in the *politics* office or in the Macdonald apartment. . . . There was a time, as I recall, when Dwight dressed almost exclusively from the *politics* barrel, choosing various plaids, stripes, and checks he found there that suited his Scotch taste.

Nancy Macdonald offered this reminiscence:

> I became an old-clothes expert. I never returned from a dinner party without a bagful. Once or twice a month a group of friends . . . came in the evening to our office in the old Bible House across from Cooper Union on Astor Place. We tried on clothing, speculated on European shoe sizes, and attempted to make the contents of the packages both useful and attractive. Once we managed to send a left shoe to Italy and the right one to France.

Among the notable recipients of Packages assistance were Andrea Caffi and George Orwell. In 1946 Orwell asked Dwight Macdonald to send him a pair of American shoes, suggesting that it would be wise to send them in separate parcels. "Then it's not worth anyone's while to pinch them," he explained, "unless there happened to be a one-legged man at the dock."[30]

The relief sent—at first the homemade parcels Nancy Macdonald described, later packages from CARE (Cooperative for American Remittances to Europe)—helped many families overseas through the first postwar winter. By February 1946, harrowing stories of survival, together with poignant expressions of gratitude, often written in halting English, began to appear in the magazine. A letter from a man operating a Rotterdam home for deported children was typical:

> It is not the first time that parcels are a benefit to me. During the German occupation, I was imprisoned in concentration camps for four years. In Dachau my life was saved by the help of German comrades, and afterwards Dutch comrades gave my wife the opportunity to send parcels to Dachau regularly. We now see again such a splendid example of international solidarity. It is not pleasant to be casted on the help of others during so many years, but something reconciles us with it. It enables us to continue our work.[31]

A French "adoptee" conveyed similar sentiments: "Yesterday I received the two packages you have send me. My heartliest thanks! More than the contents of the package rejoice me the establishing that in spite of all, there still exist yet human solidarity." This act of kindness overwhelmed the writer, who had just emerged from "three years in the hells of the Nazi camps, where every human feeling has been exterminated." A Heidelberg resident, a friend of Karl Jaspers, spoke warmly of the efforts made by a *politics* reader from Wyoming:

> I have . . . received a cordial, sympathetic letter, reflecting . . . a humanity which goes beyond barriers of nationality and hatred. Such letters stir one's heart, quickening it with hope. On the heels of the letter a package arrived, which had been got together with such care as to make one forget for the moment that our people have become beggars dependent upon the whole world. The innocent and the guilty, without distinction.[32]

The arrival of a parcel from America, filled with unexpected luxuries, was a special occasion for people living on the brink of starvation, an event to be shared with family and neighbors. A Spanish republican refugee living in Bordeaux wrote his sponsor: "I ask you to live many years so that my wife and I and my children can one day recompense you. You cannot ever imagine the joy that you bring to this house when we receive a letter, a package, the same as when a mother nurses her child, these moments are never forgotten." A German enthused about the "enormous package full of the best coffee" he received on his seventieth birthday: "The scent filled our rooms. My dear friend, you have rejoiced us as a dear Christmas man and I and my dear one are connected with you as with an old dear friend and relative. And you are doing this your lovework not like a stuffed shirt but rather yourself enjoying it. One feels it and that is such a fine way to help poor people." A correspondent in Bonn, struggling to exist on meager bread rations and forced daily to stand in long queues for the barest necessities, expressed thanks this way:

> Now I can help others who helped me in the past. In our house there live two old ladies, who for 11 years have shared our joys and sorrows. When I gave them some of the coffee they forgot their usual reserve and kissed me. To another family, where the husband is blind and the woman has to work for their living, I brought some of the bacon, coffee and cigarettes. The woman cried for joy, and the man became silent and pale.[33]

The Macdonalds put forth an extra effort to reward individuals with exemplary records of anti-Nazi resistance. One report told the story of a police inspector for a provincial French city who, during the occupation years, protected Jewish refugees from the Gestapo by conveniently "losing" their dossiers. Dwight Macdonald learned that "if by chance the Germans found the address of a refugee in the disgracefully confused files (which they probably saw as one more instance of the inefficiency of the French), a cop would be dispatched to warn the family." Macdonald was delighted to "violate every tradition of radical behavior by sending some packages to the local gendarmes."[34]

Many correspondents emphasized their appreciation for books, magazines, typewriters, and other items sent to alleviate the *cultural* deprivation they had long suffered. One donor even managed to mail the secondhand saxophone requested by an unemployed Spanish musician. A political science professor living in Berlin vividly described the claustrophobia he and his friends had endured:

> Since 1933 we are sitting in Germany like in a house without windows and in this house are living also honest persons. They are desirous to get connection with the spacious free world. Each letter, which is reaching us, is like a fresh breeze of delicate air coming into our suffocating grotto. Certainly the bodily misery is oppressing and the hunger aches. But much more aches us intellectuals the mental loneliness.

Another German antifascist, exhausted from years of persecution, reaffirmed the importance of expressions of solidarity and moral support from abroad: "During the Nazi regime we swam alone and without any help against the current. Certainly there must have been people all over the world swimming against the current. But we here in Germany did not see them and rarely heard of them. Under such circumstances the strength of resistance seems to diminish. Now help has come, not only material help."[35]

Conditions actually worsened in some parts of Europe in 1947 and 1948, and the Packages reports had to remind readers of the continuing need as contributions fell. But by late 1948 the crisis finally began to subside, thanks in large measure to the implementation of the Marshall Plan. Its massive infusions of aid, however tardy, came as a welcome development, and Dwight Macdonald speculated that *politics* may have helped force the issue of European relief onto the official agenda. In a letter to his French correspondents "Gelo and Andrea" in February 1946, he wondered if his Packages pamphlet had made the Truman administration more sensitive (at least publicly) to the shortages overseas. "It [the pamphlet] has made some stir over here," he wrote, "and while I wouldn't claim that Truman himself knew about it, some of his sub-sub-bureaucrats almost certainly do, and it may have played some modest part in changing the Government's policy." The program that ultimately became the Marshall Plan had little of the human touch distinguishing its humble precursor, however, operating as it did through state machineries as part of a larger mobilization for the cold war.[36]

Packages Abroad was an important and successful enterprise, energizing the *politics* community and fostering lasting transatlantic ties even as it helped alleviate a desperate human tragedy. Packages was a worthy model of the kind of action at the "personal" level advocated in *politics*. It involved ordinary people asserting themselves freely and spontaneously, transcending the constraints of bureaucracy, nation, and even their own daily inertia to realize impulses for friendship and solidarity. It was an inherently small-scale operation, with its practical and concrete means closely linked to immediate human ends. Still, Packages was an ad hoc, temporary project, lacking sufficient ideological content to serve by itself as the basis for a viable "third camp" in the late 1940s. Dwight Macdonald and his friends hoped another vehicle—"Europe-America Groups"—might lay broader foundations for such a movement.[37]

The Europe-America Groups Project, 1946–1949

Camus's "Civilisation du Dialogue"

Albert Camus, *moraliste*, philosopher of the "absurd," heroic symbol of the French Resistance, and 1957 recipient of the Nobel Prize for Literature as a man who "illuminates the problems of the human conscience in our times," is today better remembered for his artistic creations than for his political ideas. American observers have typically misread those ideas, and, like Orwell, his name has been appropriated for positions on all points of the political spectrum. In the 1950s commentators praised or dismissed Camus as a pro-Western liberal anticommunist. Later, the image of Camus as an advocate of existential rebellion inspired the romantic proclivities of militant young New Leftists. There has lately been a rediscovery of Camus the radical political philosopher among scholars seeking to restore subtlety and context to a thinker whose social criticism resists easy pigeonholing. It is in this connection that his brief contact with the *politics* circle in the late 1940s is of particular interest.[38]

Camus had much in common with the *politics* intellectuals, above all an instinctive aversion to centralized power and an admiration for classical Greek conceptions of moderation and limit. Like Macdonald and Chiaromonte, and like their mutual "patron saint," Simone Weil, Camus saw the hubristic violation of limit as the source of the human crisis of modernity, the root cause of the collective tragedies of the twentieth century. In 1948, Chiaromonte summarized Camus's outlook this way: "He would be willing to maintain that today we are still in the phase of the 'resistance,' when one must defend a certain stability and normalcy of human existence against the catastrophic automatism of History."[39]

The Rebel, Camus's controversial 1951 survey of the "astonishing history of European pride," presents themes he had been pondering since the end of the Second World War. In it Camus describes how the post-Christian West has constructed new messianic faiths to satisfy deep-seated longings for transcendent meaning. The ideology of "Progress" amounted, in his view, to an elaborate evasion of the tragic contingency and finitude necessarily implied by the death of God. Its chief offspring, bourgeois scientific materialism and prophetic Marxist theories of revolutionary class warfare, were nihilistic and dehumanizing in their deification of the historical process. Speaking to an audience at Columbia University in the spring of 1946, Camus explained how such "intoxicating" abstractions legitimized murder in pursuit of the absolute ends they promised to fulfill. "Whoever today speaks of human existence in terms of power, efficiency, and 'historical tasks,' " he warned, "is an actual or potential assassin. For if the problem of man is reduced to any kind of 'historical task,' he is nothing but the raw material of history, and one can do anything one pleases with him."[40]

Since 1914, Camus argued, individuals by the millions had perished as expendable bits of such "raw material," their interactions reduced to assertions of brute force culminating in Auschwitz and Hiroshima. Later in 1946—in an essay Dwight Macdonald translated and published in *politics*—he observed: "The years we have gone through have killed something in us. Mankind's long dialogue has just come to an end." Camus saw the restoration of that dialogue—the give-and-take of relations founded on tolerance and mutual respect, a democratic "sociability" antithetical to totalizing ideologies—as the first step in any effort to "preserve from History that part of man which does not belong to it." His sketch of an international *civilisation du dialogue* (sociable culture), comprised of networks of small-scale communities working to build "relative utopias" opposed to the larger world of force and polarized "mass" politics, seemed, in Macdonald's words, to offer a blueprint for "taking us where we want to go" as the threat of a new war increased. Along with Caffi's parallel notions about rebuilding a subculture of dissident "sociability," it provided the theoretical impetus for the Europe-America Groups project in the late 1940s. Because his influence on Macdonald's circle came at such a crucial juncture, it is useful to preface consideration of EAG by briefly examining Camus's background, his encounter with America, and the ideas he presented in two key postwar texts: the Columbia speech, titled "The Human Crisis," and a series of *Combat* essays collectively known as "Neither Victims Nor Executioners."[41]

Camus was born in 1913 to the cosmopolitan poverty of working-class French Algiers. He never knew his father, who died the following year at the Battle of the Marne, an event that, according to biographer Patrick McCarthy, "explains Camus's loathing for bloodshed and his sense that he belonged to a generation cursed by wars." From childhood Camus developed a natural empathy for the quiet suffering of the dispossessed and a preference for the concrete over the abstract—a perspective akin to the "peasant" sensibility of writers like Silone and Chiaromonte. He saw his family, McCarthy writes, as "tough, stoical and sceptical. Their silence contained a greater truth than the rhetoric of politicians or the theorizing of intellectuals." Camus's teachers recognized his creative gifts at an early stage, and they groomed their exceptional student for life in the French academy—a career derailed by his initial bout with tuberculosis at seventeen. Camus gravitated into literary and theatrical circles, enjoying the small-group environment that would thereafter serve as his model of community. Inspired by the hero of the moment, André Malraux, Camus joined the provincial Communist Party for a brief period in the mid-1930s, but like others he became disillusioned with the expedient policy shifts of the Popular Front, and for the rest of his life he remained hostile to party orthodoxy of any kind. He turned his energies to journalism, attracting official censure for a muckraking series in the left-wing *Alger Républicain* exposing the colonial exploitation of the native Arab population.[42]

In 1939 the war came, and Camus, rejected for military service because of his fragile health, anxiously marked time in Algeria. During the dark days of 1941, he and his friends in Oran sheltered the exiled Nicola Chiaromonte on his circuitous flight to America. In a memorial written two decades later, after the shock of his friend's death in an automobile accident, Chiaromonte offered a poignant recollection of how the encounter with Camus, like his earlier discovery of Simone Weil, lifted his spirits in the face of Nazi victories. Here, on the remote shores of North Africa, he found an oasis of affirmation and sociability in a world engulfed by barbarism:

> They lived together, passed the days on the seashore or hillside and the evenings playing records and dancing, hoping for the victory of England and giving vent to their disgust with what had happened to France and to Europe. . . . In their midst I found the France I loved and the pure, clear warmth of French friendship. I attended the rehearsals of *Hamlet*, went to the beach with them, talking about what was happening in the world. Hitler had just occupied Greece, and the swastika waved over the Acropolis. I suffered continual nausea in the face of these events. But, solitary and shut off as I was, I was the guest of those young people. To know the value of hospitality one must have been alone and homeless.[43]

Chiaromonte and Camus developed a lasting spiritual bond, and as the Italian departed for Casablanca, the next stop on his perilous journey, he said goodbye "knowing that we had exchanged the gift of friendship." Chiaromonte's words evoke millions of other fleeting but profound relationships fostered by the dislocations of the war:

> At the core of this friendship was something very precious, something unspoken and personal that made itself felt in the way they received me and in our way of being together. We had recognized in each other the mark of fate—which was, I believe, the ancient meaning of the encounter between stranger and host. I was being chased from Europe; they remained, exposed to the violence that had driven me out.[44]

Later, while in France, Camus himself became an exile, cut off from his homeland by the Nazi annexation of Vichy. He joined the clandestine Resistance organization *Combat*, and by 1944 was editing its chief organ in Paris, whose credo was "From Resistance to Revolution." Camus's stirring, anonymous editorials in the final months of the occupation gave voice to the aspirations for the moral and political rebirth of Europe held by an entire generation of French intellectuals. As we have seen, the "revolution" they sought, although vaguely socialist in content, had more to do with reasserting the values of human dignity than with 1930s-style class warfare.[45]

With the liberation of Paris Albert Camus became an international celebrity overnight. After the war he agreed to undertake a series of fundraising and public relations tours abroad for the French government, a project that brought him to the United States. Among those who greeted him at the pier in Manhattan in March 1946 was Chiaromonte, eager to resume their interrupted friendship. In the weeks that followed, the two men visited each other a number of times amid Camus's grueling round of speeches, interviews, and official functions. An entry in Camus's private journal gives an intriguing hint of what they talked about: "Sunday. Long conversation with Ch. Can we create a secular church?" Chiaromonte had by then read works like *The Stranger* and *The Myth of Sisyphus,* and he admired the way his young friend had matured since their days together in North Africa:

> He had faced the question that I considered crucial and that had so absorbed me during the days when I first met him. . . . He had succeeded in saying, in his fevered way and in an argument as taut as a bow, why, despite the horror and fury of history, man is an absolute; and he had indicated precisely where, according to him, the absolute lay: in the conscience, even if mute and stilled; in remaining true to one's self even when condemned by the gods to repeat over and over again the same vain task.[46]

Camus's reactions to America, seen primarily through the filter of New York, were mixed. Patrick McCarthy has concluded that "the US and Camus never really met: he had strayed too far from the Mediterranean." In his journal Camus confessed to being "out of his depth" in Manhattan, which, for all its exotic dynamism, was forbidding in its extreme contrasts and gigantic scale—a "prison by day and funeral pyre by night." He was struck by America's surreal, relentlessly affirmative mass culture, with its "ads filled with clouds of smiles proclaiming from every wall that life is not tragic."[47]

Like other European visitors, Camus admired the American gift for openness and informality, and he was especially taken with the vitality of the black culture he witnessed during excursions to Harlem. But beneath the billboards and lights, Camus sensed an insidious loneliness. He recorded Niccolo Tucci's terse observation that "human relationships are very easy here because there are no human relationships." Camus also detected a provincial innocence this side of the Atlantic. At one point he concluded that America was "a great country, strong and disciplined in liberty, but unaware of many things, foremost of which is Europe." During a brief trip to Canada he similarly commented: "This big country, calm and slow. One feels that it has been completely unaware of the war. In the course of a few years Europe, which was several centuries ahead in knowledge, moved several centuries ahead in moral consciousness." By witnessing to Europe's horrors, by describing the problem of radical evil to Americans, Camus hoped to contribute to the breaking down of this dangerous insularity.[48]

The public highlight of Camus's visit to America was his speech "The Human Crisis," presented to an audience of over one thousand crowded into Columbia University's McMillan Theater on the evening of March 28. Camus began his remarks—preserved for us by Chiaromonte and Lionel Abel—with an eloquent, impassioned recital of the experiences of the European Resistance generation, a grim narrative of negation and revolt:

> We were born at the beginning of the First World War. As adolescents we had the crisis of 1929; at twenty, Hitler. Then came the Ethiopian War, the Civil War in Spain, and Munich. These were the foundations of our education. Next came the Second World War, the defeat, and Hitler in our homes and cities. Born and bred in such a world, what did we believe in? Nothing. Nothing except the obstinate negation in which we were forced to close ourselves from the very beginning. The world in which we were called to exist was an absurd world, and there was no other in which we could take refuge. The world of culture was beautiful but it was not real. And when we found ourselves face to face with Hitler's terror, in what values could we take comfort, what values could we oppose to negation? None. If the problem had been one of the bankruptcy of a political ideology or a system of government, it would have been simple enough. But what had happened came from the very root of man and society. There was no doubt about this, and it was confirmed day after day not so much by the behavior of the criminals but by that of the average man. The facts showed that men deserved what was happening to them. Their way of life had so little value; and the violence of the Hitlerian negation was in itself logical. But it was unbearable, and we fought it.[49]

Camus used a series of anecdotes to illustrate the depths of the "Hitlerian negation": one was about a concierge who ignored the plight of her tenants, victims of Gestapo torture; another was about a German officer who showed mock concern for a prisoner whose ears he had helped mutilate; yet another was about an officer who had forced a mother to choose which of her sons was to be shot. His point was that for many in occupied Europe, the agonies of a fellow human being became a thing "to be examined with a feeling of indifference, with friendly or experimental interest, or without response." People brutalized by the war came to accept grief "as a somewhat boring obligation, to be classed with problems like the getting of supplies or the need to stand in line to obtain the smallest bit of butter."[50]

For Camus, the Nazi reign of terror was an extreme symptom of a deeper crisis in social relations endemic throughout the modern world. "The poison which impregnated Hitlerism has not been eliminated," he insisted to his listeners. "It is present in each of us." The fundamental issue was the destruction of human instincts for solidarity that accompanied the rise of absolute ideologies, with their "cult of efficiency and of abstraction," their worship of power and History. The structures erected to serve these ideologies had a disastrous impact on communal life. "By means of paper, bureaus, and functionaries," Camus observed, "a world has been created from which human warmth has disappeared, where no man can come in contact with another except across a maze of formalities." For the atomized inhabitants of such a world, force inexorably supplanted dialogue:

> Men live and can only live by retaining the idea that they have something in common, a starting point to which they can always return. One always imagines that if one speaks to a man humanly his reactions will be human in character. But we have discovered this: there are men one cannot persuade. It was not possible for an inmate of a concentration camp to persuade the S.S. men who beat him that they ought not to have done so.

The Nazi murderer, the apotheosis of the "men one cannot persuade," was in fact less a man than an automaton, a "mathematical theorem which nothing can impede or deflect."[51]

To reverse the dehumanization spreading, in less pronounced forms, in all advanced industrial societies, Camus first urged his audience to recognize the inescapable fact of human interdependence. The war, he said, demonstrated that "the injury done a student in Prague affected a worker in a suburb of Paris, and that the blood spilled along the shores of a central European river would lead a Texas farmer to spill his own on the soil of the Ardennes, which until then he had never seen." Beyond the recognition of our common predicament, Camus called for the development of reciprocal human relationships that could only exist in an environment of safety and equality, and in a culture purged of lies. To that end, contemporary society must abandon the search for an earthly millennium in favor of more "modest" goals aimed at "diminishing the sufferings of men." Although vague on the specifics of his program for reconstruction, Camus clearly had little faith in the conventional mechanisms of power. Like Andrea Caffi, he was "thinking outside politics":

We must all of us create outside of parties and governments communities of thought which will inaugurate a dialogue across the boundaries of nations; the members of these communities should affirm through their lives and their words that this world must cease to be a world of policemen, of soldiers and of money, and become a world for man and woman, of fruitful work and reflective leisure.[52]

During the weeks in New York, Camus had an opportunity to discuss his ideas for transnational "communities of thought" with Chiaromonte and his American friend, Dwight Macdonald. At the time Macdonald was busy with Packages Abroad and preoccupied with drafting the second installment of "The Root Is Man," which was to define a "personal" means of radical activism. With his critique of progressive ideologies and his call for the renewal of human dialogue, Camus seemed to be heading in the same direction as the *politics* circle in 1946. Macdonald had him in mind when he observed, toward the end of "The Root Is Man," that "some of us of late seem to be getting some dim notion at least of the *kind* of political activity worth engaging in." Macdonald cited Camus for the proposition that "as in arts and letters, communicability to a large audience is in inverse ratio to the excellence of a political approach." He wrote:

Albert Camus, for example, edited the underground Resistance paper, *Combat*, during the German occupation of France. After the liberation, *Combat* quickly won a large audience, and Camus became one of the most widely read and influential political journalists in France. Yet, as he told me, he found that writing about politics in terms of the great parties and for a mass audience made it impossible for him to deal with reality, or to tell the truth. And so he has withdrawn from *Combat*, giving up what in traditional terms would seem to be a supremely fortunate chance for a socially-minded intellectual to propagate his ideas among the masses, in order to cast about for some better way of communicating. This will be found, I suspect, in talking to fewer people more precisely about "smaller" subjects.[53]

We can only infer other details of what Macdonald, Chiaromonte, and Camus discussed in their meetings that spring, but it is evident that some sort of collaboration was in the works. "I don't need to tell you," Macdonald wrote Camus in a May 17 letter, "that your proposals—for an international magazine and the formation of groups of individuals in various countries 'committed' to some statement of principles—attracts me very much. They are the first practical suggestions for activity which seem to me to offer some possibility of taking us where we want to go." Macdonald still had questions about Camus's views (his apparent accommodation with violence as a member of the wartime Resistance, for example), but he was eager for them to begin working together "in a small, unpretentious, practical way."[54]

The ideas Macdonald presented in the conclusion of "The Root Is Man" reflect the influence of Camus's vision of cosmopolitan democracy. Here is Macdonald's formulation of the task:

> We must begin way at the bottom again, with small groups of individuals in various countries, grouped around certain principles and feelings they have in common. These should probably not be physically isolated communities as was the case in the 19th century since this shuts one off from the common experience of one's fellowmen. They should probably consist of individuals—*families,* rather—who live and make their living in the everyday world but who come together often enough and intimately enough to form a *psychological* (as against a geographical) community.

These "psychological communities" or "families" would, in Macdonald's scenario, function in two ways. Internally, members would get to know each other on an intimate, face-to-face basis, exchanging ideas about issues from the global to the personal ("not only the atomic bomb but also the perils of child-rearing"). Toward the "outside world" —a significant demarcation—they would act to advance their views by "preaching" ("making propaganda") at every opportunity—"trade union meetings, parent-teacher associations, committees for 'worthy causes,' cocktail parties," and the like. As with the members of Camus's "communities of thought" and Caffi's enclaves of "sociability," participants in Macdonald's international network would operate "outside politics," avoiding as a matter of principle corrupting involvement with parties and governments. They would work, through persuasion and example, to change attitudes rather than institutions.[55]

After Camus returned to Europe, his budding partnership with Macdonald and Chiaromonte lay fallow for many months. In December 1946, Macdonald wrote to Camus in Paris, expressing disappointment that he had heard nothing further on their plans for collaboration. He also requested a copy of Camus's *Combat* essays from the previous month, collectively titled "Neither Victims Nor Executioners," noting that European readers had recommended the series as "having much in common with *politics'* line of thinking." Macdonald's translation appeared in his magazine's special summer 1947 issue showcasing recent French political writing. He complained to Chiaromonte that the pieces contained "too much rhetoric and too little serious analysis," intimating a growing suspicion that "the Sartre-Camus group just don't know much about politics as yet, especially leftwing politics." Still, he found Camus's overall tone "most congenial," and "Neither Victims Nor Executioners" (an early statement of the themes of *The Rebel*) stands as a key *politics* document. It powerfully summarizes the journal's hopes for an international "third camp" founded on the proliferation of a cosmopolitan "sociable culture."[56]

Camus began by reprising the diagnosis of his "Human Crisis" speech. We live in a "century of fear," he wrote, a time when technology leaves us "cut off from the future," when men are willing to commit the most appalling crimes against their brothers in the name of incontestable ideologies. "Naturally a man with whom one cannot reason," Camus asserted, "is a man to be feared." He continued:

> We live in terror because persuasion is no longer possible; because man has been wholly submerged in History; because he can no longer tap that part of his nature, as real as the historical part, which he recaptures in contemplating the beauty of nature and of human faces; because we live in a world of abstractions, of bureaus and machines, of absolute ideas and of crude messianism. We suffocate among people who think they are absolutely right, whether in their machines or in their ideas. And for all who can live only in an atmosphere of human dialogue and sociability, this silence is the end of the world.

Camus's concern for the decline of human empathy echoed a major theme in Dwight Macdonald's wartime writings. People who accepted mass murder were, at a profound level, "unable to really *imagine* other people's death," Camus observed. "It is a freak of the times. We make love by telephone, we work not on matter but on machines, and we kill and are killed by proxy. We gain in cleanliness, but lose in understanding."[57]

Camus spoke in the fall of 1946 on behalf of the "men without a kingdom," both those physically exiled and, more fundamentally, those who were estranged from the various party orthodoxies and the two sides in the developing cold war. With the reality of "thirty million fresh corpses" in mind, he called for an "end of ideologies"—in the sense of "absolute Utopias which destroy themselves, in History, by the price they ultimately exact." Camus urged the uncommitted to search for "modest," "relative" solutions, to build alternatives based on "provisional agreement" rather than totalizing faiths. The goal of such endeavors would be something less than the millennium. "I am convinced that we can no longer reasonably hope to save everything," Camus wrote, "but that we can at least propose to save our skins, so that *a* future, if not *the* future, remains a possibility."[58]

For Camus it was clear that the world was on the verge of a new level of political integration; the only question concerned the shape this universal order would assume. There were, in his view, two possibilities. The first, and more likely, was an international dictatorship, dominated from above by the victor in a cataclysmic war between East and West. Such a war was inevitable if the structures of state power remained unchallenged. "Little is to be expected from present-day governments," Camus argued, "since they live and act according to a murderous code."[59]

The second possibility—a remote one at best—was a cosmopolitan democracy, governed by a popularly elected "World Parliament." This "relative utopia" had a chance to emerge only if a recalcitrant few, dedicated to creating "a living society inside a dying society," worked together to "reconsider everything from the ground up." Camus's peace movement would consist of communities of workers and intellectuals. The former, organized domestically into cooperatives, would "help as many individuals as possible to solve their material problems"; the latter, organized internationally, would explore ways to foster solidarity and ensure basic human rights. "The first objectives," he wrote, "might be the drawing up of an international code of justice whose Article No. 1 would be the abolition of the death penalty, and an exposition of the basic principles of a sociable culture [*civilisation du dialogue*]." Camus cautioned his readers that he was advocating a "style of life"— pluralistic, open-ended, sensitive to human needs—rather than some new, rigidly absolute "ideology." To implement their ideas, Camus's intellectuals would use the same techniques of "resistance" and moral suasion Dwight Macdonald recommended in "The Root Is Man." They would "consistently oppose to power the force of example; to authority, exhortation; to insult, friendly reasoning; to trickery, simple honor."[60]

Were Camus's "relative utopians" foolish in their desperate gamble that "words are more powerful than munitions"? Perhaps, but much less so than the ideologues who believed that expedient sacrifices in the present could lead to harmony in the future. Compared to these "progressives," Camus's chastened radicals exhibited a "positively dazzling realism." He closed on a note of defiance:

> Yes, it is fear and silence and the spiritual isolation they cause that must be fought today. And it is sociability [*le dialogue*] and the universal intercommunication of men that must be defended. Slavery, injustice and lies destroy this intercourse and forbid this sociability; and so we must reject them. But these evils are today the very stuff of History, so that many consider them necessary evils. It is true that we cannot "escape History," since we are in it up to our necks. But one may propose to fight within History to preserve from History that part of man which is not its proper province.[61]

Camus intended "Neither Victims Nor Executioners" as a diagnosis of the contemporary malaise and as a description of the preconditions for a humane reconstruction. Although it achieved those objectives brilliantly, it was much less successful as a programmatic statement, although his references to a "World Parliament" and to workers' co-ops came as close to a concrete agenda as anything written by the *politics* circle after the war. The most exciting idea presented in the essay—and the one that captured Macdonald's imagination—was the "community of dialogue." Here, it seemed, was the essence of politics on a "personal" level, an antidote to the holy wars of competing messianic ideologies. Even this was not such a new idea, however. As David Sprintzen has observed, Camus's political thought—with its commitment to "relative" solutions and "provisional," consensus-based truths, its preference for the immanent as opposed to the transcendent—bears striking parallels to the Deweyan tradition of American pragmatism that Macdonald and others often denigrated during these years.[62]

By 1947, the *politics* group was eager to get to the business of drawing up a "new social contract" in the spirit of the Caffi-Camus vision of an international "sociable culture." As cold war polarization tightened its hold on world events, they hoped to establish a grassroots movement based on an alternative set of guiding principles. Like the Packages program, the defining feature of this confederation-from-below would be its commitment to intimate human relationships "outside" politics, "outside" History, "within frontiers and across them." The multiplication of such ties might be the only hope for shaping "a living society inside a dying society."

The Elusive "Third Camp"

"Europe-America Groups," the project that ultimately emerged from the Macdonald-Chiaromonte-Camus discussions of 1946, never really got off the ground, despite the initial good intentions of its founders. As chairman and chief organizer Mary McCarthy observed in the summer of 1948, EAG turned out to be more "innocent flirtation" than substance. Undermined from the beginning by cold war factionalism, this "modest" experiment proved unable to convert hopes for a transatlantic "community of dialogue" into reality. It was not a viable answer to the increasingly difficult question, "What Is to Be Done?" EAG's failure is part of the larger story of the defeat of Resistance "third campism" in the late 1940s, and it serves to highlight the promise and limitations of the cosmopolitan "personal" politics Macdonald and his colleagues advocated after World War II.[63]

In the spring of 1947, after years of exile, Nicola Chiaromonte returned to Europe with his wife Miriam, charged by Dwight Macdonald with the mission of establishing contacts with nonaligned leftists and assessing the prospects for sponsoring organizing initiatives along the lines discussed with Camus. Chiaromonte's experiences in France and Italy in the months that followed confirmed reports, from correspondents like the Delecourts, of disaffection and anarchist ferment, of opportunities for a "new beginning" developing throughout Western Europe. In a July 1947 letter from Rome, Chiaromonte urged Macdonald to refine his ideas for "small group" activism in order to take advantage of the political vacuum: "With the rapid devaluation of Stalinism in Europe, more and more people reach the conclusion we have reached, namely that a 'negative' attitude is better than a positively false one. Hence, they fall back on some kind of 'private' existence, with only occasional contacts with the world of politics. But the question of a purposeful social existence still remains to be solved."[64]

Perhaps *politics* could play a role in rebuilding a "purposeful social existence" by facilitating contacts between scattered dissidents and by forging direct lines of communication across the Atlantic. The basis for action would be a prospectus drafted earlier by Macdonald—probably around the time of Camus's visit the previous year—calling for the formation of networks of "small groups of individuals in various countries."

What was the nature of these groups, united by principles of nonviolent resistance to coercion of the individual? In what activities would they engage? Macdonald had difficulty supplying precise answers in the prospectus. He noted Camus's suggestion that "they could be a kind of preaching brotherhood, committed to writing, talking (and I presume acting) to further their ideas in every possible context," again reciting examples like trade union meetings, cocktail parties, and functions for "worthy causes." He mentioned the idea of an international magazine. He pointed to conscientious objection to militarism and the struggle for racial democracy in the United States as issues requiring new, imaginative approaches. And he invoked the model of Packages Abroad, an enterprise that met urgent material needs while fostering human relationships "across oceans and frontiers." Further details could emerge, however, only from the experience of the groups, from the "multiplication and . intensification of each individual's powers and convictions that would take place if a truly fraternal, communal brotherhood could be established." "This would set in motion all kinds of actions," Macdonald concluded, "impossible to plan or foresee in advance."[65]

The "Europe-America Groups" project developed from these loose notions of an international "brotherhood." In the spring of 1948, the first formal version of EAG's statement of purpose circulated, drafted primarily by Mary McCarthy and signed by a wide array of New York Intellectuals. It began: "We are a group of people from many intellectual professions in America who have gotten together to provide some center of solidarity with and support for intellectuals in Europe who find themselves outside the mass parties. Like ourselves, these intellectuals are isolated not only from the great power blocs that divide the world, but also to a large extent from each other." The manifesto declared the group's intent to address the atomization and "passivity" afflicting "independent democrats and socialists" as a result of "the extreme polarity of Soviet and American power." Europeans, after more than a decade of political upheaval, war, and deprivation, faced "material" obstacles to communication; dissidents in the United States, on the other hand, complained of isolation born of an inability "to make our opposition, real as it is to us, felt in any practical way." Out of this frustration came the Americans' impulse to reach out to their European counterparts, to demonstrate to them that "they are not alone, and that certain basic ideas of freedom and social equity remain for us common ground."[66]

Apart from an assertion that Stalinism was "the main enemy in Europe," the nature of this common ground remained intentionally vague. The EAG founders sought at this early stage only "to provide an atmosphere in which new political thought is possible," to build Camus's "community of dialogue" as the basis for a "new 'left'" alternative to the cold war. "What we support in Europe today is not any specific program," the document stated, "but the reexamination of political questions through controversy and discussion." Its first two pledges of "concrete" action reproduced the Packages Abroad approach to international fraternity, announcing a commitment to send material aid, books, and magazines to individuals and small groups in France and Italy. A final proposal called for the creation of a permanent body to encourage discussion of political and cultural questions, to raise funds, and to establish "regular channels of communication" with friends in Europe.[67]

EAG began that spring with a flurry of activity. At a meeting in March, held at the Macdonalds' Tenth Street apartment, the signatories offered monetary donations and elected Mary McCarthy chairman. In the following weeks, EAG raised additional funds (eventually totaling over $2,000) through a series of public fundraisers, including an auction of "literary souvenirs" (according to the official minutes, these included a canceled check of T. S. Eliot, donated by Philip Rahv, and Delmore Schwartz's manuscript for his short story, "In Dreams Begin Responsibilities"). EAG sponsored Nicholas Nabokov's lecture "The Soviet Attack on Culture" and made plans for other, similar events—a discussion of "Jewish Policy in Palestine" by Hannah Arendt, for example, and a debate between Dwight Macdonald, Sidney Hook, and A. J. Muste on the question of "Pacifism as a Political Strategy." Decades later

McCarthy recalled a debate on the Wallace candidacy during which Hook "chased Mark Van Doren across the stage and virtually pinned him to the wall." A vote at the April 11 meeting disbursed 75 percent of the monies collected to Nicola Chiaromonte, to use "in his various capacities as the European representative of Europe-America Groups."[68]

EAG's flaws were already becoming apparent, however. The self-consciously preliminary language of its founding manifesto, deemed necessary to achieve initial consensus, masked deep differences between the *politics* faction—Macdonald, Chiaromonte, and McCarthy—and Hook, Rahv, and Phillips. The *politics* intellectuals were attempting to stake out a critically independent position on the cold war; and although they did not adopt a pacifist response, they opposed the U.S. government's tendency to see the competition with Stalin in exclusively military terms. In contrast, their putative allies (derisively dubbed "The *PR* Boys" by Macdonald and McCarthy) were by now helping to formulate the tenets of liberal anticommunism, assuming what Macdonald would call a "get-Russia-at-all-costs attitude" that made them unreliable partners in any third-camp experiments. In a letter to McCarthy, Miriam Chiaromonte captured the tenuous nature of the coalition, reporting Hook's smug comment that her husband's "metaphysical aberrations can be excused since he didn't have the benefit of an American education until too late, and it is clear that his heart is in the right place." Despite a common language, the two factions differed at a more profound level as well. For men like Sidney Hook, "totalitarianism" was something that existed in the terror states of Hitler and Stalin, and criticisms of the West had to be muted for the duration of the struggle against these external threats. For Macdonald and his friends, on the other hand, "totalitarian" tendencies pervaded to some degree the technocratic organization of *all* modern industrial societies. The "end of ideology" spoken of by Camus implied not just rejection of Marxian socialism, but a retreat from the underlying faith in "progress" manifest on both sides of the geopolitical divide.[69]

The "*PR* Boys" manifested their hostility to the founders' vision from the start, voicing reservations about assistance to "nonaligned intellectuals" and conspicuously withholding donations for that purpose (they offered "not even five dollars worth of help," McCarthy later remembered, "whereas people like Dick Rovere and Arthur Schlesinger, not at all close to us, sent checks for twenty-five dollars, quite a lot of money at the time"). At a meeting at the Rahvs' apartment, the last one before a summer hiatus, "The Boys" even attempted a coup, stacking the room with their supporters in hopes of appropriating the EAG treasury for other purposes. McCarthy got wind of the ambush in advance, however, and recruited her own sympathizers to attend the meeting en masse. She recalled with pleasure "the faces of Hook and company when they looked around Rahv's living room and realized they were not in the majority."[70]

An immediate crisis had been averted, but the deeper problem of EAG's direction remained. Over the next months the *politics* faction tried, with mixed results, to define their goals more precisely. Chiaromonte, the European liaison, sent regular reports of his activities and of the shifting political atmosphere in Italy and France. He supplied EAG funds to a number of individuals, including Andrea Caffi, Anton Ciliga, and the Delecourts and—with Camus's help—made contacts with a wide variety of dissident groups. Although the response he received during these encounters was generally favorable, his wife Miriam wrote that a skeptic interrupted one talk by "jump[ing] up to say . . . that this was just another trick of the U.S. govt. to divide the Italian workers."[71]

Dwight Macdonald remained committed to the project, but he recognized the need for some strategic fine-tuning. In July 1948 he wrote Chiaromonte:

> The PR boys made a little trouble, but it fizzled out; they aren't a menace so long as the Groups has some positive idea of what it wants to do. . . . Whatever happens, I've concluded that discussion groups plus public meetings MUST be organized by "our" set next fall. I'm constantly running into people who need and want that kind of thing, and would support it if they had a chance.

But a "positive idea of what it wants to do" was exactly what EAG lacked. For Mary McCarthy, who in one sense *was* "Europe-America Groups," the sense of drift triggered profound personal feelings of despair. After reading one of Chiaromonte's reports she confided to Macdonald her "shame at the seriousness of the European response to our very trivial and muddling efforts." "I am sick of the way I am living," she added, "the lack of accomplishment and seriousness, and one year succeeding another with nothing's being changed."[72]

As a way to give EAG some solidity and forward momentum, McCarthy suggested an "attempt at a communal program of living," and she raised again the idea of an international bulletin, offering the title, "The Situation." She also argued for opening up the membership after adopting a more forthright founding declaration:

> It seems to me obvious at this point that our aims *must* be radical; it won't do a second time to get up a statement that is simply the L.C.D. of a heterogeneous group. We must, I think, raise the military question and answer it; otherwise, we might just as well melt into the A.D.A. I

don't mean that we have to subscribe to a philosophy of non-violence; that goes too far, in my opinion, at least for this group; we simply have to oppose the militarization of Europe and of the United States. This means a break with the boys, but they only discredit us anyway, while feeling compromised themselves by the connection.[73]

Macdonald expressed less urgency about EAG's identity crisis. It was part of the same problem of meaningful action he had been grappling with for years. "I don't feel any more morally spurred to action than I had already felt," he wrote McCarthy at the end of July, "perhaps because we get so many letters from Europe and hence have come long ago to expect the seriousness of attitude that impresses you." Macdonald agreed in principle with her desire to formulate more specific aims, but was unable to suggest what they might be. "Communal living, small group activity, opposition to and evasion from the State, militarism, etc. — all these things I of course favor strongly, but surely we knew them all IN GENERAL a long time ago."[74]

In his letters from Rome, meanwhile, Chiaromonte did his best to break the impasse. In early September he wrote to Macdonald that EAG should function as a "center of information and contacts," a loose "federation" of groups and individuals committed to defending the principles of "internationalism" and "radical democracy" in a world ruled by statist realpolitik. He offered the "concrete" suggestion (consistent with his campaign against the "responsibility of peoples") of publicizing distinctions between the Stalinist regime and its anonymous subjects typically ignored by American propagandists. Perhaps EAG could also play a role in establishing unofficial, grassroots links between East and West. A month later, Chiaromonte wrote of his disgust with the lack of imagination demonstrated by Washington policymakers, who, in his view, simply mirrored the tactics of force practiced by their Soviet adversaries. America's failure to represent democratic ideals left Europeans frightened and demoralized. "Both sides have nothing to offer the world except finally war," he lamented. "Can we really blame those people who refuse to choose?" Again, EAG had an opportunity for constructive action, beginning with the task of exposing the "monstrous inertia" of the present world leadership and articulating widespread popular desires for a peaceful alternative.[75]

Prospects for EAG did not improve in the fall. One factor in the project's rapid demise was the unhappy example of international collaboration established by two of its founding fathers. If "the US and Camus never really met," the same could be said of Dwight Macdonald and Camus, and by the end of 1948 their relationship had permanently soured. As late as October of that year, Camus wrote to Macdonald, reaffirming his willingness to work with EAG and offering suggestions about how to revise its manifesto. To allay European fears of State Department involvement, Camus urged Macdonald to expand the condemnation of Stalinism into a broader denunciation of *all* forms of totalitarianism, including, presumably, those present in the technocratic capitalism of the West. Macdonald responded by explaining the factionalism in New York and, to facilitate fund-raising, he asked for details of Camus's activities on behalf of the project. He joked apologetically that the request "sounds more and more like the Marshall Plan!"[76]

Unfortunately, Camus at this time was preoccupied, both with his writing and with the frenzied political wars of postwar Paris, and EAG remained a low priority. Macdonald became infuriated with Camus's failure to answer inquiries, a neglect highlighted by his silence on the Garry Davis controversy. Davis, an American bomber pilot turned pacifist, launched his own symbolic protest against the cold war by staging a sit-in on the steps of the U.N.'s temporary Paris headquarters in September 1948, declaring himself a "citizen of the world." Although he was an object of ridicule for many observers—including those few in the American press who paid any attention—a number of respected French intellectuals, among them Camus, saw something worthwhile in the protest and wrote and spoke in Davis's defense. In December Macdonald asked Camus why there had been no word from him on the matter, adding, "we of Europe-America really have some interest in those kind of things. How can we talk about transatlantic cooperation when we don't even know what you're up to in any concrete sense?" In a letter to Chiaromonte early in the new year, Macdonald vented his anger over Camus's broken promises:

> Let him write novels and plays, but I object to his pretense that he is concerned personally about Worthy Causes like EAG or that international magazine he was going to devote his life to several years ago. How can we have a brotherhood if the Paris brothers won't answer letters or even let us know when they take an action, like the Davis case, which might concern us too? It's all bluff and hypocrisy, and you can tell Camus that from me.

This was an ignominious end indeed for the Macdonald-Camus dialogue.[77]

Ironically, Camus was engaged by 1948–49 in his own, equally abortive experiment in third-campism, *Groupes de Liaison Internationale*. The language of his manifesto for the organization resembled that of the EAG statement of principles, except that it offered more explicit reservations about the American side of the cold war equation, framed in a

critique of what Adorno and Horkheimer would call the "culture industry." It read, in part:

> We are a group of men who, in liaison with friends of America, Italy,
> Africa, and other countries, have decided to unite our efforts and our
> reflections in order to preserve some of our reasons for living.
>
> These reasons are threatened today by many monstrous idols, but
> above all by totalitarian techniques.
>
> These reasons are especially threatened by Stalinist ideology.
>
> These reasons are threatened also, at a lesser degree it is true, by
> American worship of technology. This is not totalitarian, because it
> accepts the individual's neutrality. But in its own way it is total
> because, through films, press and radio, it has known how to make
> itself loved.[78]

Camus's *Groupes* drew its membership largely from anarcho-
syndicalist circles around the periodical *Révolution Prolétarienne*. Its
activities included aid to political refugees, especially Spanish antifascists,
and the publication of a newsletter whose first issue featured articles by
Dwight Macdonald and George Orwell. Chiaromonte attended at least
two *Groupes* meetings, and he encouraged Macdonald to cultivate contacts with the organization. "The atmosphere is very nice, the discussions
often interesting," he wrote in April 1949. "In my opinion a new Left is
developing in France, and it is worthwhile to follow its manifestations,
of which Groupes de Liaison certainly are one." Macdonald, still disillusioned with Camus, declined his friend's advice. Despite its early
promise, *Groupes,* like EAG, was to lead a brief and troubled existence,
never establishing a consensus about its purposes. Meetings quickly
degenerated into desultory strategy debates and long-winded mono-
logues, and, in 1950, a discouraged Camus presided over the body's
formal dissolution.[79]

EAG's end was similarly demoralizing. Its members gathered for the
first time in months in October 1948, and the *politics-PR* schism immediately resurfaced. Even at this late date, Macdonald still hoped that the
two factions could somehow continue working together under the same
roof, but as the weeks passed each meeting became increasingly "sterile."
What emerged was a redraft of the statement of aims, a document to be
circulated among one hundred prominent writers and artists that Macdonald pronounced "unexceptionable if a bit on the dull side."[80]

Although the new statement repeated the substance of the original, it
did respond to European concerns about EAG's autonomy. "In carrying
out this work," it asserted, "we are acting as individuals and intellectuals, independent of the State Department or any other official agency."

Stalinism was still "the main enemy in Europe today," but this time the group took pains to condemn "other forms of totalitarianism"—Franco, Tito, the authoritarian tendencies of the French Gaullists and the Italian Christian-Democrats. The text continued:

> Our conception of authoritarianism is not derived from the State Department. Our opposition to the Soviet government is not based on nationalist grounds, but on our rejection of a system of ideas and a way of life which will appear to us equally repugnant, whatever its geographical locale. We are also critical of our own country. We refuse to identify ourselves with American capitalism and we oppose the social and economic and racial inequities this system perpetuates.

The drafters, obliged to address the "military question," settled on an intermediate stand, rejecting pacifism but emphasizing their conviction that "it is a mistake on the part of the two major political parties to conceive of the struggle against world communism primarily in military terms."[81]

Although this was a strong expression of the *politics* circle's opposition to armed conflict, a weary and impatient Macdonald still considered the restatement an uninspiring product of compromise. The response was equally tepid, and by the spring of 1949 the entire project was dead. This was no surprise to Macdonald, who, in a letter to Chiaromonte the previous December, had already described EAG as "moribund." "The whole fall was wasted in a series of talky-talk meetings of the in-group," he complained, and the presence of Hook and the "PR boys"—the "right opposition"—effectively "stymied" exploration of any new directions. In short, EAG as an amorphous "popular front" movement was no longer worth the trouble. "All that [it] actually proposes to *do*," Macdonald observed, "can really be done through *politics*—i.e., help individuals abroad, run meetings, bring European letters to an American audience." As presently conceived, the organization was therefore an empty vessel. He concluded: "EAG has to survive as a 'band of brothers,' or not at all. And there is not much brotherhood about it now. . . . Unless EAG is a fraternal, communal group, it is nothing."[82]

In his reply that same month, Chiaromonte continued to see potential in a reconstituted EAG, and he urged Macdonald to "keep at least the formula alive" as a way to publicize and defend humanist principles on a case-by-case basis. By then, however, it was too late. Macdonald wrote again to Chiaromonte, expressing second thoughts about the "communal" impulse that had prompted EAG's formation in the first place:

> We've long assumed that people like us want above all things a community, a band of brothers. But do we really? Myself, I'm not so

sure any more. I'm quite happy now working & thinking & reading in my own individualistic way; and I have plenty of human and social contacts here and abroad, mostly via the magazine (which might be called a kind of community, I suppose). True that these contacts are not as close and mutually trusting-and-respecting as an EAG group might be; but also true (for me) that, except for Mary and one or two others, I can't really think of individuals here in NYC with whom I am sure I want to plunge into brotherhood ... maybe a little distance (except from a *very* few people) isn't too bad a way to be able to continue loving one's fellowmen.[83]

Mary McCarthy channeled her disappointment at EAG's failure into *The Oasis*, a fictional examination of the problems of communal living raised by Macdonald. This short novel, originally published in 1949 in the British literary periodical *Horizon*, was a satirical account of an attempt by a group of urban intellectuals to build a model cooperative society in the backwoods of New England. The project was inspired by the ideas about justice, individual freedom, and the need for "small insurgent communities, peripheral movements" expressed by an Italian anarchist named "Monteverdi" (obviously Nicola Chiaromonte), now lost somewhere in war-torn Europe.[84]

The participants offered a variety of motivations for their retreat, but, as in EAG, they soon divided into two factions. The leader of the "Utopians," in search of a fresh start based on a scrupulously principled existence, was Macdougal Macdermott, the "tall, red-bearded, gregarious" editor of a libertarian magazine. The skeptics of the "Realist" camp, on the other hand, followed the cues of Will Taub (Philip Rahv), a manipulator with a vindictive streak who privately relished the thought of the experiment's collapse. Although the Realists had abandoned the dogmatic formulas of "scientific" socialism, according to McCarthy they retained its contempt for individual autonomy, the freedom of self-creation on which the entire enterprise rested. Taub viewed the Utopians as hopelessly naive, a group of "irresponsible moralists." McCarthy summarized his attitude this way: "Macdermott and a pack of school-teachers and religious types, what had they got to say to him that he had not heard before? He could read it all in Macdermott's magazines, in a series called New Roads, without paying rent on a cottage and being put to work on the land."[85]

Crises developed even before the group left the city, as the smallest decisions prompted prolonged and heated debate. What was the community's position on technology? A pragmatic compromise allowed the use of bicycles, carpet-sweepers—"any machine, in fact, to which a man contributed his own proportionate share of exertion." Should Joe Lockman, a philistine businessman with little sympathy for the project's larger aims, be admitted to membership? The ordinarily generous Macdermott betrayed a visceral elitism in his initial resistance to the idea. At a group meeting he loudly protested that Lockman was "the antithesis of everything we stand for. My God, aren't we going to have any standards? I don't hold his business against him; he may be a decent employer; but, my God, the man is uncivilized. Don't you believe in *anything*? This fellow is a Yahoo." After further discussion, Macdermott—never a prisoner of consistency—abandoned his opposition, thanks largely to the deft intervention of his humane and practical wife, Eleanor. This change of heart defused what could have been "an ugly beginning for a community devoted to brotherhood."[86]

McCarthy described the feelings of the colonists as they made their way, unmolested by the authorities, to the abandoned hotel that would serve as their new home:

> The realists suspected a trap, and the more intransigent members asked themselves what Monteverdi, the Founder, would have said if he could have seen that cavalcade of cars, well-stocked with whiskey, cans and contraceptives, winding up the mountain of Nowhere, with their papers in perfect order—doubtless, he would have smiled but they could hardly smile for him, and the evocation of his fate cast, for those who had loved him, a shadow on the Utopian hillside, comparable to the shadow of Calvary upon the militant Church. Reviewing their actions, however, in the light of the ideas of the Founder, they could find no real cause for self-reproach. Throughout, in every decision, they had respected the idea of *limit,* which seemed to them in retrospect the very definition of his thought.[87]

Once they were ensconced in their retreat, however, sectarian tensions combined with a series of mishaps and dilemmas to undermine hopes for an enduring model of sociability. Taub and Macdermott jockeyed for advantage while ideas like "Operation Peace," an ambitious scheme to aid dissident Europeans, remained mired in the talking stage. The conflict between ideals and reality exploded in a controversy over how to deal with trespassers picking the colonists' strawberries. As McCarthy's biographer Carol Gelderman notes, "The ensuing and interminable analysis about 'What To Do' parodied the typical EAG meeting," and a decision to use the threat of force (in the form of Joe Lockman's shotgun) to repel the interlopers sealed the project's failure. In the end, McCarthy's message was one of frustration: moral action, problematic enough on an individual level, remained an even more complex and elusive affair in the context of social relations.[88]

Reactions to *The Oasis* varied. Hannah Arendt called the work "a gem," but many in the New York intellectual community were upset that

McCarthy had made so public a caricature, especially in a British forum. No one was angrier than Philip Rahv, who even considered suing for the damage done to his reputation. Dwight Macdonald persuaded Rahv to drop the matter. "You realize, Phil," he wrote, "in order to win this lawsuit, you have to prove you are Will Taub. Are you prepared to make that kind of jackass out of yourself?" Macdonald and Chiaromonte found the book flawed but harmless. The former chided his Italian friend for McCarthy's reverential portrayal of "Monteverdi": "You of course are the Holy Ghost, hovering over the scene but exempt, by virtue of your sacred character, from either criticism or (alas) specific description."[89]

"New World Orders"

The search at *politics* for a vehicle to implement its vision of an international new left, founded on a synthesis of "cosmopolitan" values and "personal" activism, achieved mixed results in the period of flux after World War II. On the one hand, "Packages Abroad" represented, as Macdonald himself recognized, the journal's finest moment, a model of creative thinking and individual moral assertion whose ultimate value can never be fully calculated. On the other hand, "Europe-America Groups," an attempt to build an ideological position around the practical efforts at international fraternity established by Packages and similar initiatives, quickly aborted, and its collapse hastened Macdonald's exit from political engagement by the end of the decade. As with other expressions of the Resistance–"third camp" impulse of the late 1940s, a good part of the explanation for EAG's failure lies in the extraordinary pressures of the cold war in its acute, early stages. Some of the blame, however, resides in its own inherent limitations; EAG was a flawed blueprint for a postwar new left. Although it did offer a genuine alternative to the liberal anticommunist reading of the world situation, EAG's positive agenda, at least as set forth in its founding documents, was vague in the extreme. Its proposals for economic reform, for example, never went beyond passing reference to the need for "social equity." In addition, EAG's aversion to conventional politics was perhaps too absolute; and with its focus on communities of intellectuals, the specter of insular elitism threatened its promise from the start. Finally, given the *politics* circle's suspicions about anything they interpreted as "provincial," one wonders whether EAG's marriage of internationalism and localism would, in practice, have tilted heavily in favor of the former.

Even with its congenital deficiencies, however, EAG remains of lasting interest as an experiment in social reconstruction. It was, at bottom, an attempt to rescue the Enlightenment ideal of a universal culture, a commitment central to pre-1914 socialist thought that had resurfaced (at least rhetorically) in the Resistance movements of the Second World War. EAG should also be seen within the context of a more diffuse universalist zeitgeist peculiar to the 1940s, a sensibility that, as historian William Graebner has noted, reflected itself in such phenomena as Wendell Willkie's best-selling *One World,* the founding of the United Nations, and even Garry Davis's quixotic "world citizenship" campaign of 1948. Observers from all perspectives understood by the end of the war that the globe was shrinking at an accelerating rate, a process that would inevitably bring with it new forms of political and social integration. Camus was correct to point out in 1946 that the overriding question concerned the *kind* of world order that would develop in the face of this increasing interdependence. Would it be what he termed an "International Dictatorship," managed and administered from above by centralized superstates and other aggregations of power, legitimized only by their monopoly of the means of mass destruction? Or would it be an "International Democracy," a participatory order emerging from below, characterized by a peaceful, pluralistic associational life dedicated to the protection of human rights and the flowering of a cosmopolitan "sociable culture"—a *civilisation du dialogue?*[90]

EAG was designed to promote the latter alternative. It proceeded from two fundamental, related insights, established by the *politics* enterprise as a whole and reaffirmed by the success of the Packages project. First was the discovery of what Camus called "that thirst for fraternity which today burns in Western man," an instinctive human urge to reach out to others in friendship and solidarity in open disregard of the artificial constraints of nation, ideology, or bureaucracy. Second was the realization of the energies released when that urge found appropriate outlets. Something exciting and profound happened when individuals of different backgrounds and experiences managed to transcend "frontiers" to get to know each other in intimate, *personal* ways, forging reciprocal relationships "outside" the structures of hierarchy, "outside" politics, indeed, "outside" History. Such voluntary ties—epitomized, for example, in the bond between exile and host, or between Packages recipient and donor—were the essence of the Caffian conception of "free sociability"; they provided the setting for pure Camusian *dialogue.*

The EAG architects believed that the values of these ideal relations—equality, mutuality, friendship—could survive and flourish in a world torn by total war only if regular channels for their expression could be created. The long-term goal was an autonomous, international sphere of civil society, challenging and subverting existing regimes of rigid authority organically, from below. With a vital substratum of *pouvoirs secondaires,* linked by personal interactions and "persisting" through the vicissitudes of diplomatic crises and military confrontations, it would become increasingly difficult for governments to adhere to the dictates of "power, efficiency, and 'historical tasks' " without regard for the needs of the living human beings who bore the consequences of their decisions. As these networks multiplied, it would be harder to mobilize support for messianic crusades against demonized peoples, harder to accept the collective abstractions and one-dimensional stereotypes on which wars, hot and cold, sustained themselves.

The relevance of the cosmopolitan "personal" politics championed, in various forms, by Macdonald, Chiaromonte, Caffi, and Camus in the 1940s continues to the present. The idea that direct, intimate ties of cooperation and friendship, across frontiers and outside official channels, have a powerful resonance is the animating principle behind all manner of valuable initiatives, from Amnesty International and Havel's "Charter 77" to Physicians Without Borders and grassroots "sister cities" programs. In the 1980s, Hungarian "antipolitician" György Konrád reaffirmed "the special flavor of international friendship, the fascination of thinking along the same lines as someone who lives on the other side of the earth." Perhaps, as the cold war abates and new dangers and opportunities emerge in a multipolar world, it is time to look again to the possibilities of this kind of independent, self-constituted sphere of exchange. In that endeavor it will be important to draw on the lessons of projects like EAG, which, flawed and incomplete as they may have been, offered creative departures in the moment before the deep freeze first descended.[91]

■

EIGHT

The End of *politics*

On the world scale, politics is a desert without hope.
—DWIGHT MACDONALD, 1947

Exhaustion and Withdrawal, 1947–1949

If 1945 was the "vintage" year for *politics*, and if 1946 represented its excursion into the "rarefied atmosphere" of theoretical speculation, 1947–49 marked the journal's rapid decline. A confluence of factors—material, personal, and political—resulted in a visible loss of momentum as the enterprise limped into its fourth year. Always a shoestring operation, by the end of 1946 *politics* faced a "full-fledged financial crisis" that would not abate. Rising production costs forced the Macdonalds to appeal to readers for money and to cut back the magazine's publication schedule, first to a bimonthly and then to a quarterly basis. Although necessary to keep things going, this arrangement diminished the journal's ability to offer fresh, topical commentary, eroding the intimate sense of community that had always been its hallmark.[1]

The inner circle was also coming apart. Nicola Chiaromonte returned to Europe in early 1947, and by then the Macdonalds' marriage was beginning to deteriorate. Exacerbating these problems was a creeping despair in the face of the cold war, an evaporation of the faith in radical possibilities that had inspired the journal's founding in the first place. In a 1948 report to his readers, Dwight Macdonald frankly admitted why *politics* had not appeared on the newsstands for several months. It had been a "one-man magazine," he wrote, "and the man (myself) has of late been feeling stale, tired, disheartened, and—if you like—demoralized." This spiritual exhaustion, he explained, was a product of the relentless "psychological demands" of a little magazine, of his "growing sense of ignorance" and lack of time for reflection, and, not least, of "the ever blacker and bleaker political outlook."[2]

During this late period *politics* was not without moments of lasting significance. The magazine continued to promote fresh viewpoints: the special "French issue" of summer 1947, for example, gave many Americans their first exposure to the ideas of Camus, Sartre, and Beauvoir, among others. Its coverage also foreshadowed dominant political questions of the coming decades, like the crisis of the European imperial order. There were reports of postwar colonial unrest, especially in India and Indochina, and the December 1946 issue included a profile of revolutionary leader (and self-proclaimed democrat) Ho Chi Minh. On the domestic side, *politics* offered analysis of the official policies of surveillance and repression accompanying the onset of a new Red Scare. Macdonald flatly condemned Truman's 1947 "loyalty" purge of government employees as a "witch-hunt," a gross violation of individual rights that seemed one more step down the road to a native totalitarianism. The winter 1948 issue featured an exposé of J. Edgar Hoover's FBI, beneficiary of expanded powers and huge funding increases amid the climate of obsession with "national security." Clifton Bennett described the FBI as a "Gestapo in Knee-Pants," pointing to its Kafkaesque bureaucratic culture, its harassment of political "subversives" through wiretapping and illegal searches, and its "files bulging with anonymous gossip"—all under the arbitrary control of a publicity-hungry megalomaniac.[3]

Although at all times a staunch defender of civil liberties, during these years Macdonald escalated his own dual crusade against the "Soviet Myth" and the liberal fellow travelers ("Stalinoids") who continued to give it legitimacy. The spokesman for this group was Henry Wallace, former vice-president, editor of the *New Republic,* and in 1948, third-party presidential candidate. To many, Wallace represented the last hope for New Dealism, and his reform agenda was indeed admirably progressive, especially in the area of race relations. Foreign affairs was another matter. To Macdonald, Wallace was a naive, opportunistic demagogue, a provincial hack whose calls for cooperation with Stalin offered a dangerously fraudulent alternative to the cold war. Macdonald worked zealously to discredit Wallace, even engaging in a speaking tour of college campuses around New York and in the Midwest. His biographical treatment of Wallace, appearing in two installments in the 1947 *politics* (and also published as a book), skewered its subject as a cowardly neurotic, a man devoid of moral conviction or complexity. Not the least of Wallace's flaws, in Macdonald's view, was his weakness for uplifting rhetorical abstractions such as "Century of the Common Man," nostrums that lulled his followers into a state of sublime ignorance about geopolitical realities. "Wallese," Macdonald wrote, was the debased language of a dream world where "perpetual fogs, caused by the warm winds of the liberal Gulf Stream," came into contact with "the Soviet glacier."[4]

Macdonald devoted the spring 1948 issue of *politics* to stripping away any remaining illusions about the nature of that "glacier." In his mind, the Soviet Union under Stalin had become as closed and hostile a society as Hitler's Germany, "with the whole ghastly newsreel flickering through once more in a second showing." The special issue, which included testimony of "bottom-dog," ordinary citizens (mostly prisoners of war) and an extensive "layman's" reading list, focused in particular on the regimentation and politicization of culture then underway as part of the latest state purges. Macdonald decried the unprecedented ability of the Communist Central Committee to suppress dissent, to interfere "in the most intimate details of artistic creation," and to impose from above a mass culture of "high quantity, low quality."[5]

The irony of Macdonald's dogged crusade against Wallace is that it probably played into the hands of those committed to prosecuting the militarized cold war EAG opposed. In a political culture lacking viable left alternatives, with a rapidly shrinking space for criticism of official policies, the nuances of Macdonald's "third camp" position may well have been lost amid the passion of his anti-Stalinist rhetoric, leaving his readers with no place to turn. Robert Westbrook has made a similar point about Dewey, quoting Irving Howe on the challenges of being "an intelligent anti-communist" amid the hysteria of the late 1940s. Howe observed that such a position required "a very considerable degree of political sophistication," poise, and finesse, along with "the capacity for seeing two enemies at the same time"—a balancing act made even more difficult by the "historically unprecedented" dangers of totalitarianism. Macdonald disregarded the risks of his scorched-earth tactics under these conditions, and his words may therefore have produced some unintended consequences.[6]

The near-absolute oppression of the Soviet system highlighted for Macdonald the extent to which civil liberty and freedom of expression persisted in the United States, despite encroachments by the government and other guardians of moral and aesthetic standards. He applauded, for example, the controversial award of the 1948 Bollingen Prize to Ezra Pound as a healthy sign—"the brightest political act in a dark period"—because the prize committee had refused to consider the poet's "detestable" fascist past when evaluating the literary merits of his work. For Macdonald, this was a blow for genuine cultural freedom, a model of pluralism as opposed to totalitarian *Gleichschaltung*. He argued: "Such incomplete democracy as we of the West still possess depends on our continuing ability to make the kind of discrimination the Bollingen committee made, to evaluate each sphere of human activity separate from the rest instead of enslaving them all to one great reductive tyrant, whether it be The Church, The Proletariat, People's Democracy, The Master Race, or American Patriotism."[7]

In March 1949, Macdonald finally had a face-to-face confrontation with a commissar of "anti-culture." The occasion was the Waldorf Peace Conference in New York City, an ill-timed Soviet propaganda offensive organized in partnership with an array of prominent "Stalinoid" liberals. Macdonald and Mary McCarthy joined Sidney Hook's ad-hoc group, "Americans for Intellectual Freedom" (AIF), in a campaign to discredit attempts to portray the Eastern bloc as a haven of tolerance and diversity. At a dramatic session on contemporary Soviet writing, held before a packed house of eight hundred people, Macdonald rose to direct a series of embarrassing questions to A. A. Fadayev, secretary of the Union of Soviet Writers and Stalin's "No. 1 literary bureaucrat." Why were internationally distinguished authors like Boris Pasternak and Isaac Babel absent from the gathering? Were they dead, or perhaps imprisoned? After Fadayev's indignant and evasive response, Mary McCarthy took the floor to press critic F. O. Matthiessen on the veracity of his co-panelist's remarks. The session climaxed with Dimitri Shostakovich's nervous, formulaic replies to queries from Robert Lowell concerning his opinion of Soviet policies on music.[8]

Exchanges like these made the Waldorf Conference a public relations disaster for its sponsors. The AIF intellectuals had succeeded in their purpose, and Sidney Hook, for one, was eager to institutionalize the ideological warfare, cofounding the Congress for Cultural Freedom in Berlin the following year. Macdonald was less enthusiastic about continuing the crusade. He told his readers that the Waldorf affair, combined with Wallace's electoral debacle in 1948, convincingly demonstrated that communism had spent its force in American political life. In addition, he confessed that the "Stalinoids" he had encountered at the conference were, in general, not the automatized ideologues he had long imagined them to be. On the contrary, he found them open to reasoned debate, and he noted with surprise that they existed in a cultural-political milieu common to their anti-Stalinist adversaries. "We read the same books, went to the same art shows and foreign films, shared the same convictions in favor of the (American) underdog." In contrast, Macdonald felt little connection to the people who picketed outside the conference, provincial reactionaries who booed him "as roundly as any other delegate (since their hatred was directed against all alien-appearing intellectuals)." These comments seem to be Macdonald's tacit admission that he had gone overboard in his "red-baiting" campaigns against liberal fellow travelers. They also reveal his alienation from the "masses" and a growing sense that political engagement was futile. As the decade drew to a close, Macdonald was ready to give up that engagement to do battle in the more limited arena of cultural criticism.[9]

The intractability of the superpower military confrontation also tempered Macdonald's satisfaction at the Waldorf triumph. In his commentary on the Truman Doctrine in the May/June 1947 *politics,* he had written that the cold war presented "impossible alternatives," another clash of rival imperialisms (this time complete with an atomic arms race) from which even a victory of the "lesser evil" would produce only disaster. "On the world scale," Macdonald grimly concluded, "politics is a desert without hope," evidently "uncontrollable by man's will and consciousness." He reflected on the impasse:

> Superior insight into history used to be exhilarating for radicals; if we can see more clearly than the Enemy what is really going on, then we can use our knowledge to advance *our* values. But now the clearer one's insight, the more numbed one becomes. Thus during the war, some of us wrote articles in this magazine predicting that the conflict would *not* solve anything, . . . that the methods used by the Allies were infecting the moral atmosphere, that Russia and America would clash violently as soon as Germany was disposed of, etc., etc. Almost all the rest of the press, from liberal to conservative, was more optimistic. It turns out we were more right than they. This should make us feel prescient, confident. Instead, it is discouraging.

"As one brought up in the Progressive tradition," Macdonald admitted being shaken by the dearth of answers, the ever widening gulf between knowledge and effective action. He still held on to the possibility of working for change on a small, "personal" scale, where intentions and results were clearly linked, but prospects for the libertarian-socialist order he had once championed appeared more remote than ever.[10]

Macdonald's pessimism deepened with each new international crisis, culminating with the Soviet blockade of Berlin in the tense summer of 1948. Although he expressed admiration for the courage of the Berliners in the moment of danger, he saw their collective transmutation in the American press—from depraved totalitarians to heroic freedom fighters, only three years after the war—as ironic confirmation that the "responsibility of peoples" mythology was still alive and well. Berlin also dealt the fatal blow to Macdonald's pacifism. The last issue of *politics,* which appeared in the winter of 1949, featured a proposal by two former Oak Ridge engineers for unilateral American disarmament as a solution to the cycle of military escalation. A. J. Muste enthusiastically endorsed the plan; Sidney Hook dismissed it as naive. Macdonald, meanwhile, remained somewhere in the middle. He agreed with Hook's "realist" assessment, but was unwilling to condone a position that might lead to a nuclear war with Stalin. Neither violence nor nonviolence offered an exit from the "dilemma"; it posed the ultimate in "impossible alternatives."[11]

Macdonald's writings were often dark and cautionary, in striking contrast to the mood of affirmation prevailing, at least on the surface, in American discourse of the 1940s. Robert Westbrook has aptly termed this "rhetorical style" the "politics of fearful anticipation." By the end of the decade, however, it was difficult to discern where "anticipation" left off and description began. Consider, for example, Macdonald's evaluation of the political landscape in an article for the winter 1949 *Student Partisan,* an undergraduate publication at the University of Chicago:

> Man lives in history but is not at all comfortable there. Even at best—by which I mean in a smallish, integrated community like the ancient Greek city state—there is always a desperate struggle between what the individual wants and what happens to him as a result of living in society. . . . And at worst—by which I mean the big-scale, industrial-bureaucratic societies in which the peoples of USA, USSR, and most of Europe toss and twist—there is not even a struggle: the individual "citizen" (what a mockery!) has about the same chance of determining his own fate as a hog dangling by one foot from the conveyor belt of a Chicago packing plant.

Although quite powerful, this account also exaggerated the foreclosure of options, at least outside the world of the concentration camp. Looking back, we know that World War III was not inevitable, that the power of the state was never so complete, and that myriad forms of struggle, individual and collective, did continue, even in the grimmest days of the postwar period. Why then the unremitting despair, the loss of perspective? Why, by 1950, did Macdonald stage a "strategic retreat" from political criticism to what he called "social-cultural reportage"?[12]

Macdonald's reactions to the cold war can be understood as the reflection of his fundamentally *romantic* temperament, a characteristic of his generation of radical intellectuals. During the ideological wars of the 1930s and early 1940s, when the battle lines appeared to be sharply drawn, these writers learned to see the world in terms of conflicts between good and evil. Although more utopian than many of his peers, and therefore more resistant to "lesser-evil" choices, Macdonald nonetheless shared their dualistic vision. In a 1946 journal entry, Alfred Kazin noted his exasperation with Macdonald's dead-end *modus operandi.* "[Dwight] errs initially and almost fatally," Kazin wrote, "by setting himself the smallest amount of primary alternatives, usually in terms of the external organization of the state, and then, despondently finding them equally abhorrent, writes them all off." William Barrett admired how Macdonald tackled politics "with a passion and purity that were all his own," but he, too, was bothered by the impatience such an approach brought with it. Barrett observed: "[Macdonald] could never accept that political discourse must be plodding and prosaic, that politics itself deals with a middling region of reality where ultimate and sweeping generalizations were almost never possible. For him every venture into politics was a leap toward the Absolute."[13]

In a celebrated debate with Norman Mailer at Mount Holyoke College in 1952, Macdonald, weary of holding out for historically unavailable alternatives, finally announced his decision to "choose the West" in its struggle against the "perfect" evil of the Soviet Union. As Christopher Lasch has pointed out, Macdonald's decision was not only unenthusiastic but also "premature," based in large part on Hannah Arendt's overly static model of totalitarianism. Lasch argued that Macdonald's withdrawal from the political arena was the result of something deeper than an evaluation of the geopolitical situation. It also represented a reaction to the loss of excitement and drama inherent in a period of reduced choices and discredited ideologies, when an overwhelming inertia seemed to block any chances for dramatic positive change. This is the thrust of a revealing comment Macdonald made to Nicola Chiaromonte in the early 1950s, speculating about why his interest in the daily newspapers had declined: "Is this because I am 'escaping' from history? Or is it because history seems to have settled into a routine jog-trot in which repetition is the keynote? Like a ballet—one done by a rather unimaginative choreographer—in which each successive position can be foretold by the previous one. History seems to be 'marking time' and statesmen to be 'going through the motions.'" If not exactly "escaping from history," Macdonald *was* forfeiting the creative possibilities of a more actively engaged critical posture. As Lasch concluded, Macdonald's discussions of the problem of mass culture in the 1950s had less of an edge than his political writings of the previous decade, dealing as they did with "symptoms" rather than root causes. Whatever the motivation, Macdonald's decision to abandon politics stands as one more instance of the generational discontinuity that has plagued the American Left throughout the twentieth century.[14]

Macdonald considered a number of ideas to revitalize *politics* in the months before its final demise. At one point he hoped to transform his "one-man magazine" into a group effort, published under the direction of an editorial board that would include such confidants as Mary McCarthy, Hannah Arendt, and C. Wright Mills. In his correspondence with Chiaromonte, Macdonald also seriously entertained thoughts of moving to Paris to start a European *politics*. He felt an urgent need to remove himself, at least for a while, from the claustrophobia of New York, with its demanding pace and increasingly bitter factionalism. In an April 1949 letter to his Italian friend, Macdonald complained that he simply found himself "at the center of too many intersecting lines of force." "Never," he added, "have I been so plucked at, called up, written to, and generally asked to react or to act in one way or another by all kinds of people and groups. I've established so many personal links in NYC journalistic-intellectual-and upperclassbohemian circles by now that I'm a crossroads, a waiting-room, and can find almost no time to write & read."[15]

In the end, Macdonald's efforts to continue *politics* came to naught, and the journal's departure left a void in the radical community that could never really be filled. In the years that followed, Macdonald received countless requests to revive the magazine. He once observed that he was probably better known for *politics*, with its small but intensely devoted audience, than for his work with such mass-circulation periodicals as the *New Yorker*. Responses to Macdonald's downbeat letter to subscribers in November 1947, announcing the reduced production schedule and broaching the possibility of its indefinite suspension, provide some idea of the immediate and personal sense of loss felt by many readers. One person wrote: "Sorry you feel bad. We do, too. But we feel better when we read *politics* and find out that everybody else feels bad." Another letter sounded a similar theme:

> You say you are disheartened? What man of goodwill, what man who is both intelligent and sensitive is not disheartened these days? Our times are such that it is actually pleasant, almost exhilarating to find a person who's views are even gloomier than one's own. If for no other reason, *politics* should continue as the Journal of Gloom. . . . To us, the day when *politics* arrives is a good day. It acts like the opening of a window in a stuffy room.

Macdonald's impassioned voice of "negativism" would be missed. A third correspondent poignantly summarized the general feeling: "Your letter disturbed and saddened me," the reader began. "I've felt *involved* in the magazine as I never have done with any other. It was, to me, obviously more honest, unaffected and relevant to daily moral concerns than anything else being published."[16]

A Transatlantic Friendship, 1947–1972

Dwight Macdonald and Nicola Chiaromonte, whose partnership formed the core of *politics* magazine, maintained intimate ties throughout the quarter century after the latter's return to Europe. The two men, along with Mary McCarthy, enjoyed a kind of sibling relationship, periodically visiting one another in New York or Rome and sharing summer holidays at Bocca di Magra, a tiny fishing village on the Italian seacoast. In addition, they carried on a steady correspondence, disclosing personal information about love affairs and health problems, exchanging the latest literary gossip and debating the political questions of the day. Although this dialogue sometimes produced friction and hurt feelings, especially in the years just prior to Chiaromonte's death, the warmth and intensity of these friendships never waned.

Chiaromonte's initial reaction to the continent in the spring of 1947, following many years of exile, was positive. In his first letter to Macdonald after arriving in Rome, he reported: "As soon as I was in Europe, I felt the warmth of a sociability which in America you can feel only in a very restricted circle of friends." A few months later he wrote, in a similar vein: "Europe is in an awful state, and not very interesting intellectually either, but still Europe is a society, streets with trees, things odd and beautiful—while New York to me is a few scattered friends, a lot of concrete, and an incredible (from here) lack of quality in everything." Chiaromonte's personal situation remained unsettled, however. "Earning money here," he observed, "is a terrific problem if you don't belong to some political gang."[17]

By the end of the decade, the imperative to earn a living forced both men to submit, reluctantly, to "legitimate" jobs, Macdonald as a regular contributor to the *New Yorker* and Chiaromonte as a UNESCO official in Paris. Macdonald complained of the pressure to obey formulas in writing for a middlebrow audience, but he managed to retain a tolerable degree of independence in his new career. Chiaromonte was less fortunate, thoroughly demoralized by the "empty and absurd" routines of life in a large organization—"another example," he told his sympathetic friend, "of the superutilitarianism of our time, a form of fetishism or other hyperprimitive religion." Chiaromonte described in detail the bureaucratic wastefulness he encountered daily, glumly concluding: "So here I am, doing extremely little, but bound . . . to office hours, the language of idiots and stuffed shirts, feeling that every day I lose more hold on my own life and brains, etc." Chiaromonte's tenure at UNESCO was mercifully brief, and, in 1953, after a period of casting about, he returned to Rome with his wife Miriam to begin a fifteen-year stint as theater critic for the liberal weekly, *Il Mondo*.[18]

In the meantime, Chiaromonte had been able to resume his friendship with the aging Andrea Caffi, rescuing his mentor from the provincial isolation of southwest France, providing for his material needs (with the aid of carefully prepared packages from the Macdonalds) and, in general, trying to cheer up a man who felt "more and more lonely in the present world." "He doesn't want to confess it," Chiaromonte wrote to Macdonald, "but the few things of his that were published in Politics have helped his morale a lot." Caffi, in failing health, died in 1955. A decade later, the Chiaromontes preserved something of his legacy, editing a collection of his writings (mostly scattered correspondence) which, thanks to the efforts of Dwight Macdonald, eventually appeared in the United States under the title *A Critique of Violence*.[19]

Macdonald and Chiaromonte had only sporadic connection to political controversy during the cold war stasis of the 1950s. But even as he turned his energies toward the critique of "mass-cult" and "midcult" for which he is today best remembered, Macdonald always kept a close eye on world events. He gave qualified support to Truman's stand against Stalin in Korea, but continued to speak out against the injustices of the domestic Red Scare. In a letter to Chiaromonte, Macdonald worried that observers abroad were "coming to think of this country as a homogeneous mass of atom-bomb-makers and 'red-baiters' and dollar-imperialists." This emphasized for him the need for a reborn *politics,* or some similar vehicle, "to communicate directly, in a human voice, with European intellectuals; to express the considerable amount of disaffection . . . with official policies; and to show that the McCarthys and McCarrans don't by any means have it all their own way." In that spirit, Macdonald lobbied the American Committee for Cultural Freedom (an affiliate of the Congress for Cultural Freedom, the international anti-communist organization with which he was briefly involved) to issue a forthright repudiation of Senator McCarthy. In addition, he agreed in 1953 to serve as co-editor with Hannah Arendt, Richard Rovere, and Arthur Schlesinger Jr. (with Chiaromonte as European correspondent) on Mary McCarthy's proposed monthly *Critic,* a project that never got off the ground due to funding problems.[20]

Both Macdonald and Chiaromonte continued their indirect good-faith cooperation with the Congress for Cultural Freedom well into the next decade. In 1955–56, Chiaromonte and Ignazio Silone, with CCF financial backing, founded the monthly *Tempo Presente,* which quickly gained a reputation as one of the leading independent journals of opinion on the Italian scene. In 1956–57, Macdonald spent a "pleasurable" year in London as co-editor of *Encounter,* another CCF-sponsored publication. Upon returning to the United States, he wrote an essay that, as a rare departure from the affirmation of American life then in vogue, became the subject of a minor *cause célèbre* in intellectual circles. In "America! America!" Macdonald condemned the disturbing "shapeless-ness" and violence he saw in his native culture, describing his country-men as a profoundly "unhappy people," coarse provincials who, for all their material advantages, lacked the basic attributes of sociability—the sense of style, tradition, and community—common to the most humble of their European brethren. When, after much temporizing, the *Encounter* editors declined the piece for fear of offending the American "foundations" that underwrote them, Macdonald made the affair public, dismissing it at the time as a puzzling lapse of independent judgment. Several years later a fuller, more sinister explanation for the decision would emerge.[21]

With the resurgence of left-wing activism in the 1960s, Macdonald began gradually to regain his appetite for political combat. He presented a speech, "The Relevance of Anarchism," to the first national convention of the fledgling Students for a Democratic Society in New York in June 1960. The following year, while on another sabbatical in Britain, he participated in the Aldermaston peace march, and though encouraged by this symbolic, nonviolent display of resistance to state authority, he complained to both Chiaromonte and Mary McCarthy that the atmosphere was altogether too bohemian and sedate. Sounding like Orwell in *The Road to Wigan Pier,* dismissing the "sandal-wearers and bearded fruit-juice drinkers" of the socialist camp, Macdonald confessed to McCarthy: "I could have done with a leeetle more passion even if it had resulted in incidents I should have deplored; something wrong about such a VEGETARIAN mob."[22]

Macdonald's January 1963 *New Yorker* review of Michael Harrington's *The Other America* was to be, by the author's own estimate, the "most effective political article" of his career. It exposed the persistence of poverty in the midst of the "affluent society," exerting a direct influence on policymakers at the highest levels of the Kennedy administration. Macdonald's voice, like bestseller Mary McCarthy's, was now gaining respectful attention from media and government power-brokers, a situation that made him uneasy. Was success eroding his radical edge? In an October 1963 letter to Chiaromonte, Macdonald used picturesque imagery to convey his plight. "I feel like an old Indian fighter," he wrote, "who is now sneered at as a panty-waist and has-been by the tough cookies of the new frontier," even while being showered with honors from those he once considered "savages." How could he maintain his critical distance, he asked his friend, "when the tribes are so *friendly?*"[23]

At about the same time, an old issue from World War II—the question of responsibility for the Holocaust—suddenly resurfaced with the publication of Hannah Arendt's *Eichmann in Jerusalem.* Macdonald, McCarthy, and Chiaromonte all mobilized around their longtime friend in the face of a storm of criticism against the book, initiated by Lionel Abel in *Partisan Review* and aimed at her conclusions about the complicity of the Jewish Councils in the success of Hitler's project. For Arendt's defenders, these violent attacks distorted her views and smacked of a Stalinist-McCarthyite inquisition against heretical thinking. Macdonald carried the argument a step further in a letter to *PR*, deploring the anti-*Eichmann* campaign as an example of the chauvinist essentialism now practiced by the "Jewish Establishment," an effort to exempt Jews from criticism that he found offensive to the cosmopolitan-universalist standards the New York Intellectuals had stood for since the 1930s. Chiaromonte agreed with his friend's assessment. He wrote Macdonald: "I also dislike the Official Jewry's fuss about the book. What's the matter with them? Is Hannah a new Spinoza? Were the Jewish Councils holy institutions? Is Israel a 'chosen' State?"[24]

What finally pulled Macdonald—the "old Indian fighter"—back into the center of the political arena was his outrage at the escalation of the Vietnam War in early 1965. Taking perverse advantage of his newfound respectability, Macdonald chose an unusual venue for one of his first public protests, accepting an invitation to President Johnson's "Festival of the Arts" that June. Once on the grounds of the White House, Macdonald did his best to disrupt the proceedings, conspicuously circulating an antiwar petition right under the noses of his hosts. Although Chiaromonte registered misgivings about Macdonald's decision to attend the Festival, he was pleased with the spirit of the action. "It feels like old times," he wrote, "and very much like old Dwight indeed. . . . [Y]ou gave an important contribution to rendering undignified a ceremony that was vulgar to start with." In the months and years that followed, Macdonald became increasingly visible as an "elder statesman" to the antiwar movement, making speeches, counseling draft resistance, and participating in demonstrations such as the 1967 March on the Pentagon.[25]

From their public statements and private correspondence, it is clear that Macdonald, McCarthy, and Chiaromonte agreed from the beginning about the egregious folly of the Vietnam enterprise. Resurrecting themes from the 1940s, they saw the war, in essence, as a victory of force over limit, an exercise of imperial hubris, an example of bureaucratic-technological rationality run wild. For Macdonald it was an agonizing replay of the worst of World War II. Once again the morning paper arrived with accounts of bombs raining down on defenseless civilians, while most Americans, insulated from the horror, went about their normal activities without noticeable concern. In the July 1967 installment of his regular political column for *Esquire*, Macdonald described the "unconscious" automatism of his country's war apparatus in language that could easily have been written twenty-five years earlier. "[O]ur intervention in Vietnam," he charged, "has ceased to be intelligible. It has become a mindless, impersonal process that keeps grinding on at an accelerating tempo like a machine out of control, a blind extension of mass-industrial civilization into the life of a people who can only be damaged and corrupted by it."[26]

Chiaromonte felt a similar revulsion. In the early months of the war he told Macdonald: "There is something quite specially nauseating about American brutality. Not only because it is accompanied by so much double talk about democracy liberty and peace, but because it is so naked, so crude, so much a kind of end in itself, a sport, a technical affair." Of the war's architects, he added: "POWER POWER POWER. Don't they even suspect that power can be *spent* much more quickly and badly than money?" This was certainly the case when Americans placed their resources at the disposal of "the various Kys, the various Juntas and the various bemedalled rascals around the world." Chiaromonte warned of a coming day of "retribution," culmination of "the corruption, brutality, coarseness, that sets in the very moment power is used for the sake of itself." In the meantime, however, Europeans continued to look upon the super-charged technocratic style that America represented with a mixture of fear and envy. "The 'future' seems to lie in that direction," Chiaromonte bitterly concluded to his friend, "and everybody worships The Future, today, as you well know."[27]

Despite their shared interpretation of the Vietnam catastrophe, relations between Macdonald and Chiaromonte underwent severe strains in the late 1960s, a result of their different reactions to a scandal involving the Congress for Cultural Freedom and to the rise of the worldwide student insurgency. In 1966, the radical journal *Ramparts* issued the bombshell disclosure that the CCF had, from its inception, received secret subsidies from the American CIA. Although the true source of the money was known only to a handful of the organization's insiders, all of its activities now appeared more or less tainted. For Macdonald, the news explained *Encounter*'s curious rejection of his "un-American raspberry" of the previous decade, and, as a former guest editor of that journal, he was appalled at having been "played for a sucker" in the corrupt game of cold war geopolitics. Because his role as an "unwitting accomplice of the CIA's dirty work" was relatively minor, however, Macdonald's anger was based more on principle than any lasting sense of personal injury.[28]

For Chiaromonte the situation was more complex, and the damage caused by the revelations went much deeper. Suddenly a cloud hung over years of devotion to *Tempo Presente,* despite his innocence of the CIA-CCF connection and his efforts to defend the journal's independence (he had not hesitated, for example, to publish Macdonald's "America! America!"). The blow to his reputation for integrity left wounds that would never fully heal. Chiaromonte protested to Macdonald that he had never felt outside pressure over editorial decisions at *TP,* and that the existence of laundered funds was a "false issue" except with regard to those few who had explicit knowledge. He resented the "loftly moralizing" surrounding the scandal—in his mind, part of a New Left attitude of being "holier than you rabid anti-communists"—and he was particularly stung when he saw Macdonald's signature on a *Partisan Review* statement declaring a "lack [of] confidence" in the magazines supported by the Congress. Macdonald apologized for lending his name to the blanket condemnation, but the "poisons" of the affair would linger on. In a 1969 letter to McCarthy, he wondered whether recent events had taken a toll on Chiaromonte's work. "It may be," Macdonald confided, "that he's been deeply scarred or crippled, poor man, by the CIA experience and that whatever he writes or thinks is in some way a *justification* of it, over and over."[29]

Macdonald and Chiaromonte also disagreed sharply about the meaning of the youth rebellion of the 1960s. Macdonald had been impressed by the idealism of the civil rights and student movements in their early stages, and in many ways they fulfilled the vision of individual and small-group activism he had outlined in the final sections of "The Root Is Man" in 1946. He was troubled from the start, however, by the anti-intellectual dimensions of New Left thinking, and as the political temperature rose he worried that centrifugal forces might soon destroy the movement's promising beginnings. Macdonald had no patience for radicals who preached a gospel of violent revolution inspired by Ho, Mao, or Che Guevara; nor did he condone the separatism espoused by "Black Power hotheads." In a speech at the famous "countercommencement" at Columbia University in the spring of 1968, Macdonald offered his audience a prophetic warning about the dangers of their aggressively confrontational tactics. "I'm for . . . a (social) revolution," he said, "but I don't think it is a historical possibility in the foreseeable future in this country, and premature efforts to force it will merely damage or destroy such positive, progressive institutions as we have. Their only effect—if any—will be to stimulate a counterrevolution which will have far more chances of success."[30]

Still, there was much to admire in the young people Macdonald encountered in his antiwar activities. In 1968 he worked to raise funds for the New York branch of SDS; and following several personal visits, he pronounced the Columbia student strike a "beneficial disturbance." "I've never been in or even near a revolution before," Macdonald wrote. "I guess I like them. There was an atmosphere of exhilaration, excitement—pleasant, friendly, almost joyous excitement." He was especially cheered by the capacity for orderly, democratic self-government displayed by the students in their ad-hoc communes—islands of civility in year of escalating violence.[31]

Chiaromonte was less enamored of the student uprisings he saw occurring simultaneously in Rome and other European cities, and he was
critical of his American friend's relative enthusiasm for the New Left.
Although he sympathized with the younger generation's desire to reject
a bankrupt social order, Chiaromonte felt that their revolt had taken
mindless, "sterile," even authoritarian forms, merely reproducing the
nihilism of their elders. Once again it was a question of limits. Chiaromonte compared the ferment in Eastern Europe, which he admired, to
the messianic fevers of the West. "The freedom the Polish students are
demanding is a clear, specific challenge to a clearly and specifically
oppressive regime," he wrote, "whereas the 'global confrontation' the
Italian and German students are talking about is a formula as vague as
it is violent." In the end, Chiaromonte concluded that the "total rejection" demanded by youthful extremists amounted to "rebellion against
everything and against nothing." He could never understand Macdonald's attraction, however qualified, to a movement so clearly doomed to
futility. Chiaromonte's alternative to the shallow slogans and instant
gratification of the New Left echoed the teachings of his mentor, Caffi:

> If there is a remedy at all, it lies elsewhere and is a very long-term
> one. . . . [I]t consists of a determined secession from a society (or
> rather, from a state of affairs, since "society" implies a community and
> a purpose, which is exactly what collective life nowadays lacks) that is
> . . . deadening. People must detach themselves, must become resolute
> "heretics" . . . without shouting or riots, indeed, in silence and secrecy;
> not alone but in groups, in real "societies" that will create, as far as is
> possible, a life that is independent and wise, not utopian or phalan-
> sterian, in which each man learns to govern himself first of all and to
> behave rightly toward others, and works at his own job according to
> the standards of the craft itself, standards that in themselves are the
> simplest and strictest of moral principles and, by their very nature, cut
> out deception and prevarication, charlatanism and the love of power
> and possession.[32]

Chiaromonte's antipathy to the New Left was part of a more general
sense of pessimism and alienation he experienced in his last years. In a
July 1969 letter to Mary McCarthy, he concluded that true socialism was
possible "only in a very aristocratic society," adding: "Modern man, as
they call him, just does not give a damn for democracy, liberty, or
anything that is not crudely material and stupidly mythical at the same
time (like space travel . . .)." McCarthy shared the letter with Macdonald, who found it "a puzzling exposition."

> So much I agree with, as always in the time I've known Nick—the
> rejection of progress, democracy, marxism, socialism and communism

(as these terms are perverted by the left pietists), the refusal to be bullied in the name of "the masses," the insistence on social justice as a precondition of a new order, etc. But there's that vagueness about What Is To Be Done now, concretely . . . and also flashes of a disturbing, to me, kind of anti-popular elitism. I'm for elitism in culture but not in politics. In that sphere I'm with Nick's M. Proudhon: people know better what their interests are . . . [and] have more common sense and decency . . . than their "leaders." I do believe in people — Rousseau was more right than Hobbes — and I think Nick maybe doesn't any more.[33]

Macdonald's reading notwithstanding, Chiaromonte never completely abandoned faith in the possibilities of democratic renewal — a renewal in which his wartime refuge, for all its flaws, might still play a crucial role. In his 1970 *L'Espresso* review of *Controamerica*, the Italian translation of Macdonald's collection *Against the American Grain*, Chiaromonte paid tribute to his friend as an exemplary "free intellect," an "old-style American, a rampaging and fanciful individualist, intolerant of 'esprit de systeme,' nonconformist by temperament and training even before he became one by moral and ideological choice." For Chiaromonte, this critical spirit was a reflection of the fact that "no ready-made ideology could account for the American situation," and Macdonald's work was inextricably bound up with the struggle over his nation's future direction:

> For Macdonald it is a question today of finding the fundaments of that new culture and civilization which was and remains one of the great "promises" of America. In political terms, it is the matter of finding the bases for a new democracy. Which is not possible if it does not succeed in giving to American giganticism, and to the massification that derives from this giganticism, a humanly accessible and controllable measure. The protest against the Vietnam war, the struggle for racial equality, the revolt of the young either have this meaning and will manage to proceed to this goal, or are agitations designed to end in a further reinforcement of mass conformism.[34]

Despite the sometimes bitter arguments of the final period of their friendship, Macdonald and Chiaromonte never lost their sense of devotion to each other. In his last letter to Macdonald, on 5 January 1972, Chiaromonte offered these reassurances: "It is true that I do not hold the smallest brief for the New Left, or, for that matter, for the left in general. But what has that got to do with you and me? We have always had differences, and felt the more friendly toward each other for that." He added, in a teasing spirit, "You have not become a Weatherman, or something, have you? And even if you had, I would consider that just like Dwight . . . going to the farthest end."[35]

Less than two weeks later, Chiaromonte, age sixty-seven, dropped dead of a heart attack in an elevator of the Italian Radio Building in Rome, just after participating in a broadcast discussion of J. F. Revel's *Without Marx or Jesus*. In the following weeks messages of condolence poured in from individuals of various countries, and tributes to Chiaromonte appeared in all quarters of the Italian press, including even the Communist papers. Mary McCarthy found it striking—and appropriate—that of all the memorials, "scarcely a one had an official or conventional ring." For Dwight Macdonald, the loss of his friend of nearly three decades was devastating. As soon as he heard the news he wrote to Chiaromonte's widow, Miriam: "It's the most *depriving* death in my life since my father died—also suddenly, of a heart attack—in 1926." In addition to revealing the mentor-disciple dynamic of their relationship, Macdonald's words show that he and Chiaromonte enjoyed a true friendship in the classical sense, a bond forged not only in mutual admiration but in a common desire to advance shared moral commitments. Their friendship was a microcosm of the social ideals espoused by *politics* in the 1940s, its vision of a culture in which individuals could transcend boundaries of nation, ideology, and even temperament to create intimate bonds of human affection and solidarity. Macdonald explained:

> Ever since we met in 1944, he's been my best friend, the one person— despite recent political-cultural disagreements, w. were so painful to us both—I felt closest to, morally and intellectually, also personally. The one person, except my poor dear father, that gave me the feeling of being valued for myself, individually, not for my brains (though also for them too) or achievements, just for myself—a personal love and respect—as I felt for him too but it was not quite an equal relationship, emotionally—I now think—more like a father to a son, despite our almost equal ages.[36]

Conclusion:
The Post–Cold War
Legacy of *politics*

> Does not the perspective of a better future depend on some-
> thing like an international community of the shaken which,
> ignoring state boundaries, political systems, and power blocs,
> standing outside the high game of traditional politics, aspiring
> to no titles and appointments, will seek to make a real political
> force out of a phenomenon so ridiculed by the technicians of
> power—the phenomenon of human conscience?
>
> —Václav Havel, 1984

In 1946 young Daniel Bell, frustrated by the lack of immediate prospects
for political change in the wake of the Second World War, wrote to his
friend Dwight Macdonald about the responsibilities of the radical intellectual in the period ahead. Bell observed: "At this stage, since the future
is committed, the only constructive role we can play is that of critics,
since the men of action can only choose alternative paths within the
dominant framework. . . . [O]ur role as critics should be such so that
when some meaningful choices are possible say in fifty years, people shall
have a truly relevant body of materials to draw upon." I have attempted
to show that the work of Macdonald and his collaborators in the middle
and late 1940s is indeed a "relevant body of materials" for later generations, and that its importance goes beyond the value of its criticism.
Macdonald was undoubtedly at his best as an internal gadfly of the
Left—"tougher on himself and his own side," as he once wrote of
Orwell, than on opponents further afield—but his *politics* became more
than an organ of "negativism," more than simply a "Journal of Gloom."
Its American and European contributors articulated the outlines of a
decentered, pluralistic politics of "limits" that contrasted sharply with
the statist alternatives commonly associated with the postwar years,

demonstrating, for a time at least, that the death of Marxism and the "end of ideology" did not inevitably lead to the "vital center" of cold war liberalism.[1]

In his review of the 1953 edition of *The Root Is Man*, Czeslaw Milosz tried to explain why what he called "Macdonaldism" had relevance for the peoples of Eastern Europe and for anyone imprisoned, for the foreseeable future, in oppressive circumstances. "They are surely able to appreciate his betting on slow processes in the human mass," Milosz wrote, "and his belief that one man counts or, if we are lucky, three or four men, linked by friendship. Macdonald seems to pin his hopes on the fermentation concealed beneath the surface, which is not automatic, and to which everyone can contribute." Milosz concluded: "There is something in this anticipation of new movements, now that the forms of action that existed up till the present seem . . . to be leading to miserable outcomes."[2]

The "new movements" Macdonald and his friends sought to nurture did not develop in the years just after World War II, and there is no little irony in the fact that the writers for *politics* finally succumbed to an "oasis psychology" close to the Koestlerian version condemned so vigorously in the debut issue of the magazine. In addition, the ideas presented by Macdonald, Chiaromonte, Weil, Caffi, and Camus were by no means fully developed or entirely consistent. Individual autonomy, dialogue, "free sociability"—however attractive these might be as ethical first principles, they provide little guidance in the practical problems of organization and conflict-resolution endemic to any social order, however radically restructured. The experience of postcommunist Eastern Europe in the 1990s supports the argument that the Caffian notion of "thinking outside politics" serves best as a strategy of opposition. Václav Havel has noted that the power-mongering, dissension, xenophobia, and greed corrupting public life in his country during the first years of his presidency reaffirm that, in practice, "the way of truly moral politics is not simple, or easy."[3]

Still, half a century later, as cold war polarities break down and new sets of "meaningful choices" present themselves, it is my belief that the insights of Macdonald's circle, however fragmentary or flawed, merit a second look. The problems these writers struggled against remain with us in our own moment of crisis and opportunity: the "anti-human dynamics" of high technology and bureaucratic organization, the dangerous centralization of economic and political power, and, perhaps most fundamentally, the fear and estrangement people feel among themselves, whether caught within the machinery of armed national conflicts or merely facing each other on the streets of a crowded modern city. Too often, as Havel observes, people continue to "shrug off anything that goes beyond their everyday, routine concern for their own livelihood; they seek ways of escape; they succumb to apathy, to indifference toward suprapersonal values and their fellow men, to spiritual passivity and depression." As we ponder the reconstruction that must come soon if we are to surmount our current dilemmas, the yellowed pages of *politics*, crucible for the "First New Left," might prove a timely and inspirational resource.[4]

Today we face anew the question of the 1940s: in an ever-shrinking world, what *kind* of international society do we want? Some have predictably cast their lot with a "new world order" administered by massive state and corporate mechanisms, governed by the ancient laws of force and power politics, disguised and justified by paeans to abstractions like "democracy" and "free markets." In such an order, the "masses" around the globe are consigned to sitting before their television sets, consuming the stream of images and definitions of reality transmitted around-the-clock by CNN and other megamedia. This top-down arrangement is necessary, we are urged to believe, as the only possible check on descent into chaos and bloody tribalism.

A truly "radical" alternative to this state of affairs will not materialize overnight, but we can sow the seeds for its development by encouraging the proliferation of informal, transnational lines of dialogue and friendship, "outside" traditional structures of authority. Macdonald's insights in this regard have lost none of their relevance. "We are all human beings—as seditious, treasonable, and politically explosive a proposition as can be put forward today," he wrote in 1945. "The effort of those who want to bring about a more humanly tolerable society must be to unite with their brothers across frontiers and battle lines." Or, as Hungarian dissident György Konrád put it in 1982, "the thinking ones are frontier violators, the censors are the border guards. Our intellectual weight is in direct proportion to the number of border violations we commit."[5]

Although there should be agreement about certain rudimentary values, as the *politics* experiments show, these networks may be founded on an infinite variety of interests and objectives, political and "pre-political." They may involve efforts at group living or merely be "psychological communities." The animating principle of this grassroots renaissance is the Proudhonian imperative, "multiply your associations and be free." New communication forms can be valuable in the flowering of this "global civil society." But, in the spirit of Macdonald and his associates, we must approach the claims of postmodern cyber-utopians with utmost caution, and work to ensure that the "information superhighways" of the future do not become the exclusive province of an oppressive technocratic elite.[6]

By tapping into the vast, latent reservoirs of good will that still exist throughout human society, by providing a wide array of outlets for the universal "thirst for fraternity" that too often goes unsatisfied, a genuinely democratic, "sociable" subculture might in time be able to interrupt once and for all the "monstrous inertia" of "History with a capital 'H.' " When that happens, as Camus wrote, ours will "cease to be a world of policemen, of soldiers and of money, and become a world for man and woman, of fruitful work and reflective leisure."

Notes

Introduction

1. Carol Gelderman, *Mary McCarthy: A Life*, 118–23, 120.

2. Dwight Macdonald, cover editorial for *politics* 2 (August 1945): 225.

3. Daniel Bell, "The Mood of Three Generations," reprinted in Bell, *The End of Ideology: On the Exhaustion of Political Ideas in the Fifties*, 299–314, 307. In a preface to a later reprinting of his work from *politics*, Macdonald wrote: "The one claim I would make for these essays is that, in the pursuit of 'the concrete contemplation of the complete facts,' I have strayed across a good deal of rather rough country" (*The Root Is Man*, v).

4. See Staughton Lynd, "Marxism-Leninism and the Language of *politics* Magazine: The First New Left . . . and the Third," in G. A. White, ed., *Simone Weil: Interpretations of a Life*, 111–35, and Noam Chomsky, "The Responsibility of Intellectuals," reprinted in Chomsky, *American Power and the New Mandarins: Historical and Political Essays*, 323–66. For an example of the standard treatment of Macdonald and *politics*, see Richard Pells, *The Liberal Mind in a Conservative Age: American Intellectuals in the 1940s and 1950s*, 174–82. See also the reactions to Macdonald's 1957 volume *Memoirs of a Revolutionist*, discussed in Michael Wreszin, *A Rebel in Defense of Tradition: The Life and Politics of Dwight Macdonald*, 334–40.

5. James D. Wilkinson, *The Intellectual Resistance in Europe*; Lynd, "Marxism-Leninism and the Language of *politics* Magazine"; and Jeffrey C. Isaac, "Arendt, Camus, and Postmodern Politics," *Praxis International* 9 (April/June 1989): 48–71, and "Why Postmodernism Still Matters," *Tikkun* 4 (July/August 1989): 118–22. See also Isaac's *Arendt, Camus, and Modern Rebellion*.

6. Carol Gelderman, ed., *Conversations with Mary McCarthy*, 15–16.

One. Preface to *politics*

1. Czeslaw Milosz, "Dwight Macdonald," reprinted in Milosz, *Beginning with My Streets: Essays and Recollections;* Norman Mailer, introduction to Dwight Macdonald, *Discriminations: Essays & Afterthoughts,* viii.

2. The starting point for any consideration of Macdonald's life and career is his own autobiographical essay, "London, 1957," reprinted as the introduction to his collection *Politics Past: Essays in Political Criticism,* 3–31. Also invaluable is Michael Wreszin's *Rebel in Defense of Tradition.* For a detailed study of his early life, see Robert Cummings, "The Education of Dwight Macdonald, 1906–1928" (Ph.D. diss., Stanford University, 1988). Stephen Whitfield's *Critical American: The Politics of Dwight Macdonald* is a useful overview.

3. Cummings, "Education of Dwight Macdonald," 1–12.

4. Ibid., 28. Cummings describes Macdonald's "characteristic bifurcation of social and cultural reality into an enclave-oasis of the likeminded and elevated, a realm of harmonious communication and fecund creativity, and another world, variously described, whose central features were defined by the absence of those qualities ascribed to the oasis" (118).

5. D. Macdonald, *Politics Past,* 7–8.

6. Ibid., 8.

7. Wreszin, *Rebel in Defense of Tradition,* 136; Nancy Macdonald, *Homage to the Spanish Exiles: Voices from the Spanish Civil War,* 17, 29.

8. N. Macdonald, *Homage,* 29–33; D. Macdonald, *Politics Past,* 10.

9. D. Macdonald, *Politics Past,* 6–7, 10, 17; Neil Jumonville, *Critical Crossings: The New York Intellectuals in Postwar America,* 38.

10. D. Macdonald, *Politics Past,* 8–9, 31; Wreszin, *Rebel in Defense of Tradition,* 48.

11. D. Macdonald, *Politics Past,* 11–12. In addition to Jumonville and a host of recent autobiographies, the best studies of the New York Intellectuals are James B. Gilbert, *Writers and Partisans: A History of Literary Radicalism in the United States;* Terry A. Cooney, *The Rise of the New York Intellectuals: "Partisan Review" and Its Circle;* and Alan M. Wald, *The New York Intellectuals: The Rise and Decline of the Anti-Stalinist Left from the 1930s to the 1980s.* See also Richard Pells, *Radical Visions and American Dreams: Culture and Social Thought in the Depression Years,* esp. 330–64.

12. Jumonville, *Critical Crossings,* 36–37; William Barrett, *The Truants: Adventures Among the Intellectuals,* 17.

13. Alfred Kazin, *Starting Out in the Thirties,* 136–37. Representative of Macdonald's analysis of Stalinist culture is his 1942 *PR* essay, "The Eisenstein Tragedy," reprinted in D. Macdonald, *Politics Past,* 229–35. For Macdonald's attack on the American cultural nationalism of the late 1930s, see his 1941 essay *"Kulturbolshewismus* & Mr. Van Wyck Brooks," also reprinted in *Politics Past,* 203–14. On Macdonald, Clement Greenberg, and the early "mass culture" debate, see Diana Trilling, "Interview with Dwight Macdonald," *Partisan Review: The 50th Anniversary Edition,* ed. William Phillips, 319.

14. Jumonville, *Critical Crossings,* 1–16; Cooney, *Rise of the New York Intellectuals,* 5–7, 57–60, 264–69; David A. Hollinger, "Ethnic Diversity, Cosmopolitanism, and the Emergence of the American Liberal Intelligentsia," reprinted in Hollinger, *In the American Province: Studies in the History and Historiography of Ideas,* 56–73. Thomas Bender describes cosmopolitanism as the defining feature of New York culture in his *New York Intellect: A History of Intellectual Life in New York City, from 1750 to the Beginnings of Our Own Time.*

15. Cooney, *Rise of the New York Intellectuals,* 59–60.

16. Ibid., 126–32, 181; D. Macdonald, *Politics Past,* 10–11, 17–22; Sidney Hook, *Out of Step,* 516–18; George Scialabba, "The Lady and the Luftmensch," *Dissent* 41 (Spring 1994): 287. Macdonald was a member of the famous Committee for the Defense of Leon Trotsky, headed by John Dewey. For more on Macdonald's brief but important formal

affiliation with the Trotskyists (1939–41), see Peter Drucker, *Max Schachtman and His Left: A Socialist's Odyssey Through the "American Century,"* 121–26. Diana Trilling recalls a New Year's Eve fundraising party at the Macdonalds' apartment, decorated with a large picture of Trotsky with an axe through his skull in the wake of his assassination. Diana Trilling, *The Beginning of the Journey: The Marriage of Diana and Lionel Trilling,* 303.

17. See S. A. Longstaff, *"Partisan Review* and the Second World War," *Salmagundi* 43 (Winter 1979): 108–29; Cooney, *Rise of the New York Intellectuals,* 167–95; Dwight Macdonald, "War and the Intellectuals, Act Two," *Partisan Review* 6 (Spring 1939): 15, 8.

18. Longstaff, *"Partisan Review* and the Second World War," 117–21, 120; Cooney, *Rise of the New York Intellectuals,* 186–88.

19. Longstaff, *"Partisan Review* and the Second World War," 121–24; Cooney, *Rise of the New York Intellectuals,* 188–91, 191; N. Macdonald, *Homage,* 61–62. The *PR* split was not without acrimony. Nancy Macdonald remembered that Philip Rahv surrendered access to the journal's contributors list only after some verbal sparring in his office. See *Homage,* 62. The initial capital for *politics* consisted of Dwight Macdonald's savings and stocks from his *Fortune* years, Nancy Macdonald's small inheritance, and a donation from Margaret de Silver, widow of Carlo Tresca. D. Macdonald to Philip Young, 27 May 1947, Macdonald Papers.

20. Dwight Macdonald, 1943 draft prospectus for magazine project, Box 152, Folder 1, Macdonald Papers.

21. Mills to Macdonald, 10 October 1943, Box 34, Folder 855, Macdonald Papers; Goodman to Macdonald, [1943], Box 19, Folder 477, Macdonald Papers; Coser to Macdonald, 20 August 1943, Box 12, Folder 288, Macdonald Papers; Dwight Macdonald, "Why *politics?*" *politics* 1 (February 1944): 6–8, 6. Other names considered for the new journal included "Babylon," "Gulliver," and "Left." Mills advised against "cute" titles which might be seen as "frivolous or 'literary' in the bad sense. People play with them: ('Gulliver' equals gullible, 'Left' equals left-out—left over)" (Mills to Macdonald, 25 October 1943, Box 34, Folder 855, Macdonald Papers).

22. Dwight Macdonald, "Koestler: Some Political Remarks," *politics* 1 (February 1944): 5.

23. Hannah Arendt, "He's All Dwight," *New York Review of Books,* 1 August 1968, 31–33.

24. See Macdonald's notes for a 1968 *politics* reissue, Box 74, Folder 93, Macdonald Papers, and D. Macdonald, "Why *politics?*" 6.

25. Cooney, *Rise of the New York Intellectuals,* 3.

26. On Lionel Abel's career, see his *Intellectual Follies: A Memoir of the Literary Venture in New York and Paris.* On McCarthy, see Carol Gelderman, *Mary McCarthy,* and Carol Brightman, *Writing Dangerously: Mary McCarthy and Her World.* McCarthy's reminiscence is from a 1962 interview with Elisabeth Niebuhr, reprinted in Carol Gelderman, ed., *Conversations with Mary McCarthy,* 3–29, 12–13. See also Mary McCarthy, "My Confession," in her book *On the Contrary,* 75–105. For a decidedly negative portrait of McCarthy during the *PR* years, describing her "wholly destructive critical mind," see Kazin, *Starting Out in the Thirties,* 154–56. Among the other young contributors to *politics* who went on to larger prominence was Irving Kristol, the young historian Kenneth Stampp (then a University of Maryland colleague of C. Wright Mills), and Canadian writer Marshall McLuhan. See Kristol, "Koestler: A Note on Confusion," *politics* 1 (May 1944): 108–9; Stampp, "Our Historians and Slavery," *politics* 1 (March 1944): 58–59; and McLuhan, "Out of the Castle and into the Counting-House," *politics* 3 (September 1946): 277–79.

27. See Howard Brick, *Daniel Bell and the Decline of Intellectual Radicalism: Social Theory and Political Reconciliation in the 1940s,* esp. 91–93; Daniel Bell, "The Coming

Tragedy of American Labor," *politics* 1 (March 1944): 37–42, and "The World of Moloch," *politics* 1 (May 1944): 111–13. For Bell's reflections on *politics,* see the essay "The Mood of Three Generations," included in his book *The End of Ideology,* 299–314, esp. 305–8.

28. Irving Howe, *A Margin of Hope: An Intellectual Autobiography,* esp. 114–17.

29. Theodore Roszak, *The Making of a Counterculture: Reflections on the Technocratic Society and Its Youthful Opposition,* 180; D. Macdonald, review of Goodman's *Art and Social Nature, politics* 3 (November 1946): 361–62. For a portrait of Paul Goodman and the *PR* circle, see Alfred Kazin's memoir *New York Jew,* 67–68, 142–46. For discussions of Goodman's work, see Richard King, *The Party of Eros: Radical Social Thought and the Realm of Freedom,* 78–115, and Morris Dickstein, *Gates of Eden: American Culture in the Sixties,* esp. 74–80.

30. See Taylor Stoehr's introduction to Paul Goodman, *Drawing the Line: The Political Essays of Paul Goodman,* esp. xiii–xvi.

31. See Paul Goodman, *Growing Up Absurd: Problems of Youth in the Organized Society;* selections from Goodman, *Drawing the Line;* Paul Goodman and Percival Goodman, *Communitas;* Paul Goodman, "The Political Meaning of Some Recent Revisions of Freud," *politics* 2 (July 1945): 197–203; and Paul Goodman, "Revolution, Sociolatry, and War," *politics* 2 (December 1945): 376–80.

32. D. Macdonald, *Discriminations,* 299. For a brief overview of Mills's life, see Irving Louis Horowitz's introduction to *Power, Politics, and People: The Collected Essays of C. Wright Mills,* 1–20. On Mills and the New Left, see James Miller, *"Democracy Is in the Streets": From Port Huron to the Siege of Chicago,* 78–91. Rick Tilman provides an in-depth discussion of Mills's education in *C. Wright Mills: A Native Radical and His American Intellectual Roots.*

33. Max Weber, "Class, Status, Party," *politics* 1 (October 1944): 271–78.

34. C. Wright Mills, "The Powerless People," *politics* 1 (April 1944): 68–72; Miller, *"Democracy Is in the Streets,"* 82.

35. Mills, "The Powerless People," 71, 72. The Mills-Macdonald friendship ended acrimoniously in the early 1950s, following the latter's negative review of *White Collar.* See Macdonald, *Discriminations,* 299–300.

36. Andrea Caffi, "The Automatization of European People," *politics* 2 (November 1945): 335–37, 336.

37. Letter, *politics* 2 (September 1945): 285–86.

38. Ibid. I am indebted to Robert Cummings for bringing this passage to my attention.

39. See Longstaff, *"Partisan Review* and the Second World War," 123, and D. Macdonald, 1943 draft prospectus for magazine project, Box 152, Folder 1, Macdonald Papers, and "Trotsky, Orwell, and Socialism," in his *Discriminations,* 330–44.

40. Dwight Macdonald, "Comment," *politics* 1 (November 1944): 295–96; Orwell to Macdonald, 12 December 1946, Box 38, Folder 959, Macdonald Papers.

41. See Bernard Crick, *George Orwell: A Life,* 536; Orwell to Macdonald, 24 January 1947, Box 38, Folder 959, Macdonald Papers; George Orwell, "The Ethics of the Detective Story: From Raffles to Miss Blandish," *politics* 1 (November 1944): 310–15, and "Catastrophic Gradualism," *politics* 3 (September 1946): 268–70.

42. *Retort* 3 (Spring 1947): 30–31, 33–34, 33; Orwell to Macdonald, 24 January 1947, Box 38, Folder 959, Macdonald Papers. A decade after his death Macdonald considered writing Orwell's biography. See Macdonald to Sonia Orwell, 22 January 1960 and 14 March 1960, Box 38, Folder 959, Macdonald Papers. On the posthumous career of the Orwell myth, see John Rodden, *The Politics of Literary Reputation: The Making and Claiming of "St. George" Orwell.*

43. See George Woodcock, "London Letter," *politics* 3 (March 1946): 74–76; George Woodcock, "The Tyranny of the Clock," *politics* 1 (October 1944): 265–67; and Macdonald to Woodcock, 28 July 1948, and 10 March 1949, Box 6, Macdonald Papers. See also George Woodcock, *Letter to the Past: An Autobiography.*

44. George Woodcock, "George Orwell, 19th Century Liberal," *politics* 3 (December 1946): 384–88. These themes are elaborated in George Woodcock, *The Crystal Spirit: A Study of George Orwell.*

45. Woodcock, "George Orwell," 387; Michael Walzer, *The Company of Critics: Social Criticism and Political Commitment in the Twentieth Century,* 117–35. Christopher Lasch contrasts Orwell's faith in "common" values to the "elitism" of the New York Intellectuals in his *Minimal Self: Psychic Survival in Troubled Times,* 108–9.

46. Camus quoted in Nicola Chiaromonte, *The Worm of Consciousness and Other Essays,* 55–56.

47. N. Macdonald, *Homage,* 45–60.

48. Ibid., 53–57; Herbert Lottman, *The Left Bank: Writers, Artists and Politics from the Popular Front to the Cold War,* 92–96; Dwight Macdonald, "Small Talk," *politics* 5 (Winter 1948): 56. See also the biographical sketch in the preface to Victor Serge, *Midnight in the Century,* 11–18.

49. N. Macdonald, *Homage,* 53–57; D. Macdonald, "Small Talk," 56; Victor Serge, "The Revolution at Dead-End," *politics* 1 (June 1944): 147–51; idem, "War Communism," *politics* 2 (March 1945): 74–78; idem, "Kronstadt," *politics* 2 (April 1945): 107–11; idem, "Vignettes of NEP," *politics* 2 (June 1945): 176–80; "Peter Meyer," "The Soviet Union: A New Class Society," *politics* 1 (March 1944): 48–55, and (April 1944): 81–85; and Anton Ciliga, "A Talk with Lenin in Stalin's Prison," *politics* 3 (August 1946): 234–41.

50. Henry Jacoby, [Sebastian Franck, pseud.], "Travel Notes: Fall of 1946," *politics* 4 (January 1947): 7–8; Bruno Bettelheim, "Behavior in Extreme Situations," *politics* 1 (August 1944): 199–209. Bell quoted in Jacob Weisberg, "The Orphans: Dwight Macdonald and *politics* Magazine" (senior thesis, Yale University, 1987), 22–23. Jacoby recollects his years in exile in *Conflict and Consensus: A Festschrift in Honor of Lewis A. Coser,* ed. Walter W. Powell and Richard Robbins, 53–60.

51. Kazin, *New York Jew,* 299–307, 299; Robert Westbrook, "The Responsibility of Peoples: Dwight Macdonald and the Holocaust," 37; Hannah Arendt to Houghton Mifflin Fellowship Committee, 24 December 1946 (copy in Box 6, Folder 98, Macdonald Papers). On Arendt's life, see Elisabeth Young-Bruehl, *Hannah Arendt: For Love of the World,* and Anthony Heilbut, *Exiled in Paradise: German Refugee Artists in America from the 1930s to the Present,* 395–437. Karl Jaspers learned that his former student was alive in America when he saw her mentioned in a copy of *politics* in 1945. See Young-Bruehl, *Hannah Arendt,* 212. In 1946 Arendt wrote her teacher: "I don't belong to [Macdonald's] group politically at all; but morally they are, as people say here, all right" (Lotte Kohler and Hans Saner, eds., *Hannah Arendt and Karl Jaspers: Correspondence, 1926–1969,* 38).

52. Lewis Coser, panel comments at conference "The Legacy of the Workers Party, 1940–49: Recollections and Reflections," Tamiment Institute, New York, 7 May 1983; Lewis Coser, *A Handful of Thistles: Collected Papers in Moral Conviction,* xii–xx. See also *Conflict and Consensus,* 27–52.

53. Coser, panel comments, "Legacy of the Workers Party."

54. Macdonald, notes for 1968 *politics* reissue, Box 74, Folder 93, Macdonald Papers; Irving Howe, review of Chiaromonte's *Worm of Consciousness, New Republic,* 1 May 1976, 26–27; Lionel Abel, "Reconsideration: Nicola Chiaromonte," *New Republic,* 24 March 1986, 39; Mary McCarthy, introduction to Chiaromonte's *Worm of Consciousness,* xv; McCarthy interview with Carol Brightman in Gelderman, *Conversations with Mary McCarthy,* 234–49, 241; Macdonald to Chiaromonte, 7 April 1947, Box 10, Folder 241, Macdonald Papers.

55. On Chiaromonte's life and ideas, see *Survey* 26 (Spring 1982): 1–49.

56. Ibid. See especially Gino Bianco, "The Story of a Friendship: Chiaromonte and Caffi," 9–17.

57. Nicola Chiaromonte, "Spain: The War," reprinted in *Worm of Consciousness,* 20–30, 30.

58. Nicola Chiaromonte, "Lost Italians," reprinted in *Worm of Consciousness*, 31–40, 32–33.

59. Nicola Chiaromonte, "Albert Camus," reprinted in *Worm of Consciousness*, 50–57, esp. 51–53; Enzo Bettiza, "Chiaromonte: Citizen of the World," *Survey* (Spring 1982): 2–7.

60. Macdonald to Chiaromonte, 7 April 1947, Box 10, Folder 241, Macdonald Papers; Barrett, *Truants*, 90–91.

61. See Gelderman, *Mary McCarthy*, 118–24, 231; Brightman, *Writing Dangerously*, 271–78; and Eileen Simpson, *Poets in Their Youth: A Memoir*, 161–63.

62. Gelderman, *Conversations with Mary McCarthy*, 241, 249.

63. Ibid.

64. On Niccolo Tucci's early life, see his biographical note in *Twice a Year* 14–15 (Fall–Winter 1946–47): 332–33.

65. Niccolo Tucci, "Notes for a Political Dictionary," *politics* 2 (April 1945): 112, and 2 (May 1945): 149; draft of letter from Macdonald to National Endowment for the Humanities, 11 June 1975, Box 54, Folder 1286, Macdonald Papers. Tucci was one *politics* writer who suffered negative legal consequences for expressing heretical opinions. In the late 1940s he faced a difficult battle to gain U.S. citizenship after a New York district court denied his petition for naturalization. Its opinion cited both his 1930s "fascist" activities and the fact that "in 1945 and 1946, he wrote articles wherein he was highly critical of the Government of the United States, its leaders and policies." Perhaps influenced by the protests of Dwight Macdonald and other civil libertarians, the court later reversed its decision.

66. Abel, *The Intellectual Follies*, 186. On Caffi's life, see Bianco, "Story of a Friendship," 9–17, and Chiaromonte's introduction to Andrea Caffi, *A Critique of Violence*, vii–xxiii.

67. Chiaromonte, introduction to Caffi, *Critique of Violence*, ix–x, xii.

68. Ibid., xii–xiii, xvi. For insight on the attitudes and experiences of Caffi's generation of European intellectuals, see the work of historian Robert Wohl, including his essay, "The Generation of 1914 and Modernism," appearing in Monique Chefdor et al., eds., *Modernism: Challenges and Perspectives*, 66–78.

69. Chiaromonte, introduction to Caffi, *Critique of Violence*, xiii–xvi.

70. Ibid., xvi–xviii.

71. Bianco, "Story of a Friendship," 14.

72. Ibid., 15–17. Chiaromonte felt guilty about "abandoning" his friend to go to America—undoubtedly a common sentiment among European émigrés. At one point he wrote: "Leaving you, dear Andrea, was desertion on my part, a mutilation, a deliberate rupture of the strongest and deepest ties I have ever had, since my friendship with you was not a chance one. . . . I had promised myself to stay with you, but if I did not do so, it is because you discouraged me and made me feel that neither my staying nor my going would make much difference. That happened because of the pernicious and terrible nature of your spirit that insists on refusing offers of love and devotion."

73. D. Macdonald, *Politics Past*, 27; Arendt, "He's All Dwight," 33.

74. D. Macdonald, *Politics Past*, 26–27; Coser, panel comments, "Legacy of the Workers Party."

75. "The Fascinated Readers," *politics* 5 (Winter 1948): 59–63; "The Intelligence Office," *politics* 1 (July 1944): 191.

76. "The Intelligence Office," *politics* 2 (January 1945): 31–32; *politics* 3 (September 1946): 293.

77. Coser, panel comments, "Legacy of the Workers Party"; Macdonald, editor's note to "The Soldier Reports," *politics* 2 (August 1945): 244.

78. "The Intelligence Office," *politics* 1 (July 1944): 192; "Letter from a Sergeant," *politics* 2 (May 1945): 131–32.

79. "The Intelligence Office," *politics* 3 (December 1946): 398–99.

Two. *politics* and the Moral Crisis of World War II

1. Robert Westbrook, "The Responsibility of Peoples," 35–68, 46. For the evolution of Macdonald's early war critique, see the following articles: "Reading from Left to Right," *New International* 6 (June 1940): 104–5; "National Defense: The Case for Socialism," *Partisan Review* 7 (July–August 1940): 250–66; "What Is the Fascist State?" *New International* 7 (February 1941): 22–27; "Fascism—A New Social Order," *New International* 7 (May 1941): 82–85; and "The End of Capitalism in Germany," *Partisan Review* 8 (May–June 1941): 198–220. See also Michael Wreszin, *Rebel in Defense of Tradition*, 69–127.

2. Westbrook, "Responsibility of Peoples," 46. Macdonald expressed admiration for Bourne—"the intellectual hero of World War I"—in *politics* 1 (March 1944): 35–36, and in "The Root Is Man, Part Two," *politics* 3 (July 1946): 211. For a recent account of Bourne as a wartime critic, see Casey Blake, *Beloved Community: The Cultural Criticism of Randolph Bourne, Van Wyck Brooks, Waldo Frank, and Lewis Mumford*, 157–80. *politics*'s war critique of the 1940s was a resource for opponents of American involvement in Vietnam two decades later. See, for example, Noam Chomsky, "The Responsibility of Intellectuals," in Chomsky, *American Power and the New Mandarins*, 324.

3. Simone Weil, "The *Iliad*, or, The Poem of Force," *politics* 2 (November 1945): 328. The translation, by Mary McCarthy, became *politics* pamphlet no. 1. A good treatment of the Frankfurt School is David Held, *Introduction to Critical Theory: Horkheimer to Habermas*. Casey Blake has called Macdonald's *politics* essays "an American *Dialectic of Enlightenment*, as translated by H. L. Mencken." See Blake, "A Radical's Unorthodoxy," *Nation*, 12 January 1985, 21.

4. Dwight Macdonald, "The Responsibility of Peoples," *politics* 2 (March 1945): 86–87, reprinted in Macdonald, *Politics Past*, 33–72, 51; Albert Camus, "Neither Victims Nor Executioners," reprinted in *politics* 4 (July–August 1947): 141, trans. Dwight Macdonald.

5. Simone Weil, "Words and War," *politics* 3 (March 1946): 70 (no. 4 of the "War as an Institution" series).

6. Dwight Macdonald, "Comment," *politics* 1 (May 1944): 102, and "Atrocities of the Mind," *politics* 2 (August 1945): 227, reprinted in *Politics Past*, 92–97; Paul Fussell, *The Great War and Modern Memory*, 7.

7. On American liberals and World War II, see Richard Pells, *The Liberal Mind in a Conservative Age*, 1–40. For an example of Macdonald's criticism of the expedient morality of "totalitarian liberals" at the *New Republic* and *Nation*, see his "Comment" for *politics* 2 (August 1945): 254–56. See also Dwight Macdonald, "The (American) People's Century," *Partisan Review* 9 (July–August 1942): 294–310.

8. Dwight Macdonald, "Comment," *politics* 1 (July 1944): 162; Niccolo Tucci, "The Cause That Refreshes: Four Delicious Freedoms," *politics* 1 (April 1944); Tucci, "Commonnonsense," *politics* 2 (July 1945): 196. For a similarly critical view of Allied policies in liberated Europe, see Gabriel Kolko, *The Politics of War: The World and United States Foreign Policy*.

9. Macdonald, *Politics Past*, 110; idem, "Comment," *politics* 1 (June 1944): 129–32, 110, 125; idem, "Greece," *politics* 2 (January 1945): 1–8; idem, "Warsaw," *politics* 1 (October 1944): 257–59. On the "ideological vacuum" of World War II, see also Paul Fussell, *Wartime: Understanding and Behavior in the Second World War*, 129–43.

10. Dwight Macdonald, "War and the Intellectuals, Act Two," *Partisan Review* 6 (Spring 1939): 3–20, and *Politics Past*, 107–12, 110.

11. Dwight Macdonald, "The Two Horrors," *politics* 2 (May 1945): 130–31.

12. Robert Jay Lifton, *The Genocidal Mentality: Nazi Holocaust and Nuclear Threat*, 9–11. Contributing to Macdonald's view of the "symmetry" between the two sides in World War II was the Allies' failure to extend significant aid to Jewish refugees, a policy he consistently criticized. See, for example, Dwight Macdonald, "The Jews, 'The New

Leader,' and Old Judge Hull," *politics* 2 (January 1945): 23–25. On this point see also Monty Noam Penkower, *The Jews Were Expendable: Free World Diplomacy and the Holocaust,* and David S. Wyman, *The Abandonment of the Jews: America and the Holocaust, 1941–1945.*

13. Westbrook, "Responsibility of Peoples," 37; Dwight Macdonald, notes to *The Root Is Man;* Macdonald, "Responsibility of Peoples," 83. On Orwell, see Michael Walzer, *The Company of Critics,* 117–35.

14. Westbrook, "Responsibility of Peoples," 59. Another Macdonald scholar offers a similar conclusion: "Macdonald's work in the 1940s can be summed up as an effort to forge a radical politics that connected values with social reality, consciousness with the course of events, free action with the actual shaping of the social future. *Both* terms in each of these phrases were crucial but by no means easily harmonized. For running in tension with this normative vision was Macdonald's increasingly pessimistic description of an emerging historical and social reality that seemed impermeable to the shaping hand of human agency or consciousness" (Robert Cummings, "Resistance and Victimization: Dwight Macdonald in the 1940s," *New Politics* 1 [Summer 1986]: 213–14).

15. Bruno Bettelheim, "Behavior in Extreme Situations," *politics* 1 (August 1944): 199–209, 200; Macdonald to Bettelheim, 29 February 1944, Box 8, Folder 151, Macdonald Papers. Bettelheim recounted his camp experiences in later works as well. See his *Informed Heart: Autonomy in a Mass Age* and *Surviving and Other Essays.*

16. Bettelheim, "Behavior in Extreme Situations," 209.

17. Macdonald, "Responsibility of Peoples," 86. Bettelheim did take care to note that his account of camp life was not exhaustive, and he described the "extraordinary courage" of internees who defied the Gestapo. He did not explore these examples in any detail, however, and the message the essay conveys is clearly one of general human degradation. Bettelheim, "Behavior in Extreme Situations," 209.

18. Terrence Des Pres, "The Bettelheim Problem," *Social Research* 46 (Winter 1979): 647; Jan Levcik, "Buchenwald Before the War," *politics* 2 (June 1945): 173–74; David Rousset, "The Days of Our Death," *politics* 4 (July–August 1947): 151–57. For a critical view of these issues, see Christopher Lasch's essay, "The Discourse on Mass Death: 'Lessons' of the Holocaust," appearing in his book *The Minimal Self,* 100–129. Des Pres noted that Bettelheim's model of passive victimization influenced scholarship on the antebellum American South, including studies like Stanley Elkins's *Slavery* (1959). Recent historiography has challenged those earlier works by describing a vital black culture engaged in all manner of resistance. See, for example, Lawrence Levine, *Black Culture and Black Consciousness: Afro-American Folk Thought from Slavery to Freedom.*

19. Macdonald, "Responsibility of Peoples," 82; Dwight Macdonald, "Comment," *politics* 2 (April 1945): 102–3; Westbrook, "Responsibility of Peoples," 57. Reinhold Niebuhr wrote a letter to Macdonald praising the article, but cautioned that it failed to take full account of the "varieties and degrees of complicity." See Wreszin, *Rebel in Defense of Tradition,* 157.

20. Macdonald, "Responsibility of Peoples," 85, 83–84.

21. Ibid., 90. Macdonald quoted from a "brilliant" article by Arendt, "Organized Guilt and Universal Responsibility," published in *Jewish Frontier,* January 1945, 19–23, reprinted in Hannah Arendt, *Essays in Understanding, 1930–1954,* 121–32. See also her *Origins of Totalitarianism* and *Eichmann in Jerusalem: A Report on the Banality of Evil.*

22. Macdonald, "Responsibility of Peoples," 86–87. Paul Fussell describes the reduction of soldiers to standardized, interchangeable parts—the "G.I. Joe," distinguished only by his serial number—as one of the war's defining innovations. Fussell, *Wartime,* 66.

23. Macdonald, "Responsibility of Peoples," 88–89.

24. On this subject see also Robert Westbrook, "Horrors—Theirs and Ours: The *Politics* Circle and the Good War," *Radical History Review* 36 (1986): 9–25. Michael Walzer concurs that Anglo-American bombing policies lacked moral legitimacy, at least after 1942, when the "supreme emergency" of imminent Nazi victory had passed. See

Michael Walzer, *Just and Unjust Wars: A Moral Argument with Historical Illustrations,* 255–68.

25. Dwight Macdonald, "Notes on the Psychology of Killing," *politics* 1 (September 1944): 239–43. The essay was the first installment of a regular series, "War as an Institution." The British had a similar manual. See Fussell, *Wartime,* 284.

26. Macdonald, "Notes on the Psychology of Killing," 239.

27. Lifton, *Genocidal Mentality,* 13–14, 16.

28. Dwight Macdonald, "Comment," *politics* 1 (March 1944): 33; Macdonald, "Atrocities of the Mind," 227.

29. Dwight Macdonald, cover editorial for *politics* 2 (August 1945): 225, reprinted in *Politics Past,* 169–70. On Macdonald's place in the early response to the atomic bomb, see Paul Boyer, *By the Bomb's Early Light: American Thought and Culture at the Dawn of the Atomic Age,* 233–37.

30. Macdonald, *Politics Past,* 169.

31. Ibid., 170. It is worth noting that Macdonald's critique of the atomic bomb—and of the machinelike automatism of modern society—closely paralleled the arguments of his contemporary, Lewis Mumford. See Everett Mendelsohn, "Prophet of Our Discontent: Lewis Mumford Confronts the Bomb," in Thomas P. Hughes, ed., *Lewis Mumford: Public Intellectual,* 343–60, 359.

32. Dwight Macdonald, "The Bomb," *politics* 2 (September 1945): 257–60.

33. Ibid., 258, 259. The notion of a "Permanent War Economy"—a precursor to the "military-industrial complex" spoken of in the 1960s—appeared in the first issue of *politics.* See Walter J. Oakes, "Toward a Permanent War Economy?" *politics* 1 (February 1944): 11–17.

34. Macdonald, "The Bomb," 258.

35. Ibid., 260. Excerpts from Macdonald's commentary on the atomic bomb appeared in *Time* (October 15, 1945). Even before Hiroshima, Macdonald noted how little the policies of Truman, "the colorless mediocre narrowminded provincial machine-politician," differed from those of his predecessor, the allegedly "brilliant masterful cosmopolitan charmer." Again the reason was that "the governmental mechanism is so massive and has so compelling a logic of its own." See Dwight Macdonald, "Comment," *politics* 2 (August 1945): 253–54.

36. Staughton Lynd, "Marxism-Leninism and the Language of *politics* Magazine," in George Abbott White, ed., *Simone Weil,* 111–35, 131; Dwight Macdonald, "Weil: The Intellectual as Saint," *New Leader,* 5 May 1952, 23–24.

37. Macdonald, "Intellectual as Saint," 23; Simone Weil, "Factory Work," *politics* 3 (December 1946): 369–77. There are a number of biographies of Weil. A standard work is *Simone Weil: A Life* (1976), written by her friend Simone Petrement, who also provided a profile of Weil for *politics* magazine. An excellent recent study is David McLellan, *Utopian Pessimist: The Life and Thought of Simone Weil.* See also Macdonald's note (as "Candide") in *politics* 2 (February 1945): 55–56. Weil, like Macdonald, had drawn the wrath of Leon Trotsky in the 1930s for her political "deviations." See McLellan, *Utopian Pessimist,* 62.

38. Weil's work on postwar France later appeared as *L'Enracinement* (*The Need for Roots,* 1949). In a later review of the volume, Macdonald applauded Weil's analysis of the problem of "uprootedness," but he found her ideas about disciplining the free press "horrifying." See Macdonald, "Intellectual as Saint," 24. On Weil's complex psychology, see Robert Coles, *Simone Weil: A Modern Pilgrimage.*

39. Nicola Chiaromonte, "Simone Weil's *Iliad,*" reprinted in Chiaromonte, *The Worm of Consciousness and Other Essays,* 183–90, 184.

40. Simone Weil, "Reflections on War," *politics* 2 (February 1945): 51–56 (no. 4 of the "War as an Institution" series). Weil's 1930s essays on Stalinism are collected in the volume *Oppression and Liberty.*

41. Weil, "Words and War," *politics* 3 (March 1946): 69–73.

42. Weil, "*Iliad*," 321.
43. Ibid., 321–22.
44. Ibid., 326, 324.
45. Ibid., 324, 325.
46. Ibid., 331.
47. Chiaromonte, *Worm of Consciousness*, 184; Macdonald, "The Root Is Man, Part Two," 206–7.
48. Westbrook, "Responsibility of Peoples," 55–56; Weil, "*Iliad*," 328.
49. Macdonald, "Responsibility of Peoples," 93.
50. Macdonald, "The Bomb," 360. Michael Walzer has challenged this view of the "irresponsibility" of the atomic scientists. He argues that in urging Roosevelt to approve a program to develop the bomb before Hitler, Einstein and his colleagues were acting as "complete men" rather than "specialists": "Many of them [were] European refugees, with an acute sense of what a Nazi victory would mean for their native lands and for all mankind. They were driven by a deep moral anxiety, not (or not most crucially) by any kind of scientific fascination; they were certainly not servile technicians." See Walzer, *Just and Unjust Wars*, 263.
51. Macdonald, "Notes on the Psychology of Killing," 242–43.

Three. The Appeal of the European Resistance

1. Dwight Macdonald, "Resistance: A Semantic Note," *politics* 2 (March 1945): 66.
2. Robert Westbrook, "The Responsibility of Peoples," 46–47.
3. Dwight Macdonald, " 'Dual Power' in France," *politics* 1 (November 1944): 290–94, 290; Howard Brick, *Daniel Bell and the Decline of Intellectual Radicalism*, 106. On the political climate in France before and after the war, see Tony Judt, *Past Imperfect: French Intellectuals, 1944–1956*.
4. Irving Howe, *A Margin of Hope*, 106.
5. Dwight Macdonald, "Allied Policy in Europe," *politics* 1 (July 1944): 161–64.
6. Ibid., 162.
7. For a similar analysis of the Allies' "counterrevolutionary" policies in liberated Europe, see Gabriel Kolko, *The Politics of War*.
8. Dwight Macdonald, "Comment," *politics* 1 (December 1944): 326–27. For more on the Italian situation, see James D. Wilkinson, *The Intellectual Resistance in Europe*, 195–260, and Kolko, *Politics of War*, 43–63, 436–39.
9. For other accounts of the birth and revolutionary possibilities of the French Resistance, see Wilkinson, *Intellectual Resistance in Europe*, 25–106, and Kolko, *Politics of War*, 64–98, 439–45.
10. Victor Serge, Letter, *politics* 1 (August 1944): 222–23.
11. Albert Camus, *Resistance, Rebellion, and Death*, 35–37. For more on the Paris uprising, see Herbert R. Lottman, *The Left Bank*, 210–15; Wilkinson, *Intellectual Resistance in Europe*, 57–59; and Kolko, *Politics of War*, 85. Wilkinson describes how the Underground saw the liberation of Paris as "a lesson in civic responsibility"; Kolko observes that leaders of the Paris Resistance, "the heart and inspiration of the movement, sought to atone for its passivity and give meaning and life to its words and promises by acting in an essentially irrational and heroic way." Socialist Party elder statesman Leon Blum, veteran of an earlier generation of failed revolutionary hopes, expressed the nature of the task at hand: "to seize this possibility of enthusiasm, to maintain it and forge with it a creative spark during what may be a rather short period open to useful action, before it exhausts itself in wearying struggles and before it recedes into daily routine" (Wilkinson, *Intellectual Resistance in Europe*, 53).
12. Dwight Macdonald, "The Liberation of Paris," *politics* 1 (October 1944): 262–63.

13. Ibid., 263.

14. Lewis Coser, "The France of Tomorrow: What the French Underground Wants," *politics* 1 (September 1944): 227.

15. Ibid., 227.

16. Ibid., 226.

17. Ibid., 229.

18. Ibid., 230.

19. Ibid., 230; Arendt's letter is reproduced in Lotte Kohler and Hans Saner, eds., *Hannah Arendt and Karl Jaspers*, 66. In her analysis of the Resistance phenomenon for American readers, Arendt expressed admiration for the cosmopolitan horizons of its spokesmen throughout the continent: "That they achieved such unity without uniformity under the conditions of a German-occupied Europe shows how deeply they must have felt that none of their problems—the pressing social question any more than that of political reorganization—could be solved along strictly national lines" (Hannah Arendt, "Parties, Movements, and Classes," *Partisan Review* 12 [Fall 1945]: 511–12). She also noted the absence of a desire for blanket vengeance against the German people. See Hannah Arendt, "Approaches to the 'German Problem,' " *Partisan Review* 12 (Winter 1945): 99, reprinted in Hannah Arendt, *Essays in Understanding, 1930–1954*, 106–20.

20. Coser, "The France of Tomorrow," 227.

21. Ibid., 231.

22. Macdonald, "Allied Policy in Europe," 164; Coser, "The France of Tomorrow," 226–27. According to *politics,* the expedient nationalism of the French CP also infected its cultural products. See, for example, the following critiques of writer Louis Aragon: Jean Malaquais, "Louis Aragon, or the Professional Patriot," *politics* 2 (August 1945): 233–35, and Ed Seldon, "The Resistance Poetry of Aragon and Eluard," *politics* 2 (November 1945): 347–49. Seldon condemned the latest works of "the principal poet of the French Resistance" as Stalinist agitprop, "narrowly nationalistic in the worst tradition."

23. Coser, "The France of Tomorrow," 232.

24. Macdonald, " 'Dual Power' in France," 290–91.

25. Ibid.

26. Ibid.

27. Ibid., 292–93. The *politics* correspondents were not in complete agreement concerning the nature of the Stalinist threat. The February 1945 issue featured a letter from Victor Serge criticizing what he saw as naive misreadings of the European situation by Coser and Macdonald. Abandoning his earlier optimism, Serge insisted that, contrary to Coser's reports of the existence of independent libertarian elements, the French Resistance was in fact "completely dominated by the Communist Party." Serge also rejected out of hand Macdonald's speculation that, as in China, the French CP might be able to assert some degree of autonomy from Moscow in order to maintain popular support. ("One should not make the mistake . . . of attributing to Russia a godlike omnipotence," Macdonald had observed in his article "Dual Power.") After decades of opposition to Stalin, Serge would tolerate no departures from a monolithic totalitarian model: "I am convinced, or rather I *know* that the Communist apparatus controls inexorably and completely all the movements it influences, including peripheral organizations. This formidable apparatus is a new historical fact whose enormous significance is not yet appreciated enough. *Politics* exists in too free an environment for this to be clearly realized" (letter, *politics* 2 [February 1945]: 61–62).

28. Macdonald, " 'Dual Power' in France," 292.

29. Dwight Macdonald, "Footnote on the European Revolution," *politics* 1 (December 1944): 323.

30. Lewis Coser, "European Newsreel," *politics* 2 (February 1945): 56–57.

31. Ibid.

32. Ibid. Kolko summarizes the "conservative" impact of the CP this way: "The major party of the Left took upon itself, with the guidance of the Soviet Union, the responsibility

of managing and restoring a tottering system during its moment of greatest danger" (*Politics of War,* 444–45).

33. Coser, "European Newsreel" (February 1945), 57.

34. Lewis Coser, "The Stalintern over Europe," *politics* 2 (March 1945): 68–71, 68–69.

35. Ibid., 69.

36. Lewis Coser, "European Newsreel," *politics* 2 (June 1945): 174–75.

37. Lewis Coser, "The Big 3 Against Europe," *politics* 2 (September 1945): 272.

38. Ibid., 272–73.

39. Andrea Caffi, "The Automatization of European People," *politics* 2 (November 1945): 335.

40. Ibid.

41. Ibid.

42. Ibid.

43. Ibid.

44. Ibid., 337. For a recent discussion of the ambiguities of Resistance mythology, see Henri Rousso, *The Vichy Syndrome: History and Memory in France since 1944.*

45. Caffi, "Automatization," 337. In an article appearing in the special "French Issue" of *politics* (summer 1947), Caffi described the Resistance defeat as the latest manifestation of a long-term degeneration of French political life, another example of the "inability of 'thinking France' (a synonym for 'society'), despite its great influence on public opinion, to insinuate its ideas into the actual functioning of the State machinery." With the "liberation" of 1944 "new men animated by generous visions apparently came to the top—and yet the machinery of the State, more weighty and fantastic than ever, is once more lumbering along, brushing aside like straws the most solemn promises of a New Order. And it is the Men of the Resistance themselves, the very ones who then appeared so ardent for change, who today drive, pull, or push the sinister mechanism along" (Andrea Caffi, "The French Condition," *politics* 4 [July/August 1947]: 133).

46. Coser, "Why the Resistance Failed," 117.

47. Ibid., 116–17. The "immaturity" motif was a common one; here is the chastened testimony of a *Combat* editor: "Following the war, many of us believed that new social forms would be born. Something had to emerge from such an upheaval. It seemed to us that we had acquired a certain wisdom that could favorably replace the systems and doctrines we felt had failed. . . . In truth, we had believed that the conduct of public affairs required more good faith than experience, more imagination than systematic thinking, more common sense than ruse. We were childish" (quoted in Wilkinson, *Intellectual Resistance in Europe,* 77).

48. Coser, "Why the Resistance Failed," 116–17; Arendt, "Parties, Movements, Classes."

49. Coser, "Why the Resistance Failed," 117.

50. Ibid. See also Erich Fromm, *Escape From Freedom.*

51. Coser, "Why the Resistance Failed," 118.

52. Wilkinson, *Intellectual Resistance in Europe,* 263.

53. Ibid., 261–79.

54. Ibid., 274.

55. Ibid., 268–69. In the 1950s Jean-Paul Sartre reflected on the circumstances that caused him and his comrades such adjustment problems: "Choice [during the Resistance] was easy, even if a great deal of energy and courage was required to adhere to it. One was for or against the Germans. . . . [S]ince 1945 the situation has grown more complex. One needs less courage to choose, perhaps, but the choices are far more difficult" (quoted in Wilkinson, *Intellectual Resistance in Europe,* 106).

56. "Gelo and Andrea," "Anti-Capitalist 'Revolution' in France," *politics* 3 (November 1946): 341–44. See also the periodicals review section of *politics* 4 (January 1947): 29–30,

and H. Stuart Hughes, *The Obstructed Path: French Social Thought in the Years of Desperation, 1930–1960*, 153–64, 161.

57. Wilkinson, *Intellectual Resistance in Europe*, 270.

58. "Realistically considered," Hughes concludes, it was not surprising that the French people refused to follow the radical Resistance: "The latter, after all, had never been more than a devoted minority: most people, in common with the run of mankind throughout history, had adopted an attitude of *attentisme*—of wait-and-see. The final victory had proved the *résistants* right—but this did not necessarily endear them to the rest of their countrymen . . . [who] could not forgive the heroic minority for the air of moral superiority with which their triumph in 1944 and 1945 had endowed them" (Hughes, *Obstructed Path*, 163–64).

59. See, for example, "The Soldier Reports," *politics* 2 (August 1945): 244–46; "Gelo and Andrea," "Letters from France," *politics* 2 (September 1945): 276–79; and "A.B.C.," "The Communists and the National Question," *politics* 3 (May 1946): 142–44. A useful introduction to the dynamics and aftermath of the "Revolution of 1989" is Vladimir Tismaneanu, *Reinventing Politics: Eastern Europe from Stalin to Havel*.

60. "Gelo and Andrea," "The Decline of the French Communists," *politics* 2 (December 1945): 366–67; "Gelo and Andrea," "French Letter," *politics* 3 (April 1946): 125–26.

Four. Domestic Alternatives

1. Dwight Macdonald, "Comment," *politics* 1 (July 1944): 161–67, 161.

2. Daniel Bell, "The Coming Tragedy of American Labor," *politics* 1 (March 1944): 37–42, and "The Political Lag of Commonwealth," *politics* 2 (May 1945): 139–43; Walter J. Oakes, "Toward a Permanent War Economy?" *politics* 1 (February 1944): 11–17; and Dwight Macdonald, "The Root Is Man," *politics* 3 (April 1946): 97–115, esp. 106–9, 112–15, and "Comment," *politics* 1 (November 1944): 294. Simone Weil's "Factory Work," reprinted in *politics* 3 (December 1946): 369–77, depicted workers as atomized victims reduced, like Bettelheim's concentration camp inmates, to a "brutish stupor" by totalitarian technology and organization. Thus, she concluded, "the comradeship of working men, never moving to some positive crystallization, remains but an unshapen, weakened volition, a mere velleity."

3. Dwight Macdonald, "A Theory of 'Popular Culture,'" *politics* 1 (February 1944): 20–23. For a consideration of the connections between Macdonald's cultural and political views, see Thomas S. Edwards, "The Pursuit of the Ideal: Mass Culture and Mass Politics in the Works of Dwight Macdonald" (Ph.D. diss., Bowling Green State University, 1989). In a letter from Europe, published in the November 1946 issue of *politics*, Andrea Caffi added the notion of "Anti-Culture" to Macdonald's typology to describe the effects of modern propaganda machines like those perfected under Hitler and Stalin. Macdonald's and Caffi's ideas received qualified endorsement from T. S. Eliot in the preface to his 1949 study, *Notes Toward the Definition of Culture*, 7.

4. On the labor militancy of the 1940s, see, for example, Staughton Lynd, "Marxism-Leninism and the Language of *Politics* Magazine," in George Abbott White, ed., *Simone Weil*, and Nelson Lichtenstein, *Labor's War at Home: The CIO in World War II* and "The Making of the Postwar Working Class: Cultural Pluralism and Social Structure in World War II," *Historian* 51 (November 1988): 42–63. A useful critique of the concept of "mass culture" advanced in the 1940s and 1950s is Christopher Lasch, "Mass Culture Reconsidered," *democracy* 1 (October 1981): 7–22. See also Andrew Ross, *No Respect: Intellectuals and Popular Culture*, 42–64, and George Lipsitz, "Listening to Learn and Learning to Listen: Popular Culture, Cultural Theory, and American Studies," *American Quarterly* 42 (December 1990): 615–36.

5. On the shift in focus from class to race and other issues in the American political culture of the 1940s, see Steve Fraser and Gary Gerstle, eds., *The Rise and Fall of the New Deal Order, 1930–1980,* esp. xix, 185–95.

6. Dwight Macdonald, "Whither *politics?*" *politics* 3 (May 1946): 138–42, 141.

7. On political ferment within the C.O. communities of the 1940s, see Lawrence S. Wittner, *Rebels Against War: The American Peace Movement, 1941–1960,* 62–96, 151–212; Richard Polenberg, *War and Society: The United States, 1941–1945,* 54–60; Maurice Isserman, *If I Had a Hammer: The Death of the Old Left and the Birth of the New,* 125–69; and Gretchen Lemke-Santangelo, "The Radical Conscientious Objectors of World War II: Wartime Experience and Postwar Activism," *Radical History Review* 45 (Fall 1989): 5–29. See also Penina M. Glazer, "From the Old Left to the New: Radical Criticism in the 1940s," *American Quarterly* 24 (December 1972): 584–603. The role played by *politics* in the pacifist movement is highlighted in Robert Cooney and Helen Michalowski, eds., *The Power of the People: Active Nonviolence in the United States,* 88–123.

8. Isserman, *If I Had a Hammer,* 132–33.

9. Editor's note prefacing Milton Mayer, "How to Win the War," *politics* 1 (March 1944): 45–46.

10. Don Calhoun, "The Political Relevance of Conscientious Objection," *politics* 1 (July 1944): 177–80.

11. Ibid., Don Calhoun, "Conscientious Objection Again," *politics* 1 (October 1944): 287. For more on the Danbury strike, see James Peck, "A Note on Direct Action," *politics* 3 (January 1946): 21–22. See also Don Calhoun, "Non-Violence and Revolution," *politics* 3 (January 1946): 17–21. David Dellinger recounts his experiences at Danbury and Lewisburg in his memoir *From Yale to Jail: The Life Story of a Dissenter,* 81–98, 119–37.

12. Macdonald's reply to Calhoun, *politics* 1 (July 1944): 179–80.

13. Ibid.

14. "Conscription and Conscientious Objection," *politics* 2 (June 1945): 165–68.

15. Don Calhoun, "The Non-Violent Revolutionists," *politics* 3 (April 1946): 118–19.

16. Ibid., 119.

17. Macdonald to Calhoun, 12–13 March 1946, Box 9, Folder 209, Macdonald Papers.

18. Isserman, *If I Had a Hammer,* 136–37; Dwight Macdonald, "The Root Is Man, Part Two," *politics* 3 (July 1946): 208.

19. George Woodcock, "The English Community Movement," *politics* 3 (August 1946): 231–33, and "Conscientious Objection in England," *politics* 2 (October 1945): 296–97, 296. Woodcock noted that the inspiration for the community movement of the 1940s was the *Society of Brothers (Bruderhof),* a pacifist German sect that had fled the Nazis to found a farming settlement of several hundred people in western England.

20. Woodcock, "Conscientious Objection," 296–97, and "English Community Movement," 231.

21. Woodcock, "English Community Movement," 233. For more on the problems of small-group democracy, see Jane J. Mansbridge, *Beyond Adversary Democracy.*

22. David R. Newton, "The Macedonia Community," *politics* 5 (Winter 1948): 27–30.

23. Ibid., 30. David Shi provides historical context to this sensibility in *The Simple Life: Plain Living and High Thinking in American Culture.*

24. Dwight Macdonald, "The CPS Strikes," *politics* 3 (July 1946): 177–80; James Peck, "You CAN Strike Against the Government," *politics* 3 (July 1946): 215–16. See also "Individual Responsibility: Some Recent C.O. Actions," *politics* 2 (November 1945): 342–44, and Arthur Wiser, "Letter to Judge," *politics* 2 (December 1945): 364–65.

25. Albert Votaw, "Resistance in C.P.S." *politics* 3 (September 1945): 272–74, 273.

26. Ibid.

27. "An Appeal for Action," *politics* 4 (January 1947): 31. Macdonald was also an activist in the War Resisters League during this period. See Wittner, *Rebels Against War,* 153.

28. Dwight Macdonald, "Why Destroy Draft Cards?" *politics* 4 (March/April 1947): 54–55.

29. "Peacemakers," *politics* 5 (Spring 1948): 136–37.

30. "Gandhi," *politics* 5 (Winter 1948): 1–11.

31. Ibid., 6–7.

32. Ibid.

33. Dwight Macdonald, "Pacifism and the USSR," *politics* 5 (Summer 1948): 145–49.

34. See the appendix to the 1953 edition of Macdonald's book *The Root Is Man,* 62.

35. Macdonald, "Why Destroy Draft Cards?" 55. For Macdonald's views on draft resistance during the Vietnam War, see "Civil Disobedience: Theory and Practice," in Macdonald, *Discriminations,* 441–49.

36. The pacifist and civil rights movements of the 1940s shared close links. Congress of Racial Equality (CORE) activists like Bayard Rustin and James Farmer learned about Gandhian direct action while they were C.O.'s during the war. See August Meier and Elliot Rudwick, *CORE: A Study in the Civil Rights Movement, 1942–68,* 3–46, and Wittner, *Rebels Against War,* 64–69. Although *politics* rarely referred to CORE's activities, the May/June 1947 issue did note the results of the first "freedom ride" ("Journey of Reconciliation") through the upper South earlier that year. See *politics* 4 (May/June 1947): 126. On blacks in the 1940s, see Neil Wynn, *The Afro-American and the Second World War;* John Morton Blum, *V Was for Victory: American Politics and Culture during World War II,* 182–220; and Polenberg, *War and Society,* 99–130. During World War I many African Americans, hopeful that loyal service to their country would enhance prospects for domestic reform, followed W. E. B. Du Bois's advice: "Let us, while this war lasts, forget our special grievances" (Polenberg, *War and Society,* 100).

37. See Dwight Macdonald, "The Novel Case of Winfred Lynn," *Nation,* 20 February 1943, 268–70, reprinted as MOWM pamphlet, "The War's Greatest Scandal."

38. Ibid. On Dwight and Nancy Macdonald's involvement with MOWM, see Michael Wreszin, *A Rebel in Defense of Tradition,* 115–16. On the final years of race separation in the military, see Richard M. Dalfiume, *Desegregation of the U.S. Armed Forces: Fighting on Two Fronts, 1939–1953,* and Philip McGuire, ed., *Taps for a Jim Crow Army: Letters from Black Soldiers in World War II.*

39. Macdonald, "Winfred Lynn."

40. Ibid.

41. Ibid.; "Free and Equal," *politics* 1 (February 1944): 23–26; "Free and Equal," *politics* 1 (April 1944): 85–88; Dwight Macdonald, "Comment," *politics* 1 (June 1944): 133. See also Dalfiume, *Desegregation of the U.S. Armed Forces,* 52–53.

42. Isaac McNatt, "I Was a Seabee," *politics* 1 (June 1944): 137–40, 140; "Free and Equal," *politics* 2 (May 1945): 150.

43. "Bombardier," "The Story of the 477th Bombardment Group," *politics* 1 (June 1944): 141–42.

44. Ibid.

45. Dwight Macdonald, "How 'Practical' Is a Racially Segregated Army?" *politics* 1 (July 1944): 184–86.

46. Ibid. Journalist Walter White came to similar conclusions during his tour of battle zones in Italy and North Africa in 1944. "As men approach combat and the dangers of death," he observed, "the tendency becomes more manifest to ignore . . . race prejudice" (Blum, *V Was for Victory,* 209–10).

47. "Free and Equal," *politics* 2 (May 1945): 150–51; Dwight Macdonald, *Politics Past,* 46.

48. "Free and Equal," *politics* 1 (July 1944): 181–82. William Graebner places Myrdal within the context of the "assimilationist forties" in his study *The Age of Doubt: American Thought and Culture in the 1940s*, 92, 96. See also Ralph Ellison's 1944 review of *An American Dilemma*, reprinted in his *Shadow and Act*, 303–17.

49. "Free and Equal," *politics* 1 (May 1944): 121–23; Wilfred H. Kerr, "Negroism: Strange Fruit of Segregation," *politics* 1 (August 1944): 212–17.

50. "Free and Equal," *politics* 2 (July 1945): 209–10.

51. Richard King, *The Party of Eros*, 7–8. For a general account of the war's impact on sexual mores in the United States and Great Britain, see John Costello, *Virtue under Fire: How World War II Changed Our Social and Sexual Attitudes*, esp. 257–74. See also Estelle B. Freedman and John D'Emilio, *Intimate Matters: A History of Sexuality in America*. It is worth noting here that the *politics* audience included bohemian, proto-"Beat" cultural radicals like Kenneth Rexroth, Jack Kerouac, and Allen Ginsberg. See, for example, Dennis McNally, *Desolate Angel: Jack Kerouac, the Beat Generation, and America*, 95–96.

52. Robert Duncan, "The Homosexual in Society," *politics* 1 (August 1944): 209–11. Duncan rejected Macdonald's advice to withhold his identity, and his literary career suffered as a result. After publication of the essay, he found himself blacklisted from major journals. See Ekbert Faas, *Young Robert Duncan: Portrait of the Poet as Homosexual in Society*, 145–60. On homosexuals and the war, see Freedman and D'Emilio, *Intimate Matters*, 288–90, and Allan Berube, *Coming Out Under Fire: The History of Gay Men and Women in World War II*, esp. 250–51.

53. Ethel Goldwater, "The Independent Woman: A New Course," *politics* 3 (May 1946): 145–49; " 'The Independent Woman'—Discussion," *politics* 3 (September 1946): 276–80 (includes a response by young Canadian writer Marshall McLuhan). In his article "A Theory of 'Popular Culture' " (*politics* 1 [February 1944]: 20–23, 23), Macdonald speculated that the fact that radio soap operas and other "modern folk sagas" almost always portrayed women as victims demonstrated the superficiality of their much-heralded "emancipation."

54. Paul Goodman, "The Political Meaning of Some Recent Revisions of Freud," *politics* 2 (July 1945): 197–203; Paul Goodman, "Revolution, Sociolatry and War," *politics* 2 (December 1945): 376–80.

55. Goodman, "Political Meaning," 201, and "Revolution," 379; King, *Party of Eros*, 83–88, 84.

56. See Stephen L. Tanner, *Lionel Trilling*, 102–6; Dwight Macdonald, "The Root Is Man, Part Two," *politics* 3 (July 1946): 194–214, esp. 197–98; King, *Party of Eros*, 88. Tanner notes, at page 105 of his study, that "while some find Freud's biological determinism pessimistic, Trilling found it a bracing and possibly liberating idea in that it allows that at least some part of man is safe from determination by culture." C. Wright Mills accused Goodman of retreating into a privatist "metaphysics of biology." See exchange in "The Barricade and the Bedroom," *politics* 2 (October 1945): 313–16.

Five. "Ancestors"

1. Dwight Macdonald, "The Root Is Man, Part Two," *politics* 3 (July 1946): 194, 208.

2. Nicola Chiaromonte, *The Paradox of History: Stendhal, Tolstoy, Pasternak, and Others*, 141.

3. Dwight Macdonald, 1968 notes, Box 74, Folder 93, Macdonald Papers. Christopher Lasch made a similar critique of the New Left's descent into "nihilistic," anti-intellectual militancy in his book *The Agony of the American Left*, esp. 180–88.

4. Dwight Macdonald, editorial note to D. S. Savage, "Socialism in Extremis," *politics* 2 (January 1945): 15.

5. Dwight Macdonald, editorial note to "Ancestors (1): Proudhon," *politics* 2 (October 1945): 297.

6. Alasdair MacIntyre, *After Virtue: A Study in Moral Theory*, 206–7. For another discussion of the selective reconstruction of the past, see Edward Shils, *Tradition*.

7. "Ancestors (3): Tolstoy," *politics* 3 (May 1946): 161–67, 161. For Jane Addams's view on Tolstoy, see her *Twenty Years at Hull House*, 151–63. Casey Blake describes Tolstoy's influence on Van Wyck Brooks in *Beloved Community*, 59–63. For more on Tolstoy's life and politics, see George Woodcock, *Anarchism: A History of Libertarian Ideas and Movements*, 222–35; Andrzej Walicki, *A History of Russian Thought: From the Enlightenment to Marxism*, 326–48; and Peter Brock, *Freedom from War: Nonsectarian Pacifism, 1814–1914*, 185–204.

8. "Ancestors (3): Tolstoy," 161; Dwight Macdonald, *Politics Past*, 30–31. For more on Macdonald's hostility to religion, see his response to a 1950 *Partisan Review* questionnaire, reprinted in *Politics Past*, 369–73.

9. "Ancestors (3): Tolstoy," 161–64.

10. Ibid., 164–67.

11. Max Weber, "Class, Status, Party," *politics* 1 (October 1944): 271–78; H. H. Gerth and C. Wright Mills, eds., *From Max Weber: Essays in Sociology*. On Mills's interest in Weber, see Rick Tilman, *C. Wright Mills*, 42–50.

12. Macdonald, "The Root Is Man, Part Two," 214. One scholar explains the Frankfurt School's evolution from the 1930s to the 1950s and 1960s as "a shift in theoretical orientation away from Marx to Weber." See David Held, *Introduction to Critical Theory*, 65.

13. See Wolfgang Mommsen, *The Age of Bureaucracy: Perspectives on the Political Sociology of Max Weber*; Weber, "Class, Status, Party," 271; James T. Kloppenberg, *Uncertain Victory: Social Democracy and Progressivism in European and American Social Thought, 1870–1920*, 321–48, 385–91. Kloppenberg emphasizes the contrast (not lost on the *politics* circle) between Weber's gloom and the more hopeful assumptions of writers like John Dewey: "In ethics, then, Weber's mood of heroic pessimism distinguished him from the other theorists of progressivism, all of whom hitched the idea of individual moral growth to a larger scheme of steady, although hardly inevitable, cultural progress" (*Uncertain Victory*, 347).

14. Meyer Schapiro, "A Note on Max Weber's Politics," *politics* 2 (February 1945): 44–48; H. H. Gerth, " 'Max Weber's Politics'—a Rejoinder," *politics* 2 (April 1946): 119–20; Gerth and Mills, *From Max Weber*, 43. Kloppenberg presents a similar defense of Weber's "cultural nationalism" in *Uncertain Victory*, 322.

15. "Ancestors (4): Godwin," *politics* 3 (September 1946): 260–67, 262. See also Woodcock, *Anarchism*, 60–93.

16. "Ancestors (4): Godwin," 263.

17. Ibid., 267.

18. Woodcock, *Anarchism*, 83–85, 82; Macdonald to Woodcock, [1959], Box 6, Macdonald Papers.

19. Henry Jacoby, "De Tocqueville: Prophet of the Total State," *politics* 3 (April 1946): 127–28.

20. Ibid.

21. Ibid. Tocqueville's concerns about the fragility of self-government in the United States continue to attract the attention of social critics. The best-known recent examination of the difficulties of constructing a vital, mediating public sphere founded on a common moral language is Robert N. Bellah, et al., *Habits of the Heart: Individualism and Commitment in American Life*.

22. Jacoby, "De Tocqueville," 128.

23. "Ancestors (1): Proudhon," 297–99. See also Woodcock, *Anarchism*, 106–44; J. Hampden Jackson, *Marx, Proudhon, and European Socialism*; and Aileen Kelly,

"Herzen and Proudhon: Two Radical Ironists," *Common Knowledge* 1 (Fall 1992): 36–62.

24. "Ancestors (1): Proudhon," 299–300, 304.

25. Nicola Chiaromonte, "Social Law, After Proudhon," *politics* 2 (January 1945): 25–28, 28, 26.

26. Ibid., 26.

27. Nicola Chiaromonte, "P. J. Proudhon: An Uncomfortable Thinker," *politics* 3 (January 1946): 27–29, 28, 29. Chiaromonte was responding to J. Salwyn Schapiro, "Pierre Joseph Proudhon, Harbinger of Fascism," *American Historical Review* 50 (July 1945): 714–37.

28. See Woodcock, *Anarchism*, 13: "The strong point in anarchist writings has always been their incisive criticism of . . . institutions; in comparison their plans of reconstruction have been oversimplified and unconvincing." See also Chiaromonte, "P. J. Proudhon," 27.

29. Macdonald, "The Root Is Man, Part Two," 202–4.

30. Richard King, *The Party of Eros*, 36.

31. Macdonald, "The Unconscious War," reprinted in *Politics Past*, 107–12, 111.

32. "Ancestors (5): Alexander Herzen," *politics* 5 (Winter 1948): 40–51, 40. See also *My Past and My Thoughts: The Memoirs of Alexander Herzen*, edited by Dwight Macdonald. Macdonald added a terse comment about the spectatorial distance that inhibited understanding on his side of the Atlantic: "That we read about (the outrages) in the papers rather than experiencing them in our own lives was, and is, symptomatic of the quality of American intellectual life." For more on Herzen, see Woodcock, *Anarchism*, 402–6, and Walicki, *History of Russian Thought*, 127–34, 162–80.

33. "Ancestors (5): Alexander Herzen," 44.

34. Ibid., 48.

35. Ibid., 50–51; Macdonald, *Politics Past*, 112.

36. "Ancestors (5): Alexander Herzen," 51.

37. "Ancestors (6): Kurt Tucholsky," *politics* 5 (Summer 1948): 171–76. See also Istvan Deak, *Weimar Germany's Left-Wing Intellectuals*, 36–48.

38. "Ancestors (6): Kurt Tucholsky," 171–73. One commentator has concluded that "in their wholesale rejection of Weimar Germany as an inadequate society, in jeering where they might have helped," critics like Grosz and Tucholsky "unwittingly contributed to the tragedy which engulfed both it and them" (A. J. Ryder, *Twentieth Century Germany: From Bismarck to Brandt*, 235–36).

39. King, *Party of Eros*, 43; Cornel West, *The American Evasion of Philosophy: A Genealogy of Pragmatism*. West's advocacy of a socially engaged "prophetic pragmatism," based on the American "evasion" of "epistemology-centered philosophy," is part of a larger contemporary rediscovery of immanent intellectual traditions. Robert Westbrook, another "discriminating scavenger" in this project, offers a good discussion of the revival of interest in American pragmatism in his epilogue to *John Dewey and American Democracy*, 537–52. See also Alan Ryan, *John Dewey and the High Tide of American Liberalism*.

40. Macdonald, *Politics Past*, 28; William Cain, "An Interview with Irving Howe," *American Literary History* 1 (Fall 1989): 554–64. For Howe's second thoughts about the radical possibilities of Emersonian thought, see his study *The American Newness: Culture and Politics in the Age of Emerson*.

41. Dwight Macdonald, "Our Golden Age," *politics* 1 (June 1944): 144–46. Macdonald was reacting to Alice Felt Tyler's study *Freedom's Ferment: Phases of American Social History to 1860*. Compare Paul Goodman's ideas about the anarchic pluralism of the early United States, presented in his article "A Conjecture in American History, 1783–1815," *politics* 6 (1949): 11–13.

42. Lasch, *Agony of the American Left*, 33–59, 47. Richard King offers similar criticism of American overreliance on European traditions in *Party of Eros*, 3–4.

Six. "New Roads"

1. Dwight Macdonald, editorial note, *politics* 2 (December 1945): 369. Other participants in the "New Roads in Politics" series were Will Herberg ("Personalism Against Totalitarianism," *politics* 2 [December 1945]), Helen Constas ("A Critique of Marxian Ideology," *politics* 3 [January 1946]), Paul Goodman ("Revolution, Sociolatry and War," *politics* 2 [December 1945]), and Don Calhoun ("Non-Violence and Revolution," *politics* 3 [January 1946]).

2. Dwight Macdonald, *Politics Past*, 75, and "The Bomb," *politics* 2 (September 1945): 258. "Zero hour" has often been used to indicate the radical historical break represented by 1945. See, for example, John Lukacs's study *1945: Year Zero*, dedicated to his friend Dwight Macdonald.

3. Nicola Chiaromonte, *The Paradox of History*.

4. Ibid., 30.

5. Macdonald, "The Root Is Man, Part Two," *politics* 3 (July 1946): 211.

6. Ibid., 213.

7. Dwight Macdonald, "New Roads," *politics* 3 (October 1946): 334–35.

8. Richard King, *The Party of Eros*, 43; Dwight Macdonald, "Why *politics?*" *politics* 1 (February 1944): 6–8.

9. Macdonald, *Politics Past*, 28–29. The essay's title is from a statement by Marx, expressing his early humanist aspirations: "To be radical is to grasp the matter by its root," he wrote. "Now the root for mankind is man himself."

10. Dwight Macdonald, *The Root Is Man*, v.

11. Macdonald was referring to Trotsky's article, "The USSR in War," originally appearing in *New International* 5 (November 1939); reprinted in *The Basic Writings of Trotsky*, ed. Irving Howe, 305–14. See also Isaac Deutscher, *The Prophet Outcast: Trotsky, 1929–1940, Vol. 3*, 463–64. Trotsky admitted that the failure of the proletariat to seize this latest opportunity would mean that the "bureaucratic relapse" of Stalinism was not merely a temporary setback but instead was the result of the "congenital incapacity" of the workers to become a ruling class.

12. Dwight Macdonald, "The Root Is Man," *politics* 3 (April 1946): 98.

13. Ibid., 106.

14. Ibid., 109–12. The idea of "bureaucratic collectivism" had been in the air since the 1930s. One of the first accounts of this development appeared in Bruno Rizzi, *La Bureaucratisation du Monde* (Paris, 1939). Macdonald explicitly referred to Ciliga's work, *The Russian Enigma*, but he was also influenced by the pioneering analyses of the Soviet Union by Victor Serge, Josep Gutman ("Peter Meyer"), and Simone Weil. He dismissed James Burnham's famous study, *The Managerial Revolution*, as "flimsy" and superficial. See Macdonald, *Politics Past*, 20.

Even as early as 1933 Weil understood the nature of Stalinism, a system that defied the assumption "that there can . . . be only two types of State, the capitalist State and the workers' State." To Weil, the Soviet Union represented the culmination of "a new species of oppression, oppression exercised in the name of management"—a phenomenon also advancing in the United States, home of Taylorism and Fordism. Although "certainly Marx never foresaw anything of this kind," she concluded, "not even Marx is more precious to us than the truth" (*Oppression and Liberty*, 6, 8–9).

15. Macdonald, "The Root Is Man," 112–15, 113. Cf. Weil on this point: "Marx and Engels, in their analysis, omitted one factor: war. Marxists have never analyzed the phenomenon of war, nor its relation to the economic system; for I do not call the simple assertion that capitalist greed is the cause of wars as analysis. What a gap! And what credence can be given to a theory which claims to be scientific and is capable of such an omission?" (*Oppression and Liberty*, 151).

16. Macdonald, "The Root Is Man," 99; Macdonald, "The Root Is Man, Part Two," 214.

17. Macdonald, "The Root Is Man," 99–101.

18. Ibid.

19. Ibid.

20. Ibid., 100; Macdonald, "The Root Is Man, Part Two," 204, 209. Macdonald's arguments here put him, along with collaborator Paul Goodman, within a long tradition of Thoreau-inspired critics of the Western cult of material progress. See David Shi, *The Simple Life*. A recent version of this position appears in Christopher Lasch, *The True and Only Heaven: Progress and Its Critics*. Macdonald expressed the opinion that "there is a point of technological development beyond which the bad human results *must* outweigh the good ones under any conceivable social system." For an influential continental critique of technocracy along the same lines, see Jacques Ellul's classic, *The Technological Society*.

21. Macdonald, "The Root Is Man, Part Two," 212, 197, 198. Macdonald's comments here should be seen within the context of a larger discourse about humankind's "tragic" limitations in the 1940s, especially prominent among intellectuals attempting to articulate a tougher, more "realistic" liberalism to compete with its totalitarian rivals. Among the most noteworthy representatives of this group were Reinhold Niebuhr, Lionel Trilling, and Arthur Schlesinger. See Richard Pells, *The Liberal Mind in a Conservative Age*, 136–38.

22. Steven Lukes, *Marxism and Morality*, 141. One example of this "congenital defect" is Marx's rhetorical tendency to dismiss individual rights as "bourgeois" fictions. "It is one thing," Lukes concludes, "to reject liberal views of freedom as too narrow; it is another to try to deny bourgeois freedoms the status of genuine freedoms" (*Marxism and Morality*, 78).

23. Bourne's critique of Dewey and his liberal followers appears in the essays "The War and the Intellectuals" and "Twilight of Idols," reprinted in the collection *The Radical Will: Randolph Bourne Selected Writings, 1911–1918*, 307–18 and 336–47. Howard Brick has also argued that despite attempts at repudiation, Macdonald reinvented many Deweyan principles. See Brick, *Daniel Bell and the Decline of Intellectual Radicalism*, 121. On Dewey's critique of the "Quest for Certainty," and his argument with Trotsky, see Robert B. Westbrook, *John Dewey and American Democracy*, 348–61 and 463–76. For a discussion of Dewey's influence on the Students for a Democratic Society in the early 1960s, see James Miller, *"Democracy Is in the Streets,"* 16.

24. Macdonald, "The Root Is Man, Part Two," 197, 195.

25. Ibid., 197–98. Macdonald applied this "subjective" approach to his own journalistic judgments. He once advised Norman Mailer always to follow his instincts, remarking: "If something feels bad to you, it is bad." See Mailer's introduction to Dwight Macdonald, *Discriminations*, viii.

26. Macdonald, "The Root Is Man, Part Two," 196.

27. Chiaromonte to Macdonald, [1946], Box 10, Folder 241, Macdonald Papers. In a footnote to the 1953 reprinting of "The Root Is Man," Macdonald acknowledged Chiaromonte's objections, conceding that acting on ideals may indeed often require present sacrifices. "But," he added, "the prevailing morality, Christian or Marxian, I think involves far too much of that kind of thing, going to the extremes of the Puritan and of the Communist fanatic. I think pleasure and virtue ought to be reintroduced to each other, and that if there's too much of the sacrificial and not enough of the enjoyable about one's political or ethical behavior, it's a bad sign." Robert Cummings pointed out to me that this exchange reveals much about the temperamental differences between Macdonald and Chiaromonte. See Macdonald, *The Root Is Man*, 49–50.

28. Nicola Chiaromonte, "On the Kind of Socialism Called 'Scientific,' " *politics* 3 (February 1946): 33–44.

29. Ibid., 35.

30. Ibid., 39–40.

31. Ibid., 35, 42. Cf. Simone Weil on the contradictions between Marxist means and ends: "Marx's revolutionary materialism consists in positing, on the one hand, [the idea] that everything is exclusively regulated by force and, on the other, that a day will suddenly come when force will be on the side of the weak" (*Oppression and Liberty*, x).

32. Chiaromonte, *Paradox*.

33. Ibid., xix.

34. Ibid., 100, 9; Joseph Frank, "Nicola Chiaromonte: The Ethic of Politics," *Dissent* 21 (Winter 1974): 83–89, 89.

35. Chiaromonte, *Paradox*, xiii, xix.

36. Ibid., 1–16, 3, 4.

37. Ibid., 7, 15.

38. Ibid., 17–50, 19, 26, 46. Chiaromonte's immediate purpose in writing this essay was to contest Isaiah Berlin's famous thesis that, while by nature Tolstoy was a "fox," knowing "many things," he longed to be a "hedgehog," knowing "one big thing." See Isaiah Berlin, *The Hedgehog and the Fox: An Essay on Tolstoy's View of History*. Gary Saul Morson also finds an antihistoricist critique in Tolstoy in his *Hidden in Plain View: Narrative and Creative Potentials in "War and Peace,"* esp. 83–189.

39. Chiaromonte, *Paradox*, 27, 36.

40. Ibid., 21.

41. Ibid.; Randolph Bourne, "Below the Battle," *Seven Arts* 2 (July 1917): 270–77.

42. Chiaromonte, *Paradox*, 30. Cf. Hannah Arendt's rejection of historical absolutism, summarized by Jeffrey Isaac: "It is the effort to foretell the ending of a story that is not yet complete and is inherently open-ended. To be human is to act with imperfect knowledge, without knowing the ultimate causes or consequences of our activity" (*Arendt, Camus, and Modern Rebellion*, 108–9).

43. Ibid., 101–18, 137–48, 111.

44. Ibid., 145–46.

45. Ibid., 147. Compare Theodor Adorno on this point: "And which driver is not tempted, merely by the power of his engine, to wipe out the vermin of the street, pedestrians, children and cyclists? The movements machines demand of their users already have the violent, hard-hitting jerkiness of Fascist maltreatment" (*Minima Moralia: Reflections from a Damaged Life*, 40).

46. Isaac, *Arendt, Camus, and Modern Rebellion*, 148.

47. Chiaromonte, "On the Kind of Socialism," 37; Macdonald to Chiaromonte, [1946], Box 10, Folder 241, Macdonald Papers.

48. Nicola Chiaromonte, "Reply," *politics* 3 (July 1946): 188–89.

49. Nicola Chiaromonte, "Remarks on Justice," *politics* 4 (May/June 1947): 88–93, 88.

50. Ibid., 89.

51. Ibid., 91.

52. Ibid.

53. Ibid., 92.

54. Ibid., 92–93.

55. See Michael Walzer, "The Idea of Civil Society: A Path to Social Reconstruction," *Dissent* 38 (Spring 1991): 293–304, and John Keane, *Democracy and Civil Society*, for useful introductions to this important concept. For a social model close to Chiaromonte's, see Walzer's *Spheres of Justice: A Defense of Pluralism and Equality*.

56. Chiaromonte, *Paradox*, 72.

57. "Whither *politics?*" *politics* 3 (May 1946): 138.

58. Don Calhoun, "Science, Politics, and the Absolute," *politics* 3 (September 1946): 281–85, 283.

59. Dwight Macdonald, "politicking," *politics* 3 (January 1946): 31.

60. Lionel Abel, *The Intellectual Follies*, 187–88.

61. Sebastian Franck, "Escapism v. Marxism," *politics* 3 (July 1946): 189. Christopher Lasch offered a similar analysis of the effects of isolation on radical intellectuals in his study *The Agony of the American Left*, 43–59.

62. "New Roads: Discussion," *politics* 3 (August 1946): 249–53. Although he admired much about *politics*, decades later historian and labor activist Staughton Lynd would advance a similar criticism of Macdonald's "aloofness" from workers' struggles. See Staughton Lynd, "Marxism-Leninism and the Language of *Politics* Magazine," 111–35.

63. "New Roads: Discussion" (August 1946), 252–53; "Whither *politics?*" 140.

64. "New Roads: Discussion," *politics* 3 (March 1946): 89–93.

65. Ibid., 92.

66. Louis Clair [Lewis Coser], "Digging at the Roots, or Striking at the Branches?" *politics* 3 (October 1946): 323–28.

67. Ibid., 326–27.

68. Irving Howe, "The 13th Disciple," *politics* 3 (October 1946): 329–34. In his memoir, Howe reiterated these criticisms, despite sympathy for Macdonald's good intentions. He commented: "['The Root Is Man'] was in many ways a poignant expression of the plight of those few intellectuals—Macdonald, Nicola Chiaromonte, Paul Goodman—who wished to dissociate themselves from the new turn to *Realpolitik*, but could not find ways of transforming sentiments of rectitude or visions of utopia into a workable politics. It was also a leftist rationale for a kind of internal emigration of the spirit, with some odd shadings of similarity to the Salinger cult of the late fifties. One need not be a Marxist to suspect that such ideas will usually lead away from politics entirely" (*Margin of Hope*, 116).

69. Dwight Macdonald, "Reply," *politics* 3 (October 1946): 334–35.

70. Macdonald described a Caffi essay to Chiaromonte as "one of the things I'm proudest of having published," and he chose to conclude a 1953 reprinting of "The Root Is Man" with Caffi's "Mass Politics and the Pax Americana," a piece that had arrived too late to appear in the final issue of *politics*. Macdonald to Chiaromonte, 7 April 1947, Box 10, Folder 241, Macdonald Papers; "Appendix C" to Dwight Macdonald, *The Root Is Man*, 62–63.

71. Andrea Caffi, "Violence and Sociability," *politics* 4 (January 1947): 25. See also Andrea Caffi, "Towards a Socialist Program," *politics* 2 (December 1945): 374–76, and "Is a Revolutionary War a Contradiction in Terms?" *politics* 3 (April 1946): 128–30.

72. See Gino Bianco, "Chiaromonte and Caffi," *Survey* 26 (Spring 1982): 8–17, 14.

73. On the development of a subversive public sphere of "convivial sociability" in eighteenth-century France, see Roger Chartier, *The Cultural Origins of the French Revolution*, esp. 16–17, 161–68, and 196–97, and Daniel Gordon, "The Idea of Sociability in Pre-Revolutionary France" (Ph.D. diss., University of Chicago, 1990). On Simmel's ideas about "sociability," see David Frisby, *Georg Simmel*, esp. 124–25, and Peter Lawrence, *Georg Simmel: Sociologist and European*, 78–93. Important recent discussions of Enlightenment "sociability" include Richard Sennett, *The Fall of Public Man*, and Jürgen Habermas, *The Structural Transformation of the Public Sphere: An Inquiry into a Category of Bourgeois Society*, 27–56, esp. 36–37. On Freemasonry as the basis for a cosmopolitan civil society, see Margaret C. Jacob, *Living the Enlightenment: Freemasonry and Politics in Eighteenth-Century Europe*.

74. Abel, *Intellectual Follies*, 177.

75. Andrea Caffi, "Violence and Sociability," *politics* 4 (January 1947): 26–27.

76. Ibid., 27–28.

77. Ibid.

78. See "Appendix C" to Macdonald, *The Root Is Man*, 62–63.

79. Martin Luther King, Jr., *The Trumpet of Conscience*, 63–64.

80. Václav Havel, *Disturbing the Peace*, 166, 180, and "The Power of the Powerless," in Havel, *Living in Truth*, 36–122. For another discussion of affinities between the

Resistance generation's "rebellious politics" of the 1940s and the strategies of Soviet bloc dissidents, see Isaac, *Arendt, Camus, and Modern Rebellion*, 248–59.

81. Havel, *Living in Truth*, 57, 58, 56.

82. Ibid., 118, 103; György Konrád, *Antipolitics: An Essay*, 208–43, 197.

83. See Macdonald review of Paul Goodman, *Art and Social Nature*, in *politics* 3 (November 1946): 361–62.

84. Irving Howe later shouldered some of the responsibility for what he saw as the decline of *politics* after 1945. "Toward its end *Politics* became boring," he wrote, "more earnest . . . less captivating. Its last few issues were choked with lengthy polemics, including attacks on Macdonald by me and my friend Lewis Coser. We 'corrected' Dwight, all right, but our polemics helped sink the magazine" (*Margin of Hope*, 117).

Seven. The Search for a Vehicle

1. See interview with Mary McCarthy in *Paris Review* 27 (January 1962): 76–77.

2. Dwight Macdonald, "Fourth Report on Packages Abroad," *politics* 3 (May 1946): 171.

3. Louis Clair [Lewis Coser], "European Newsreel: AMG in Wasteland," *politics* 2 (May 1945): 134.

4. Ibid., 132.

5. Dwight Macdonald, "The Two Horrors," *politics* 2 (May 1945): 131.

6. In addition to Coser's "European Newsreel" and the many letters from Europe appearing in *politics,* see the reports on Germany in the following issues: June 1945 (170–74), August 1945 (244–45), September 1945 (264), October 1945 (294–95), January 1946 (4–7), and October 1946 (314–19). For other eyewitness accounts of cities reduced to "rubble heaps," see Richard Brett-Smith, *Berlin '45: The Grey City;* Victor Gollancz, *In Darkest Germany;* and Jeffry M. Diefendorf, *In the Wake of War: The Reconstruction of German Cities after World War II,* esp. 3–17. After surveying the wreckage, General Eisenhower is reported to have remarked: "It is quite likely, in my opinion, that there will never be any attempt to rebuild Berlin." See Mark Wyman, *DP: Europe's Displaced Persons, 1945–51,* 16. For an exposé of Soviet behavior in occupied Germany, see Peter Blake, "AMG in Germany," *politics* 5 (Summer 1948): 194–202.

7. For Macdonald's criticisms of Lerner, see his "Comment" for *politics* 2 (April 1945): 102–3.

8. See Lewis Coser, "European Newsreel," *politics* 2 (May 1945): 134; and Lewis Coser and Werner Bloch, "Under the Lid," *politics* 1 (July 1944): 169–70. *politics* continued its campaign to show Americans another Germany by publishing translations of two key postwar statements by Karl Jaspers. One was an editorial, "A Beginning Must Be Made," appearing in the first issue of the cultural magazine *Die Wandlung* in November 1945. The other was a speech given at the reopening of the medical faculty of Heidelberg University on 15 August 1945. In each statement, Jaspers insisted that Germans engage in dialogue about their past as the first step toward a democratic future. See "Culture in the Ruins," *politics* 3 (February 1946): 51–55.

9. On the "No Fraternization" rule, see cover editorial for *politics* 2 (March 1945): 65.

10. "Letter from a Sergeant," *politics* 2 (May 1945): 131–32.

11. Dwight Macdonald, "Here's ONE Thing We Can Do!" *politics* 2 (October 1945): 289; "Comment," *politics* 2 (September 1945): 286–87.

12. Dwight Macdonald, "Starvation! America's Christmas Gift to the European Peoples," *politics* 2 (December 1945): 353–64 (reprinted as the pamphlet "Shall Europe Starve?"). For discussions of the postwar food crisis similarly critical of Allied efforts, see Gabriel Kolko, *The Politics of War,* 496–99, and Wyman, *DP,* 52–54. For an analysis more sympathetic to occupation authorities, see Stephen E. Ambrose, "Ike and the Disappearing Atrocities," *New York Times Book Review,* 24 February 1991.

13. D. Macdonald, "Starvation!" 354.

14. Ibid., 358.

15. Ibid., 357.

16. Ibid., 359–60. "Save Europe Now" was largely the work of Victor Gollancz, the liberal Jewish editor of the "Left Book Club" whose newspaper accounts, compiled in the volume *In Darkest Germany* (1947), helped alert the British public to postwar conditions in central Europe. An excerpt of these writings appeared in *politics* in January 1947 under the title "The German Catastrophe," 6–7. Gollancz, like Dwight Macdonald, was particularly worried about the "intellectual and spiritual starvation" imposed on the German people during the early stages of occupation. See *In Darkest Germany*, 110–12. Gollancz also shared Macdonald's concern about Allied plans for a "hard peace" and the lingering effects of the idea of collective guilt. In December 1946 he observed: "If we had to concentrate the major part of our energy on Germany during the last eighteen months, that is not because we believe that Germans are more important than anyone else: it is because we believe that they are not less important, and because they had few, and at first very few, to appeal in their name to the decency of the world." For Gollancz, the victors bore "a very special responsibility before the bars of history and of our own consciences" to treat the vanquished with humanity. See *In Darkest Germany*, 17–18.

17. D. Macdonald, "Starvation!" 363.

18. "The German Catastrophe," *politics* 4 (January 1947): 2 (reprinted as a pamphlet).

19. Ibid., 5.

20. Ibid., 3.

21. Ibid., 15.

22. Dwight Macdonald, "Fourth Report on Packages Abroad," *politics* 3 (May 1946): 171–74, 171; Nancy Macdonald, "They Need Help," *politics* 4 (May–June 1947): 83.

23. D. Macdonald, "Here's ONE Thing," 289.

24. Dwight Macdonald, "Here Is What YOU Can Do," *politics* 2 (October 1945): 320.

25. Ibid.

26. Nancy Macdonald, *Homage to the Spanish Exiles*, 65.

27. "Report on Food Packages," *politics* 2 (December 1945): 383–84.

28. Ibid., 383.

29. D. Macdonald, "Fourth Report on Packages Abroad," 171–72.

30. Ibid., 171; N. Macdonald, *Homage*, 17, 65; Orwell to Macdonald, 12 May 1946, and 26 February 1947, Box 38, Folder 959, Macdonald Papers.

31. "Third Report on Packages," *politics* 3 (February 1947): 60–61.

32. Leaflet, " 'How Can I Tell You . . .?': The Story of the *politics* Packages-to-Europe Plan"; "German Catastrophe," 15. Hannah Arendt wrote to Jaspers explaining the reciprocal nature of the Packages project: "Macdonald and his circle feel a total solidarity with European antifascists and also feel, if you will, responsible for their fate. They aren't looking for anyone to 'thank' them at all. On the contrary, they are grateful for any opportunities given them" (Lotte Kohler and Hans Saner, eds., *Hannah Arendt and Karl Jaspers*, 38).

33. "Packages-to-Europe," *politics* 5 (Spring 1948): 142, 141; "German Catastrophe," 12.

34. D. Macdonald, "Fourth Report on Packages Abroad," 173.

35. N. Macdonald, "Packages Abroad," 206–7; "Packages-to-Europe," 139. Among the texts included in the "standard book bundle" were Koestler's *Darkness at Noon*, Fromm's *Escape from Freedom*, Faulkner's *Light in August*, and the Lynds' *Middletown*. See Carol Brightman, *Writing Dangerously*, 306.

36. Dwight Macdonald to Gelo and Andrea Delacourt, 5 February 1946, Box 13, Folder 320, Macdonald Papers.

37. After the Macdonalds' marriage ended in the early 1950s, Nancy Macdonald continued her relief efforts with Spanish Refugee Aid (SRA), a program very much in the

spirit of Packages Abroad devoted to the "forgotten" veterans of the civil war living in exile in southwestern France. For decades she worked to assist these individuals and to keep their plight visible. Many of her contacts from the *politics* days served as SRA sponsors, including Dwight Macdonald, Mary McCarthy, Hannah Arendt, Albert Camus, Bruno Bettelheim, and George Woodcock. For the SRA story, see Nancy Macdonald, *Homage to the Spanish Exiles.*

38. Literary critic Germaine Bree helped shape the standard cold war reading of Camus in America. See, for example, her book *Camus and Sartre: Crisis and Commitment.* James Miller noted the influence of Camus on such New Left activists as Tom Hayden and Robert Moses in *"Democracy Is in the Streets,"* 41, 51, 58, 98, 146. For a neoconservative view of Camus, see Norman Podhoretz, "Camus and His Critics," reprinted in *The Bloody Crossroads: Where Literature and Politics Meet,* 33–49. Examples of the recent interest in Camus as a radical political thinker include Michael Walzer, *The Company of Critics,* 136–52; David Sprintzen, *Camus: A Critical Examination;* and Jeffrey Isaac, *Arendt, Camus, and Modern Rebellion.*

39. See Fred Rosen, "Marxism, Mysticism, and Liberty: The Influence of Simone Weil on Albert Camus," *Political Theory* 7 (August 1979): 301–19; Nicola Chiaromonte, "Albert Camus and Moderation," *Partisan Review* 15 (October 1948): 1142–45. Camus shared Macdonald's revulsion against nuclearism. After the attack on Hiroshima, he editorialized in *Combat:* "Our technological civilization has just reached its greatest level of savagery" (*Between Hell and Reason: Essays from the Resistance Newspaper "Combat," 1944–1947,* 110–11).

40. Albert Camus, *The Rebel: An Essay on Man in Revolt;* Nicola Chiaromonte, *The Worm of Consciousness and Other Essays,* 55–56; Albert Camus, "The Human Crisis," *Twice a Year* 14–15 (Fall/Winter 1946–47): 19–33.

41. Albert Camus, "Neither Victims Nor Executioners," *politics* 4 (July/August 1947): 141.

42. On Camus's life see Herbert Lottman's exhaustive *Albert Camus: A Biography* and Patrick McCarthy's more analytical—and critical—study, *Camus.* Quotations are from McCarthy, *Camus,* 11, 15.

43. Chiaromonte, *Worm of Consciousness,* 51.

44. Ibid., 52–53.

45. On Camus and the French Resistance, see Lottman, *Albert Camus,* 285–337.

46. Chiaromonte, *Worm of Consciousness,* 53. On the visit to New York, see Lottman, *Albert Camus,* 376–95, and Albert Camus, *American Journals,* 19–55 (the reference to Chiaromonte is on page 42). Camus experienced a particularly ugly introduction to America. Upon arriving in New York, immigration officials detained him aboard ship for several hours for his refusal to answer questions about connections to the Communist Party. Lottman, *Albert Camus,* 377–78.

47. McCarthy, *Camus,* 216. In addition to Camus's *American Journals,* see his essay "The Rains of New York," in *Albert Camus: Lyrical and Critical Essays,* ed. Philip Thody, 182–86, for the flavor of his ambivalent reactions to the American metropolis.

48. Camus, *American Journals,* 43, 48–49.

49. Chiaromonte, *Worm of Consciousness,* 55–56.

50. Camus, "Human Crisis," 22.

51. Ibid., 22–24.

52. Ibid., 27, 31.

53. Macdonald, "The Root Is Man, Part Two," 212.

54. Macdonald to Camus, 17 May 1946, Box 10, Folder 214, Macdonald Papers. Unlike Macdonald, Camus never claimed to be an absolute pacifist in the late 1940s. He recognized situations where the use of force might be necessary, within narrow limits and as a last resort. What Camus opposed was the *legitimation* of violence by transcendent ideologies. See the discussion in Sprintzen, *Camus,* 190–93.

55. Macdonald, "The Root Is Man, Part Two," 209.

56. Macdonald to Camus, 16 December 1946, Box 10, Folder 214, Macdonald Papers; Macdonald to Chiaromonte, 19 June 1947, Box 10, Folder 241, Macdonald Papers. "Neither Victims Nor Executioners" is reprinted in Camus, *Between Hell and Reason*, 115–40. Macdonald's conflation of Sartre and Camus—writers headed in very different directions after the war—was a typical American misunderstanding, indicating a superficial grasp of the French political scene. For a discussion of their varying conceptions of the cold war responsibilities of intellectuals, see Chiaromonte's "Sartre versus Camus: A Political Quarrel," *Partisan Review* 19 (1952): 680–86.

57. Camus, "Neither Victims," 141–42. Macdonald's translation of Camus's essay appeared in the special summer 1947 issue of *politics* ("French Political Writing"). Largely the work of Lionel Abel, the issue opened with an analysis of the decadence of French sociability by Andrea Caffi ("European"), "The French Condition," and provided a sampling of the ideas of a number of prominent postwar intellectuals, including Sartre ("Materialism and Revolution"), Simone de Beauvoir ("Eye for Eye"), Georges Bataille ("On Hiroshima"), David Rousset ("The Days of Our Death"), and Maurice Merleau-Ponty ("Marxism and Philosophy").

58. Camus, "Neither Victims," 142. It is important to note that Camus, like Macdonald and Chiaromonte, focused his condemnation of Marxism on its progressive, "prophetic" dimensions; he took care to insist that its critical insights about the oppressive tendencies of capitalism retained their value. See Camus, "Neither Victims," 143, and Sprintzen, *Camus*, 298 n. 2.

59. Camus, "Neither Victims," 145.

60. Ibid., 146.

61. Ibid.

62. Sprintzen, *Camus*, xv, 260–65.

63. Carol Gelderman, *Mary McCarthy*, 139–42.

64. Chiaromonte to Macdonald, 8 July 1947, Box 10, Folder 241, Macdonald Papers.

65. Dwight Macdonald, preliminary draft of EAG prospectus, Box 108, Folder 516, Macdonald Papers.

66. EAG Manifesto, [1947–48], Box 108, Folder 516, Macdonald Papers.

67. Ibid.

68. Gelderman, *Mary McCarthy*, 139–42; EAG minutes, [1948], Box 108, Folder 516, Macdonald Papers; McCarthy to Walter Goldwater, 3 September 1982, McCarthy Papers.

69. Macdonald to Chiaromonte, 10 December 1948, Box 10, Folder 241, Macdonald Papers; Brightman, *Writing Dangerously*, 309. On the formation of the anticommunist consensus in the late 1940s, see Richard Pells, *The Liberal Mind in a Conservative Age*, 96–107. For a now-classic critique of the liberal "End of Ideology" made famous by Daniel Bell, see C. Wright Mills's 1960 letter to the British "New Left," reprinted in Mills, *Power, Politics and People*, 247–59.

70. McCarthy to Goldwater, 3 September 1982. In her letter to EAG treasurer Goldwater, McCarthy speculated that the *PR*-Hook faction wanted to divert EAG funds to a predecessor of the American Committee for Cultural Freedom.

71. Miriam Chiaromonte to the Macdonalds, 1 October 1948, Box 10, Folder 240, Macdonald Papers.

72. Macdonald to Chiaromonte, 9 July 1948, Box 10, Folder 241, Macdonald Papers; McCarthy to the Macdonalds, July 1948, Box 31, Folder 779, Macdonald Papers.

73. McCarthy to the Macdonalds, July 1948, Box 31, Folder 779, Macdonald Papers.

74. Macdonald to McCarthy, 30 July 1948, Box 31, Folder 779, Macdonald Papers.

75. Chiaromonte to Macdonald, 3 September 1948, and 15 October 1948, Box 10, Folder 241, Macdonald Papers. See also Nicola Chiaromonte, "European Letter," *politics* 5 (Summer 1948): 159–61.

76. Camus to Macdonald, 6 October 1948, and Macdonald to Camus, 21 October 1948, Box 10, Folder 214, Macdonald Papers.

77. Macdonald to Camus, 10 December 1948, Box 10, Folder 214, Macdonald Papers; Macdonald to Chiaromonte, 6 January 1949, Box 10, Folder 242, Macdonald Papers. On the Davis affair, see Lottman, *Camus*, 449–52.

78. On *Groupes de Liaison Internationale,* see Lottman, *Camus,* 453–66, and McCarthy, *Camus,* 241–42, 246. The *Groupes* manifesto is reprinted in Gilbert Walusinski, "Camus et les Groupes de Liaison Internationale," *La Quinzaine Littéraire,* 3 January 1979, 21–24.

79. Chiaromonte to Macdonald, 11 April 1949, Box 10, Folder 242, Macdonald Papers. The winter 1948 *politics* featured a translation of the manifesto for another "third camp" project emerging from Paris—Sartre's *Rassemblement Démocratique Révolutionnaire* (RDR)—which Macdonald dismissed as platitudinous. See *politics* 5 (Winter 1948): 35–36, 56–57.

80. Macdonald to Chiaromonte, 10 December 1948, Box 10, Folder 241, Macdonald Papers. One of the participants in the EAG meetings that fall was recent émigré Paul de Man, whose collaboration with the Nazis had not yet been discovered. See Macdonald to Camus, 21 October 1948, Box 10, Folder 241, Macdonald Papers.

81. Revised EAG statement of purpose, [1948], Box 108, Folder 516, Macdonald Papers.

82. Macdonald to Chiaromonte, 10 December 1948, Box 10, Folder 241, Macdonald Papers.

83. Chiaromonte to Macdonald, 15 December 1948, Box 10, Folder 241, and Macdonald to Chiaromonte, 6 January 1949, Box 10, Folder 242, Macdonald Papers.

84. Mary McCarthy, *The Oasis.* See also Gelderman, *Mary McCarthy,* 142–48, and Brightman, *Writing Dangerously,* 312–17. McCarthy told an interviewer that the title was an explicit reference to Arthur Koestler's ideas about the formation of libertarian communities—ironically, a program Dwight Macdonald attacked in *politics* as "self-liquidating." See Gelderman, *Mary McCarthy,* 142–43, and Macdonald, "Koestler: Some Political Remarks," *politics* 1 (February 1944): 5.

85. McCarthy, *The Oasis,* 8, 24, 37.

86. Ibid., 31–32, 7, 12.

87. Ibid., 30–31.

88. Gelderman, *Mary McCarthy,* 144.

89. Ibid., 146; Macdonald to Chiaromonte, 14 April 1949, Box 10, Folder 242, Macdonald Papers.

90. See William Graebner, *The Age of Doubt,* 69–100. On postwar ideas about "world government," see Paul Boyer, *By the Bomb's Early Light,* 33–45. The *politics* intellectuals invested little hope in the democratic possibilities of the UN. Dwight Macdonald dismissed it as both a front for neo-imperialist power politics and, equally damning, as "a bore." See his "Comment" in *politics* 3 (November 1946): 338.

91. György Konrád, *Antipolitics* 210. On the origins of Charter 77, see Václav Havel, *Disturbing the Peace,* 125–45.

Eight. The End of *politics*

1. Dwight Macdonald, *Politics Past,* 26; "Reply," *politics* 3 (May 1946): 141; and "Politiking," *politics* 3 (November 1946): 367.

2. Dwight Macdonald, "A Report to the Readers," *politics* 5 (Winter 1948): 58.

3. "French Political Writing," *politics* 4 (July/August 1947); K. L. N. Sinha, "A Green International?" *politics* 3 (February 1946): 50–51; Dwight Macdonald, "Comment," *politics* 3 (March 1946): 66; George Padmore, "The Story of Viet Nam," *politics* 3 (December 1946): 388–90; Dwight Macdonald, "Notes on the Truman Doctrine," *politics* 4 (May/June 1947): 85–87; Clifton Bennett, "The F.B.I.," *politics* 5 (Winter 1948): 19–25. Recently released documents reveal that FBI agents kept a close watch on Dwight and Nancy Macdonald during their *politics* years, opening their mail and even following

them in the streets. See Natalie Robins, *Alien Ink: The FBI's War on Freedom of Expression,* 152–54.

4. Dwight Macdonald, "Henry Wallace," *politics* 4 (March/April 1947): 33–44; 4 (May/June 1947): 96–117. See also Macdonald, *Henry Wallace: The Man and the Myth.* Richard Pells discusses Wallace's postwar rise and fall in his *Liberal Mind in a Conservative Age,* 63–71, 108–16. Macdonald abstained from voting in the 1948 election on anarchist principles, and he saw evidence of a similar temperament in at least some of the 47 million Americans who joined him in that exercise of "civic irresponsibility." See Dwight Macdonald, "On the Elections," *politics* 5 (Summer 1948).

5. Macdonald, *Politics Past,* 201.

6. See Robert Westbrook, *John Dewey and American Democracy,* 494–95. Richard King offered a similar critique of Macdonald's late-1940s "red-baiting" in *The Party of Eros,* 197 n. 64. See also Michael Wreszin, *Rebel in Defense of Tradition,* 204–5. For a sympathetic account of Wallace, see Richard J. Walton, *Henry Wallace, Harry Truman and the Cold War.*

7. Dwight Macdonald, "Homage to Twelve Judges: An Editorial," *politics* 6 (Winter 1949): 1–2. Macdonald's praise of the Bollingen decision ignored the complexity of the questions raised by Pound's politics, which, as Robert Casillo has demonstrated, infused his art. See Casillo, *The Genealogy of Demons: Anti-Semitism, Fascism, and the Myths of Ezra Pound.*

8. See Dwight Macdonald, "The Waldorf Conference," *politics* 6 (Winter 1949): 32(A)–32(D). See also S. A. Longstaff, "The New York Intellectuals and the Cultural Cold War, 1945–1950," *New Politics* (Winter 1989): 156–70, and Neil Jumonville, *Critical Crossings,* 1–48. For Sidney Hook's account of the affair, see his autobiography *Out of Step,* 382–86.

9. See Hook, *Out of Step,* 432–60, and Macdonald, "The Waldorf Conference," 32(A), 32(D). On the AIF as precursor to the Congress for Cultural Freedom, see Longstaff, "New York Intellectuals and the Cultural Cold War," 164; Jumonville, *Critical Crossings,* 34; and Hugh Wilford, "An Oasis: The New York Intellectuals in the Late 1940s," *Journal of American Studies* 28 (1994): 209–23.

10. Dwight Macdonald, "Notes on the Truman Doctrine," *politics* 4 (May/June 1947): 85–87.

11. Macdonald, *Politics Past,* 75–79, and "Pacifism and the USSR," *politics* 5 (Summer 1948): 145–49; C. Daniel and A. Squires, "A First Step Toward World Disarmament," *politics* 6 (Winter 1949): 28–36, 56–57. Macdonald saw a parallel irony in the transformation of American pilots "from executioners into relief workers delivering coal and food instead of bombs." See Macdonald, *Politics Past,* 75.

12. Robert B. Westbrook, "The Responsibility of Peoples," 55; Macdonald, *Politics Past,* 75, 31. In his *New Radicalism in America, 1889–1963: The Intellectual as a Social Type,* 324, Christopher Lasch calls Macdonald's cold war trajectory a "strategic retreat." For a discussion of the darker side of the American consciousness during the period, see William Graebner, *The Age of Doubt.*

13. Kazin quoted in Jumonville, *Critical Crossings,* 60; William Barrett, *The Truants,* 91–92.

14. Macdonald, *Politics Past,* 197–201; Lasch, *New Radicalism,* 322–34; Macdonald to Chiaromonte, [n.d.], Box 10, Folder 242, Macdonald Papers. In the face of the post-Stalin reforms of the mid-1950s, Macdonald, as Lasch notes, was among the first to admit that the Arendtian model of a "perfectly dead, closed society" had been overstated. On the problem of generational discontinuity, see Christopher Lasch, *The Agony of the American Left,* 33–59.

15. Macdonald to Chiaromonte, 10 December 1948 and 14 September 1948, Box 10, Folder 241, Macdonald Papers; Macdonald to Chiaromonte, 14 April 1949, Box 10, Folder 242, Macdonald Papers.

16. Macdonald, *Politics Past*, 27; Macdonald, "Report to the Readers," 58. Russell Jacoby laments the disappearance of independent "public intellectuals" like Macdonald in *The Last Intellectuals: American Culture in the Age of Academe.*

17. Chiaromonte to Macdonald, 2 April 1947 and 8 July 1947, Box 10, Folder 241, Macdonald Papers.

18. Macdonald to Chiaromonte, 21 December 1950, and Chiaromonte to Macdonald, 7 June 1949, Box 10, Folder 242, Macdonald Papers.

19. Chiaromonte to Macdonald, 8 July 1947 and 10 July 1965, Box 10, Folder 241, Macdonald Papers; Andrea Caffi, *A Critique of Violence.*

20. Macdonald to Chiaromonte, 21 December 1950 and 7 November [1951?], Box 10, Folder 242, Macdonald Papers; Macdonald to McCarthy, 18 March 1952, McCarthy Papers; Carol Gelderman, *Mary McCarthy*, 175–77. Macdonald sympathized with *Dissent*, the journal founded in 1954 by his protégés Irving Howe and Lewis Coser, but he found it a lackluster substitute for *politics*. In a 10 December 1959 letter he declined Chiaromonte's suggestion that he contribute articles to a journal "less advanced than we were" in the 1940s. "I've never cared much about making the record or carrying the banner," he wrote. "If the epigones of socialism cannot put out a good lively mag, then let them go under, and take socialism too." See also Dwight Macdonald, *Discriminations,* 343–44.

21. Chiaromonte to Macdonald, 13 January 1956, Box 10, Folder 242, Macdonald Papers; Macdonald, "America! America!" reprinted in *Discriminations,* 44–59.

22. Wreszin, *Rebel in Defense of Tradition,* 371–72; Macdonald to McCarthy, 6 April 1961, McCarthy Papers. For Macdonald's comments on Orwell's critique of the "vegetarian" Left, see his *Discriminations,* 341.

23. Macdonald, "Our Invisible Poor," reprinted in *Discriminations,* 75–98, 97; Macdonald to Chiaromonte, 9 October 1963, Box 10, Folder 243, Macdonald Papers. Macdonald noted in 1974 that despite the federal government's "War on Poverty," the poor "seem to be as much with us as ever" (*Discriminations,* 98).

24. Macdonald, "Hannah Arendt and the Jewish Establishment," reprinted in *Discriminations,* 308–17; Chiaromonte to Macdonald, 5 October 1963, Box 10, Folder 243, Macdonald Papers. To Macdonald, the *Eichmann* controversy was the latest episode in a long battle against the aggressive nationalism he saw in some of his Jewish colleagues. See, for example, the discussion of his row with Clement Greenberg in Macdonald to Chiaromonte, 7 April 1949, and Chiaromonte to Macdonald, 7 June 1949, Box 10, Folder 242, Macdonald Papers.

Macdonald's reading of "semitism" is summarized in a handwritten note attached to his 1967 comments for a proposed *politics* reader: "Postwar reaction of Jews to death camps was to become collectively conscious as Jews—understandable—but dismaying to a non-Jew. Thus my own experience. . . . old friends (Jewish) attacked me as "anti-semitic" when I objected to Israel expropriating land of Arab refugees—and not letting them back. . . . reaction of Jewish intellectuals to Arendt's book. A retreat into tribal collectivity—cf. 30's attitude." Despite his claim to be a neutral defender of cosmopolitan universalism, some observers detect traces of a latent anti-Semitism in Macdonald's career, rooted in the genteel prejudices of his days at Exeter and Yale. See the discussion in Wreszin, *Rebel in Defense of Tradition,* 226–32.

25. Macdonald, "A Day at the White House," reprinted in *Discriminations,* 140–54; Chiaromonte to Macdonald, 10 July 1965, Box 10, Folder 244, Macdonald Papers. For a sampling of Macdonald's Vietnam writings, see *Discriminations,* 397–449. For vivid portraits of Macdonald, Paul Goodman, Robert Lowell, and Norman Mailer at the Pentagon march, see Mailer's *Armies of the Night: History as a Novel, The Novel as History,* esp. 21–66.

26. Macdonald, *Discriminations,* 416. For Mary McCarthy's views on the war, and her account of a controversial trip to Hanoi, see her book *The Seventeenth Degree.*

27. Chiaromonte to Macdonald, 10 July 1965, and 23 December 1965, Box 10, Folder 244, Macdonald Papers. In a 20 February 1966 letter to Macdonald, Chiaromonte described what was at stake this way: "There is a principle involved in the Vietnam war, and it is what kind of America one wants. If one wants America to be the allpowerful, overrich, overmechanized, utterly technological and electronically-calculated country some people seem to dream for (and possibly more than just 'some'), then Johnson is right.... But if one thinks that American power has an utterly different meaning and destination, and that imperialism is utterly foreign to its nature, because it is entrusted to 'natural expansion,' not to military force, then one has to be quite firm, and quite opposed to any kind of talk of 'national prestige' or 'savefacing,' or expediency."

28. Macdonald, Discriminations, 57–59. For a fuller account of the scandal, see Christopher Lasch, "The Cultural Cold War: A Short History of the Congress for Cultural Freedom," in The Agony of the American Left, 61–114.

29. Chiaromonte to Macdonald, 13 June 1967, 25 June 1967, 4 September 1967, 16 October 1967, and Macdonald to Chiaromonte, 10 October 1967, Box 10, Folder 244, Macdonald Papers; Macdonald to McCarthy, 22 May 1969, McCarthy Papers.

30. Macdonald quoted in Scialabba, "The Lady and the Luftmensch," Dissent 41 (Spring 1994): 288. For more on Macdonald's ambivalence toward the New Left, see Discriminations, 450–52.

31. See "An Exchange on the Columbia Student Strike of 1968," in Macdonald, Discriminations, 450–66.

32. Chiaromonte to Macdonald, 16 October 1967, 6 May 1970 and 1 June 1970, Box 10, Folder 244, Macdonald Papers; Chiaromonte, "The Student Revolt," in The Worm of Consciousness and Other Essays, 58–65, esp. 64–65.

33. Chiaromonte to McCarthy, 27 July 1969, and Macdonald to McCarthy, 12 September 1969, McCarthy Papers.

34. Trans. draft of Nicola Chiaromonte, "A Journey Among the Sins of Giant America," published in Italian in L'Espresso, 16 November 1970, Box 10, Folder 244, Macdonald Papers.

35. Chiaromonte to Macdonald, 5 January 1972, Box 10, Folder 244, Macdonald Papers.

36. McCarthy, preface to Chiaromonte, Worm of Consciousness, xiii–xvi; Macdonald to Miriam Chiaromonte, 19 January 1972, Box 10, Folder 244, Macdonald Papers. On the Aristotelian ideal of "civic friendship," see Robert N. Bellah et al., Habits of the Heart: Individualism and Commitment in American Life, 115–16. On Macdonald's final years (he died in December 1982), see Wreszin, a Rebel in Defense of Tradition, 471–91.

Conclusion. The Post–Cold War Legacy of politics

1. Daniel Bell quoted in Howard Brick, Daniel Bell and the Decline of Intellectual Radicalism, 124–25; Dwight Macdonald, Discriminations, 341.

2. Czeslaw Milosz, Beginning with My Streets, 186–87.

3. Václav Havel, "Paradise Lost," New York Review of Books, 9 April 1992, 6–8, 8.

4. Václav Havel, Open Letters: Selected Writings, 1965–1990, 57.

5. Dwight Macdonald, conclusion to the pamphlet edition of "The Responsibility of Peoples" (1945), 14; György Konrád, Antipolitics, 218.

6. For more on the notion of a developing "global civil society," see John Keane, Democracy and Civil Society, 23; Paul Ekins, A New World Order: Grassroots Movements for Global Change; Jeremy Brecher, John Brown Childs, and Jill Cutler, eds., Global Visions: Beyond the New World Order; Paul Wapner, "Environmental Activism and Global Civil Society," Dissent 41 (Summer 1994): 389–93; and David Held, "Democracy: From City-States to a Cosmopolitan Order?" in Held, ed., Prospects for Democracy: North, South, East, West, 13–52.

Index